STUDENT BOOK 1

The LITERATE MUSICIAN

HOW TO HEAR, SPEAK, THINK, READ & WRITE THE LANGUAGE OF MUSIC

REVISED 2ND EDITION

ANDY MULLEN

© 2020 The Improving Musician

The companion course for this book can be found on *The Improving Musician* website:
www.TheImprovingMusician.com/courses

TABLE OF CONTENTS

Introduction **9**

PART I: FOUNDATIONS OF MUSICAL THOUGHT 17

Section 1: The Whole of Music 19
Major Tonality **20**
Minor Tonality **21**
Dorian Tonality **22**
Mixolydian Tonality **23**
Phrygian Tonality **24**
Lydian Tonality **25**
Aeolian Tonality **26**
Locrian Tonality **27**
Duple Meter **28**
Triple Meter **29**
Unusual-Paired Meter **30**
Unusual-Unpaired Meter **31**

Section 2: Rhythm 33
Lesson 1: Introduction to Rhythm Concepts **34**
Lesson 2: Echoing Rhythm Patterns, Duple, Aural/Oral **36**
Lesson 3: Echoing Rhythm Patterns, Triple, Aural/Oral **37**
Lesson 4: Verbal Association, Duple Meter **38**
Lesson 5: Verbal Association, Triple Meter **40**
Lesson 6: Improvisation **41**
Lesson 7: Comparing Duple and Triple Meters #1 **42**
Lesson 8: Rhythmic Translation #1 **43**
Lesson 9: Divisions in Duple Meter **44**
Lesson 10: Divisions in Triple Meter **46**
Lesson 11: Comparing Duple and Triple Meters #2 **47**
Lesson 12: Duple Elongations **48**
Lesson 13: Triple Elongations **49**
Assessment **50**

Section 3: Harmony 51
Lesson 1: Introduction to Tonal Concepts **52**
Lesson 2: Major Tonality, Aural/Oral **53**
Lesson 3: Minor Tonality, Aural/Oral **54**
Lesson 4: Verbal Association, Major Tonality **55**
Lesson 5: Verbal Association, Minor Tonality **58**
Lesson 6: Improvisation **60**
Lesson 7: Comparing Major and Minor Tonalities **62**
Lesson 8: Singing Bass Lines **63**
Lesson 9: Harmonic Translation **65**
Lesson 10: I/V Conversations **66**
Assessment **67**

TABLE OF CONTENTS

Section 4: Melody 69
Lesson 1: Introduction to Melody **70**
Lesson 2: Stepwise Acculturation Patterns, Major Tonality **71**
Lesson 3: Stepwise Acculturation Patterns, Minor Tonality **72**
Lesson 4: Melodic Conversations **73**
Lesson 5: Comparing Major and Minor Melodies **73**
Lesson 6: Translation of Stepwise Patterns **74**
Lesson 7: Connecting Melody and Harmony I **75**
Lesson 8: Connecting Melody and Harmony II **77**
Assessment **79**

PART II: READING MUSICAL THOUGHT 81

Reading Sequence 1 83
Lesson 1.1 Macrobeats and Microbeats in Duple Meter (2/4) **84**
Lesson 1.2 Macrobeats and Microbeats in Triple Meter (6/8) **87**
Lesson 1.3 Reading Longer Rhythm Patterns, Macro/Microbeat **89**
Lesson 1.4 Introduction to Tonal Reading and FPIFO **90**
Lesson 1.5 Tonic Patterns, Major Tonality **93**
Lesson 1.6 Generalizing New Tonic Patterns, Major Tonality **95**
Introduction to Reading Benchmarks **97**
Reading Benchmark 1 **100**

Reading Sequence 2 102
Lesson 2.1 Introduction to Reading Stepwise Patterns, Major Tonality **103**
Lesson 2.2 Stepwise Patterns (DRM, MRD, DTD), Major Tonality (F-DO, Eb-DO) **104**
Lesson 2.3 A New DO: DRM, MRD, DTD in G-DO **106**
Lesson 2.4 Generalizing New Stepwise Patterns **107**
Reading Benchmark 2A **111**
Lesson 2.5 Enrhythmic Patterns in Duple Meter (4/4) **113**
Lesson 2.6 Enrhythmic Patterns in Triple Meter (3/4) **115**
Lesson 2.7 Longer Rhythm Patterns **117**
Reading Benchmark 2B **118**
Reading Benchmark 2C **119**

Reading Sequence 3 121
Lesson 3.1 How to Find DO & Two New DO-Signatures (D-DO and C-DO) **122**
Lesson 3.2 Combining Harmonic and Stepwise Patterns **125**
Reading Benchmark 3A **127**
Lesson 3.3 Divisions in Duple Meter (2/4 and 4/4) **128**
Reading Benchmark 3B **131**
Lesson 3.4 New Stepwise Patterns in Major Tonality (MFM, RMFS, SLS) **132**
Lesson 3.5 Generalization in Major Tonality (tDRMFSL) **136**
Reading Benchmark 3C **140**
Reading Benchmark 3D **142**
Lesson 3.6 Combining Stepwise and Harmonic Patterns **143**
Reading Benchmark 3E **144**

TABLE OF CONTENTS

Reading Sequence 4 146
Lesson 4.1 New Duple Time Signature: Cut Time **147**
Reading Benchmark 4A **150**
Lesson 4.2 Divisions in Triple Meter (6/8 and 3/4) **151**
Reading Benchmark 4B **156**
Lesson 4.3 Longer Rhythm Patterns in Duple and Triple **157**
Reading Benchmark 4C **160**
Lesson 4.4 Two New DO-Signatures (Bb and A) **162**
Lesson 4.5 Dominant Patterns, Major Tonality **164**
Lesson 4.6 Generalizing New Dominant Patterns, Major Tonality **169**
Lesson 4.7 Combining Familiar and Unfamiliar Tonic and Dominant Patterns **172**
Reading Benchmark 4D **174**

Reading Sequence 5 176
Lesson 5.1 The Letter System **177**
Lesson 5.2 The Math of Rhythm **179**
Lesson 5.3 Combining Stepwise and Harmonic Patterns, Major Tonality **180**
Reading Benchmark 5A **182**
Lesson 5.4 Elongations in Duple Meter; 2/4, 4/4, Cut Time **184**
Reading Benchmark 5B **189**
Lesson 5.5 Elongations in Triple Meter; 6/8, 3/4 **190**
Reading Benchmark 5C **193**
Lesson 5.6 Longer Rhythm Patterns **194**
Reading Benchmark 5D **197**

Reading Sequence 6 199
Lesson 6.1 Minor Harmonic FPIFO **200**
Lesson 6.2 Tonic Patterns, Minor Tonality **202**
Lesson 6.3 Generalizing New Minor Tonic Patterns **204**
Reading Benchmark 6A **206**
Lesson 6.4 Division/Elongations in Duple Meter; 2/4, 4/4, Cut Time **207**
Reading Benchmark 6B **209**
Lesson 6.5 Division/Elongations in Triple Meter **210**
Reading Benchmark 6C **212**
Lesson 6.6 Longer Rhythm Patterns **213**
Reading Benchmark 6D **214**
Reading Benchmark 6E **216**

Reading Sequence 7 217
Lesson 7.1 Introduction to Minor Stepwise Patterns; FPIFO in G-LA and E-LA **218**
Lesson 7.2 Stepwise Patterns in Minor Tonality (LTD, DTL, LsiL) **219**
Lesson 7.3 Generalizing New Minor Stepwise Patterns (LTD and si) **221**
Reading Benchmark 7A **222**
Lesson 7.4 Macrobeat Rests, Duple and Triple **224**
Reading Benchmark 7B **226**
Reading Benchmark 7C **228**
Lesson 7.5 Three New LA-Signatures (C-LA, D-LA and F-LA) **229**
Reading Benchmark 7D **233**

TABLE OF CONTENTS

Reading Sequence 8 235
Lesson 8.1 Combining Harmonic and Stepwise Patterns **236**
Reading Benchmark 8A **238**
Lesson 8.2 New Stepwise Patterns in Minor Tonality (TDRM, MFM, MRDTL) **240**
Lesson 8.3 Generalizing New Minor Stepwise Patterns (siLTDRMF) **244**
Reading Benchmark 8B **247**
Lesson 8.4 Two New LA-Signatures (B-LA and A-LA) **249**
Lesson 8.5 Combining Stepwise and Harmonic Patterns **251**
Reading Benchmark 8C **253**
Lesson 8.6 Microbeat Rests, Duple and Triple **255**
Lesson 8.7 Longer Rhythm Patterns **257**
Reading Benchmark 8D **258**
Reading Benchmark 8E **260**

Reading Sequence 9 262
Lesson 9.1 Dominant Patterns, Minor Tonality **263**
Lesson 9.2 Generalizing New Dominant Patterns, Minor Tonality **268**
Lesson 9.3 Combining Familiar and Unfamiliar Tonic and Dominant Patterns, Minor Tonality **271**
Reading Benchmark 9A **273**
Lesson 9.4 Combining Stepwise and Harmonic Patterns **275**
Reading Benchmark 9B **277**
Lesson 9.5 Ties, Duple and Triple **279**
Reading Benchmark 9C **281**
Reading Benchmark 9D **282**

Reading Sequence 10 283
Lesson 10.1 Major vs. Minor **284**
Reading Benchmark 10A **285**
Lesson 10.2 Extending Into Other Octaves **286**
Reading Benchmark 10B **288**
Reading Benchmark 10C **289**
Lesson 10.3 Upbeats **290**
Reading Benchmark 10D **291**
Lesson 10.4 Introduction to Subdominant **292**
Reading Benchmark 10E **295**
Lesson 10.5 Crash Course in Chord Roots **297**
Reading Benchmark 10F **298**

Appendices **299**
End Notes and References **311**

ACKNOWLEDGMENTS

I would like to thank all of my former music teachers who contributed to my development, both as a student of music, and as a student of music learning. I am indebted to their countless degrees, hours of practice, and depth of scholarship.

In particular, I owe a tremendous amount of gratitude to the faculty of The Gordon Institute for Music Learning, many of whom contributed in one way or another to the contents of the book. Most notably, I would like to acknowledge Dr. Alison Reynolds and Dr. Suzanne Burton who taught Elementary General Level 1 at Temple University; Heather Kirby and Natasha Sigmund who taught Early Childhood Level 1 at Bridgewater State University; Jennifer Bailey and Dr. Jill Reese who taught Elementary General Level 2 at Baldwin State University; and Dr. Cynthia Taggart and Dr. Heather Shouldice who taught Elementary General Level 2 at Michigan State University.

Additionally, several other GIML faculty have had a notable influence on me, either from their publications or workshops. These persons include Dr. Herbert "Butch" Marshall of Kent State University; Dr. Christopher Azzara of Eastman University; Dr. Richard Grunow of Eastman University; Dr. Beth Bolton of Temple University; and Dr. Wendy Valerio of the University of South Carolina.

Special thanks also go out to Dr. Scott Edgar, who agreed to pilot the first edition of this book in his college music course. If it weren't for this deadline, I don't think I would have gotten this done in such a timely manner. I hope the book finds purchase with his students.

Finally, thanks to Ryan Dunn for his keen graphic eye.

DEDICATION

This book is dedicated in its entirety to Dr. Edwin E. Gordon.

Not a day, nor a period goes by where I do not feel Dr. Gordon's spirit subtly guiding my decisions. His writing, research and teaching have given my previously very-entertaining-but-not-quite-heading-anywhere-specific classroom techniques and lessons a direction, a laser-like focus.

I'm sure I speak for many music educators when I say that Dr. Gordon brought a precision to music education, the results of which the profession at large still has not fully come to terms with. But, with time, as more and more teachers learn about Music Learning Theory, and more importantly, see the **results** of good teaching that MLT inevitably produces, the music education profession and the future of musical understanding in the world will be forever in his debt.

INTRODUCTION

MUSIC AS A LANGUAGE

Although music isn't a language in the **strictest** sense, we can certainly communicate and interact with each other through music. In order to communicate, we need to have something to say.

In language, we have **words**, which are given contextual meaning through the sentences we put them in. In music, we have **patterns**, which are given contextual meaning when we put them in a tonal or rhythmic context (like a tonality or a meter). Once we have patterns (words) and can give them context (sentences), we can begin to **think musically**.

> Thinking in music is called **AUDIATION**.

AUDIATION

The same way that we can visualize an image in our brain and bring meaning to it, we can "hear" music. We can have musical thoughts. But to truly audiate, we must **understand** the thoughts we are having.

Analogy: thought:language::audiation:music.

Are you audiating? If you are listening to a piece of music, here are some questions to ask yourself:

- Do you know what tonality or meter the music is in?
- Can you pick out the various pitches and give them an aural label?
- Do you know the underlying harmonic progression?
- Would you know what chords to play on the piano or guitar?
- Do you know if a modulation took place?
- Could you transcribe the rhythm?

If you can do all of those things, you are well on your way to being able to audiate! This book will arm you with the tools to audiate, and teach you to be able to **read** your musical thoughts as well as the musical thoughts of others.

BREAKING THE MUSIC CODE

Believe it or not, music is **noise** to many people. They hear it as a collection of sounds, and are not able to hear the individual parts that make up the whole, let alone make any contextual meaning of what they are hearing.

Music has two overarching frameworks:
- Tonality
- Rhythm

Tonality can be broken up into two categories: **Melody** and **Harmony**. Melody can be thought of as horizontal, whereas harmony can be thought of as vertical.

To break the code of music, your goal is to learn:
- Rhythm Patterns
- Tonal Patterns

To put it another way, you need to learn musical **words**, which you will be able to put together to make musical **sentences**.

MUSIC AS A SECOND LANGUAGE

Although there are no **direct** correlations, think of learning music like learning a foreign language. You can't think in a new language unless you have nouns, adjectives, verbs, and adverbs. Once you have those in place, you can combine them to make logical statements, to ask or answer questions, or think in that language.

Part of Speech	Job	Example
Nouns	You give things a name	**dog**
Adjectives	You describe the noun	**The big** dog
Verbs	You do something with or to each noun.	The big dog **jumped**
Adverbs	How are you doing it?	The big dog jumped **quickly**

Although music doesn't have parts of speech the way language does, we learn music in a very similar way that we learn language. We will learn many types of musical **words**, and then be able to put them into sentences, and even paragraphs. Once we have a musical vocabulary, then it makes sense to learn to **read (and write!)** what we can **already think**.

WHOLE-PART-WHOLE

Good learning takes place in a **Whole-Part-Whole** manner.

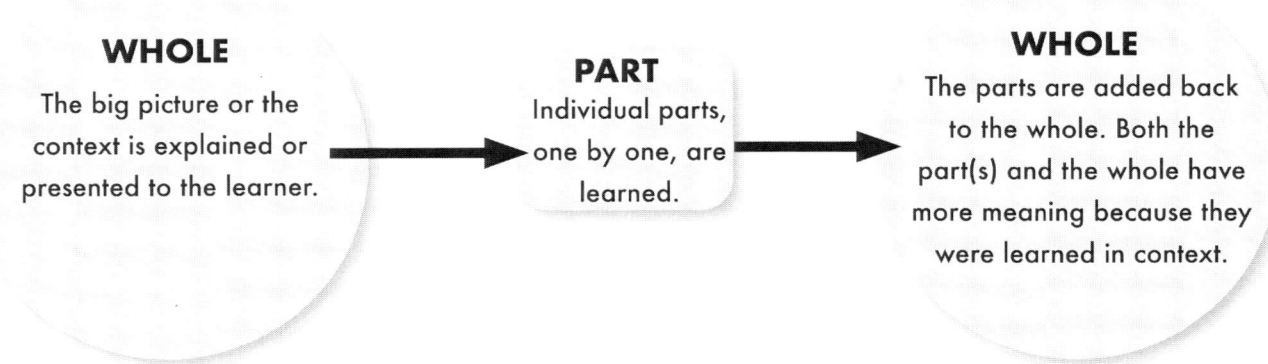

Consider a parent teaching his child how to mow the lawn. If done using a Whole-Part-Whole manner, the parent might do the following:

WHOLE
Explain to the child that he is going to learn how to mow the lawn. Then, the parent instructs the child to simply watch as the parent mows the lawn himself. This gives the child the opportunity see the **Whole** of the task in action.

PART
Next, various aspects of the task at large are explained. For example:
- How to start the lawnmower
- How to turn it off
- What are safety protocols that must be followed?
- How to add gasoline
- How to clean up afterwards

All of the PARTS make more sense because the child got to experience them during the first WHOLE **in context**.

WHOLE
Lastly, the child does it on his own, with parent guidance and repetition as necessary. He assimilates the parts into the whole because he has experienced both.

WHOLE-PART-WHOLE IN LANGUAGE

When we are born, we learn **language** in a Whole-Part-Whole manner.

WHOLE
For the first year of our life, we simply **listen** to the language as a whole before we ever attempt to speak it. We hear whole conversations with sophisticated vocabulary spoken around us all the time.

PART
When we are around one year old, we begin to learn individual words by **naming** things around us: Mommy. Daddy. Bottle. Doggy. Kitty. Brother. We learn the all-important words "yes" and "no" which, combined with the nouns we know, give us the ability to improvise with language. ("Mommy, no bottle.")

WHOLE
Then, slowly but surely, those words begin to make sense in the context of the first **Whole**. This process continues with more **Wholes** and more **Parts** in a very effective cyclical process until we are masters of our native language, and have a significant vocabulary with which we can improvise in order to communicate.

WHOLE-PART-WHOLE IN MUSIC

If we accept that we learn music in a very similar way that we learn language, we can use Whole-Part-Whole to teach ourselves music. This concept will come up again and again in a variety of ways throughout this book. Our first Whole-Part-Whole in music will help us establish the big picture.

WHOLE
Like in language, we need a sense of the **big picture** of music. That is to say, we need exposure to many tonalities and many meters. If we simply listen to pop radio, that is not a sufficient listening vocabulary. That would be as if our parents only spoke very short sentences with minimal words. We wouldn't get a sense of our language at large.

PART
We will learn specific musical patterns (words) in specific musical contexts (tonalities and meters) in a very systematic way.

WHOLE
Then, slowly but surely, those patterns within tonalities and meters begin to make sense in the context of music at large. This process continues by adding more patterns and tonalities and meters in more Whole-Part-Wholes within Whole-Part-Wholes within Whole-Part-Wholes.

THE MUSICALLY LITERATE CITIZEN

If you ask almost any adult on earth what 2+2 is, you are likely to get the correct answer. Or if you asked them what H2O meant, they would know you are referring to water. These are things that a citizen generally knows.

Music is everywhere: movies, TV shows, the radio, video games, elevators, stores. What this book puts forth are the very basic concepts that a **musical citizen** should know: the acquisition of a musical vocabulary, and the ability to think, speak and read in the "language of music." This is what it truly means to be a **literate musician**. In Part 2 of this book, we will become a literate musician by learning to read the musical vocabulary we have acquired, and learn how to put those words together to read musical sentences and paragraphs. Here is what we will learn in Part 1:

	Musical Citizenship, Book 1
Rhythm	In duple and triple meters, students will be able to • Move to macrobeats and microbeats simultaneously • Echo rhythm patterns with a neutral syllable and solfege • Name the meter and rhythmic functions • Improvise patterns • Aurally compare meters • Translate from neutral syllable to solfege
Tonal	In major and minor tonalities, students will be able to • Echo tonic/dominant (I/V) and stepwise patterns using a neutral syllable and solfege • Name the tonality and sing its resting tone and harmonic functions • Name and sing chord roots • Memorize musical "sight words" • Aurally compare tonalities • Translate from neutral syllable to solfege

A MUSIC LEARNING THEORY

Music psychologist Dr. Edwin Gordon developed a learning theory for how the human being learns music. This theory, which is called **Music Learning Theory**, is the foundation for the lessons and explanations in this book.

Dr. Gordon created a **Skill Learning Sequence** which gives teachers and students a framework for the acquisition of musical skills. The skills appear in the chart below with a brief explanation. As you go through the book, I will make reference when necessary to these skills.

There are two types of learning: **discrimination learning** and **inference learning**. In discrimination learning, you learn by rote. That is to say, all of the information is given to you. All of the patterns you learn are familiar, in both familiar and unfamiliar order.

Skill Learning Sequence - Discrimination Learning

Aural/Oral
- We listen to patterns, and repeat them back.

Verbal Association
- We give the patterns an aural label

Partial Synthesis
- We are taught how to discriminate between tonalities and meters using familiar patterns.

Symbolic Association
- We can read and write familiar patterns

Composite Synthesis
- We can read and write a series of familiar patterns, as well as identify tonality and meter.

Then, once you are given information, you put that information to use in the form of **inference learning**. In inference learning, you are essentially taught how to teach yourself. In inference learning, the patterns will be familiar **and unfamiliar**, and will be in necessarily unfamiliar order.

Skill Learning Sequence - Inference Learning

Generalization
- We can tell same from different.
- We can give labels to unfamiliar patterns.
- We can identify tonalities and meters.
- We can label rhythmic and harmonic functions.
- We can read unfamiliar music.

Creativity/Improvisation
- We can take familiar and unfamiliar patterns, and rearrange them in order to create new music. We can write this new music down in the form of a composition.

Theoretical Understanding
- We learn the technical aspects of music that are the "why" behind what we have already learned in all of the previous levels of learning.

The **Skill Learning Sequence** allows you to acquire information in a very logical way. However, we don't follow this sequence from beginning to end. Rather, skill development weaves in and out of all of the levels. Remember: we learn music in a very similar way that we learn language. When we learn language, we learn new words, we learn definitions, we learn how to use them in a sentence, we learn new words, we learn how to spell different words, etc.

This book will focus on major and minor tonalities and duple and triple meters. If we think of our Whole-Part-Whole concept, the skills learned in Book 1 are the **Parts**. However, just as you were exposed to your language as a whole before you learned your first words, you should expect to do the same in music.

	WHOLE-PART-WHOLE FOR STUDENT BOOK 1
Whole	Expose yourself to a broad range of tonalities and meters. You will not be learning them all, at least not in the context of this book, but rather you will be **acculturating** yourself to music as a whole to get a fuzzy sense of the big picture.
Part	This book will teach you to **audiate** a very specific set of parts (Part I).
Whole	Then, in Part II, you will learn to **read** those parts, and then assimilate them into a whole by reading them in the context of musical whole. The whole will, in turn, make greater and greater sense as you continue to fit more pieces of the musical jigsaw puzzle together.

HOW TO USE THIS BOOK

This book is not meant to be read from beginning to end. Through the help of a teacher, or by following the upcoming suggestions, you may bridge and spiral about the book. There are navigation suggestions throughout the book which will give you some guidance. Some basic principles to consider:

1. Any time you learn a new piece of content (functions and patterns within a tonal or rhythmic context), learn it first at the Aural/Oral level. **The sound of the pattern itself is fundamental**.
2. Before you attempt to read (either tonally or rhythmically), it is wise to achieve moderate success at the **Partial Synthesis** level lessons. That is to say, be sure that you have a good handle on tonal and rhythmic **context** before you attempt to read. Be sure to achieve success at the following lessons before attempting to read:
    - **Tonal Lesson 7: Comparing Major and Minor Tonalities**
    - **Rhythm Lesson 7: Comparing Duple and Triple Meters**
3. Any time you learn a new piece of content in Part I, you have several options
    - You may **spiral** to Part II and learn to **read (or write!)** that particular piece of content (provided you have the readiness as described above).
    - You may **bridge** to Inference learning and challenge yourself to engage with the content in more challenging ways. For example, you could try to translate the patterns from a neutral syllable to solfege. Or, you could improvise with the patterns. Or you could compose with them. Or, you could listen to unfamiliar music and see if you can find examples of the content (functions and patterns) that have been presented in this book. Inference learning gives you the opportunity to **apply** what you have learned, and to help you make the determination if you have truly learned the content.

The following navigational symbols will be used throughout this book:

 Bridge from discrimination to inference learning

 A specific spiral which asks you to **write** content after you learn to read it.

 Spiral forward to another skill or piece of content

 There is supporting video content on **The Improving Musician** YouTube channel or companion course.

 A specific spiral which asks you to read after you learn the content aurally.

 There is supporting audio content on the internet.

 Make an instrumental association with the ukulele.

 Make an instrumental association with the keyboard.

NOTE TO TEACHERS:

1. A companion teacher's edition is available as of February 2021. It is titled **MLT Any Music Teacher Can Du...De: Teacher's Guide to "The Literate Musician."**
2. Dr. Edwin Gordon's Music Learning Theory is the basis of this book. However, there are some notable deviations from Gordon's theory as it was left at the time of his passing in 2015. It is my opinion that a theory is ever-evolving, and continues to be refined based upon **practice** of the theory. The changes I put forth in this book, most notably the inclusion of Kodály-inspired stepwise patterns, are, in a sense, my own contribution to music learning theory (lack of capitalization is intended), the sum total of which could be considered a **new** music learning theory. Any deviations from "pure" Music Learning Theory are intentional, and are informed by practice of the theory.

   "Who knows what [MLT] will look like in 2020. There might need to be a new music learning theory. As someone said...'truth isn't forever.' This is something I'm doing in my lifetime, and I hope it'll help you, but that's not to say that somebody in 20 years will say 'You know, that Gordon had some good ideas, BUT...' As long as I've helped them discover something more worthwhile, I think I've done a great job, and I'm very happy with my life."
   -Dr. Edwin E. Gordon, 1997
3. Teachers who are interested in learning more about how to navigate Music Learning Theory should consider taking a 2-week certification course with **The Gordon Institute for Music Learning**. Information can be found on their website, www.GIML.org.

PART I
FOUNDATIONS OF MUSICAL THOUGHT

SKILLS, CONTEXT & CONTENT

Throughout this book, you will experience **Skills, Context and Content**.

Skills: What Are You Doing?

These are the verbs that you will be attending to in regards to music. In this book, you will experience the follow skills:

- Audiating
- Comparing
- Translating
- Recognizing
- Echoing
- Reading
- Improvising
- Identifying
- Listening
- Writing
- Composing
- Labeling

Then, you will need something with which to execute these skills, and a contextual framework on which to hang them.

Context: Bringing Meaning to Musical Sounds

In language, context is everything. Take the word "read," for example. In one context ("I **read** that book."), it is in the past tense. In another, ("My son just learned how to **read** music."), it is in the present tense. Or, if it were only spoken language, "I lost my **reed**" would have a totally different meaning!

Throughout this book, we will seek to put all music into a tonal or rhythmic context (major tonality, duple meter, for example) so that the patterns we learn (the upcoming content) have meaning because they are learned within the organizational framework of a tonality or meter.

Content: Functions and Patterns

Finally, in addition to understanding context, we will learn **content** within the context. What is content? Functions and patterns.

Functions represent working aspects of tonality or meter, and explain what is "going on" musically underneath the proverbial hood. In rhythm, the layers of the beat (macrobeat, microbeat, division) are functions, as are any other way that rhythm functions (elongations, ties, rests, upbeats, etc.). Tonally, the primary functions Gordon has identified are harmonic functions (tonic, dominant, subdominant), but melodic devices are functions, as well.

Patterns are specific examples of those functions. For example, major tonic would be a harmonic function, and "Do Mi So" would be a pattern within that function. Duple macrobeat/microbeat would be a rhythmic function, and "Du Du Du-de Du" would be a pattern representing that function.

MUSIC AS AN AURAL ART

Because music is an aural art, there are times when musical examples will be necessary to explain concepts. Because we are still in the pre-notation stage of learning, using notation to explain concepts would be counter-intuitive. However, due to the nature of the printed medium, such accommodations will undoubtedly be necessary.

When it is feasible, you will be directed to **The Improving Musician YouTube channel** or the **companion course** to listen to selected exercises, tonal and rhythm patterns, songs, études, and sundry musical examples.

Companion Course: www.TheImprovingMusician.com/courses

ORGANIZATION OF PART I

Part I is divided into four sections.
- **Section 1, CONTEXT:** introduces the big picture of music: tonality and meter
- **Section 2, RHYTHM:** how to audiate rhythmically
- **Section 3, HARMONY:** how to audiate harmonically
- **Section 4, MELODY:** how to audiate melodically

SECTION 1: CONTEXT

MUSICAL CONTEXT: TONALITY & METER

Just as there is context in language, there is context in music. If you were to say "I love you" to someone, that could mean something completely different in different contexts. Imagine saying "I love you" to your parent as you say goodnight. Now imagine saying "I love you" to your best friend after she threw a pie in your face. Same words. Different context.

You will find out that a note or a chord or a rhythm pattern can have completely different meaning based upon **musical context**. Context in music is the **tonality** or **meter** the music is in.

THE FIRST WHOLE: ACCULTURATION

Your task in this first section is to simply be **immersed** in the language of music, to experience many musical contexts (tonalities and meters).

Imagine that you went to a foreign country whose language you did not know. You would spend a great deal of time simply listening to the nuances, the cadences, the inflections. Soon, you would learn some simple phrases for important everyday tasks. "My name is Andy." "Where is the train station?" "Thank you." "Yes." "No." If enough time passed, you would eventually learn how to **think** in that new language.

The purpose of this section is simply to experience being **in** a tonality or meter by listening to songs and chants, and having some key experiences. Do not rush this, or feel like you need to **learn** anything that is presented. For your future reference, information about each tonality or meter is presented. Feel free to ignore that for now, and just **experience** the tonality or meter.

> Some experiences you might have:
> - Listen to a song in a new tonality
> - Listen to a chant in a new meter
> - Sing the bass line along with a presented song
> - Sing a song in a new tonality
> - Move to an unfamiliar meter in creative ways
> - Chant the macrobeats or microbeats along with a chant in a new meter
> - Echo patterns in an unfamiliar tonality or meter

Before you proceed with learning the **Parts** in Sections 2, 3 and 4, spend some time getting acculturated to Major and Minor tonalities and Duple and Triple meters. Throughout the rest of the book, you will be prompted to experience other tonalities and meters.

TONALITIES

MAJOR TONALITY

LISTENING EXPERIENCES

It shouldn't be hard to listen to songs in Major Tonality. A vast majority of the songs you hear on the radio are in major. But it's important now to **know** that a song is in major as you are listening and experiencing the tonality. Unless otherwise stated, all of the listening examples can be found on *The Improving Musician* YouTube channel.

 Watch the video **Major Tonality Acculturation.** Sing along with the melody and the bass line.

 Locate the **Singing Bass Lines** playlist. Watch the first video for instructions, and then any subsequent videos in major tonality.
- "Down By The Station"
- "Are You Sleeping?"

 Watch any of the **Harmonic Loops** videos in major tonality.

REFERENCE INFORMATION

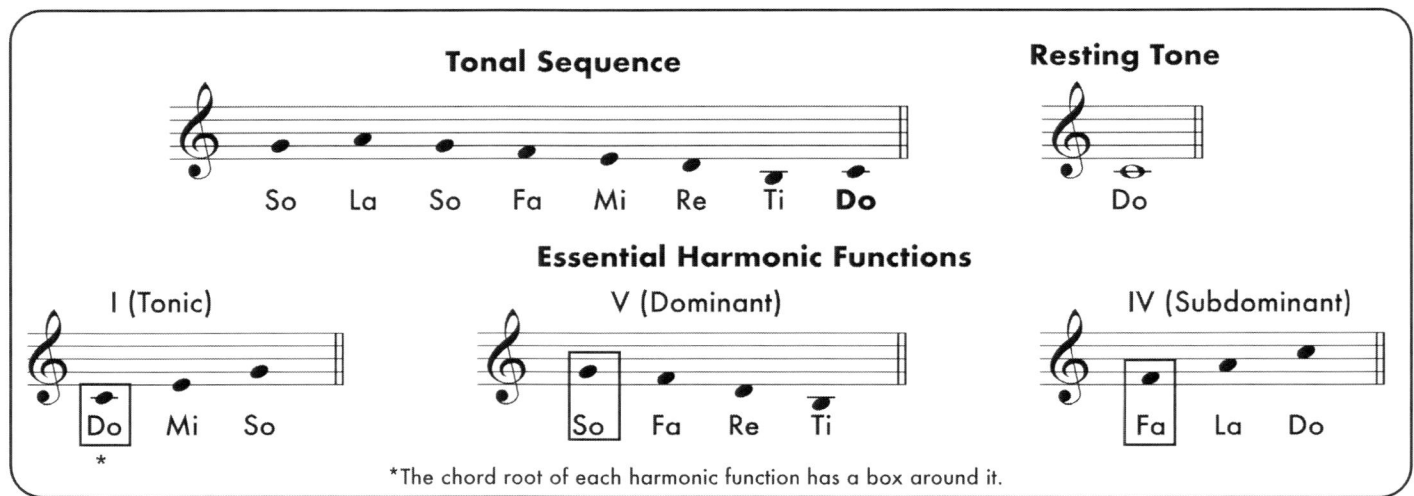

Major Acculturation Tune

TONALITIES

MINOR TONALITY

LISTENING EXPERIENCES

Minor tonality is another of the most prevailing tonalities in our culture. It is much less common than major, but there are many songs in minor. Although not as popular today, many songs from the classical and folk traditions are in minor.

 Watch the video **Minor Tonality Acculturation**. Sing along with the melody and the bass line on a neutral syllable.

 Locate the **Singing Bass Lines** playlist. Watch any videos in minor tonality.
- "Joshua"
- "Wade in the Water"

 Watch any of the **Harmonic Loops** videos in minor tonality.

 Search YouTube or Spotify for any of the following Minor songs:
- "Havana" (Camila Cabello)
- "Don Gato" (Traditional)
- "Babylon" (Traditional Round)

REFERENCE INFORMATION

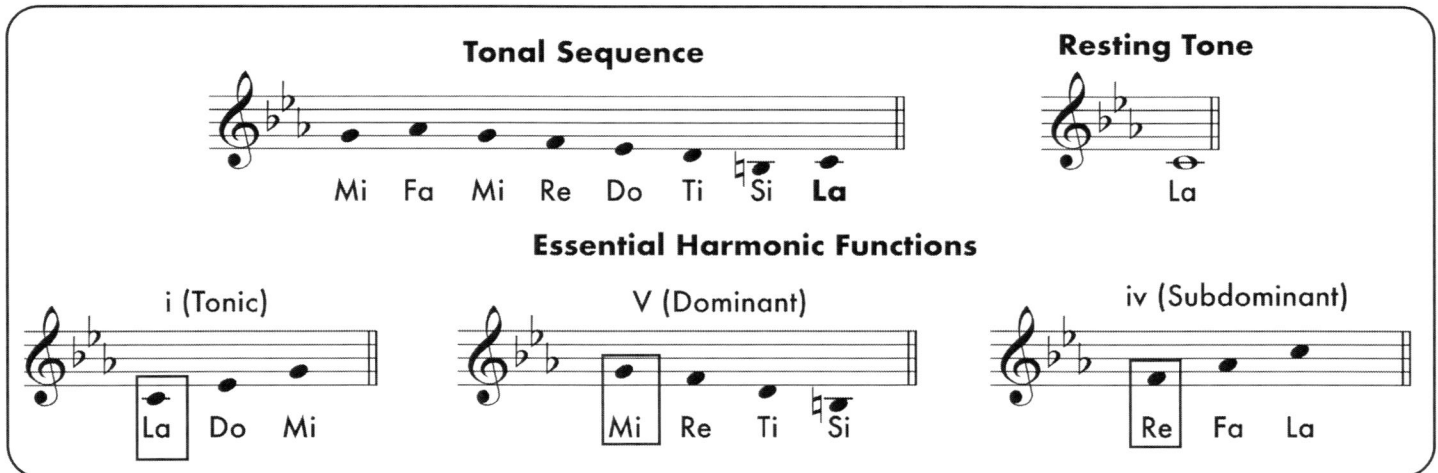

Minor Acculturation Tune

TONALITIES

DORIAN TONALITY

LISTENING EXPERIENCES

Dorian tonality is another of the most prevailing tonalities in our culture. It is much less common than major, but appears almost as frequently as minor. Many songs from the Reggae genre and several folk traditions are in Dorian. It is a popular tonality in Old Time and Irish fiddle tunes, characterized by the major IV chord.

 Watch the video **Dorian Acculturation**. Sing along with the melody and the bass line on a neutral syllable.

 Search YouTube or Spotify for any of the following Dorian songs:
- "Shady Grove" (Folk Song)
- "So What" by Miles Davis
- "Oye Como Va" by Santana

 Watch the **Harmonic Loop** video in Dorian tonality. Hum along with the bass line.

REFERENCE INFORMATION

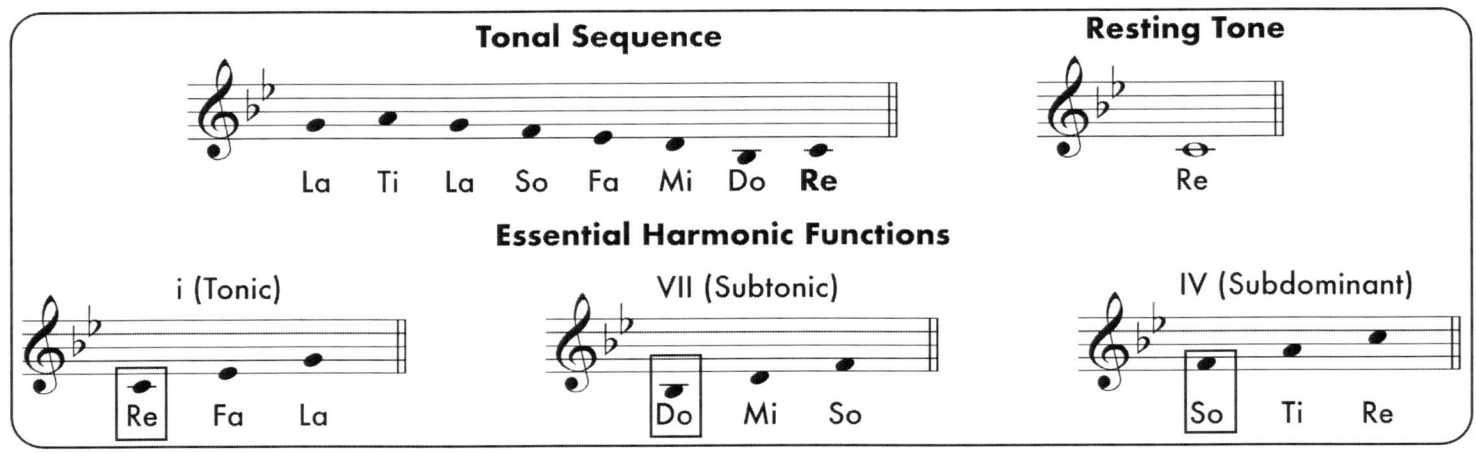

FPIFO

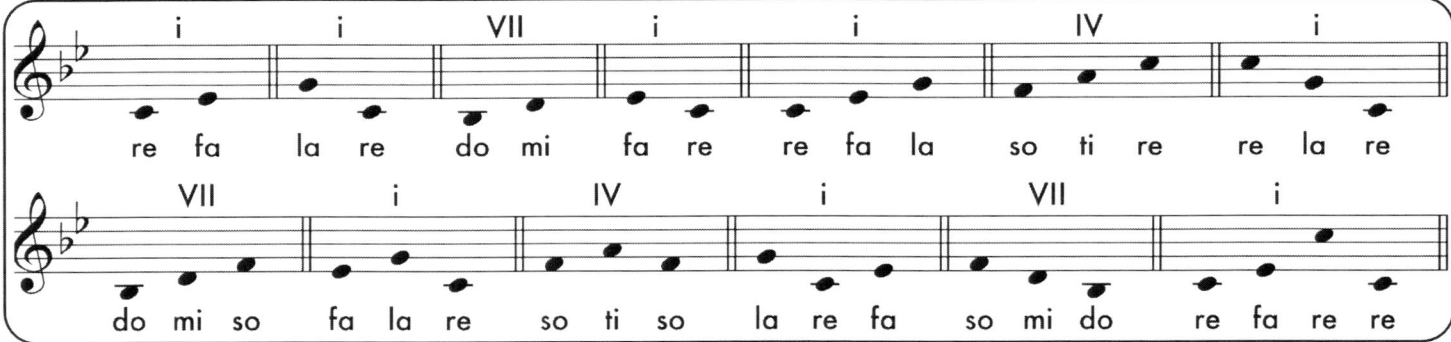

Dorian Acculturation Tune

TONALITIES
MIXOLYDIAN TONALITY

LISTENING EXPERIENCES

Along with Dorian, Mixolydian is another of the most prevailing tonalities in our culture. It is a very popular in Blues and Rock, and elements of the tonality are found everywhere. It is a favored tonality in Old Time and Irish fiddle tunes.

 Watch the video **Mixolydian Acculturation** Sing along with the melody and the bass line.

 Search YouTube or Spotify for any of the following Mixolydian songs:
- "Old Joe Clark" (Folk Song)
- "Stuck in the Middle With You" (Stealer's Wheel)
- "Royals" by Lorde

 Watch the **Harmonic Loop** video in Mixolydian tonality. Hum along with the bass line.

REFERENCE INFORMATION

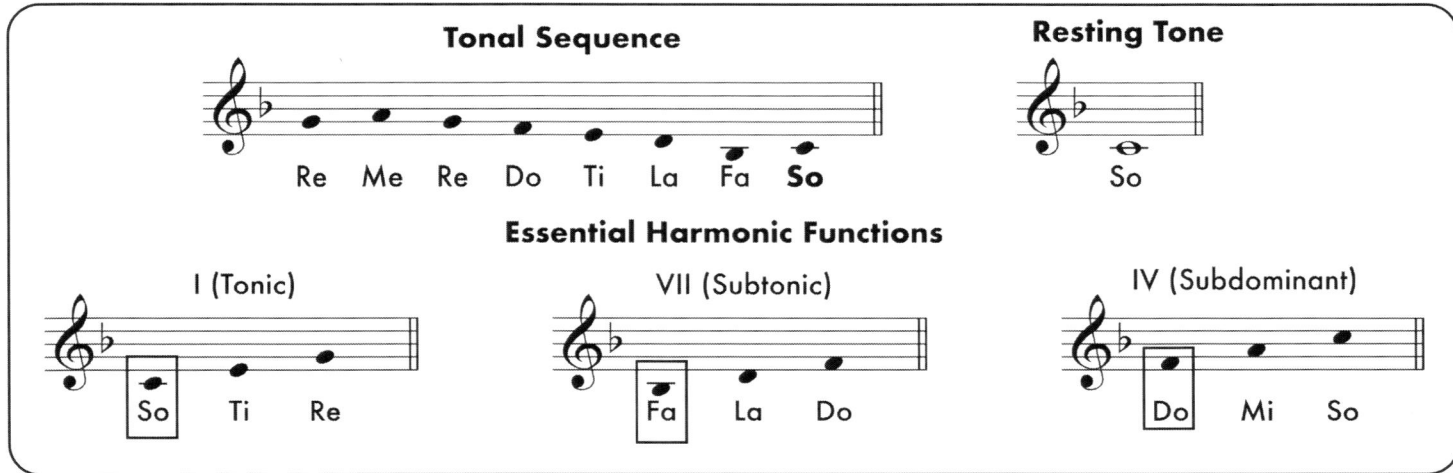

FPIFO

Mixolydian Acculturation Tune

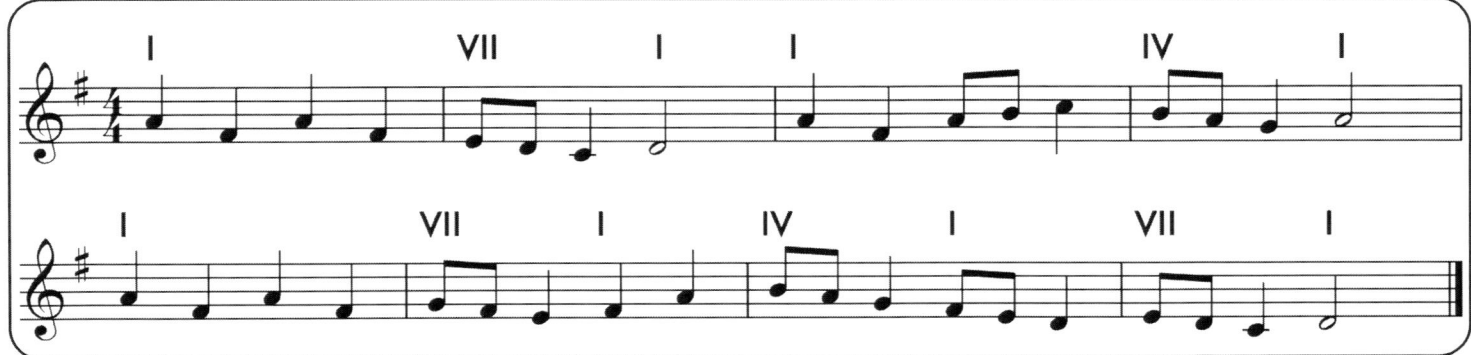

TONALITIES
PHRYGIAN TONALITY

LISTENING EXPERIENCES

Phrygian is an ancient tonality (sometimes referred to as a mode) whose use is infrequent in the music of our culture. Phrygian, and elements of Phrygian, can be found in European and Eastern European music, particularly in Greek, Spanish and Jewish cultures. It is characterized by the flattened second scale degree.

 Watch the video **Phrygian Acculturation**. Sing along with the melody and the bass line.

 Search YouTube or Spotify for any of the following songs (some only have Phrygian **flavor**):
- "White Rabbit" by Jefferson Airplane (flavor only)
- "Hava Nagila"
- "Fiselekh, Fiselekh"

 Watch the **Harmonic Loop** video in Phrygian tonality. Hum along with the bass line.

REFERENCE INFORMATION

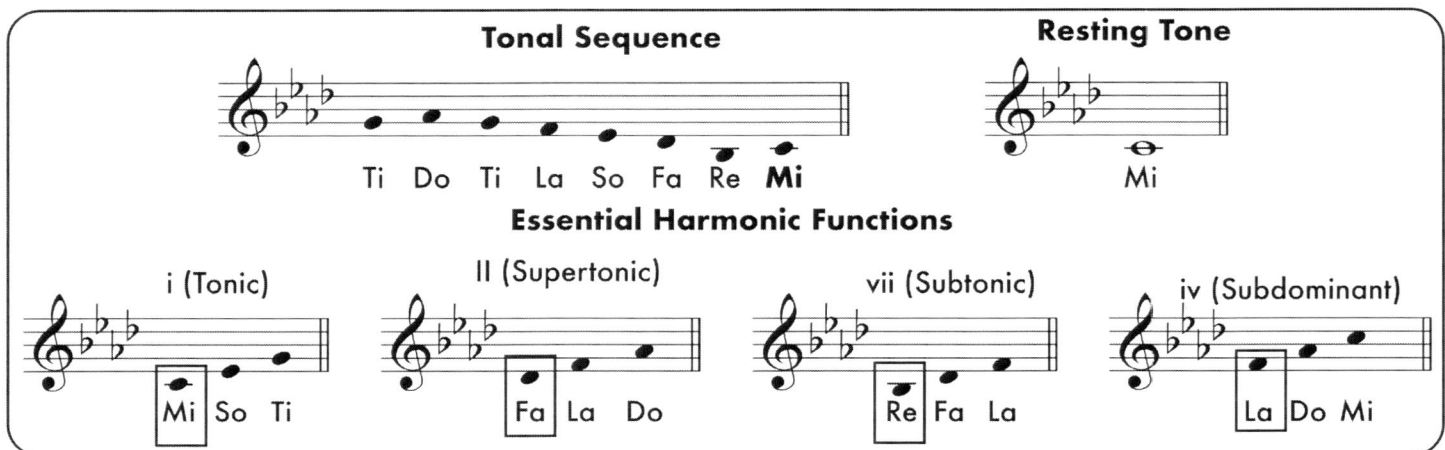

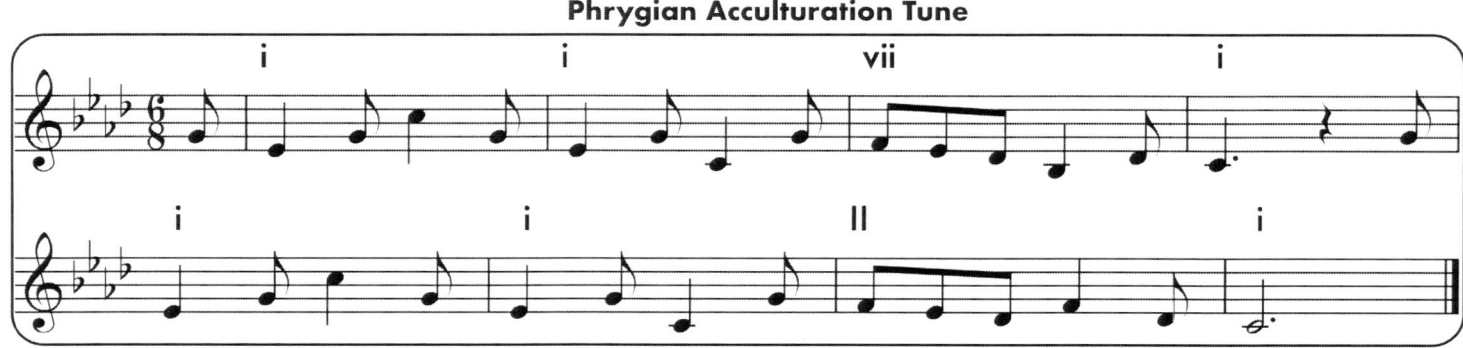

TONALITIES

LYDIAN TONALITY

LISTENING EXPERIENCES

Lydian is another tonality that you don't hear that much in current pop songwriting. However, it is very prevalent in film scores. Elements of it appear in many television and movie themes. The so called "sharp four," a nod to Lydian, is a tried and true motif.

 Watch the video, **Lydian Acculturation**. Sing along with the melody and the bass line on a neutral syllable.

 Search YouTube or Spotify for any of the following movie or TV themes with heavy Lydian influences:
- "The Simpsons" (TV theme song)
- "The Jetsons" (TV theme song)
- "Super Mario Galaxy" (video game music)
- "E.T." (movie theme)
- "Mrs. Doubtfire" (movie theme)

REFERENCE INFORMATION

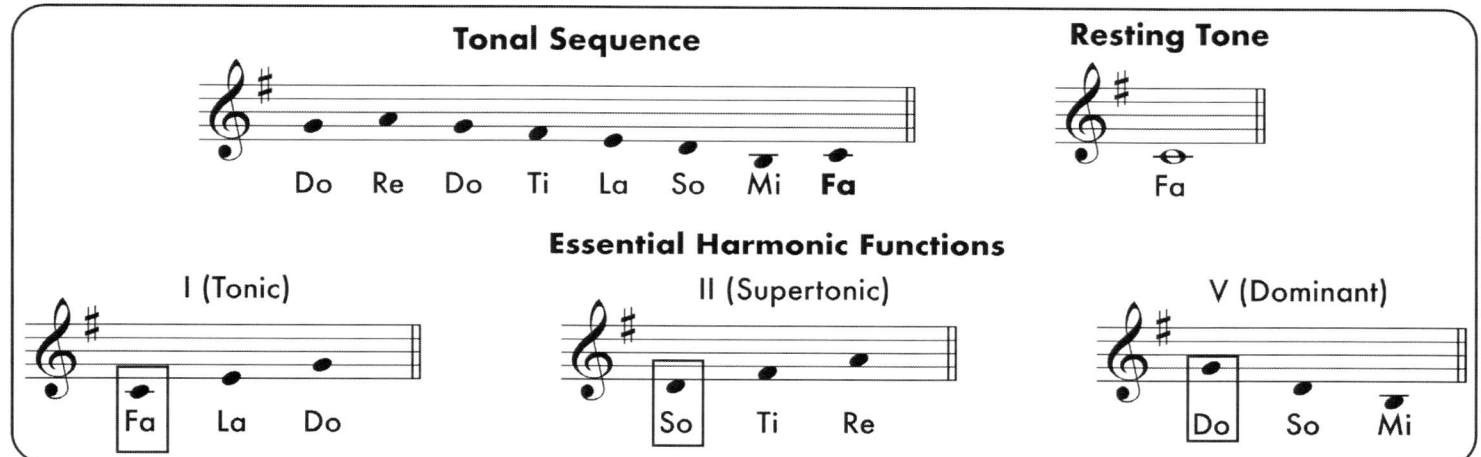

FPIFO

Lydian Acculturation Tune

TONALITIES
AEOLIAN TONALITY

LISTENING EXPERIENCES

Aeolian, which appears very frequently in our culture, is the cousin of Minor tonality because they share a resting tone. In fact, many songs labeled as minor are, in fact, more specifically Aeolian (also known as "natural minor"). They share many of the same harmonic functions (chords), however Aeolian uses a VII chord as opposed to a V7 chord.

 Watch the video **Aeolian Acculturation**. Sing along with the melody and the bass line on a neutral syllable.

 Search YouTube or Spotify for any of the following Mixolydian songs:
- "Living On a Prayer" by Bon Jovi
- "All Along the Watchtower" by Jimi Hendrix
- "Stairway to Heaven" by Led Zeppelin

REFERENCE INFORMATION

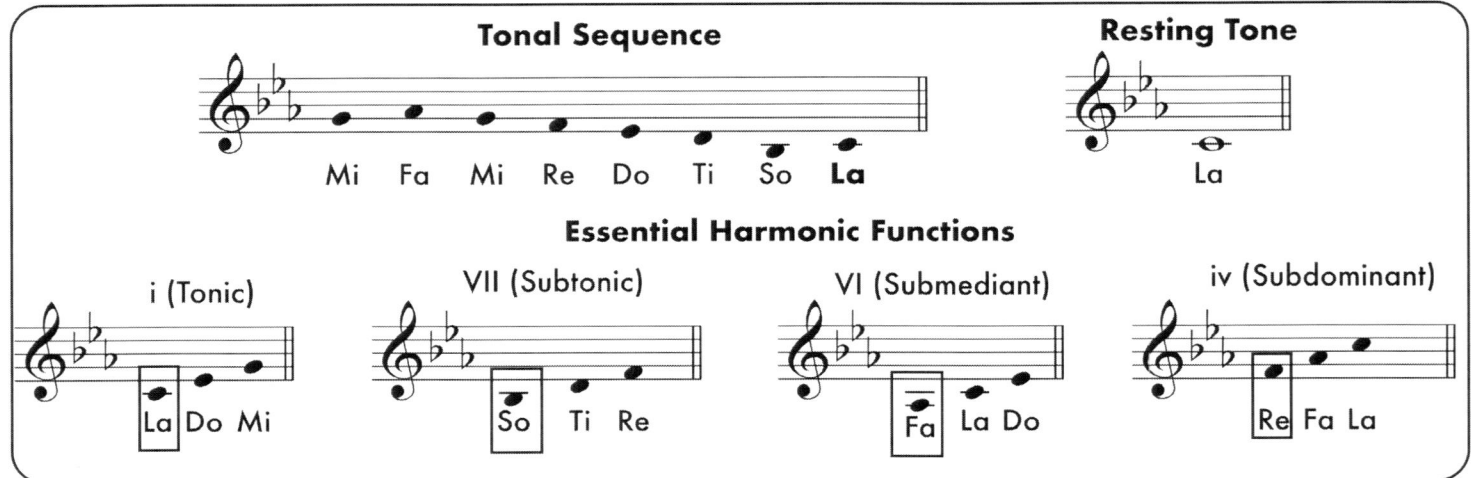

FPIFO

Aeolian Acculturation Tune

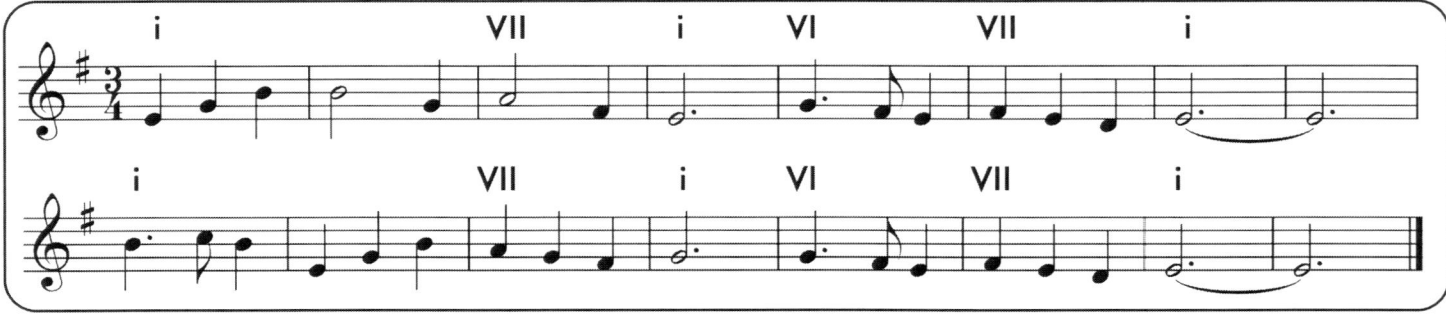

TONALITIES
LOCRIAN TONALITY

LISTENING EXPERIENCES

It is very difficult to find pure examples of songs in the Locrian mode "out in the wild," particularly because of its unstable nature with a diminished tonic chord.

 Watch the video, **Locrian Acculturation**. Sing along with the melody and the bass line on a neutral syllable.

 Search YouTube or Spotify for the following Locrian song:
- "Dust to Dust" (folk song by John Kirkpatrick)

 Watch the **Ah, Poor Snail** video. Try it as a round.

REFERENCE INFORMATION

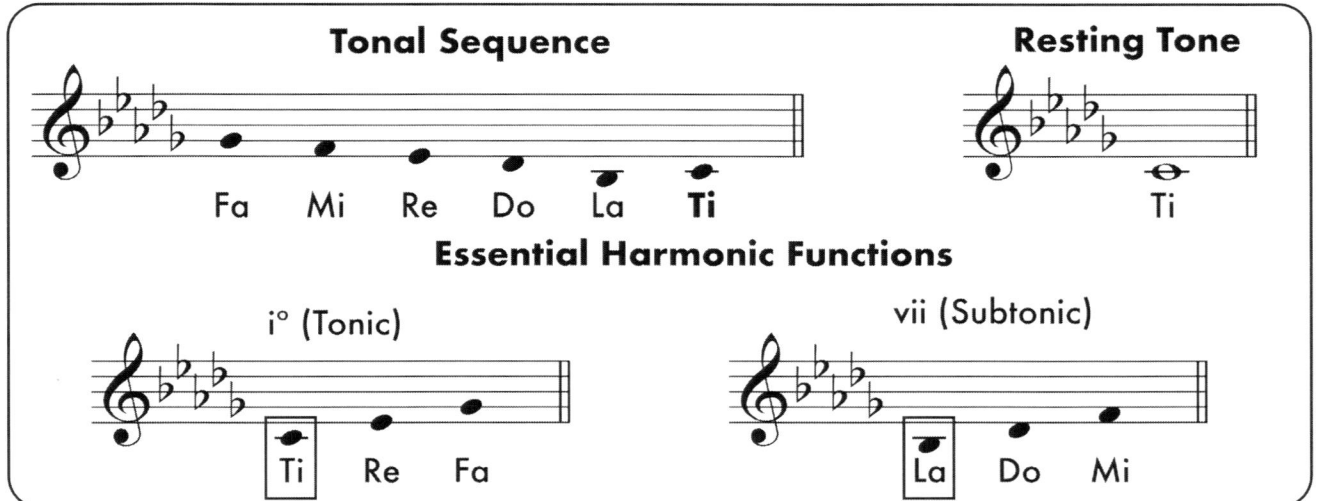

FPIFO

Locrian Acculturation Tune

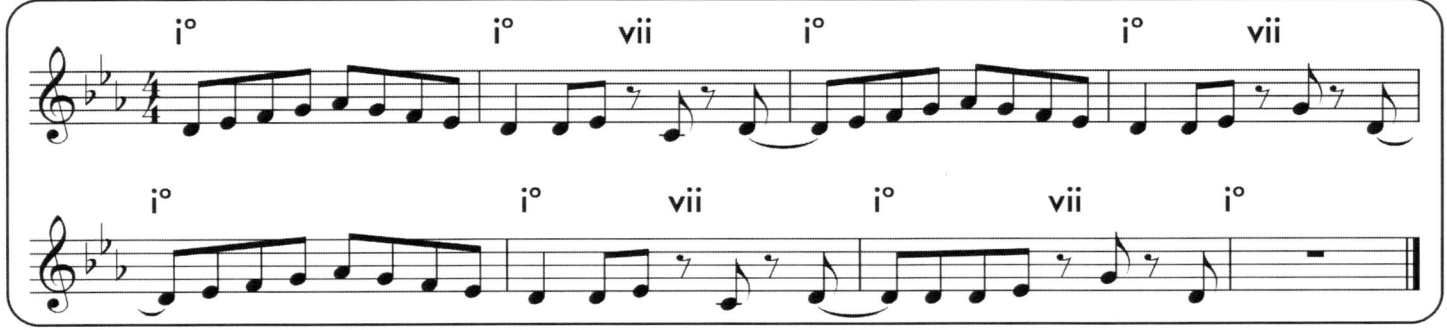

METERS
DUPLE METER

LISTENING EXPERIENCES

Duple meter is the most prevailing meter of our culture, and compromises the majority of the songs on the radio. Like major tonality, as a growing musician, you should know some songs that are decidedly duple.

 Watch the video, **Duple Acculturation**. Sing along with the melody and the bass line on a neutral syllable.

 Begin by revisiting some songs and nursery rhymes from your (perhaps not too distant) childhood. The following are in duple:
- "Twinkle, Twinkle Little Star"
- "Bah Bah Black Sheep"
- "Hot Cross Buns"
- "Are You Sleeping?"
- "Five Little Monkeys"

 On the album "Chucka Chucka Wawa," the songs "Ba Dum, Ba Dum, Ba Dum," "Bum Bum Bum," "Choo Choo", "Pa Ba, Ka Ga, Ta Da," and "Ya Ya Ya" are in duple meter. Try some of the movement activities on p. 35.

> The reference charts for meters on the following pages only show a sampling of rhythm patterns, functions, and possibilities. It is not meant to be exhaustive.

REFERENCE INFORMATION

Time Signature	Macrobeats	Microbeats	Divisions*	Elongations
2/4	♩ ♩ Du Du	♫ ♫ Du De Du De	♬♬ Du Ta De Ta	♩ (half) Du ♪ ♩. Du De ♩. ♪ Du De
4/4	♩ ♩ ♩ ♩ Du Du Du Du	♫ ♫ ♫ ♫ Du De Du De Du De Du De	♬♬ Du Ta De Ta	o Du ♩ ♩ Du Du ♩. ♩. Du Du ♩ ♩. Du Du
¢	♩ ♩ Du Du	♩ ♩ ♩ ♩ Du De Du De	♫ ♫ Du Ta De Ta	o Du ♩. ♩. Du De ♩ ♩. Du De

*incomplete measures

METERS
TRIPLE METER

LISTENING EXPERIENCES

Triple is also a very prevalent meter in our culture. It is not as popular in music today, however if you know what to listen for, you will certainly hear it.

 Watch the video, **Triple Acculturation**. Sing along with the melody and the bass line on a neutral syllable.

 Here are some nursery rhymes and childhood songs in triple meter:
- "Here We Go 'Round the Mulberry Bush"
- "Row, Row, Row Your Boat"
- "Hickory Dickory Dock"
- "Jack and Jill"
- "Three Blind Mice"

 On the album "Chucka Chucka Wawa" the song "Shum Puh Puh" is in triple meter. Can you hear **elements** of triple in "Gum Zoo?"

 On the album "Every Day Songs With Words" the songs "Who's the Cutest Baby?" and "Sleepy Head" (also in Locrian!) are in triple meter. Try some of the movement activities on p. 35.

REFERENCE INFORMATION

Time Signature	Macrobeats	Microbeats	Divisions	Elongations
6/8	♩. ♩. Du Du	♫♫ ♫♫ Du Da Di Du Da Di	* ♬♬♬ Du Ta Da Ta Di Ta	♩ ♪♪ ♩. Du Di Du Da Du
3/4	♩. Du	♩ ♩ ♩ Du Da Di	♫ ♫ ♫ Du Ta Da Ta Di Ta	♩ ♩ ♩ ♩ Du Da Du Di
3/8	♩. Du	♫♫ Du Da Di	♬♬ Du Ta Da Ta Di Ta	♪ ♩ ♩ ♪ Du Da Du Di

*incomplete measure

METERS

UNUSUAL-PAIRED METER

LISTENING EXPERIENCES

Although the name of this meter is perhaps culturally insensitive, its name implies that macrobeats are paired, but are of unequal length. This usually encompasses music written with a "5" as the top number in the time signature. If you try to move to this music, your beat will be uneven, and you might look like you are walking with a limp.

 Listen to the song, "Walking Through Mud Just Seems Impossible." Try walking to the beat of the song. Notice its uneven macrobeats. Try some of the movement activities on p. 35.

 Search YouTube or Spotify for any of the following songs in 5:
- "Take Five" by Dave Brubeck
- "Mission Impossible" Theme Song
- "River Man" by Nick Drake

 On the album "Every Day Songs With Words" listen to the song "Do You Love Your Mama?"

 On the album "Chucka Chucka Wawa" listen to the song "Chucka Chucka Wawa."

Please note that microbeats in unusual meters can be divided into various configurations of twos and threes. In 5/8, for example, microbeats can be grouped 2+3 or 3+2. For space purposes, I only indicated one grouping.

REFERENCE INFORMATION

Time Signature	Macrobeats	Microbeats	Divisions	Elongations
5/8	Du Du	Du Ba Bi Du Be	Du Ta Ba Ta Bi Ta Du Ta Be Ta	Du Ba Du
5/4	Du Du	Du Be Du Ba Bi	Du Ta Be Ta Du Ta Ba Ta Bi Ta	Du Du Ba

METERS
UNUSUAL-UNPAIRED METER

LISTENING EXPERIENCES

In Unusual-Unpaired meter, the macrobeats are also of unequal length (that is, some are two microbeats long and some are three microbeats long). The main difference is that since there are three macrobeats, they are not paired. If you try moving to the macrobeats in music in 7's and 8's, you might look like you are dizzy.

 Listen to the song, "Look at All the Happy Faces." Try walking to the beat of the song. Notice its uneven macrobeats. Try some of the movement activities on p. 35.

 Search YouTube or Spotify for any of the following songs in 7 and 8:
- "Unsquare Dance" by Dave Brubeck [7]
- "Money" by Pink Floyd [7]
- "Tin Man" by America [8]

 On the album "Every Day Songs With Words" listen to the song "All Done With Dinner Time."

 On the album "Chucka Chucka Wawa" listen to the song "Cuckoo."

Note that there are several possible combinations of twos and threes to equal 7 (2+2+3, 3+2+2, 2+3+2) and 8 (3+3+2, 2+3+3, 3+2+3). For space purposes, I only indicated one grouping.

REFERENCE INFORMATION

Time Signature	Macrobeats	Microbeats	Divisions	Elongations
7/8	Du Du Du	Du Ba Bi Du Be Du Be	Du Ta Ba Ta Bi Ta Du Ta Be Du Be Ta	Du Ba Du
8/8	Du Du Du	Du Ba Bi Du Ba Bi Du Be	Du Ta Ba Bi Du Ba Ta Bi Du Ta Be Ta	Du Ba Du Bi Du

SECTION 2: RHYTHM

SECTION 2 AT A GLANCE

	Lesson Sequence
Lesson 1	Introduction to Rhythm Concepts
Lesson 2	Echoing Rhythm Patterns, Duple, Aural/Oral
Lesson 3	Echoing Rhythm Patterns, Triple, Aural/Oral
Lesson 4	Verbal Association, Duple Meter
Lesson 5	Verbal Association, Triple Meter
Lesson 6	Improvisation
Lesson 7	Comparing Duple and Triple Meters #1
Lesson 8	Rhythmic Translation #1
Lesson 9	Duple Divisions
Lesson 10	Triple Divisions
Lesson 11	Comparing Duple and Triple Meters #2
Lesson 12	Duple Elongations
Lesson 13	Triple Elongations
Assessment	

LESSON 1
INTRODUCTION TO RHYTHM CONCEPTS

Rhythm exists on 3 fundamental levels:
- Macrobeats (Big Beats)
- Microbeats (Little Beats)
- Rhythm Patterns (Melodic Rhythm)

These levels interact with each other in musical **space** to form the rhythmic foundation of music.

MACROBEAT

The **macrobeat**, or, the big beat, is the pulse of music. It is what you would likely tap your foot to, or the beat you would move to, if you were dancing. The macrobeat defines the **tempo** of the music.

MICROBEAT

We can take that macrobeat and divide it into either two or three parts. These parts are called **microbeats**. These are the little beats in music. The microbeat defines the **meter** of the music.

If we divide each macrobeat into **two** microbeats, the music is in duple meter. If we divide each macrobeat into **three** microbeats, the music is in triple meter. There are, of course, more meters than just duple and triple. But rhythm, at a very fundamental level, is really just twos and threes, and any combination you wish to imagine.

Duple Meter
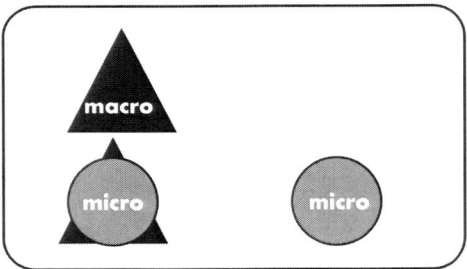

Triple Meter
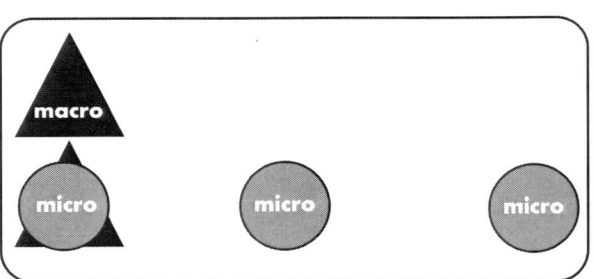

RHYTHM PATTERNS

Macrobeats and microbeats form the foundation for rhythm, and should be constantly swirling around in your audiation as you make music. On top of those two layers is the **melodic rhythm** of the song. The melodic rhythm is comprised of combinations of **rhythm patterns**, or rhythmic words.

```
X X  X  X XX    X
Mary had a little lamb
```

We will learn rhythm by learning rhythm cells (which can be thought of as rhythmic **words**), and combining them with other rhythm cells to make longer rhythm patterns (which can be thought of as rhythmic **sentences**).

RHYTHM AND MOVEMENT

Rhythm and movement go hand in hand. Rhythm requires coordination. In order to have a true sense of rhythm, one must be able to move their body to macrobeats and microbeats and the **space** in between. The amount of **space between the macrobeats** will determine how fast or slow the tempo is. Moving **not** to the beat is just as important as moving **to** the beat.

Try the movement activities listed under **Movement Exploration**. These are demonstrated in the videos below.

 Watch the following videos on The Improving Musician YouTube channel:
- **Rhythm Lesson 1**
- **Duple Acculturation**
- **Triple Acculturation**

	Movement Exploration
Continuous Flow in Space (CFS)	As you are listening to music, move as much of your body as you feel comfortable moving in free-flowing continuous space. Imagine that you are in the deep end of a pool, and you are wading your arms through the water. This is very important in order to feel **the space in-between the beats**.
Microbeats	While moving in CFS, try adding microbeat "flicks" or pulses. Then take the flow away and just try moving to the microbeats. Next, gently pat your lap with the tips of your fingers.
Macrobeats	Try gently lifting your heels up and down on the macrobeat. Try shifting your weight from side to side.
Variations	Try all of these variations: • Combine macrobeats with the feet and microbeats with the hands • Alternate between beat (macro/micro) and CFS • Put macrobeats in your feet and flow with the arms • Flick the microbeats with the hands, and walk with CFS **not** to the beat. Imagine you are walking through mud. Feel the resistance.

LESSON 2
ECHOING RHYTHM PATTERNS (DUPLE, AURAL/ORAL)

AURAL/ORAL

We will learn rhythm patterns through the first discrimination level skill, **Aural/Oral**. You will hear a pattern (aural), and then **echo** it back (oral). Think of the way that your parents taught you your first words. The process is very similar. Furthermore, after you chant the pattern (oral), you listen to the pattern again as you echo it (another aural) to check yourself for accuracy. So this cyclical process really could be called Aural/Oral/Aural.

RHYTHM PATTERNS AND THE BREATH

Most rhythm patterns will be four macrobeats in length. Before you echo back the rhythm pattern, it's important to take a full **breath** on the **4th macrobeat**. It is during the breath that audiation happens.

 If you take time to notice, when someone asks you a thoughtful question, you will pause, think (audiate?), and **take a breath** before you speak. It's **during that breath** that your brain organizes and summarizes the information about to be spoken.

Visual representation of Aural/Oral pattern with breath on 4th macrobeat

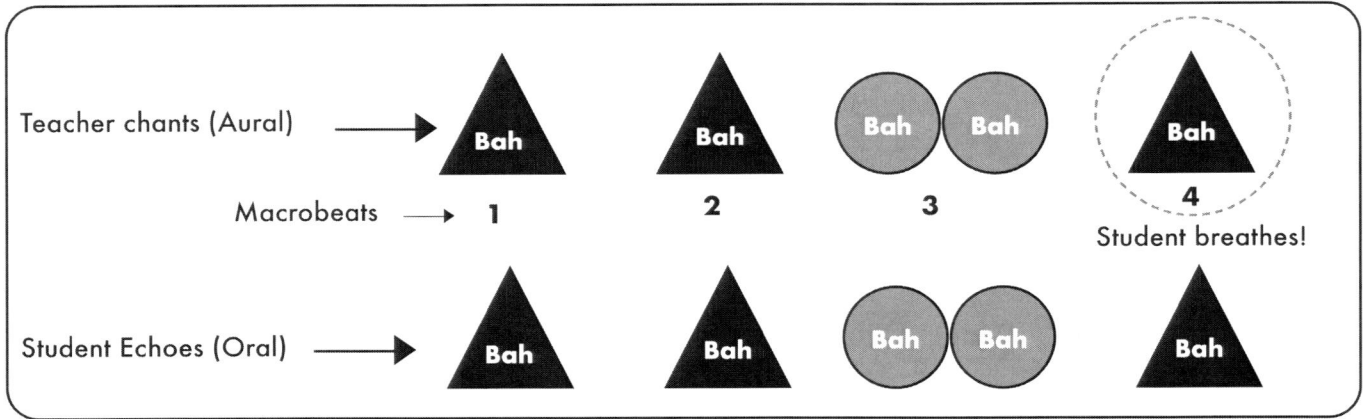

ECHOING RHYTHM PATTERNS IN DUPLE

 Listen to and echo the patterns chanted on the following companion course videos. Use a neutral syllable ("Bah").
- **Rhythm Lesson 2: Echoing Rhythm Patterns in Duple Meter**
- **Rhythm Lesson 2: Patterns Only**

Be sure to take a breath on the **4th macrobeat**. Try various movements while you are listening and chanting. **Rhythm patterns should have inflection, and be conversational.** The patterns appear on the following page for your reference.

Duple Meter, Macrobeats and Microbeats

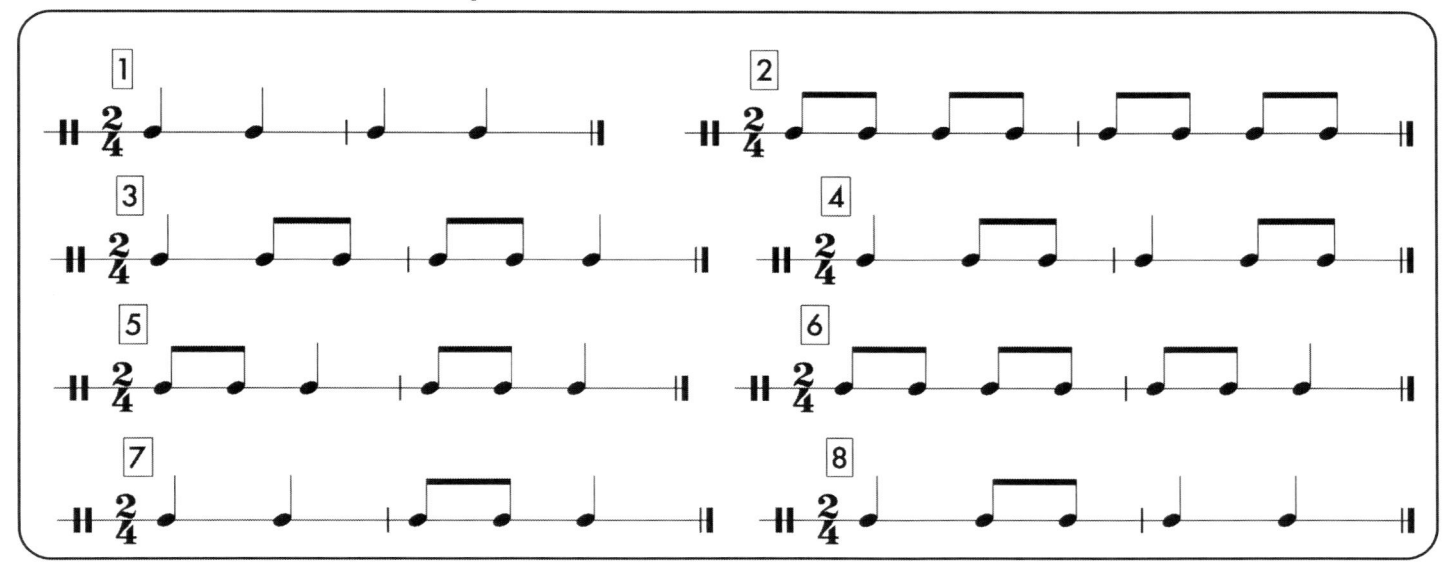

LESSON 3
ECHOING RHYTHM PATTERNS (TRIPLE, AURAL/ORAL)

Follow the same procedures as you did for Lesson 2. Listen to and echo the patterns chanted on the following companion course videos. Use a neutral syllable ("Bah"). The patterns appear below for your reference.

- **Rhythm Lesson 3: Echoing Rhythm Patterns in Triple Meter**
- **Rhythm Lesson 3: Patterns Only**

Triple Meter, Macrobeats and Microbeats

Try bridging to inference learning with the patterns you just learned at the Aural/Oral level.
- Improvisation-Aural/Oral: Watch the video **Two Chatty Sheep**.
- Generalization-Aural/Oral: Try the **Same vs. Different Test-Rhythm**.

LESSON 4
VERBAL ASSOCIATION, DUPLE METER

Once we can successfully move to macrobeats and microbeats simultaneously, and echo patterns at the Aural/Oral level, it's time to label the patterns with a **Verbal Association**.

In language, we don't need this step because we can visually see the object (Mommy, Daddy, bottle) or label it as a feeling or emotion (happy, sad, angry). **In music, we need an extra step to label and organize the sound we hear**.

The most effective system for labeling the layers of rhythm is the **Beat-Function Rhythm Solfege** system developed by Edwin Gordon and James Froseth.

▶ Watch **How to "Du De": The Gordon/Froseth Syllable System Explained** for a thorough explanation of this system with notational examples.

BEAT FUNCTION SYLLABLE SYSTEM

To begin to use this syllable system, we only need to label macrobeats and microbeats in duple and triple meters.

Macrobeats, regardless of meter, will get the syllable **"DU"** (pronounced "Doo"). **Microbeats** get different syllables based upon meter.

In duple, microbeats are **"DU DE"** (pronounced "Doo Day"). In triple, microbeats are **"DU DA DI"** (pronounced "Doo Dah Dee").

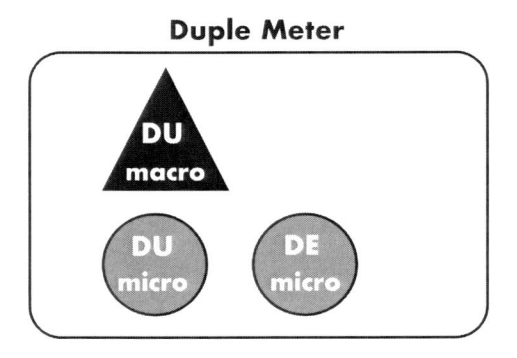

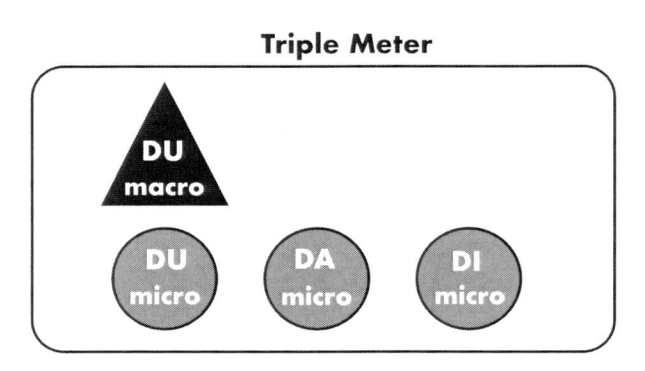

Duple Meter

- DU macro
  - DU micro
  - DE micro

Triple Meter

- DU macro
  - DU micro
  - DA micro
  - DI micro

Notice that the first syllable of the microbeat is the same syllable as the macrobeat. This allows one to hear the rhythm syllables based upon **beat function**.

Later, as we begin to read music, you'll see that this syllable system works in all time signatures. It is based on how music is **felt** first in the body, rather than how it is notated. Music, after all, is an **aural art** first, and a written art second.

Lesson 4   39

LABELING DUPLE METER

As stated, when you audiate "DU DE" as the microbeat, the music is in **duple meter**. Chant this to yourself:

"Macrobeats in **duple** meter are DU DU DU DU. Microbeats in duple meter are DU DE, DU DE, DU DE, DU DE."

ECHOING RHYTHM PATTERNS IN DUPLE METER

▶ Listen to and echo the patterns chanted on the following companion course videos. **Use rhythm syllables**.
- **Rhythm Lesson 4: Verbal Association, Duple Meter**
- **Rhythm Lesson 4: Patterns Only (Duple, Macro/Micro)**

Alternatively, you can have someone chant the patterns to you. They appear in notation below with rhythm syllables for your reference. Be sure to take a breath on the **4th macrobeat**. Try various movements while you are listening and chanting. **Rhythm patterns should have inflection, and be conversational.**

! Note: As much as possible, do not rely on seeing the rhythm solfege syllables written out. Solfege is primarily an **aural** tool. Your focus should be on listening to the patterns and echoing them back. You will have plenty of time to read patterns at the appropriate time when we get to Symbolic Association in Part 2.

Duple Meter, Macrobeats and Microbeats

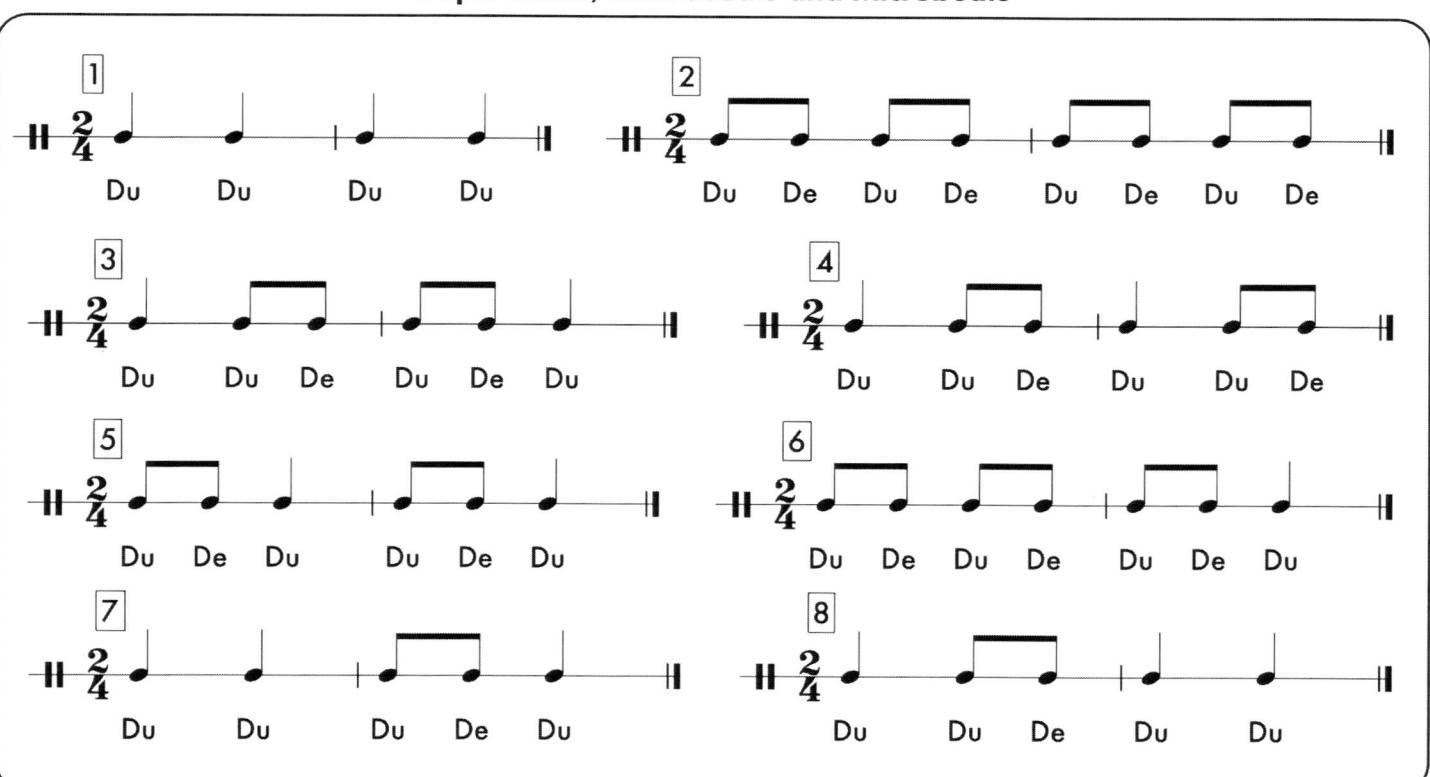

1. Du Du Du Du
2. Du De Du De Du De Du De
3. Du Du De Du De Du
4. Du Du De Du De
5. Du De Du Du De Du
6. Du De Du De Du De Du
7. Du Du Du De Du
8. Du Du De Du Du

LESSON 5
VERBAL ASSOCIATION, TRIPLE METER

LABELING TRIPLE METER

As stated, when you audiate "DU DA DI" as the microbeat, the music is in **triple meter**. Chant this to yourself:

"Macrobeats in **triple** meter are DU (4 x's) ... Microbeats in triple meter are DU DA DI (4 x's)."

ECHOING RHYTHM PATTERNS IN TRIPLE METER

Listen to and echo the patterns chanted on the following companion course videos. **Use rhythm syllables**.
- **Rhythm Lesson 5: Verbal Association, Triple Meter**
- **Rhythm Lesson 5: Patterns Only (Triple, Macro/Micro)**

Alternatively, you can have someone chant the patterns to you. They appear in notation below with rhythm syllables for your reference. Be sure to take a breath on the **4th macrobeat**. Try various movements while you are listening and chanting. **Rhythm patterns should have inflection, and be conversational.**

Triple Meter, Macrobeats and Microbeats

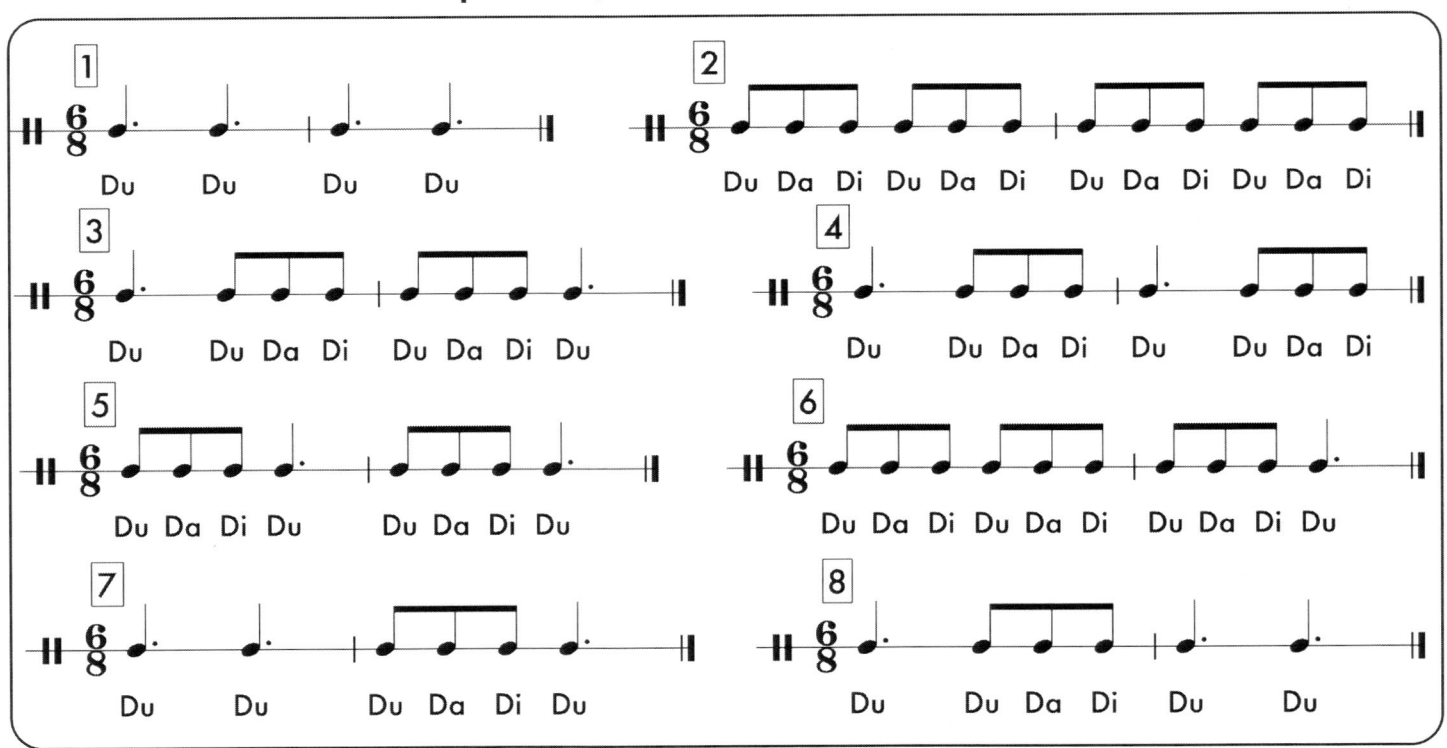

1. Du Du Du Du
2. Du Da Di Du Da Di Du Da Di Du Da Di
3. Du Du Da Di Du Da Di Du
4. Du Du Da Di Du Du Da Di
5. Du Da Di Du Du Da Di Du
6. Du Da Di Du Da Di Du Da Di Du
7. Du Du Du Da Di Du
8. Du Du Da Di Du Du

LESSON 6
IMPROVISATION

IMPROVISATION IN LANGUAGE

In language, we communicate with each other through conversation. We ask questions, and we get answers. We offer a point of view, and someone agrees or disagrees. We ask for something, and someone tells us yes or no, and why. Although we can't communicate specific information to each other in music, we can certainly have **musical conversations**, and convey underlying feelings or emotions through our expression.

SAME VS. DIFFERENT

Up to this point, you have only echoed back patterns. Once we have learned a language, it would be silly if we had a conversation where we were simply echoing back what the other person said. In fact, that might infuriate your conversation partner.

But now that you know eight duple and eight triple rhythm patterns with macrobeats and microbeats, (and have the knowledge to make up your own!) **you have something different to say**.

▶ Watch the following videos for some opportunities for rhythmic improvisation:
- **Rhythm Lesson 6: Improvisation**
- **Rhythm Lesson 6: Patterns Only (Duple)**
- **Rhythm Lesson 6: Patterns Only (Triple)**

RHYTHMIC CONVERSATIONS

Try to have **rhythmic conversations** with your musical friends. It's not until you can fluently speak "DU DE" that you fully own this. Have inflection, and pretend like you're having an actual conversation. Do this in duple meter and in triple meter!

	Rhythmic Conversation Example			
	BEAT 1	**BEAT 2**	**BEAT 3**	**BEAT 4**
Friend 1:	Du	Du	Du De	Du?
Friend 2:	Du De	Du De	Du!	Du!
Friend 1:	Du	Du De.	Du	Du De.
Friend 2:	Du?	Du?	Du De	Du!

LESSON 7
COMPARING DUPLE & TRIPLE METERS #1

Ultimately, your goal is to be able to listen to a piece of music and audiate its rhythm. That is to say, when you listen to a piece of unfamiliar music, your ears should tell you:
- What meter is it in?
- Can you audiate the various rhythmic layers that are happening simultaneously?
- Can you give labels (macrobeats, microbeats, divisions, elongations) to the sounds you are hearing?
- Is your audiation subconsciously assigning solfege syllables to the rhythms you are hearing?

The aforementioned skills are indeed the goal, but are decidedly **inference** skills that come with much practice. We are now going to practice distinguishing between duple and triple meters using **familiar** patterns. This will give you the opportunity to learn **how** to distinguish between duple and triple meters with familiar **or** unfamiliar music. This skill is called **Partial Synthesis**.

Since Partial Synthesis is an aural skill, it is difficult, nay impossible, to convey with only the written word.

▶ Watch the video **Rhythm Lesson 7: Comparing Duple and Triple #1**. The salient text appears below.

> ## COMPARING DUPLE AND TRIPLE
>
> Listen to these two musical sentences. One will be in duple, and the other will be in triple.
>
> Now, I will turn my thinking inside out, and explain what I was audiating. In the first musical sentence, I was audiating DU DE as the microbeats. When you audiate DU DE as the microbeats, the music is in **DUPLE METER**.
>
> In the second musical sentence, I was audiating DU DA DI as the microbeats. When you audiate DU DA DI as the microbeats, the music is in **TRIPLE METER**.
>
> Listen to these very similar musical sentences, and you will name the meter by stating the **microbeats** you are audiating: DU DE or DU DA DI.

When trying to distinguish between meters, try to focus your ears on the **microbeat**. They will give you your first clue to being able to identify the meter. What are you audiating? DU DE? Or DU DA DI? Try quietly chanting the microbeats as you are listening. If the music is in duple or triple, one or the other will fit.

▶ Take the assessment **Duple vs. Triple Test #1**.

> If you **are** successful at comparing duple and triple, you can **spiral** forward to read duple and triple macro/microbeat patterns at the Symbolic Association level in Part II.

LESSON 8
RHYTHM PATTERN TRANSLATION #1

INTRODUCTION

If you ever learn a foreign language, one of the ways your teacher might assess you is to ask you to translate words and phrases from one language into another. Your teacher might give you a list of familiar vocabulary words in English and have you translate them into Spanish, for example. Or, they might give you familiar words you have been taught in Spanish, and have you translate them to English. We can do the same thing in music!

▶ Watch the video **Rhythm Lesson 8: Translation #1** for a demonstration of the skill. Then, watch the **Patterns Only Videos** in duple and triple to try it by yourself
  - Listen to the pattern on a neutral syllable. These will all be patterns that you are familiar with from previous lessons. Translate the pattern from neutral syllables to rhythm syllables.
  - First, try it with four macrobeats of "think time." Then, try it with two macrobeats of "think time." And finally, translate in real time.
  - You will do some in duple, and some in triple.

⚠ If You're Having Trouble ⚠

Translating rhythm patterns is part of Generalization, which is an **inference** skill. It really works your brain in ways that it may not have worked before. If you are having difficulty, please go back to previous lessons and review the syllables, and then try again. Continue this process until the syllables become second nature.

Can you fluently "speak 'Du De'"? If not, try more improvisation!

LESSON 9
DIVISIONS IN DUPLE METER

The next rhythmic function you will learn is called a **division**. Before any explanations about how a divisions work, it's best that you hear, experience, and echo some division patterns at the **Aural/Oral** level with a neutral syllable before we put the syllables to them.

▶ Watch the video **Rhythm Lesson 9.1: Divisions in Duple Meter**
- Echo the patterns using the syllable "BAH."
- Be sure to breathe on the 4th macrobeat before you echo.
- Keep the microbeats somewhere on your body as you listen and echo.

DIVISIONS EXPLAINED

When you take a microbeat, and divide it again, it's called a **division**. We'll use the syllable "TA" to represent the division of a microbeat.

To get the syllables moving fluidly, try chanting four macrobeats, four pairs of microbeats, and then four sets of divisions. Then try it in reverse: divisions, then microbeats, then macrobeats.

To make divisions flow more easily off the tongue, you might consider pronouncing them "TUH."

3 Levels of Rhythm in Duple Meter

DIVISION RHYTHM CELLS

There are three possible division rhythm cells, which you might think of as musical **vocabulary words** that we can learn. They appear below. Try saying them over and over again. We will put these words into musical sentences. When we combine these, both with each other and with macrobeats and microbeats, this will open up a whole new rhythmic world.

As with previous rhythmic functions, try **improvising** with them as much as possible, either with yourself, or in a rhythmic conversation with another musician.

Division Pattern Possibilities

1. DU macro — TA division — DE micro — TA division
2. DU macro — TA division — DE micro
3. DU macro — DE micro — TA division

▶ • Watch the video **Rhythm Lesson 9.2: Divisions in Duple Meter** for an explanation.
• Then, watch the **Patterns Only Video** to practice echoing them.

Lesson 9   45

Although we have not come to Symbolic Association, here are the twelve Duple Division patterns for your reference. Try having another musician chant the patterns to you as you echo them back.

Macrobeats, Microbeats and Divisions in Duple Meter

1. Du   Du   Du Ta De Ta Du
2. Du   Du Ta De Ta   Du De Du
3. Du De Du   Du Ta De Ta Du
4. Du Ta De Ta   Du De   Du De Du
5. Du   Du Ta De Ta   Du Ta De Ta Du
6. Du Ta De Ta Du Ta De Ta   Du   Du
7. Du Ta De   Du Ta De   Du De Du
8. Du De Ta Du De Ta   Du De Du
9. Du Ta De Du   Du De Ta Du
10. Du De Ta Du Ta De   Du Ta De Ta Du
11. Du Ta De Ta Du Ta De   Du De Ta Du Ta De Ta
12. Du Ta De Du Ta De Ta   Du De Ta Du

TRANSLATION

▶ Watch the video **Rhythm Lesson 9.3: Rhythm Translation #2**.

In this lesson, you will translate duple division patterns from a neutral syllable to solfege. You will translate at the **word level**, the **phrase level** and at the **sentence level**. If we were to make a connection to learning a foreign language, we might think of those patterns in the following way:

- **Word level** (rhythm cell). For example, "gato" means "cat."
- **Phrase level** (two macrobeat pattern). For example, "el gato negro" means "the black cat."
- **Sentence level** (four macrobeat pattern). For example, "El gato negro esta en mi casa" means "The black cat is in my house."

After you achieve moderate success at improvisation and translation, learn to **read** these patterns in Part II.

Try to strum these rhythms on the ukulele. Be sure to keep your wrist loose!

LESSON 10
DIVISIONS IN TRIPLE METER

We will follow the same procedures as we did with duple divisions by listening to the patterns first with a neutral syllable.

▶ Watch the beginning of the video **Rhythm Lesson 10.1: Triple Divisions (Aural/Oral)**
- Echo the patterns using the syllable "BAH." Be sure to breathe on the 4th macrobeat before you echo, and keep the microbeats somewhere on your body as you listen and echo.

TRIPLE DIVISIONS EXPLAINED

Just as we did in duple meter, we'll use the syllable "TA" to represent the division of a microbeat.

To get the syllables moving fluidly, try chanting four macrobeats, four sets of microbeats, and then four sets of divisions. Then try it in reverse: divisions, then microbeats, then macrobeats.

Again, to make divisions flow more easily off the tongue, you might consider pronouncing them with a neutral schwa sound ("TUH").

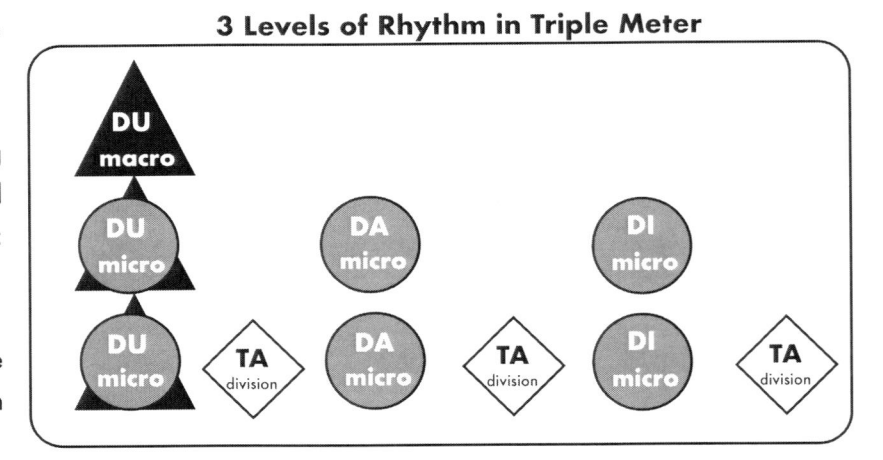

3 Levels of Rhythm in Triple Meter

TRIPLE DIVISION RHYTHM CELLS

Since there are three microbeats, there are more possibilities of division patterns in triple meter. In this book, we will focus on just four triple division vocabulary words. Later, you will have the opportunity to learn the rest.

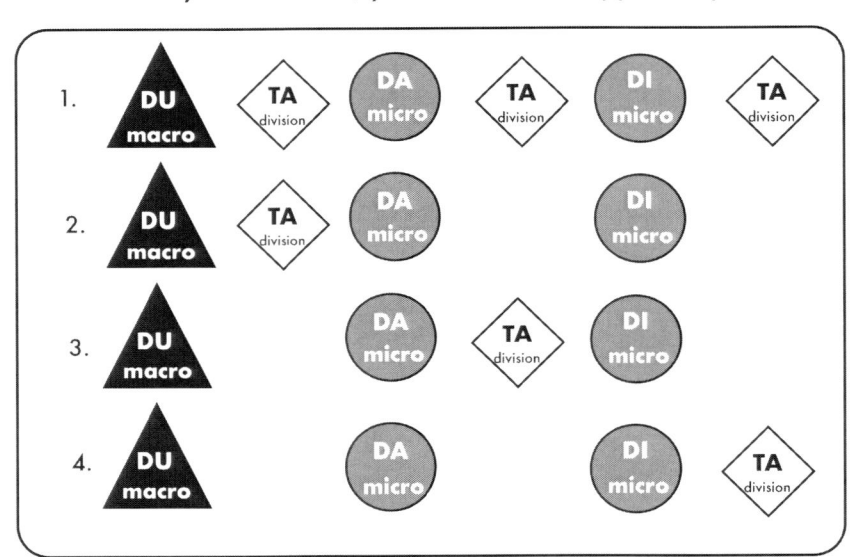

1. DU macro — TA division — DA micro — TA division — DI micro — TA division
2. DU macro — TA division — DA micro — DI micro
3. DU macro — DA micro — TA division — DI micro
4. DU macro — DA micro — DI micro — TA division

▶ • Watch the video **Rhythm Lesson 10.2: Triple Divisions, Solfege** for an explanation.
- Then, watch the **Patterns Only Video** to practice echoing them.

Although we have not come to Symbolic Association, here are the eight Triple Division patterns for your reference.

Macrobeats, Microbeats and Divisions in Triple Meter

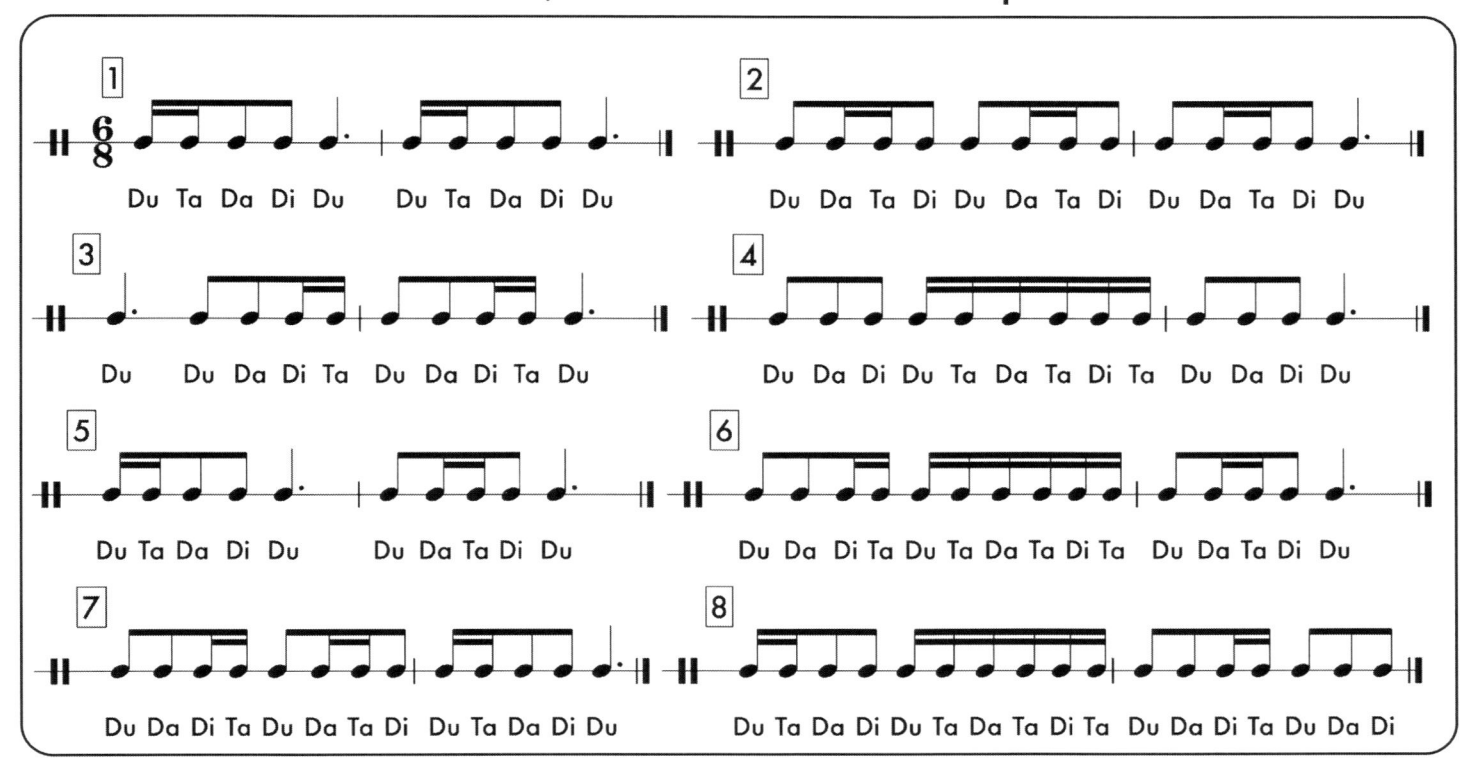

1. Du Ta Da Di Du | Du Ta Da Di Du
2. Du Da Ta Di Du Da Ta Di Du Da Ta Di Du
3. Du | Du Da Di Ta Du Da Di Ta Du
4. Du Da Di Du Ta Da Ta Di Ta Du Da Di Du
5. Du Ta Da Di Du | Du Da Ta Di Du
6. Du Da Di Ta Du Ta Da Ta Di Ta Du Da Ta Di Du
7. Du Da Di Ta Du Da Ta Di Du Ta Da Di Du
8. Du Ta Da Di Du Ta Da Ta Di Ta Du Da Di Ta Du Da Di

TRANSLATION

▶ Watch the video **Rhythm Lesson 10.3: Rhythm Translation #3**. In this lesson, you will translate triple division patterns from a neutral syllable to solfege. As you did with duple divisions, you will translate at the **word level**, the **phrase level** and at the **sentence level**.

💬 Try to have another triple rhythmic conversation. However, this time, add some triple divisions.

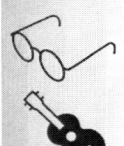

👓 After you achieve moderate success at improvisation and translation, learn to **read** these patterns in Part II.

🎸 Try to strum these rhythms on the ukulele. Be sure to keep your wrist loose!

LESSON 11
COMPARING DUPLE & TRIPLE METERS #2

▶ Watch the video **Rhythm Lesson 11: Comparing Duple and Triple #2**. In this lesson, you will follow the same procedures as Lesson 7, but we will add in duple and triple divisions.

▶ Take the assessment **Duple vs. Triple Quiz**.

LESSON 12
ELONGATIONS IN DUPLE METER

The next rhythmic function you will learn is called an **elongation**. Before any explanations about how elongations work, it's best that you hear, experience, and echo some elongation patterns at the Aural/Oral level with a neutral syllable before we put the syllables to them.

▶ Watch the video **Rhythm Lesson 12.1: Duple Elongations (Aural/Oral)**
   • As always, echo the patterns using the syllable "BAH," breathe on the 4th macrobeat before you echo and keep the microbeats somewhere on your body as you listen and echo.

ELONGATIONS EXPLAINED

An elongation is an **extension** of a macrobeat or a microbeat. You simply extend whatever syllable you're using ("DU" or "DE") and **audiate the underlying macrobeats and microbeats.** In the example to the right, one performs the syllables "DU DE" and audiates "DU DE" while they sustain the syllable "DE.")

Elongation Examples in Duple Meter

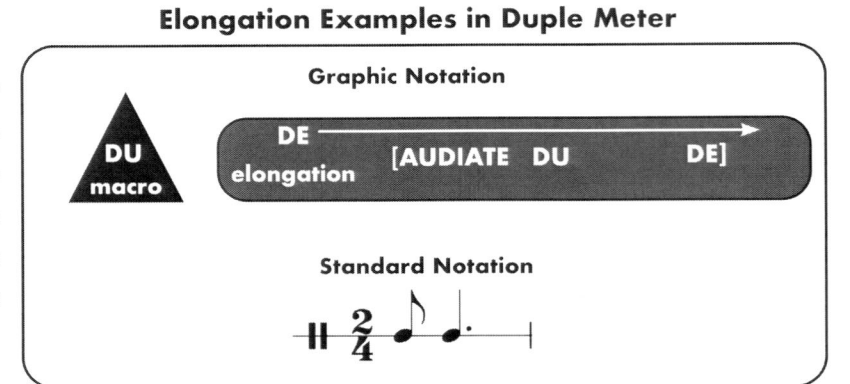

Graphic Notation

DU macro

DE elongation [AUDIATE DU DE]

Standard Notation

‖ 2/4 ♩. ♪ |

▶ Watch the video **Rhythm Lesson 12.2: Duple Elongations (Solfege)**
   • Listen to the explanation, and then echo the familiar elongation patterns you hear.
   • **REMINDER!** Keep the microbeats somewhere on your body as you listen and echo. This will help you to know whether or not you are hearing an elongation.

DUPLE ELONGATION RHYTHM CELLS

Here are the Duple Elongation rhythm cells for your reference in standard notation.

Duple Elongation Rhythm Cells
♩. ♪   ♪ ♩.   ♪ ♩ ♪   𝅗𝅥
Du De   Du De   Du De De   Du

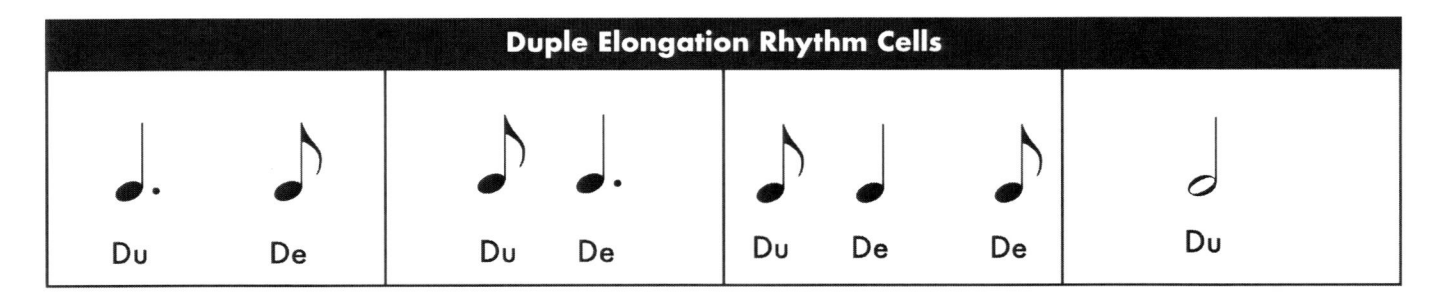

As usual, add Duple Elongations to your conversational vocabulary.

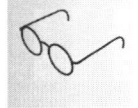

After you can improvise with this new functions, learn to **read** them in Part II.

LESSON 13
ELONGATIONS IN TRIPLE METER

We will follow the same procedures as we did with duple elongations by listening to the patterns first at the Aural/Oral level with a neutral syllable.

▶ Watch the beginning of the video **Rhythm Lesson 13.1: Triple Elongations (Aural/Oral)**
  • Echo the patterns using the syllable "BAH." Be sure to breathe on the 4th macrobeat before you echo, and keep the microbeats somewhere on your body as you listen and echo.

ELONGATIONS EXPLAINED

As explained previously, an elongation is an **extension** of a macrobeat or a microbeat. You simply extend whatever syllable you're using ("DU," "DA" or "DI") and **audiate the underlying macrobeats and microbeats.** In the example to the right, one performs the syllables "DU DA" and audiates "DI" while they sustain the syllable "DA.")

Elongation Examples in Triple Meter

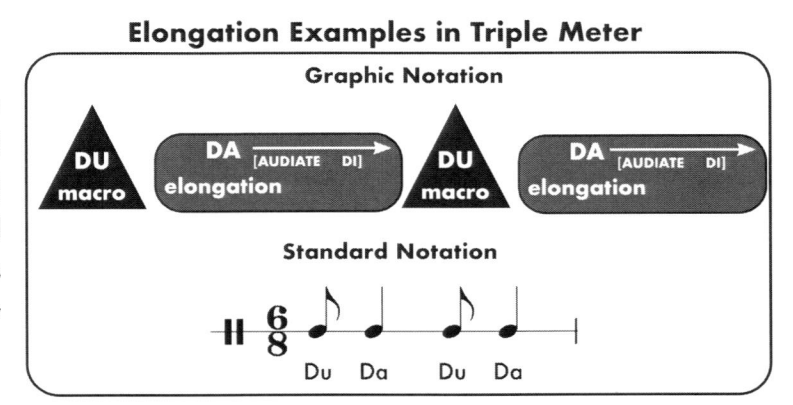

Graphic Notation

| DU macro | DA elongation [AUDIATE DI] | DU macro | DA elongation [AUDIATE DI] |

Standard Notation

6/8 — Du Da Du Da

▶ Watch the video **Rhythm Lesson 13.2: Triple Elongations (Solfege)**
  • Listen to the explanation, and then echo the familiar elongation patterns you hear.
  • **REMINDER!** Keep the microbeats somewhere on your body as you listen and echo. This will help you to know whether or not you are hearing an elongation.

TRIPLE ELONGATION RHYTHM CELLS

Here are the Triple Elongation rhythm cells for your reference in standard notation.

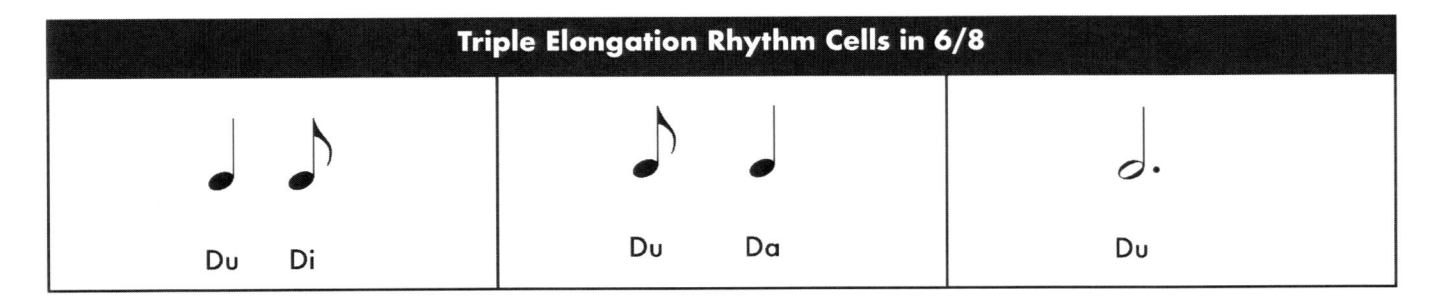

Triple Elongation Rhythm Cells in 6/8		
♩ ♪	♪ ♩	♩.
Du Di	Du Da	Du

💬 As usual, add Triple Elongations to your conversational vocabulary.

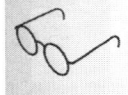

👓 After you can improvise with this new functions, learn to **read** them in Part II.

MORE RHYTHMIC FUNCTIONS

At this point, you should have a very ample listening and improvisational vocabulary of rhythmic functions in duple and triple meters. You have likely spiraled down to the Symbolic Association level of learning and read these patterns, both at the rhythm cell level and the sentence level. There are several other rhythmic functions that we will learn to audiate, improvise with, and read with multiple time signatures. However, they will be introduced in Part II. The additional functions that we will learn are:
- Division/Elongations
- Rests
- Ties
- Upbeats

SKILLS

Below is a list of the **discrimination** skills you have acquired. In duple and triple meters, you can:
- move to macrobeats, microbeats and the space between.
- take an audiation breath.
- echo macrobeat/microbeat patterns with a neutral syllable and with solfege syllables.
- name the syllables for macrobeats, microbeats and divisions.
- echo division patterns with a neutral syllable and with solfege syllables.
- echo elongation patterns with a neutral syllable and with solfege syllables.
- recognize division and elongation patterns by listening for the correct syllable.
- distinguish between duple and triple meter using familiar musical sentences by listening for the microbeat.

Below is a list of the **inference** skills you have been introduced to. In duple and triple meters, you are working on the ability to:
- translate patterns with macrobeats/microbeats from neutral syllables to solfege syllables.
- translate patterns with divisions and elongations from neutral syllables to solfege syllables.
- identify the meter of familiar **and unfamiliar** patterns.
- identify the rhythmic functions heard in familiar **and unfamiliar** patterns.
- improvise patterns with macrobeats, microbeats, divisions and elongations.

TESTS

Try taking the following tests on *The Improving Musician* YouTube channel:

▶ **Duple vs. Triple Test #1** (only macrobeats and microbeats)

▶ **Duple vs. Triple Test #2** (macrobeats, microbeats and divisions)

SECTION 3: HARMONY

SECTION 3 AT A GLANCE

Lesson Sequence	
Lesson 1	Introduction to Tonal Concepts
Lesson 2	Major Tonality, Aural/Oral
Lesson 3	Minor Tonality, Aural/Oral
Lesson 4	Verbal Association, Major Tonality
Lesson 5	Verbal Association, Minor Tonality
Lesson 6	Improvisation
Lesson 7	Comparing Major and Minor Tonalities
Lesson 8	Singing Bass Lines
Lesson 9	Harmonic Translation
Lesson 10	I/V Conversations
Assessment	

LESSON 1
INTRODUCTION TO TONAL CONCEPTS

Music has two overarching frameworks: rhythm and tonality. There are two main parts to tonal learning: **harmony** and **melody**. We will begin with harmony because it will establish the aural foundation (context!) for melody.

MELODY VS. HARMONY

Melody can be thought of as pitches moving in a forward, **horizontal** manner. Harmony, however, should be initially conceptualized **vertically**. Eventually, melody and harmony weave in and out of each other in unique and interesting ways. However, when we are first learning to audiate tonally, it's best to separate the elements, and learn one at a time.

BUILDING ANALOGY

Think of learning to audiate harmony and melody like constructing a building.

Harmony, along with resting tone, provide a foundation and frame. Since you have no stairs at first, you need a scaffold. Tonic and dominant harmonic functions form the foundation and frame of each floor, as well as the basement.

Melody would be analogous to laying down the concrete of the individual floors, as well as creating the stairs so that one can navigate between the floors. One can travel up several flights, and then return back to the bottom to get more material to build additional floors.

In the diagram below, the melody and harmony of the first phrase of "Mary Had a Little Lamb" are represented graphically. The black dots represent the melody moving in a horizontal manner. The gray boxes represent the harmonic functions you will be learning about very shortly. Notice how the melody moves through the tonic and dominant harmonic functions, which are stacked vertically.

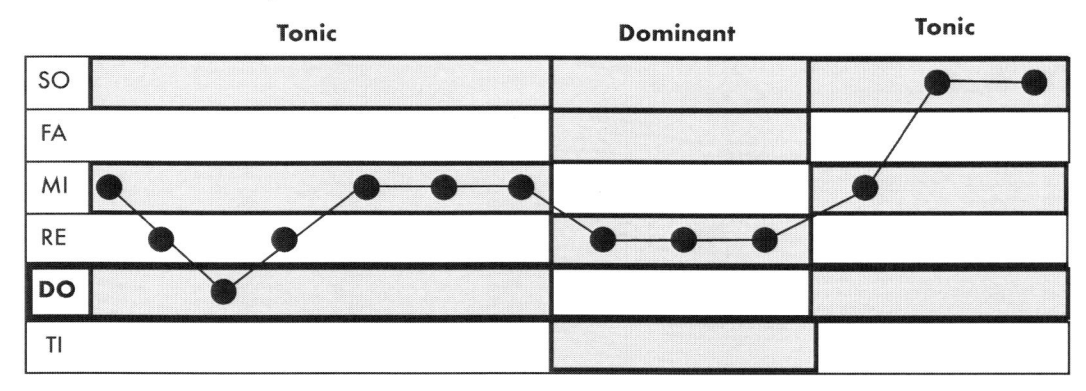

▶ Watch the video **Harmony Lesson 1: Introduction to Tonal Concepts.**

LESSON 2
MAJOR TONALITY, AURAL/ORAL

FIRST STEPS

Just as we did with rhythm, you should first experience harmony at the **Aural/Oral** level with musical **patterns**. You will use the following sub-skills to build your harmonic vocabulary:
- **First Pitch**: Listen to a pattern, sing only the first pitch you hear, and audiate the rest. Use the syllable "BUM."
- **Resting Tone**: Listen to a pattern, and sing only the resting tone on "BUM".
- **Whole pattern**: Echo the entire pattern using "BUM."

You will begin by listening to a series of **familiar patterns in a familiar order (FPIFO)**. We will listen to the patterns first without syllables. Then, we will add syllables. Eventually, these will be the same patterns you will learn to read in Part 2.

▶ Watch the video **Harmony Lesson 2: Major Tonality, Aural/Oral**. Follow the directions. Be sure to take an **audiation breath** before you perform the task.

After you have watched the video lesson, you may wish to review the **Patterns-Only Videos**. There are videos in two keys (D and Bb). Vary the performance tasks.
- 1st time: just listen to the patterns.
- 2nd time: sing the first pitch.
- 3rd time: sing the resting tone.
- 4th time: sing the whole pattern.

Although we have not come to Symbolic Association, here are the patterns in notation for your reference. They are notated in the key of C for purposes of consistency.

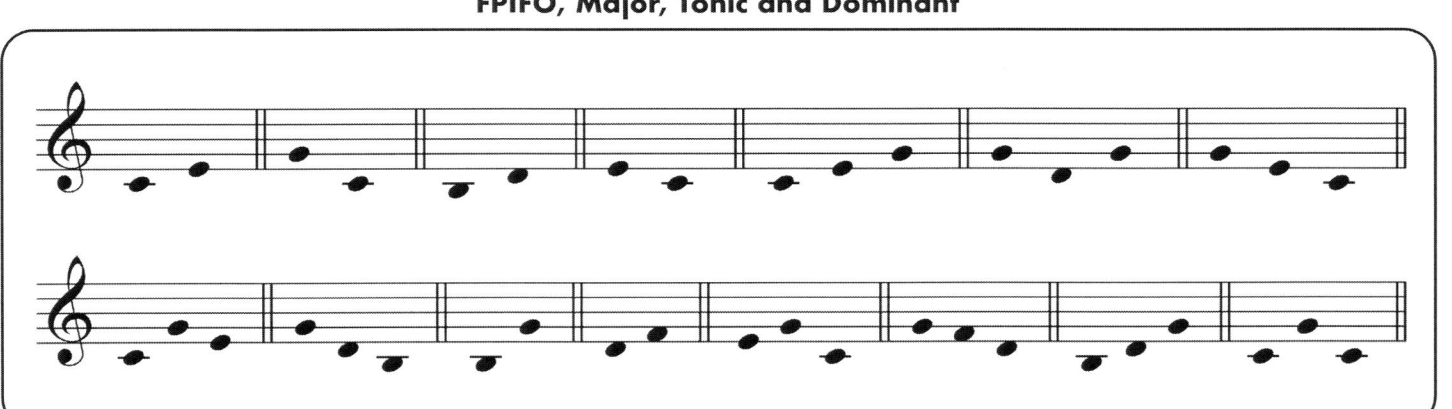

FPIFO, Major, Tonic and Dominant

LESSON 3
MINOR TONALITY, AURAL/ORAL

We will follow the same procedures as you did for Major Tonality, except in this lesson, we will be in Minor.

▶ Watch the video **Harmony Lesson 3: Minor Tonality, Aural/Oral**. Follow the directions. Be sure to take an **audiation breath** before you perform the task.

After you have watched the video lesson, you may wish to review the **Patterns-Only Videos** in two different keys. Vary the performance tasks.
- 1st time: just listen to the patterns
- 2nd time: sing the first pitch
- 3rd time: sing the resting tone
- 4th time: sing the whole pattern

Although we have not come to Symbolic Association, here are the patterns notated in C minor for your reference.

FPIFO, Minor, Tonic and Dominant

Try bridging to Inference learning with the patterns you just learned at the Aural/Oral level.
- Improvisation-Aural/Oral: Watch the videos **Listen, People, to My Song** in major and minor.
- Generalization-Aural/Oral: Try the **Same vs. Different Test-Tonal**.

ACCULTURATION

Have you had the opportunity to experience some more advanced tonalities? Try watching the Acculturation videos in **Dorian** and **Mixolydian** tonalities. The comparisons you will make between major and minor will be challenging to your audiation.

LESSON 4
VERBAL ASSOCIATION, MAJOR TONALITY

VERBAL ASSOCIATION

Once we can successfully echo patterns at the Aural/Oral level, it's time to label tonality and harmonic functions with a **Verbal Association**. The most effective system for labeling tonality is **Movable-DO with a LA-Based Minor**. In this system, the name of the resting tone changes with each **tonality**.

TONALITY DEFINED

A tonality is defined by its **resting tone**, its tonal center. Each tonality has a resting tone, a place where the music comes to a logical conclusion through a musical gravitational force. The tonalities are classified and organized in relation to their resting tone using movable-DO solfege.

Movable-do solfege is very effective because the half step relationship between MI and FA and TI and DO always remains consistent amongst tonalities (with the single exception of the raised leading tone [SI] in Minor).

It is called "movable-DO" because, as you'll find out in Part II of this book, you can put **DO** anywhere, and the relationship between pitches will stay the same.

THE TONALITIES AND THEIR RESTING TONES

Tonality	Resting Tone
Major	DO
Minor	LA
Dorian	RE
Mixolydian	SO
Phrygian	MI
Lydian	FA
Aeolian	LA
Locrian	TI

As **musical citizens**, we need to learn certain information about each tonality. We need to learn:
- the resting tone
- essential harmonic functions and their associated solfege syllables

In this book, we will learn to audiate, and then read, only major and minor tonalities. However, as you go through this book, hopefully you are experiencing other tonalities, and are being acculturated to their sound.

▶ Watch the following video. **Harmony Lesson 4: Verbal Association (Major Tonality)**

RESTING TONE

Good intonation (pitch accuracy, be it singing or on a string or wind instrument) doesn't happen in a bubble. That is to say, pitches are always correct **in relation to another pitch**. When you're first learning to audiate, that pitch will be the resting tone.

A very useful exercise to jolt your audiation is to listen to a series of patterns, and respond by **only singing the resting tone**. This forces your musical mind to make comparisons between pitches in relation to your aural anchor, the resting tone. (Be sure to take an **audiation breath** before you sing.) You did this in Lessons 2 and 3, however you have more context now that we have named the pitch.

TONAL SEQUENCE

Dr. Gordon created a tonal sequence that includes all of the pitches of each tonality. The scale degree numbers for the sequence are **56543271**. It always ends on the resting tone. In major tonality, the sequence is SO LA SO FA MI RE TI DO. In major tonality, the resting tone is DO. Therefore, the tonal sequence ends on DO. Try singing the tonal sequence.

So La So Fa Mi Re Ti Do

LABELING HARMONIC FUNCTIONS, MAJOR TONALITY

Now that you have echoed patterns at the Aural/Oral level in both major and minor tonalities, and had experience singing the resting tone using solfege, you are ready to label harmonic functions. We will give syllables to the pitches and names to the same patterns you learned at the Aural/Oral level.

Any combination of DO, MI and SO is called a **major tonic pattern**. It is often called the "one chord." Or even simpler: "1." If you were in the key of D, and you were to strum a C chord on the ukulele, you would be hearing a combination of DOs, MIs and SOs. This is the tonic function in major. **Sing "DO MI SO."**

Any combination of SO, FA, RE and TI is called a **major dominant pattern**. It is often called the "five chord." Or even simpler: "5." If you were in the key of C, and you were to strum an G7 chord on the ukulele, you would be hearing a combination of SOs and FAs and REs and TIs. This is the dominant function in major. **Sing "SO FA RE TI."**

HARMONIC FUNCTIONS IN MAJOR TONALITY

Proper Name	Nicknames	Roman Numeral	Pitches
Tonic	One chord ("1")	I	DO, MI, SO
Dominant	Five chord ("5")	V	SO, FA, RE, TI

Graphic Notation

TONIC (I) — DO, MI, SO
DOMINANT (V) — TI, RE, FA, SO

CHOOSE YOUR VERBAL ASSOCIATION

In language, there are often many words to describe the same thing. Such synonyms include: fall/autumn; groundhog/woodchuck; twelve/a dozen; soda/pop; car/automobile; laugh/giggle/chuckle/guffaw etc. Music is no exception.

If you take a music theory course in high school or college, you will use the terms tonic and dominant, but will also label harmony using **Roman numerals**. If you play popular music in a band, musicians only use the terms "1" and "5." You and/or your teacher will choose the most appropriate term. We will use the terms interchangeably throughout the remainder of this book. As you move forward in your musical life, you will likely encounter both.

FAMILIAR PATTERNS IN FAMILIAR ORDER

In every academic subject, you have vocabulary words that you need to know. The same is true with music. For each tonality and harmonic function, there are **pattern sets** of musical "vocabulary words." Our first set includes tonic and dominant patterns in major tonality. These are the same familiar patterns in the familiar order used in Lesson 2.

PATTERN LEARNING TOOLS

There are several tools that you can use to help yourself learn these patterns. These tools will become part of your audiational **tool kit** which you will continue to use throughout this book, and to help you problem-solve out in the real world of music-making. When you listen to the patterns, you should be able to engage with them in several ways:

1. You should be able to sing only the **first pitch** of each pattern, and audiate the rest.
2. You should be able to listen to a pattern and sing the **resting tone** DO.
3. You should be able to **echo the pattern** using solfege.
4. You should be able to **name the harmonic function** by singing its name on the chord root. Use your chosen verbal association. (You could sing "Major tonic" and "Major dominant" or just simply "One" and "Five.")

▶ Listen to the patterns and engage with them in the above ways until you feel like you have mastered them.
- **Harmony Lesson 4: Patterns Only (Key of D)**
- **Harmony Lesson 4: Patterns Only (Key of Bb)**

Eventually, after enough repetitions, these patterns will become familiar in their familiar order. Can you perform these patterns from memory? Try to **sing along with the patterns** in several keys on the following video:

▶ **Tonal Pattern Recital, Major, I and V**

The patterns appear below for your reference in the key of C for consistency.

FPIFO, Major, Tonic and Dominant

I	I	V	I	I	V	I
do mi so do	ti re mi do	do mi so	so re so	so mi do

I	V	V	V	I	V	V	I
do so mi	so re ti	ti so	re fa	mi so do	so fa re	ti re so	do so do

INSTRUMENTAL ASSOCIATION

To give yourself harmonic support, try to also accompany yourself using a harmony instrument as you perform these patterns. This will assist you in getting the **gestalt** sound of the harmonic function in your audiation. A keyboard or ukulele are good instruments for this task. Play a **C** chord for tonic and a **G7** chord for dominant. See the appendix for a ukulele chord chart. Inexperienced keyboard players can use a **Keyboard Card** (see p. 294 for an explanation). These cards can be printed from this page: www.shorturl.at/irEIU

Spiral forward to Lesson 8, **Singing Bass Lines**.

Try bridging to Inference learning with the patterns you just learned with solfege
- Improvisation: Have a **harmonic conversation** in major. (See lesson 10)
- Generalization-Verbal: Try to translate the patterns from a neutral syllable to solfege. (See lesson 9)

LESSON 5
VERBAL ASSOCIATION, MINOR TONALITY

We will follow the same learning model that we used in major tonality for our second tonality: **Minor.** Here is the tonal sequence:

Mi Fa Mi Re Do Ti Si La

LABELING RESTING TONE & HARMONIC FUNCTIONS

In minor tonality, the resting tone is **LA**.

Any combination of LA, DO and MI is called a **minor tonic pattern**. It is often called the "1 chord." Or even simpler: "1." If you were in the key of D minor, and you were to strum a Dm chord on the ukulele, you would be hearing a combination of LAs and DOs and MIs. This is a tonic pattern in minor. **Sing LA DO MI.**

Any combination of MI, RE, TI and SI is called a **minor dominant pattern**. It is often called the "5 chord." Or even simpler: "5." If you were in the key of D minor, and you were to strum an A7 chord on the ukulele, you would be hearing a combination of MIs and REs and TIs and SIs. This is a dominant pattern in minor. **Sing MI RE TI SI.**

HARMONIC FUNCTIONS IN MINOR TONALITY			
Proper Name	Nicknames	Roman Numeral	Pitches
Tonic	One chord ("1")	i	LA, DO, MI
Dominant	Five chord ("5")	V	MI, RE, TI, SI

Graphic Notation

TONIC (i) — FA, MI, RE, DO, TI, LA, SI (highlighted: MI, DO, LA)

DOMINANT (V) — FA, MI, RE, DO, TI, LA, SI (highlighted: MI, RE, TI, SI)

Traditionally, a lowercase Roman numeral is used to indicate a chord with a minor quality, whereas a capital letter is used to indicate a chord with a major quality.

▶ Watch the following video. **Harmony Lesson 5: Verbal Association (Minor Tonality)**

MINOR TONAL PATTERNS

Just as you did with major, listen to and engage with these patterns in minor tonality. This set includes tonic and dominant patterns in minor tonality. When you listen to the patterns, you should be able to engage with them using pattern learning tools from your **toolkit**.

1. You should be able to sing only the **first pitch** of each pattern, and audiate the rest.
2. You should be able to sing the **resting tone** LA.
3. You should be able to **echo the pattern** using solfege.
4. You should be able to **name the harmonic function** by singing its name on the chord root. Use your chosen verbal association. (You could sing "Minor tonic" and "Minor dominant" or just simply "One" and "Five.")

▶ Listen to the patterns and engage with them in the above ways until you feel like you have mastered them.
- **Harmonic Lesson 5: Patterns Only (Key of D minor)**
- **Harmonic Lesson 5: Patterns Only (Key of Bb minor)**

Eventually, after enough repetitions, these patterns will become familiar in their familiar order. Can you perform these patterns from memory? Try to **sing along with the patterns** in several keys on the following video:

▶ **Tonal Pattern Recital, Minor, i and V**

The patterns appear below for your reference in the key of C minor for consistency.

FPIFO, Minor, Tonic and Dominant

Spiral forward to Lesson 8, **Singing Bass Lines**.

Try bridging to Inference learning with the patterns you just learned with solfege
- Improvisation: Have a **harmonic conversation** in minor. (See lesson 10)
- Generalization-Verbal: Try to translate the patterns from a neutral syllable to solfege. (See lesson 9)

Make an instrumental association. Accompany yourself with the chords **Cm** and **G7** as you sing these patterns.

BENCHMARK

These patterns, as well as the Major I/V patterns, as a whole are now considered **familiar patterns** in a **familiar order (FPIFO!)**. You are now tasked with being able to **memorize** these pattern sets in their familiar order. This will likely happen whether you try to or not. You will begin to develop a sense of anticipation.

When you are learning vocabulary in any other academic subject, sometimes you simply need to memorize information so that you can recall it at a later time. For example:
- In math class, you need to memorize your times tables so that they become second nature.
- In science class, you need to memorize the abbreviation of elements.
- In history class, you need to know important dates so that when you are learning future historical concepts, you have a broad frame of reference.

The primary reason for memorizing these patterns is to make **reading** them much easier in Part 2 because you will be reading **familiar patterns.**

LESSON 6
IMPROVISATION

If we continue to follow the language analogy, then we all improvise all of the time. We don't walk around with a script that we read from all day. We select **words** from our vocabulary that fit the situation. In music, we choose **patterns** that fit the tonal or rhythmic context of the musical situation.

IMPROMPT

When you are first learning to create and improvise, it's helpful to have a few tools you can use to spark your creativity. An **Imprompt** will be a musical scenario that is set up in order to give you the opportunity to try out the skill of improvisation.

IMPROMPT #1: UNFINISHED SONG

This first imprompt is called "Unfinished Song" and is designed to see what is lurking underneath the auditional waters of your mind.

▶ Watch the following videos:
- **Harmonic Lesson 6.1: Tonic Improvisation #1** Listen to the lesson and hear the examples.
- **Harmonic Lesson 6.1: Five Unfinished Songs** Improvise your own endings to these unfinished songs.

Procedures for Unfinished Song
1. Listen to the unfinished song, and see if an ending emerges in your audiation. (Don't sing, just audiate!)
2. Listen again, and quietly sing the ending that emerges. Use a neutral syllable (like "La" or "Bum"). It's OK if it's different than the first ending you audiated! **As you're improvising, try to audiate the underlying harmony that you're hearing. A good way to end a song is with a dominant chord followed by a tonic chord.**
3. Listen again, and then try to sing the same ending with more confidence.
4. Listen again, and try a different ending!

IMPROMPT #2: BE DIFFERENT

In this imprompt, you will listen to a tonic pattern, and sing back a different tonic pattern. This will give you the opportunity to perform the patterns you have already learned (using the vocabulary!), and to enlarge your musical vocabulary by **teaching yourself new musical words** (composition).

▶ Watch the following video: **Harmonic Lesson 6.2: Tonal Improvisation #2**. Listen to the lesson and hear the examples. You will have the opportunity to review the tonic patterns you have already learned. They appear below for your reference.

Familiar Major Tonic Patterns

do mi | so do | mi do | do mi so | so mi do | do so mi | mi so do | do so do

TASK: You will listen to a tonic pattern. Your task is to sing back a **different** tonic pattern in response. You may either sing a different familiar pattern, or you could make up your own pattern.

When trying to create your own pattern, and you are bereft of ideas on how to complete such a task, you could try any of the following improvisation tools:

1. **Reverse the Pattern**: Listen to each pattern, and sing the pattern in reverse. For example, if you hear DO MI, sing MI DO. If you hear DO MI SO, sing SO MI DO.
2. **Eliminate a Pitch**: Listen to the pattern, and eliminate the first, second, or third pitch. For example, if you hear DO MI SO, you could sing DO MI or MI SO.
3. **Scramble the Pitches**: Listen to the pattern, and scramble the order of the pitches. For example, if you hear DO MI SO, you could sing MI SO DO.

Next, try the whole procedure again, but this time with **minor tonality**. The familiar minor tonic patterns appear below for your reference.

Familiar Minor Tonic Patterns

la do | mi la | do la | la do mi | mi do la | la mi do | do mi la | la mi la

Spiral forward to Lesson 10, **I/V Conversations**. This is another opportunity for improvisation.

Play the C chord on the keyboard. Use the **Major I & V** Keyboard Card. Try improvising just using pitches of the C chord. Then, try it in minor.

ACCULTURATION

Have you had the opportunity to experience some more advanced tonalities? Try watching the Acculturation videos in **Phrygian** and **Lydian** tonalities.

LESSON 7
COMPARING MAJOR AND MINOR TONALITIES

Ultimately, your goal is to be able to listen to a piece of music and audiate it tonally. That is to say, when you listen to a piece of unfamiliar music, your ears should tell you:
- What tonality is it in? What is the resting tone?
- Can you audiate the various tonal layers that are happening simultaneously? Can you separate the pitches of the melody from the underlying harmonic structure?
- Can you give labels (tonic, dominant) to the harmonies you are hearing?
- Is your audiation subconsciously assigning solfege syllables to the melodic pitches you are hearing?

The aforementioned skills are indeed the goal, but are decidedly **inference** skills that come with much practice. We are now going to practice distinguishing between major and minor tonalities using **familiar** patterns. This will give you the opportunity to learn **how** to distinguish between major and minor tonalities. This skill is called **Partial Synthesis**. Since Partial Synthesis is an aural skill, it is difficult, nay impossible, to convey with only the written word.

▶ Watch the video **Harmony Lesson 7: Comparing Major and Minor Tonalities**. The salient text is below. Then, watch the **Patterns Only** video.

> ## COMPARING MAJOR AND MINOR
> Listen to these two musical sentences. One will be in major, and the other will be in minor. ♪♩♪
>
> Now, I will turn my thinking inside out, and explain what I was audiating. In the first musical sentence, I was audiating DO MI SO as the tonic chord, and DO as the resting tone. When you audiate DO MI SO as the tonic chord, and DO as the resting tone, the music is in **MAJOR TONALITY**.
>
> In the second musical sentence, I was audiating LA DO MI as the tonic chord, and LA as the resting tone. When you audiate LA DO MI as the tonic chord, and LA as the resting tone, the music is in **MINOR TONALITY**
>
> Listen to these very similar musical sentences, and you will name the tonality by stating the tonic chord you are audiating (either DO MI SO or LA DO MI).

The first step in distinguishing between major and minor tonalities is to listen for the quality of the **tonic chord**. This will give you your first clue to being able to identify the tonality. The very powerful process of hearing one tonality paired against the other will train your ears to hear the difference. Remember, we never learn what something **is**, we learn what it is **not**. In fact, that is part of the importance of discrimination learning: we learn major and minor and duple and triple concurrently so that we always have a means of comparison. We learn to discriminate between and among tonalities and meters.

▶ Do the assessment in the video **Major vs. Minor Quiz**. Note your results.

If you **are** reasonably successful at comparing major and minor in the assessment (approximately 75%, or 15/20), you can **spiral** forward to read tonic patterns at the Symbolic Association level in Part II.

LESSON 8
SINGING BASS LINES

WHY SING BASS LINES?

As previously stated, tonality can be broken up into two parts: melody and harmony. The bass line of a song provides a direct link to the harmonic progression because it focuses on the **chord roots** of each chord. If you listen to the bass line, you will dramatically improve your ability to hear harmonic changes.

I have created videos which will give you the opportunity to sing the bass line to very simple tunes with only tonic and dominant harmonic functions.

▶ Watch the following video:
- **Harmony Lesson 8: Singing Bass Lines**

The procedures outlined in the video are as follows:

1. Listen to the melody of a familiar tune. This first video uses the folk chestnut, "Skip To My Lou." If the song is unfamiliar, you may wish to listen a few times to familiarize yourself with the melody.
2. Listen again, and hum along with the tune. Ask yourself if you hear the harmonic changes that accompany the tune. Do you hear where the I and V should go?
3. Hum along again. This time, the bass line will be added. Tune your ears to both parts. When the bass line changes notes, that indicates that there is a harmonic change.
4. After you are comfortable with that, "bum" along with the bass line in whatever octave feels comfortable. You will be hearing two parts simultaneously - the melody and the bass line. The bass line provides the chord root for the harmonic function.
5. Next, add a verbal association. This gives your brain a label for the sound. I use the words "one" and "five" on the pitches DO and SO. (For minor, sing the words "one" and "five" on the pitches LA and MI.
6. Finally, alternate between singing the melody while listening to the bass line, and singing the bass line while listening to the melody. Do each one three times. Begin by singing the melody.

Follow the same procedures for the rest of the tunes in the **Singing Bass Lines** playlist on *The Improving Musician* YouTube channel. The notation appears on the following page for your reference.

If you feel like you have the readiness, you could spiral forward to Reading Lesson 10.5 to see what bass lines look like in standard notation.

Play the chord roots on the keyboard. Use the **Chord Roots** Keyboard Card. Try singing a melody while you play the chord roots.

TUNES IN MAJOR TONALITY

"Skip To My Lou"

"Are You Sleeping?"

"Down By The Station"

TUNES IN MINOR TONALITY

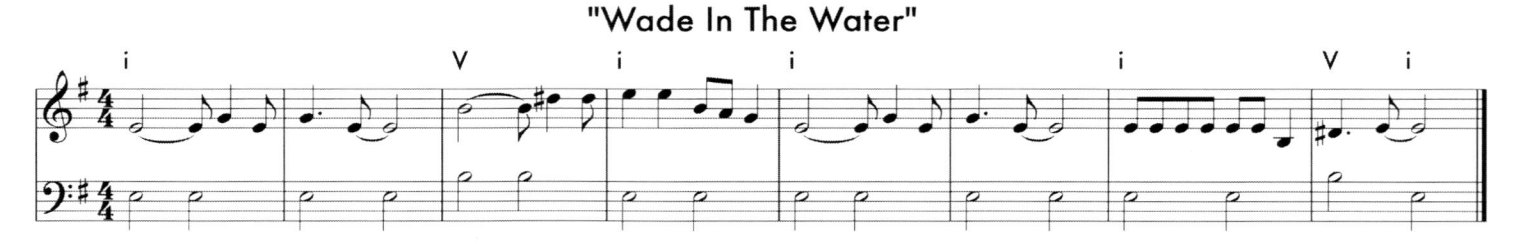

"Joshua"

"Wade In The Water"

ADDING RHYTHMIC INTEREST

Taking one tune at a time, try adding rhythmic interest to the bass line by adding in more rhythmic functions in the following order:

- Add microbeats in addition to macrobeats
- Add division patterns
- Add elongation patterns
- Add combinations of macrobeats, microbeats, divisions, and elongations
- Finally, go "hog wild" and let your musical imagination take over. Do not constrain yourself to just the rhythmic functions above.

LESSON 9
HARMONIC TRANSLATION

Just as we did with rhythm patterns, we will practice the inference skill of **translating** harmonic patterns from a neutral syllable to solfege. With any skill, there are varying levels of scaffolding from the easier to the more complex. We will explore three of those levels today:

1. Translating familiar patterns in a **familiar** order (FPIFO)
2. Translating familiar patterns in an **unfamiliar** order (FPIUFO)
3. Translating **unfamiliar** patterns

When we translate **familiar** patterns (those we have previously echoed), we are assessing our own ability to marry the pitch to the syllable in our audiation. When we translate **unfamiliar** patterns, we are truly generalizing by using the tonal information from familiar patterns to teach ourselves new patterns.

For example, by being able to translate the familiar pattern DO MI SO, you are able to use that information to also translate any number of tonic patterns, both familiar **and** unfamiliar.

- Watch the video **Harmony Lesson 9.1: Harmonic Translation (Major)** to see the three types of translation in action. Then, try them by yourself on the **Patterns Only** video.
- Then, watch the video **Harmony Lesson 9.2: Harmonic Translation (Minor)** to see the three types of translation in action in minor tonality. Then, try them by yourself on the **Patterns Only** video.

If You're Having Trouble...

Translating harmonic patterns is an **inference** skill. It really works your brain in ways that it may not have worked before. In particular, the minor syllables are less ingrained in our culture than major. If you are having difficulty, please go back to previous lessons and review the patterns at both the Aural/Oral, Verbal Association and Improvisation levels. Then try again. Continue this process until the syllables become second nature.

Additionally, don't consider this a "one and done" exercise. In fact, you very well might want to stretch these videos out over several days, if not weeks, or months. Alternate between echoing the patterns, improvising with the patterns, and then translating the patterns.

You should also revisit this skill before you read unfamiliar patterns in Part 2.

ACCULTURATION

Have you had the opportunity to experience some more advanced tonalities? Try watching the Acculturation videos in **Aeolian** and **Locrian** tonalities.

LESSON 10
I/V CONVERSATIONS

Now that you have listened to, echoed, and now memorized harmonic patterns in both major and minor tonalities, it is time to put those patterns to work. It is important to sing these patterns from memory in unfamiliar order before you read them. If we use our language analogy, we learn words, and then use them in unfamiliar order in sentences **long before** we read them.

HARMONIC CONVERSATIONS

Procedures

1. Establish major tonality. Listen to the harmonic pattern that one musician sings. Sing a **different** harmonic pattern in response. Continue having this harmonic conversation until all of the patterns have been used at least once.

2. Try any of the following conversation parameters:
   - If one person sings a tonic chord, the other person sings a different tonic chord in response. If one person sings a dominant chord, the other person sings a different dominant chord in response.
   - If one person sings a tonic chord, the other person sings a dominant chord in response. If one person sings a dominant chord, the other person sings a tonic chord in response.

3. Extend the reach of the conversation in any of the following ways:
   - Create and insert **new** harmonic words. You could sing one of the patterns backwards (For example, DO MI SO could become SO MI DO). You could eliminate a pitch from one of the patterns. (For example, DO SO MI could become DO SO, or SO MI.) You could repeat a pitch. For example, DO MI SO could become DO MI SO MI.
   - Instead of limiting yourself to harmonic patterns, you could also include stepwise patterns from Section 4.
   - Instead of limiting yourself to one pattern at a time, sing multiple patterns.
   - Create new conversation rules for you and your partners.

4. Follow steps 1-3 in minor tonality.

5. Follow the same procedures, but add subdominant chords (the IV chord) into the conversation (see Reading Lesson 10.4 for a crash course in subdominant.)

Improvise using pitches from tonic and dominant chords (C and G7 will be the easiest) on the keyboard. Use the **Major I & V** Keyboard Card. Try it in minor, as well.

SUMMARY

Below is a summary of the musical citizenship skills you have acquired in Section 3.

Questions for review:
- What is the resting tone in major tonality?
- What is the resting tone in minor tonality?
- What are the syllables for tonic and dominant harmonic functions in major tonality?
- What are the syllables for tonic and dominant harmonic functions in minor tonality?
- What is the difference between melody and harmony?

SKILLS

Below is a list of the **discrimination** skills you have acquired. In major and minor tonalities, you can:
- take an audiation breath.
- echo tonic and dominant patterns with a neutral syllable and with solfege.
- sing the first pitch of patterns that are performed for you, both at the aural/oral and verbal association levels.
- sing the resting tone when both a tonic and dominant pattern is performed for you.
- name the syllables for tonic and dominant harmonic functions.
- provide the chord root for familiar tonic and dominant patterns.
- distinguish between major and minor tonalities using familiar musical sentences by listening for the quality of the tonic chord.

Below is a list of the **inference** skills you have been introduced to. In major and minor tonalities, you are working on the ability to:
- translate patterns with tonic and dominant functions from neutral syllables to solfege syllables.
- identify the tonality of familiar **and unfamiliar** patterns.
- aurally identify harmonic functions in a series.
- create new tonic and dominant patterns.
- improvise tonic and dominant patterns in conversation form.

TESTS

Try taking the following tests on *The Improving Musician* YouTube channel:

▶ **Major vs. Minor Test #1**. This test gives you an aural anchor by playing chords underneath the patterns.

▶ **Major vs. Minor Test #2**. This test is harder in that you are not given chords as an aural anchor.

Now that you have had experience identifying the harmonic function of **familiar** patterns, can you try to distinguish between I and V when listening to the patterns as a whole in context? These tests ask you to indicate whether or not the progression you hear matches the progression displayed on the screen.

▶ **Match the Progression #1**. Major tonality.

▶ **Match the Progression #2**. Minor tonality.

SECTION 4: MELODY

SECTION 4 AT A GLANCE

Lesson Sequence	
Lesson 1	Introduction to Melody
Lesson 2	Stepwise Acculturation Patterns, Major Tonality
Lesson 3	Stepwise Acculturation Patterns, Major Tonality
Lesson 4	Melodic Conversations
Lesson 5	Comparing Major and Minor Melodies
Lesson 6	Translation of Stepwise Patterns
Lesson 7	Connecting Melody and Harmony I
Lesson 8	Connecting Melody and Harmony II
Assessment	

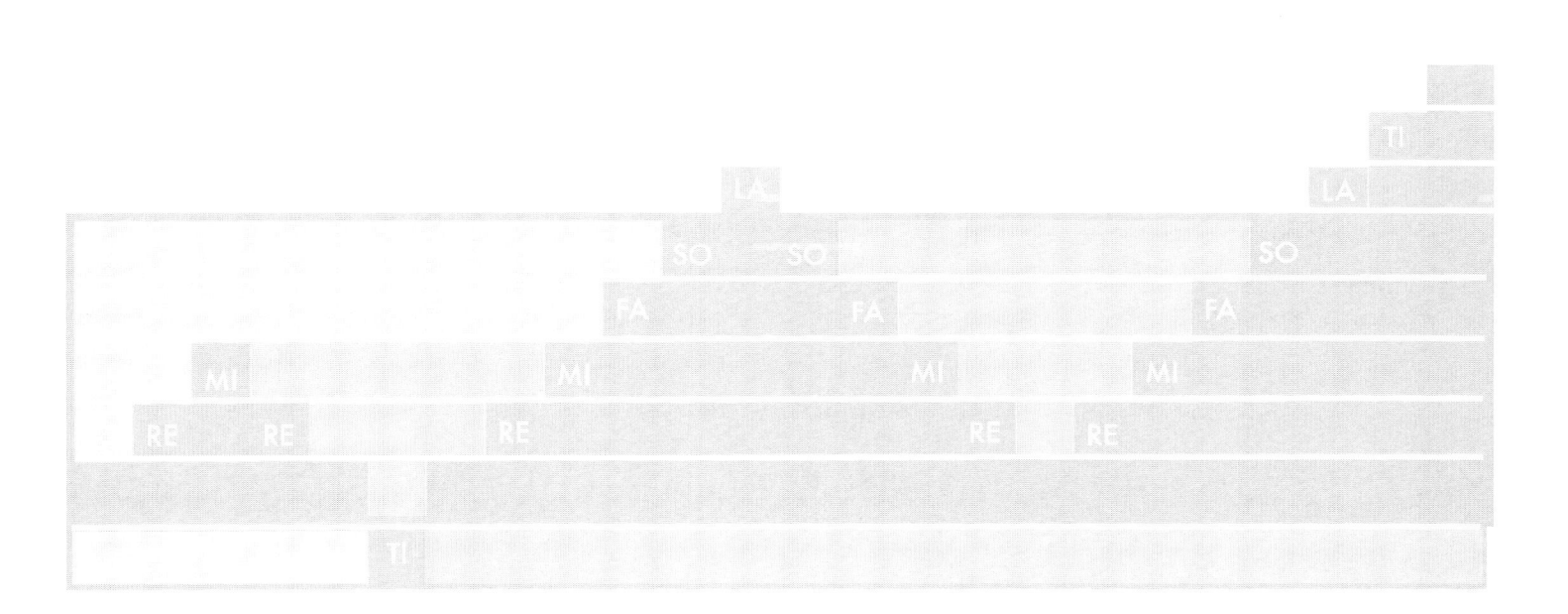

LESSON 1
INTRODUCTION TO MELODY

Melody is a succession of notes that move in a forward manner. As previously stated, melody should initially be conceived in a **horizontal** manner as compared to the **vertical** organization of harmony. We learned harmony first because it provides the tonal **context** for melody.

LEARNING MELODY

Melody inherently has rhythm. However, when we are first learning, it is advantageous to isolate the elements. That is to say, we will remove the rhythm from melody, and just focus on the building up of the pitches of the scale, step by step, in major and minor tonalities.

Just as we did with harmony, we will learn using patterns. These **Stepwise Acculturation Patterns** are always stepwise, and contain no leaps or jumps within a pattern. The purpose of these patterns is to acculturate you to all of the diatonic pitches inherent in the scale of each tonality. By building the pitches up, step by step, the logic of the harmonic patterns becomes clearer, and will greatly assist when we begin to read in Part II.

EXAMPLE MELODIES

Below are four very simple melodies in all combinations of major, minor, duple and triple. They all follow the same basic format.

▶ Listen to the lesson, and learn these songs on the video: **Melody Lesson 1: Introduction to Melody.**

"Little Johnny Johnson" — Duple, Major

"Sister Mary Margaret" — Duple, Minor

"Principal Pinkerton" — Triple, Major

"Admiral Anderson" — Triple, Minor

LESSON 2
STEPWISE ACCULTURATION PATTERNS, MAJOR

AURAL/ORAL

We will now learn **Stepwise Acculturation Patterns** in major tonality. Just as we did with harmony, you should first experience these rhythymless melodic patterns at the **Aural/Oral** level.

▶ Listen to the lesson, and echo the patterns on this video: **Melody Lesson 2.1: Stepwise Patterns, Major Tonality (Aural/Oral).** Then, echo the patterns on the **Patterns Only** video. Perhaps your brain is subconsciously making an inference and assigning solfege!

VERBAL ASSOCIATION

After you have experienced the patterns at the Aural/Oral level, add a Verbal Association using tonal solfege. All of the syllables should be familiar to you since you already used them with major and minor harmonic patterns.

▶ Listen to the lesson, and echo the patterns on this video: **Melody Lesson 2.2: Stepwise Patterns, Major, Solfege.** Then, echo the patterns on the **Patterns Only** video.

These patterns are now familiar patterns in a **familiar order.** You should make every effort to **memorize these patterns**. Just like in language, when we first learn to read, we learn to read **familiar** words, not unfamiliar words. The patterns appear with solfege below for your reference. However, do not rely on seeing the solfege written out as a crutch. Solfege is an aural tool.

FPIFO, Major, Stepwise

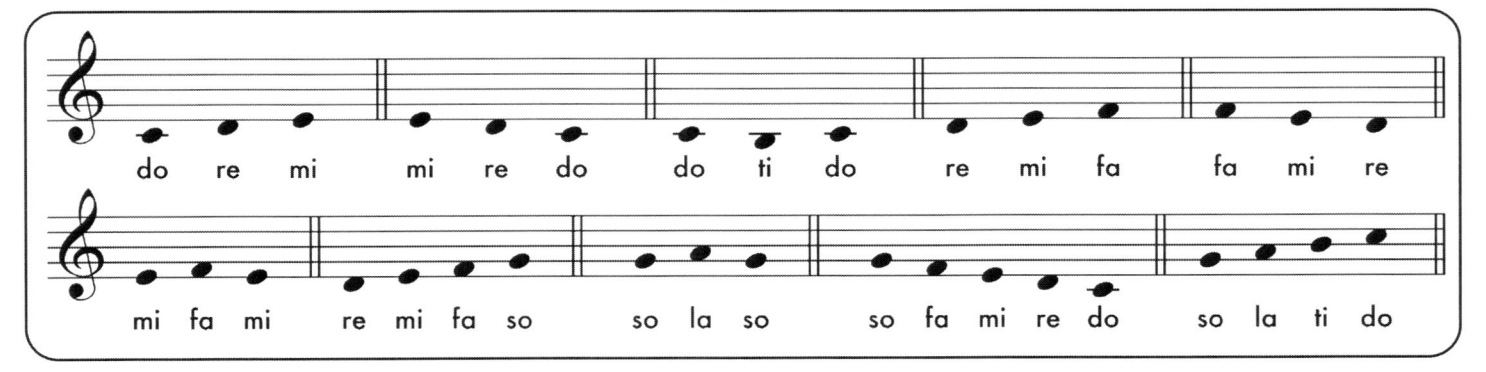

do re mi | mi re do | do ti do | re mi fa | fa mi re
mi fa mi | re mi fa so | so la so | so fa mi re do | so la ti do

👓 Spiral forward to Lesson 2.1 in Part II and read these stepwise patterns.

🏃 Try bridging to Inference learning with the patterns you just learned with solfege
• Generalization-Verbal: Try to **translate** the patterns from a neutral syllable to solfege. Use the video **Melody Lesson 2.1 (Patterns Only)**.
• Improvisation: Add some stepwise patterns to your harmonic conversations.

🎹 Play these patterns on the keyboard. Use the **Solfege** Keyboard Card.

LESSON 3
STEPWISE ACCULTURATION PATTERNS, MINOR

AURAL/ORAL

Let's repeat the same process we used for Major Tonality, but for Minor Tonality. You will first experience minor Stepwise Acculturation Patterns at the **Aural/Oral** level.

▶ Listen to the lesson, and echo the patterns on this video: **Melody Lesson 3.1: Stepwise Patterns, Minor Tonality (Aural/Oral).** Then, echo the patterns on the **Patterns Only** video. Perhaps your brain is subconsciously making an inference and assigning solfege!

VERBAL ASSOCIATION

After you have experienced the patterns at the Aural/Oral level, add a Verbal Association using tonal solfege. All of the syllables should be familiar to you since you already used them with major and minor harmonic patterns.

▶ Listen to the lesson, and echo the patterns on this video: **Melody Lesson 3.2: Stepwise Patterns, Minor, Solfege.** Then, echo the patterns on the **Patterns Only** video.

These patterns are now familiar patterns in a **familiar order.** You should make every effort to **memorize these patterns**. Just like in language, when we first learn to read, we learn to read **familiar** words, not unfamiliar words. The patterns appear with solfege below for your reference. However, do not rely on seeing the solfege written out as a crutch. Solfege is an aural tool.

FPIFO, Minor, Stepwise

| la ti do | do ti la | la si la | ti do re | re do ti |
| do re do | ti do re mi | mi fa mi | mi re do ti la | mi fa si la |

👓 Spiral forward to Lesson 7.1 in Part II and read these stepwise patterns.

🏃 Try bridging to Inference learning with the patterns you just learned with solfege
- Generalization-Verbal: Try to **translate** the patterns from a neutral syllable to solfege. Use the video **Melody Lesson 3.1 (Patterns Only)**.
- Improvisation: Add some stepwise patterns to your harmonic conversations.

🎹 Play these patterns on the keyboard. Use the **Solfege** Keyboard Card.

LESSON 4
MELODIC CONVERSATIONS

Now that you have listened to, echoed, and now internalized stepwise patterns in both major and minor tonalities, it is time to put those patterns to work. Try having melodic conversations in a small group. The procedures appear below.

MELODIC CONVERSATIONS
Procedures

1. Establish major tonality. Listen to the stepwise pattern that one musician sings. Sing a different stepwise pattern in response. Continue having this melodic conversation until all of the stepwise patterns have been used at least once.
2. Establish minor tonality. Have a melodic conversation in minor.
3. Extend the reach of the conversation in any of the following ways:
   - Create and insert **new** stepwise patterns. You could sing one of the patterns backwards (For example, RE MI FA SO could become SO FA MI RE). You could eliminate a pitch from one of the patterns. (For example, DO RE MI could become DO RE, or RE MI.) You could repeat a pitch. For example, DO RE MI could become DO RE MI RE.
   - Instead of limiting yourself to stepwise patterns, you could also include harmonic patterns from Section 3.

LESSON 5
COMPARING MAJOR AND MINOR MELODIES

Just as we did in Section 3, it is important to train our ears to distinguish between major and minor tonalities. We will do this in conjunction with the very simple songs we learned in Lesson 1. This is a **Partial Synthesis** skill.

▶ Listen to and participate in the following video: **Melody Lesson 5: Comparing Major and Minor Melodies**

Listen to the song "Little Johnny Johnson." This song is in major tonality because the resting tone is DO. Listen to a snippet of the song, and then sing the resting tone, DO. Continue until the song is completed. Then, listen to the song "Sister Mary Margaret." This song is in minor tonality because the resting tone is LA. Listen to a snippet of the song, and then sing the resting tone, LA. Continue until the song is completed.

Then, you will hear a snippet of one of the above tunes.
- If you are audiating major tonality, sing the resting tone, DO.
- If you are audiating minor tonality, sing the resting tone, LA.

In Partial Synthesis, it is important to hear one tonality right after the other so we can train our brain to hear the difference. To quote Dr. Gordon, "We learn what something is by what it's not."

LESSON 6
TRANSLATION OF STEPWISE PATTERNS

Just as we did with rhythm patterns and harmonic, we will practice the inference skill of **translating** stepwise patterns from a neutral syllable to solfege. With any skill, there are varying levels of scaffolding from the easier to the more complex. We will explore three of those levels today:

1. Translating familiar patterns in a **familiar** order (FPIFO)
2. Translating familiar patterns in an **unfamiliar** order (FPIUFO)
3. Translating **unfamiliar** patterns

When we translate **familiar** patterns (those we have previously echoed), we are assessing our own ability to marry the pitch to the syllable in our audiation. When we translate **unfamiliar** patterns, we are truly generalizing by using the tonal information from familiar patterns to teach ourselves new patterns.

For example, by being able to translate the familiar pattern DO RE MI, you are able to use that information to also translate any number of stepwise patterns with the same pitch combinations, both familiar **and** unfamiliar.

- Watch the video **Melody Lesson 6.1: Translation of Stepwise Patterns (Major)** to see the three types of translation in action. Then, try them by yourself on the **Patterns Only** video.
- Then, watch the video **Harmony Lesson 6.2: Translation of Stepwise Patterns (Minor)** to see the three types of translation in action in minor tonality. Then, try them by yourself on the **Patterns Only** video.

As previously stated, remember that translation is an inference skill, and will require persistence on your part. If you are struggling, that is merely an indication that you need more practice at the discrimination level of learning. Go back to echoing the patterns, and then try this lesson again.

LESSON 7
CONNECTING MELODY AND HARMONY I

If you were to listen to any of our four simple songs, would you know how to **harmonize** them? That is to say, could you accompany the songs on a piano or ukulele using simple chords? Or, could you sing a bass line to accompany the songs? In this lesson, we will learn some simple rules for **harmonization**. Harmonization is when you assign harmony to melody. In Lesson 8, we will do the opposite: we will create a melody from harmony.

Let's review the pitches for tonic and dominant chords in major and minor tonalities.

| HARMONIC FUNCTIONS IN MAJOR TONALITY ||||
Proper Name	Nicknames	Roman Numeral	Pitches
Tonic	One chord ("1")	I	DO, MI, SO
Dominant	Five chord ("5")	V	SO, FA, RE, TI
HARMONIC FUNCTIONS IN MINOR TONALITY			
Tonic	One chord ("1")	i	LA, DO MI
Dominant	Five chord ("5")	V	MI, RE, TI, SI

A graphic representation of the melody of the song "Little Johnny Johnson" would look like this:

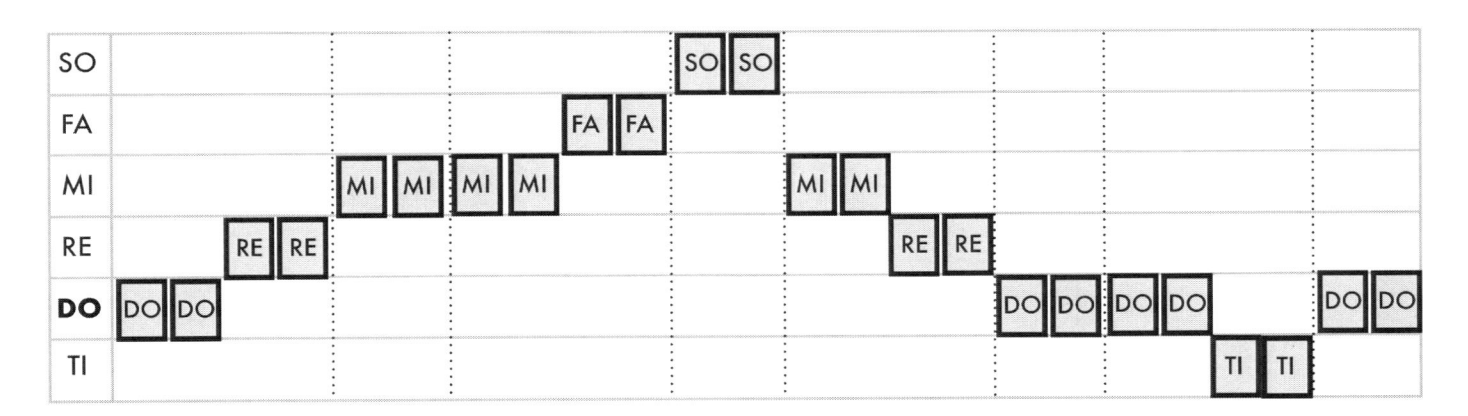

SO							SO	SO								
FA						FA	FA									
MI			MI	MI	MI	MI			MI	MI						
RE		RE	RE								RE	RE				
DO	DO	DO											DO	DO	DO	DO	DO	DO
TI															TI	TI		

If, for the purposes of this book, we limited our harmonic choices to only tonic and dominant, we could establish the following rules for **major tonality**:
- If a strong melodic note is on DO or MI, we will harmonize it with a tonic chord.
- If a strong melodic note is on TI, RE or FA, we will harmonize it with a dominant chord.
- If a strong melodic note is on SO, we can use a I or a V.

If a note is a passing tone, or an unimportant note on a weak beat (like, for example, the pitch RE in the first phrase of "Mary Had a Little Lamb" on p. 50), we need not harmonize it. For the purposes of this book, we are learning a **rule** which you will learn, and eventually, learn how to **break**. (Remember "I before E, **except** after C.")

The first phrase has the stepwise pattern DO RE MI. If we follow the rules above, and ignore the repeated pitches, we would harmonize those three pitches with I V I.

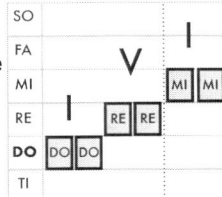

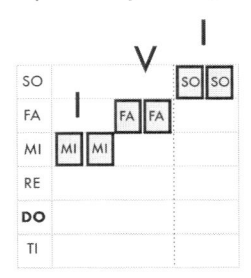

The second phrase has the stepwise pattern MI FA SO. If we follow the rules above, and ignore the repeated pitches, we would harmonize those three pitches with I V I. (We could have harmonized SO with a dominant chord, but the pattern I V I has been established.)

The third phrase has the stepwise pattern MI RE DO. If we follow the rules above, and ignore the repeated pitches, we would again harmonize those three pitches with I V I.

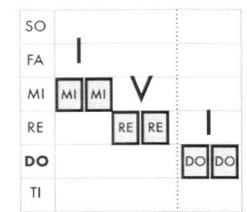

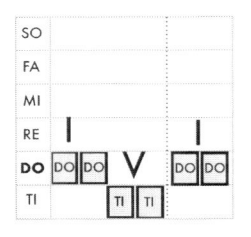

The final phrase has the stepwise pattern DO TI DO. If we follow the rules above, and ignore the repeated pitches, we would again harmonize those three pitches with I V I.

▶ Listen to the song in the video for **Melody Lesson 1** and sing the bass line along with the song using the pitches DO for tonic and SO for dominant.

The rules for **minor tonality** are very similar. If, for the purposes of this book, we limited our harmonic choices to only tonic and dominant, we could establish the following rules for minor tonality:
- If a melodic note is on LA or DO, we will harmonize it with a tonic chord (i).
- If a melodic note is on SI, TI or RE, we will harmonize it with a dominant chord (V).
- If a melodic note is on MI, we can use a tonic or dominant.

A graphic representation of the melody and harmonization of the song "Sister Mary Margaret" would look like this:

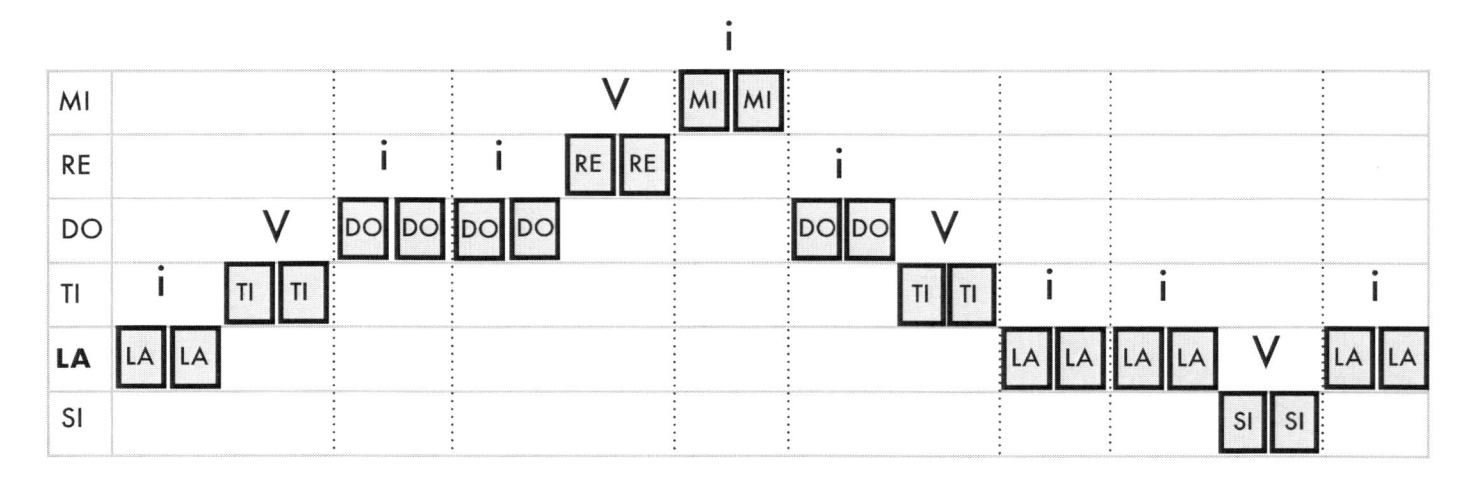

Can you listen to our other two songs ("Principal Pinkerton" and "Admiral Anderson") and make inferences about how to harmonize these very similar songs? The solfege pitches appear below:

"Principal Pinkerton" (Major): | D D D R R R | M M | M M M F F F | S S | M M M R R | D D | D D D T T T | D D |

"Admiral Anderson" (Minor): | L L L T T T | D D | D D D R R R | M M | D D D T T T | L L | L L L si si si | L L |

LESSON 8
CONNECTING MELODY AND HARMONY II

Now that we have done a simple harmonization of a melody, we need to create a melody from harmony, and find the melodic connections between our harmonic functions in major and minor.

The harmonic progression in all of our simple songs is I-V–I. We can move in-between these chords in a very logical way if we explore the **melodic pathways** between tonic and dominant chords. There are certain directions that pitches like to go. Music theorists call these **tendency tones**. Pitches tend to follow the path of least resistance. Interestingly, when changing from tonic to dominant, a correct pitch is always only one step away.

Look at the digram below for **one way** to navigate melodically from tonic to dominant to tonic in **major** tonality only moving by step.

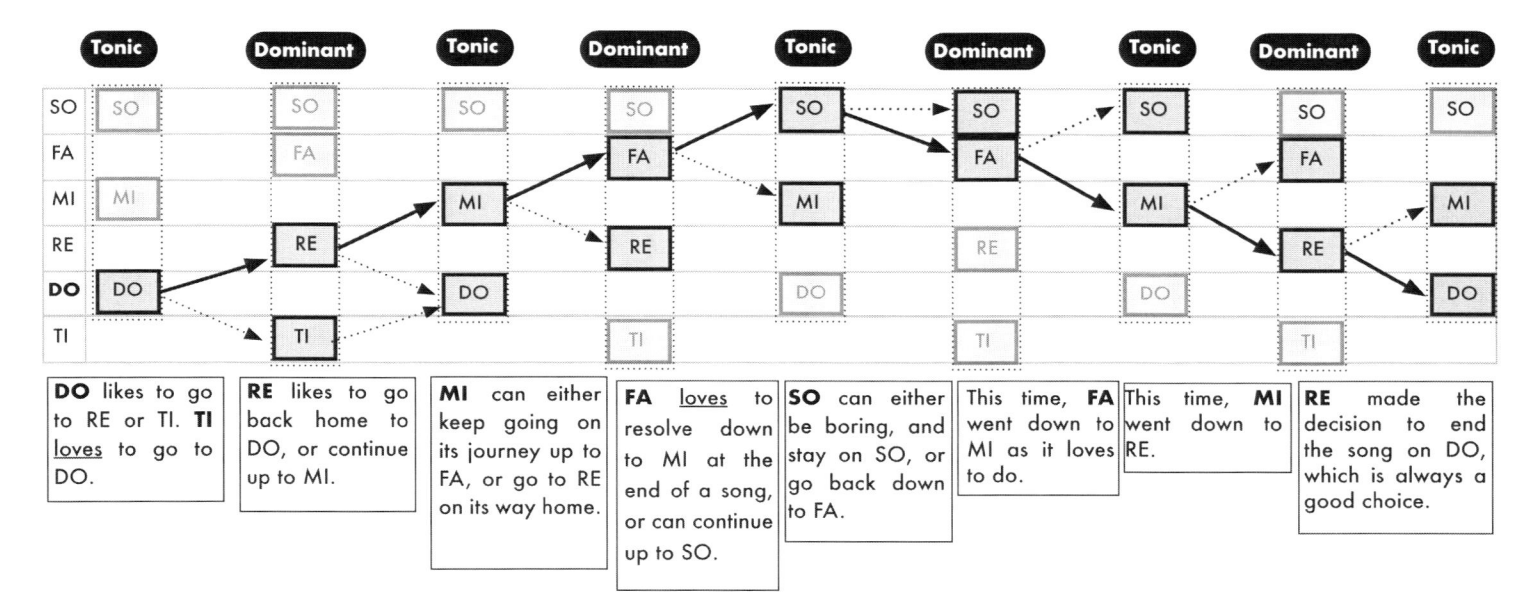

DO likes to go to RE or TI. **TI** loves to go to DO.	**RE** likes to go back home to DO, or continue up to MI.	**MI** can either keep going on its journey up to FA, or go to RE on its way home.	**FA** loves to resolve down to MI at the end of a song, or can continue up to SO.	**SO** can either be boring, and stay on SO, or go back down to FA.	This time, **FA** went down to MI as it loves to do.	This time, **MI** went down to RE.	**RE** made the decision to end the song on DO, which is always a good choice.

Look at the digram below for **one way** to navigate melodically from tonic to dominant to tonic in **minor** tonality. The commentary about movement options should be obvious by following the arrows.

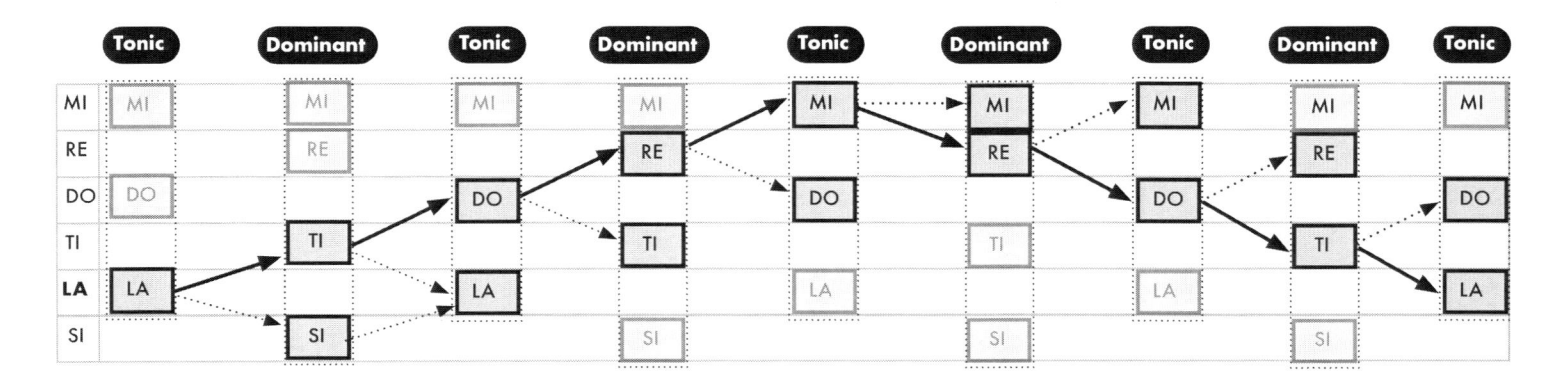

Try singing different pathways through tonic and dominant progressions in major and minor. You may wish to provide some simple harmony by playing an alternating tonic and dominant progression on a ukulele, keyboard or guitar.

CHOOSE YOUR OWN MELODIC ADVENTURE

Using the harmonic foundation of our simple songs, create a **new** melodic pathway through the harmonic progression. Use the options from the diagrams below. (You may feel free to extend into higher or lower octaves should you feel inspired.) Do one in major and one in minor. Make note of your new pathway. **Record them** in Garageband or BandLab (or another DAW [Digital Audio Workstation]) if possible.

Major Harmonic Progression

| I V | I I | I V | I I | I V | I I | I V | I I |

Minor Harmonic Progression

| i V | i i | i V | i i | i V | i i | i V | i i |

On the second tonic chord of the second half of each phrase, you may either:
- Stay on the same pitch, or
- Leap up or down to another pitch of the tonic chord.

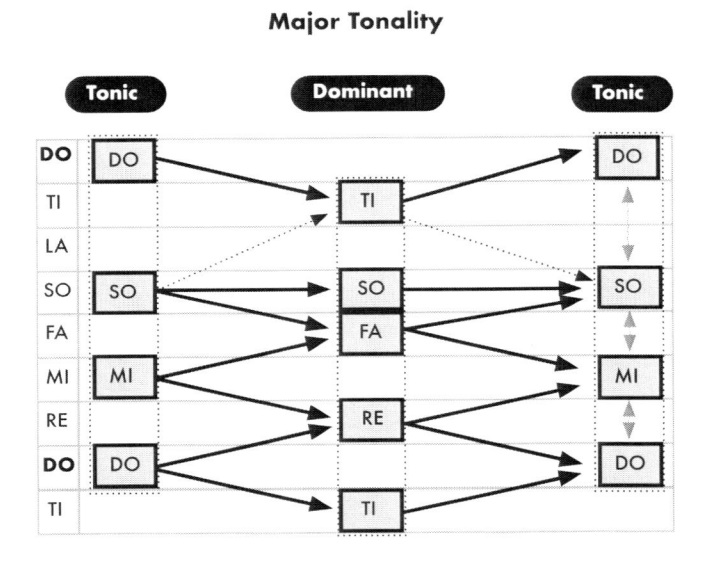

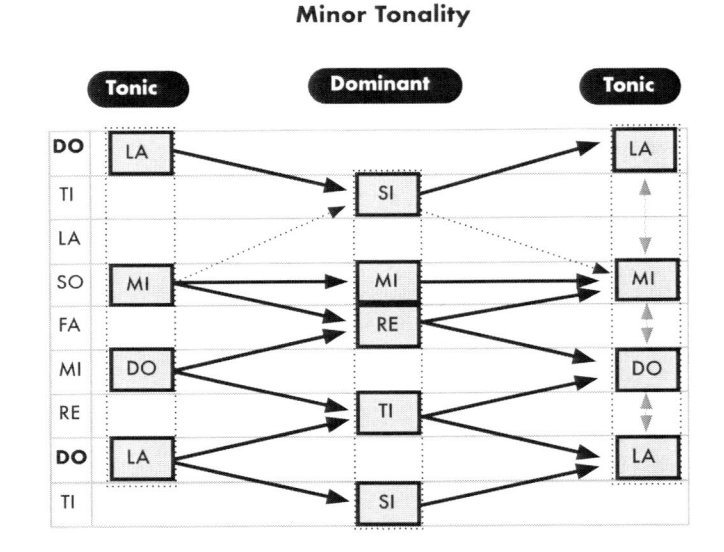

Major Tonality

	Tonic	Dominant	Tonic
DO	DO		DO
TI		TI	
LA			
SO	SO	SO	SO
FA		FA	
MI	MI		MI
RE		RE	
DO	DO		DO
TI		TI	

Minor Tonality

	Tonic	Dominant	Tonic
DO	LA		LA
TI		SI	
LA			
SO	MI	MI	MI
FA		RE	
MI	DO		DO
RE		TI	
DO	LA		LA
TI		SI	

▶ For practice with connecting I and V chords, watch the following videos on *The Improving Musician* YouTube channel: **Harmonic Connections, Major, I & V; Harmonic Connections, Minor i & V; Harmonic Loops, Major, I & V; Harmonic Loops, Minor, i & V**

ADD A BASS LINE

Look back at the new bass lines you created in Lesson 7. Try singing them along with the new melody that you composed. Make any adjustments as necessary. Create a new track, and record your bass line along with the melody. You could either sing the bass line if your voice is low enough, or you could use a Virtual Instrument to record the bass line. Repeat this process for your other three tunes.

Major Tonality

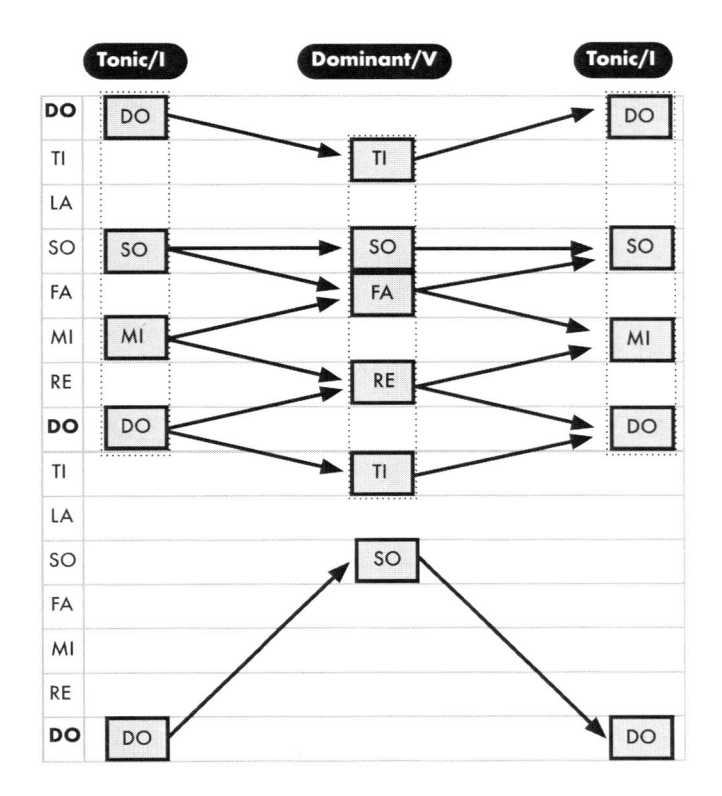

Minor Tonality

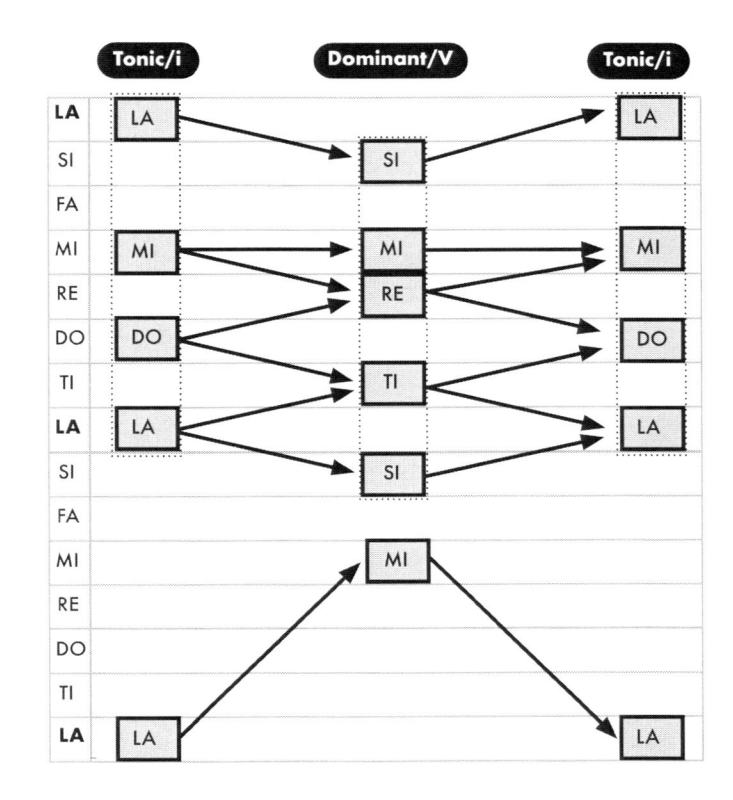

Can you play any of these parts on the keyboard?

SKILLS

Below is a list of the **discrimination** skills you have acquired. In major and minor tonalities, you can:
- echo stepwise patterns with a neutral syllable and with solfege syllables.
- recite the series of stepwise patterns **from memory** in familiar order.
- distinguish major from minor when listening to familiar melodies in contrasting tonalities.

Below is a list of the **inference** skills you have been introduced to. In major and minor tonalities, you are working on the ability to:
- translate stepwise patterns from neutral syllables to solfege syllables.
- create new stepwise patterns by singing the pitches in a different order.
- improvise stepwise patterns in conversation form.

ASSESSMENT

PART II
READING MUSICAL THOUGHT

INTRODUCTION

If we continue our analogy that music is like a language of sorts, then we are now ready to begin **reading** the language of music. Consider a child who is entering school, and will soon learn to read. The child has already amassed a significant vocabulary of words and can use those words in complicated sentences which communicate a myriad of ideas and concepts. You could say that the child is a fluent "improviser" in his native language. Now that child is ready to read.

Hopefully at this point, you have amassed a vocabulary of tonal patterns and rhythm patterns, have had experience improvising musical sentences, and have had success at comparing major vs. minor and duple vs. triple. You are ready to begin to read musical words, and then, soon enough, attend to the complicated task of reading musical sentences **with comprehension**.

ORGANIZATION OF PART II

You will learn to read the content that was explicitly taught to you in Part I. Furthermore, you will learn to combine those elements together (rhythm and melody; rhythm and harmony; rhythm and melody and harmony) to form musical sentences.

Part II is broken up into ten **Reading Sequences**. Each sequence contains tonal content and rhythm content. Within each sequence, there are a number of **Reading Benchmarks**. Reading Benchmarks, with a few exceptions, combine tonal content and rhythm content into real-life musical examples that a student should be able to read if he has achieved success at the preceding lessons. If one is not successful, he need only go back, one lesson at a time, and attend to the reading problem.

PREPARING FOR READING

Although you often will be specifically prompted, it is imperative that you can **speak** the musical vocabulary before you **read** it. Do take time to review the concepts and musical vocabulary words from Part 1 before you attempt to read the notation in Part 2. Being musically literate involves good listening, speaking and thinking vocabularies in addition to reading and writing vocabularies. It is **always** a good idea to review the lesson from Part 1 that specifically prepares you for reading in Part 2.

VIDEO LESSONS

▶ Many of these lessons are presented as video lessons in the companion course on *The Improving Musician* website and YouTube channel. Since it is difficult to communicate musical ideas in written form, it is recommended that you experience the lessons **first** in video format when available. Then, use the text as a review.

READING SEQUENCES

This is the broad layout of the **content** of the Reading Sequences in Part II.

Sequence	New Tonal Content	New Rhythm Content
1	Major; Tonic Function	Duple and Triple; Macro/Microbeats (2/4 and 6/8)
2	Major; Stepwise patterns with tDRM	Enrhythmic time signatures (4/4 and 3/4)
3	Major; Stepwise patterns with tDRMFSL	Duple Divisions
4	Major; Dominant Function	Triple Divisions; Cut Time
5	The Letter System	Duple and Triple Elongations
6	Minor; Tonic Function	Duple and Triple Division/Elongations
7	Minor; Stepwise patterns with siLTD	Macrobeat Rests
8	Minor; Stepwise patterns with siLTDRMF	Microbeat Rests
9	Minor; Dominant Function	Ties
10	Extending the Octave; Subdominant; Bass Clef	Upbeats

WRITING

Although not addressed in any one specific lesson, it is assumed that you will engage in the **writing** of musical notation in addition to reading. When writing musical notation (as in language writing), there are always two things to consider:

1. The **technical** components of writing. That is to say, can you actually draw the notes, rests, beams, and accidentals? When you first learn to write in your native language, you likely spent time learning how to write letters, words, and then sentences. The same is true in music. Do spend time copying the note heads, stems, beams, time signatures, and key signatures. A wonderful resource is **Reading and Writing Music Notation** by Marilyn Lowe. This book is also aligned with the principles of Music Learning Theory.

2. The **audiational** components of writing. When, you write, you want not just to simply copy music notation, but rather to **write it from your audiation**. You want to be able to hear music in your head, and bring it to the page. One simple technique is to look at the notation, chant or sing it, hide it from your view, and try to write without looking at it. Try this at the cell level, the sentence level and beyond.

This symbol will be used when you will be asked to write music notation.

The following abbreviations will at times be used for tonal solfege syllables. All chromatic solfege (SI, FI, etc.) will always be written out in full. Solfege written as a lowercase letter will indicate a lower octave (tDRM; siLTD).

DO = **D**   RE = **R**   MI = **M**   FA = **F**   SO = **S**   LA = **L**   TI = **T**

READING SEQUENCE 1

SEQUENCE 1 AT A GLANCE

Reading Content	
TONAL	**RHYTHM**
• Tonality: Major • Pitches: Major Tonic • Keys: F-DO, Eb-DO	• Meters: Duple and Triple • Functions: Macrobeats and Microbeats • Time Signatures: 2/4, 6/8
Lesson Sequence	
1.1 Rhythm	Duple, Macro/Micro; 2/4
1.2 Rhythm	Triple, Macro/Micro; 6/8
1.3 Tonal	Reading Longer Rhythm Patterns, Macro/Microbeat
1.4 Tonal	Introduction to Tonal Reading and FPIFO
1.5 Tonal	Tonic Patterns, Major Tonality
1.6 Tonal	Generalizing New Tonic Patterns, Major Tonality
Introduction to Reading Benchmarks	
Reading Benchmark 1 • Major (F & Eb); Tonic chord only; Starts and ends on DO • Macro/micro; Duple & Triple; 2/4; 6/8	

IMPORTANT REMINDER

If, at any time, you are having a difficult time reading the patterns, it's important to remember that you can (and should!) **review the patterns at the Aural/Oral and Verbal Association levels**. Trying to read a pattern that you can't audiate is like trying to read a word that you can't understand or pronounce. There is no shame in reviewing. In fact, it

LESSON 1.1

MACROBEATS AND MICROBEATS IN DUPLE METER
TIME SIGNATURE: 2/4

REVIEW

Take a moment to review macrobeats and microbeats in duple meter. Review Lesson 4 on p. 38 if necessary. Say the following to yourself:

"**Macrobeats** in duple meter are DU DU DU DU."

"**Microbeats** in duple meter are DU DE, DU DE, DU DE, DU DE."

TIME SIGNATURE

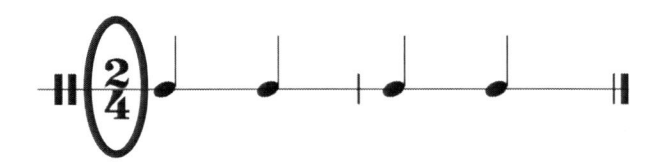

The stacked numbers circled in the picture above are called a **time signature**. It tells you what to audiate rhythmically. Technically, it's a mathematical representation of how much of a whole note is in a measure. However, that theoretical knowledge is not important when first learning how to read. (When you first learned to read the word "cat," did you need to know it was a noun??) Notice how far down on the Skill Learning Sequence theoretical understanding is.

To guide you when you are first learning to read, I will simply **tell you** what each time signature is telling you to audiate.

READING MACROBEATS AND MICROBEATS IN 2/4

The time signature $\frac{2}{4}$ tells us that the macrobeats (DU) will be represented by a quarter note, and that microbeats (DU DE) will be represented by paired eighth notes.

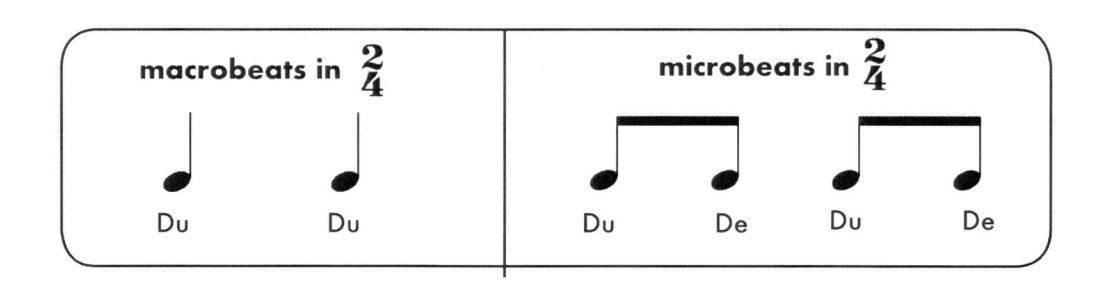

RHYTHM CELLS

Let's look at the possible combinations of macrobeats and microbeats in duple meter. There are only four possible combinations. These are called **rhythm cells**. You might think of these as musical words. Chant each of these rhythm cells several times.

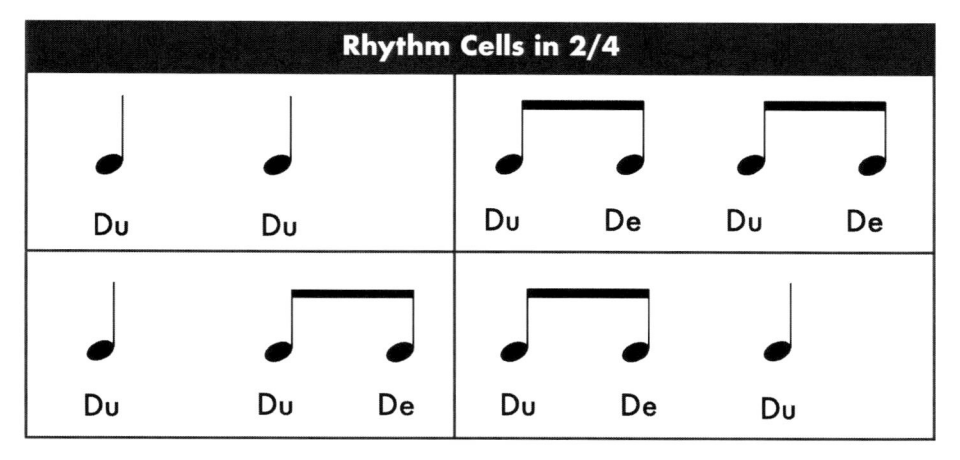

Rhythm Cells in 2/4	
Du Du	Du De Du De
Du Du De	Du De Du

COMBINING RHYTHM CELLS

Now we will combine these rhythm cells into four-macrobeat rhythm patterns. You might think of these as very simple **musical sentences**. These eight rhythm patterns will be part of your musical vocabulary.

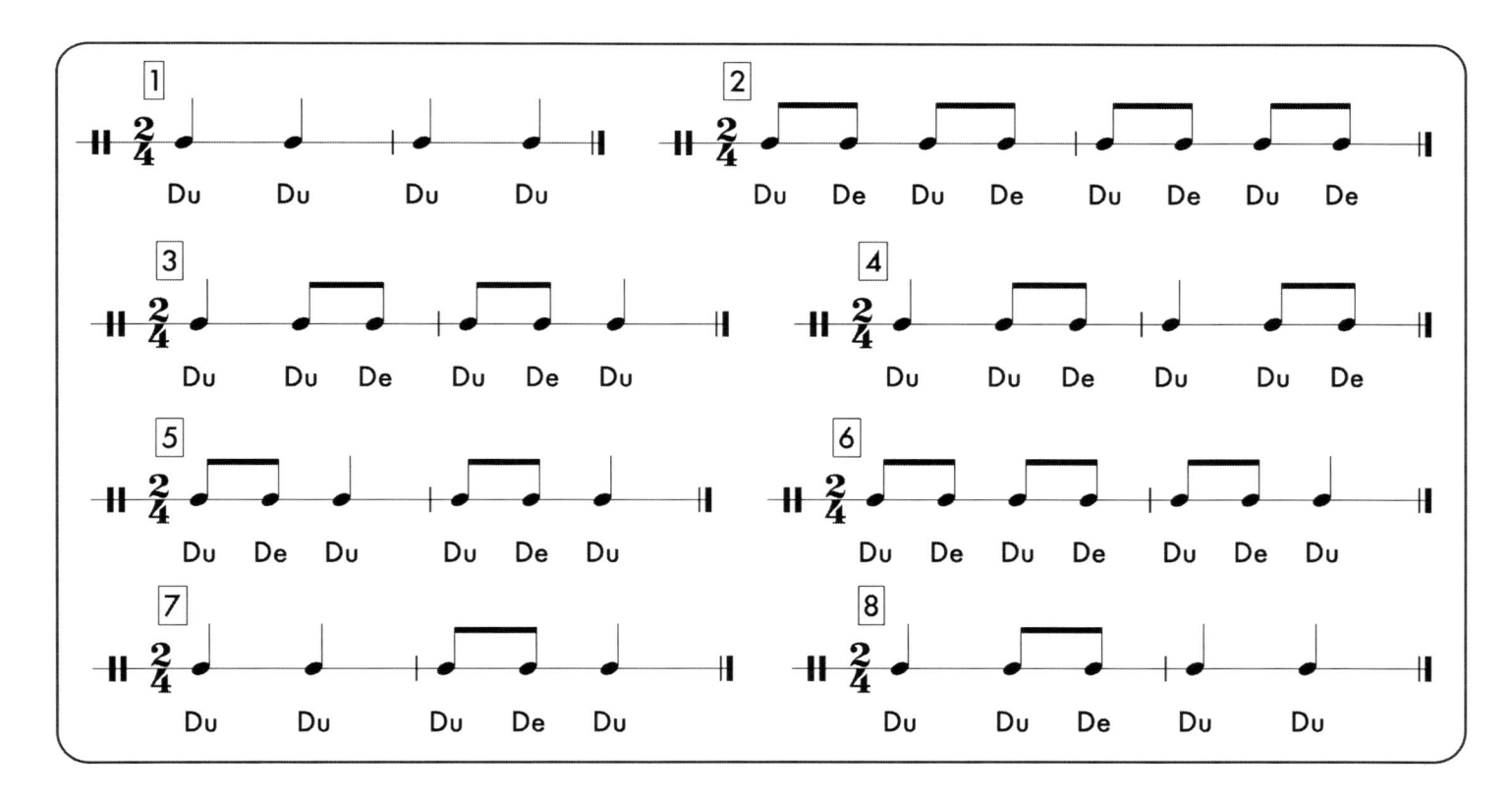

1. Du Du Du Du

2. Du De Du De Du De Du De

3. Du Du De Du De Du

4. Du Du De Du Du De

5. Du De Du Du De Du

6. Du De Du De Du De Du

7. Du Du Du De Du

8. Du Du De Du Du

IMPORTANT CONCEPT

Do not become dependent upon seeing DU and DU DE below the notation. Solfege should primarily be an **aural tool**. They are written here only for means of communicating how to read.

READING FAMILIAR PATTERNS

Now, read those same eight patterns using rhythm syllables without using the written solfege as a visual crutch. The same eight patterns appear below in their familiar order. Read these with DU and DU DE. Read them both in their familiar **and** unfamiliar orders. Try varying the tempo. Set your metronome so that the macrobeats are at the following tempos: 60, 120, 160, 30. As you are reading these patterns, continue to **move** as you read. Move your heels to the macrobeats and gently tap the microbeats on your lap with "spider fingers."

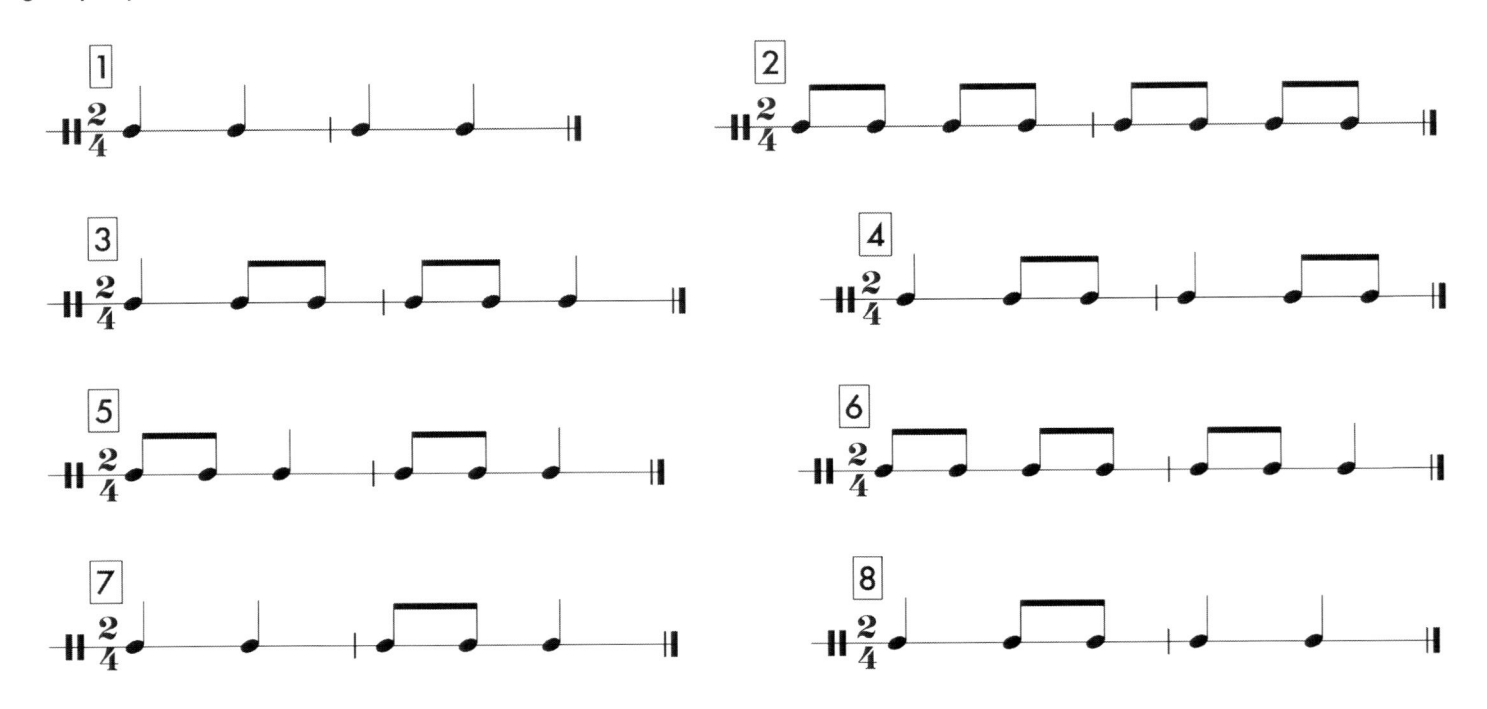

Try to write these patterns. Look at the pattern, audiate it, read it aloud, cover up the pattern, and try to write it **from your audiation**. This is a skill that, like anything else, you will get better at with more practice. You may then wish to challenge yourself further by writing two or more patterns.

Once you get comfortable with writing patterns, you may want to try writing a rhythmic composition.

LESSON 1.2
MACROBEATS AND MICROBEATS IN TRIPLE METER
TIME SIGNATURE: 6/8

REVIEW

Take a moment to review macrobeats and microbeats in triple meter. Review Lesson 5 on p. 40 if necessary. Say the following to yourself: "**Macrobeats** in triple meter are DU DU DU DU. **Microbeats** in triple meter are DU DA DI, DU DA DI, DU DA DI, DU DA DI."

READING MACROBEATS AND MICROBEATS IN 6/8

The time signature 6/8 tells us that the macrobeats (DU) will be represented by a dotted quarter note, and that microbeats (DU DA DI) will be represented by three paired eighth notes.

RHYTHM CELLS

Let's look at the possible combinations of macrobeats and microbeats in triple meter. There are only four possible combinations. Chant each of these rhythm cells several times.

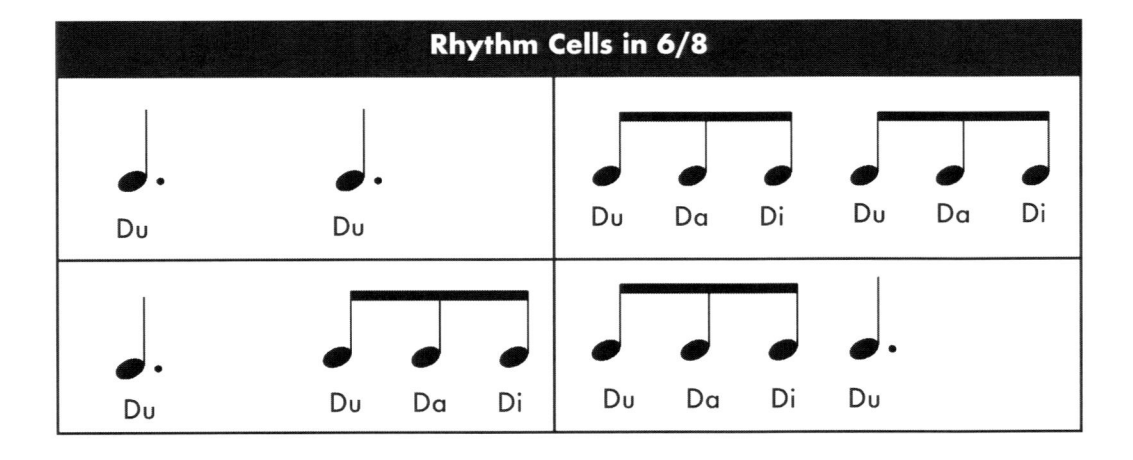

COMBINING RHYTHM CELLS

Just as we did in duple meter, we will combine these rhythm cells into four-macrobeat rhythm patterns. These eight rhythm patterns will be part of your musical vocabulary.

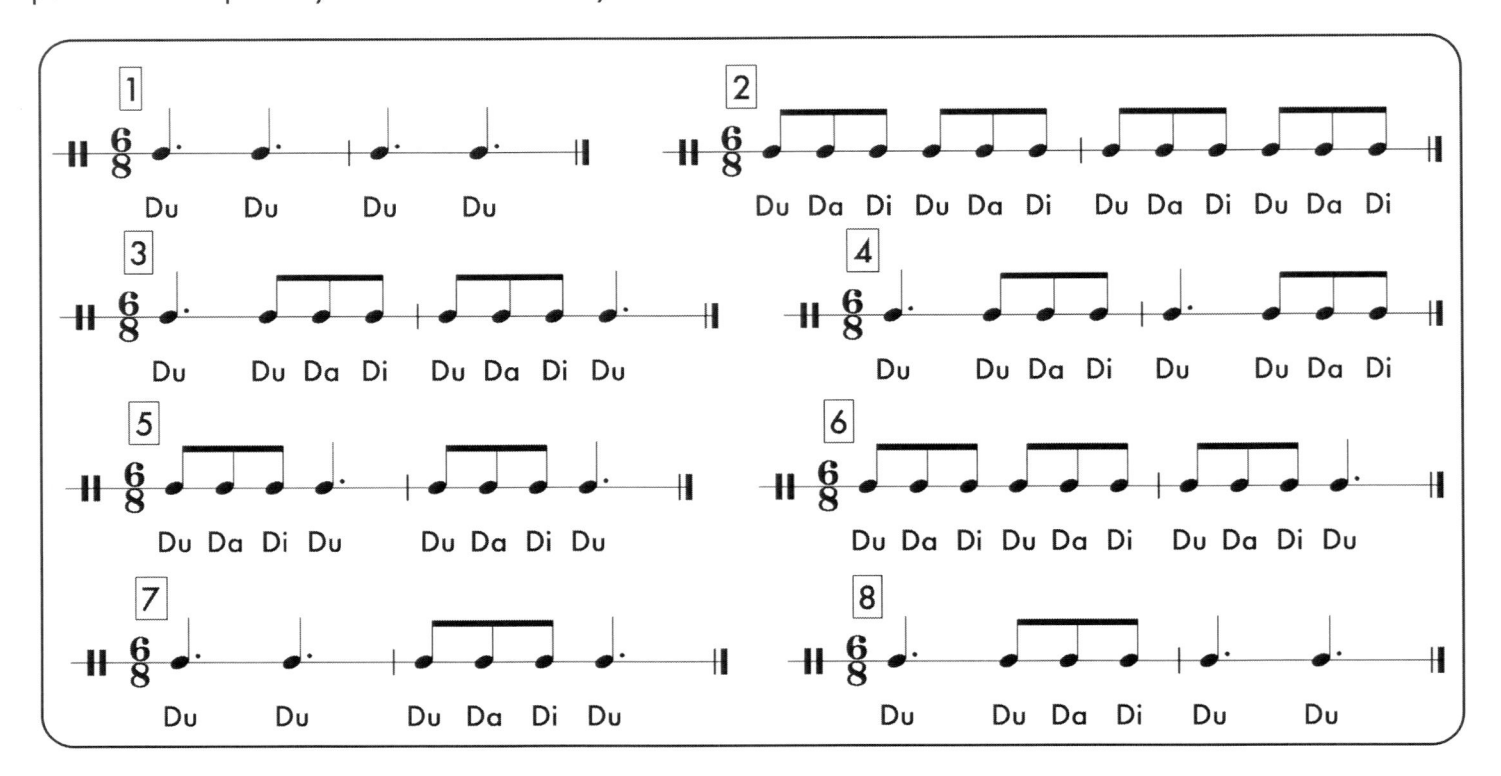

READING FAMILIAR PATTERNS

The same eight patterns appear below without solfege. Read them with rhythm syllables in their familiar and unfamiliar order without using written solfege as a visual crutch.

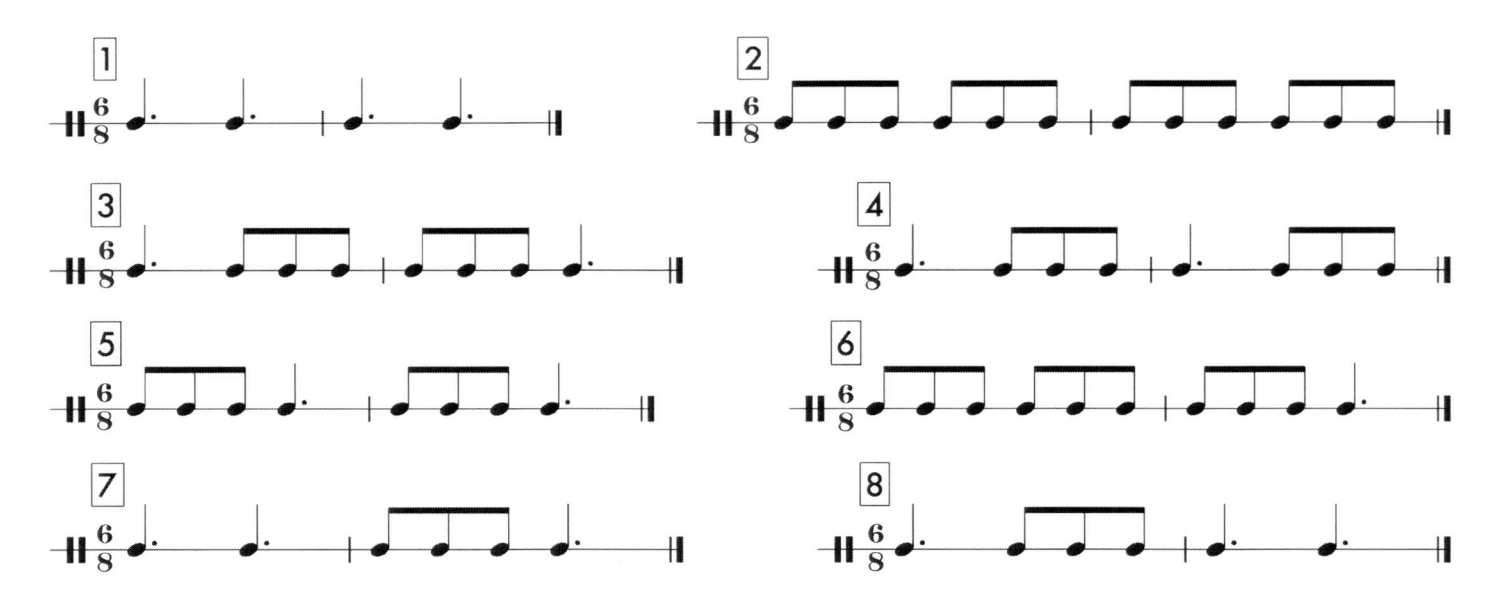

Just as you did in duple meter, try to write these patterns, one at a time, from your audiation.

Once you get comfortable with writing patterns, you may want to try writing a rhythmic composition.

LESSON 1.3
READING LONGER RHYTHM PATTERNS
DUPLE & TRIPLE

Up to this point, all of the rhythm patterns we have looked at have been 2-4 measures long. You can think of these as short sentences. In the upcoming Reading Benchmarks, you will be reading longer, more complicated sentences. You will also need to recognize the meter without being explicitly told. This skill is called **Composite Synthesis**.

First, **identify the meter.**
- Look at the time signature and the rhythm patterns. Are you audiating DU DE or DU DA DI as the microbeats?
- If you are audiating DU DE, the music is in duple meter. If you are audiating DU DA DI, the music is in triple meter.

Next, **remind yourself of the rhythm solfege** representing macrobeats and microbeats. Chant them to yourself. Scan the entire piece for **familiar rhythm patterns**. Chant the rhythm of the exercise **using rhythm solfege**.

LESSON 1.4
INTRO TO TONAL READING & "FPIFO"

In Part I of this book, you learned several series of familiar tonal patterns in a familiar order (abbreviated FPIFO, and pronounced "Fuh-Pi-Fo"). Let's now look specifically at what the major harmonic patterns look like in musical notation.

DO-SIGNATURES

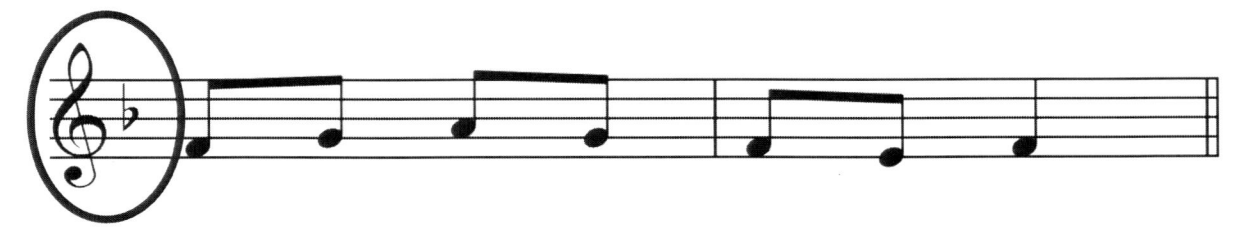

Just as we needed a time signature to tell us what to audiate rhythmically, we need a **key signature** to tell us what to audiate tonally. However, since we are using solfege, it is more beneficial to think about them as **"DO Signatures"** because that should be their main use for us: to tell us where DO is.

In the case of this DO-Signature, DO is on the first space from the bottom. Since this note is named F, we will refer to this as **F-DO**. I have highlighted this space in light gray for clarification purposes.

You can put DO anywhere on the staff, which is one of the amazing thing about learning to read with solfege. The relationships between the notes will be the same, but they just start in a different place. This will become very obvious soon!

TONIC AND DOMINANT PATTERNS IN NOTATION

The first thing you should realize is that you can think about harmonic patterns happening in two directions: **vertically and horizontally.** When you conceive of a harmonic function vertically, the individual pitches happen concurrently, and you have a chord (as if you strummed a chord on the ukulele). This is what our initial tonic and dominant chords look like when conceived **vertically** in F-DO.

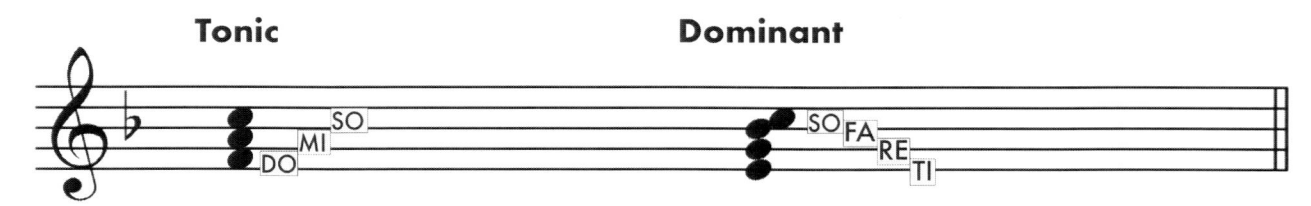

Strum an F (tonic) and C7 (dominant) on the ukulele to hear the gestalt sound. Sing **DO MI SO** as you strum tonic, and **SO FA RE TI** as you strum dominant.

You can also conceive of the pitches of these patterns happening **horizontally**, one after the after, as when you echoed the patterns.

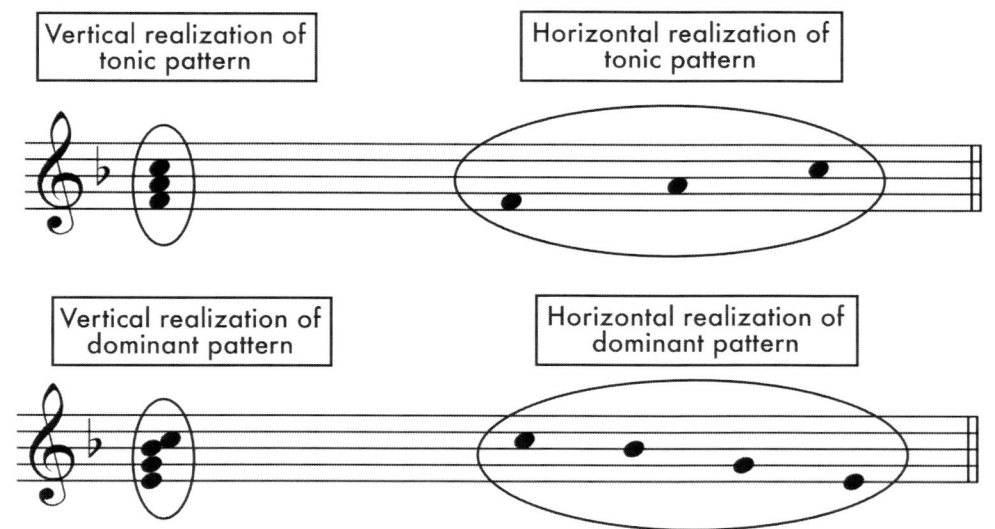

Vertical realization of tonic pattern

Horizontal realization of tonic pattern

Vertical realization of dominant pattern

Horizontal realization of dominant pattern

Regardless of whether they are played together (as in a chord strummed on a ukulele) or performed pitch by pitch, they should still be audiated as a gestalt, as one harmonic function.

FAMILIAR PATTERNS IN FAMILIAR ORDER (FPIFO)

Below are the familiar harmonic patterns in their familiar order (FPIFO) in major tonality with F as DO. Engage with these patterns in the following ways.

- Watch the **Patterns Only** video from Part I, and as you echo each pattern, point to the notation.
- Watch the **Tonal Pattern Recital** video from Part I, and point to each pattern as you sing.

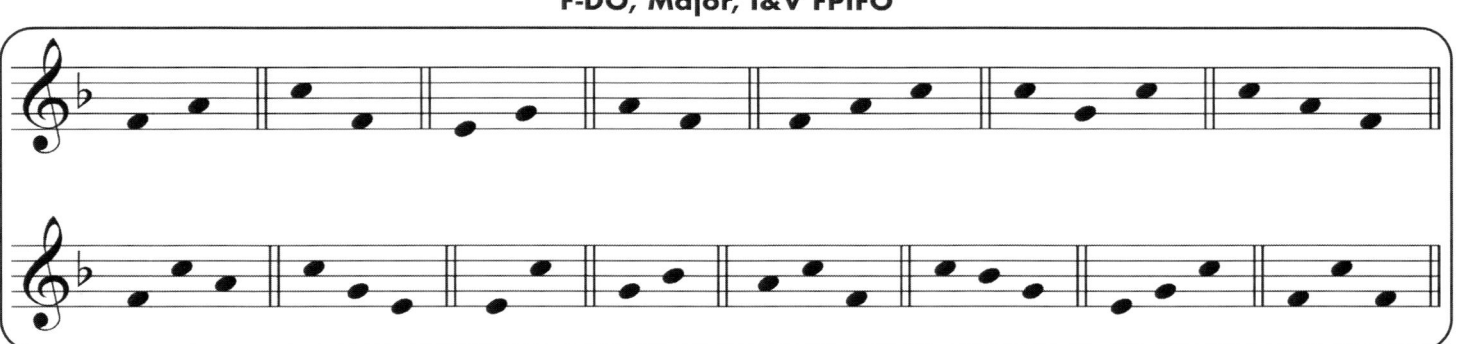

F-DO, Major, I&V FPIFO

MOVABLE DO

Once we learn how to read patterns in one DO-signature, the same patterns can be put in a different place, and the **relationship between pitches will remain constant**. The only thing that will change is **where DO is**. Once you understand and internalize this concept, music reading becomes a lot easier.

LETTERS The letters of the musical alphabet answer the question, **"Which DO?"** Since DO is movable, we need to distinguish between DO-signatures. Letters help us do that. Think of them like proper nouns vs. common nouns: Which boy? Todd.

FPIFO IN A NEW DO: Eb-DO

Let's now follow the exact same procedure in a new DO, Eb-DO.

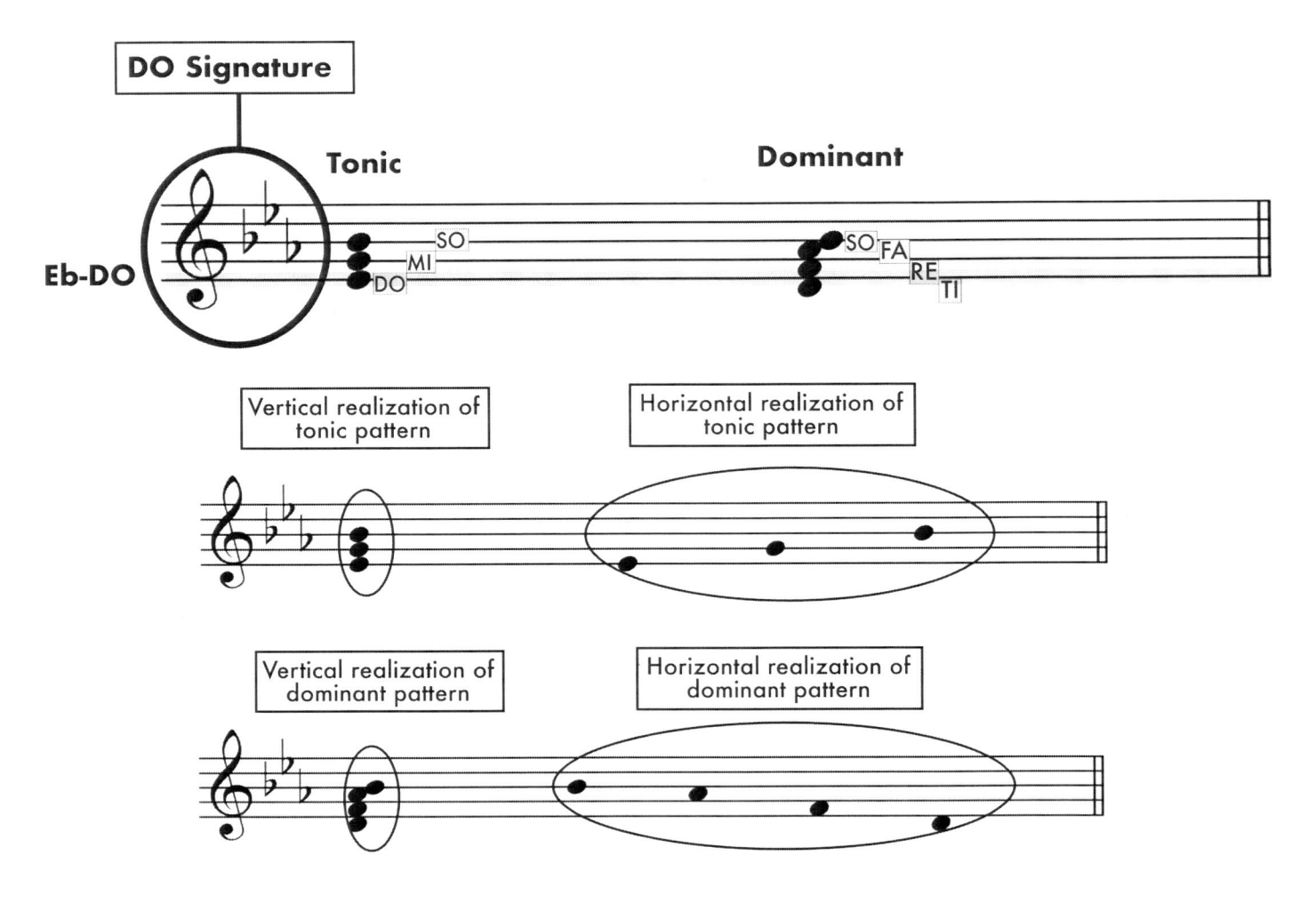

We will not go through this arduous detail for every new DO-signature, but I hope you see that the patterns **look exactly the same**, but they are just in different places on the staff.

Follow the same procedures for reading the patterns below as you did for the FPIFO in F-DO.

Eb-DO, Major, I&V FPIFO

LESSON 1.5
TONIC PATTERNS, MAJOR TONALITY

Now that we have read familiar patterns in familiar order, it is time to read familiar patterns in an unfamiliar order ("FPIUFO," pronounced "Fuh-pyu-fo").

THREE TONIC PATTERNS: DO MI SO, SO MI DO, DO SO DO

We will learn three familiar tonic patterns by rote, and then use those patterns to teach ourselves many more patterns!

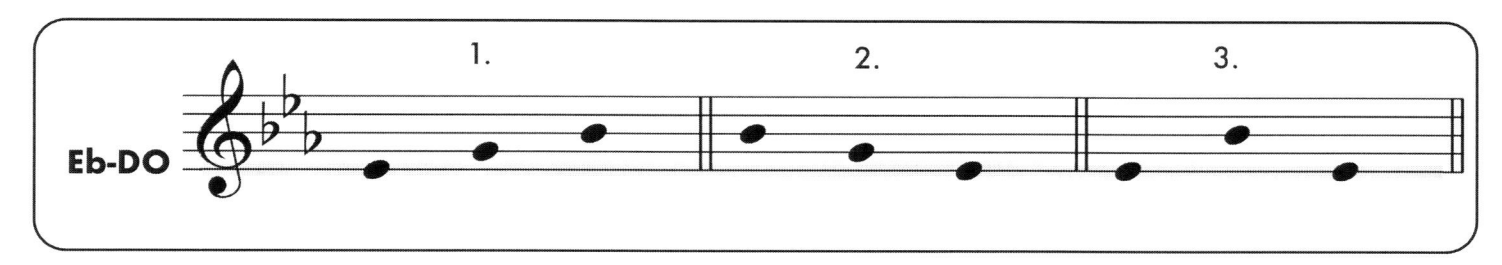

The first pattern is **DO MI SO**. Look at the notation, take a breath and sing **DO MI SO**. Just as you did when you echoed the patterns, keep the pitches separated. The second pattern is **SO MI DO**. Look at the notation, take a breath and sing **SO MI DO**. The third pattern is **DO SO DO**. Look at the notation, take a breath and sing **DO SO DO**. Read these three patterns, one after the other with a short pause in-between.

When you read a tonic pattern, take note of where each pitch is on the staff **in relation to DO**.

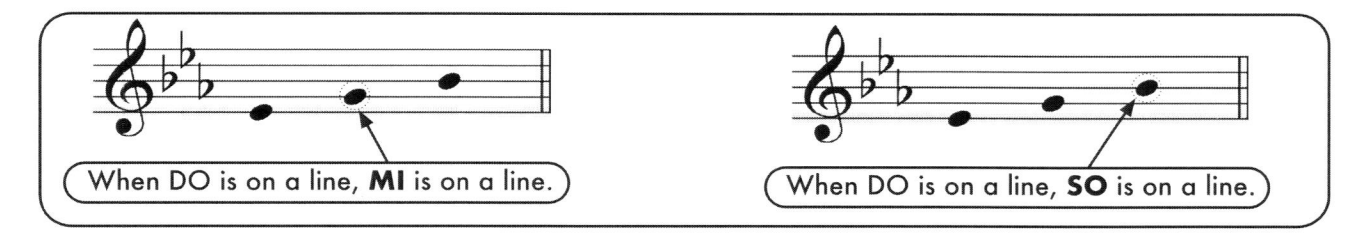

When DO is on a line, **MI** is on a line.

When DO is on a line, **SO** is on a line.

FAMILIAR PATTERNS, UNFAMILIAR ORDER

Read the same three familiar patterns, but this time, read them in an unfamiliar order.

SAME PATTERNS IN F-DO

It bears repeating that when you read the same patterns in new DO-signatures, the patterns look the same **in relation to themselves**, however, they just start in different places on the staff. Let's read those same 3 patterns in F-DO.

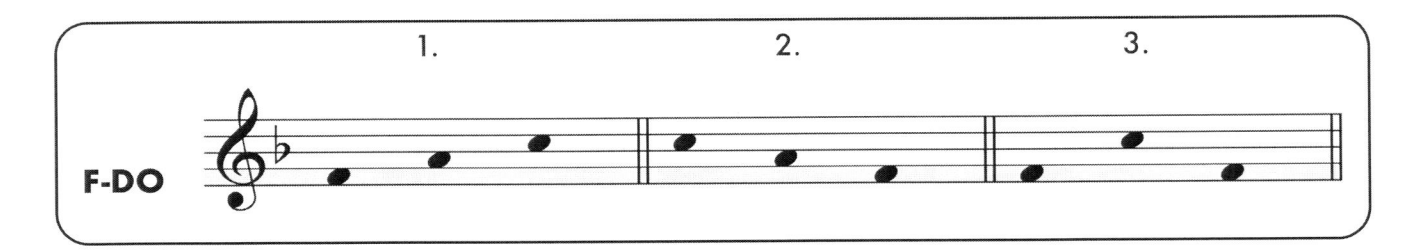

In F-DO, **DO** is on a space. Take note of where each pitch is on the staff **in relation to DO**.

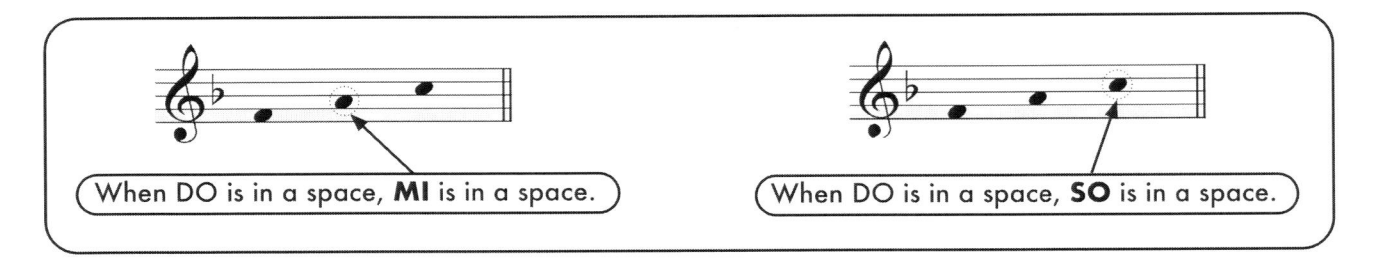

When DO is in a space, **MI** is in a space.

When DO is in a space, **SO** is in a space.

Read these familiar harmonic patterns in unfamiliar order in **F-DO**

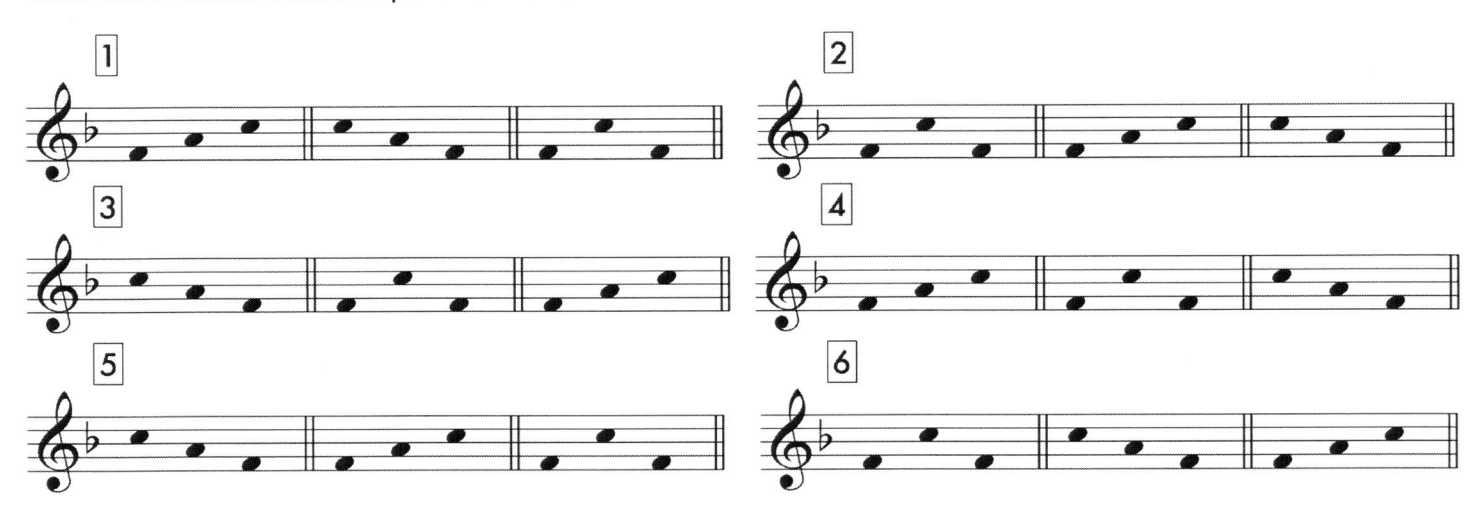

! If you need an aural reminder of these three patterns, review them in the companion course videos. Remember: we are learning to read **familiar patterns**. !

Write these musical sentences one at a time. Look at the pattern, audiate it, remove it from your view, and then write it **from your audiation**.

Try to play these patterns on the keyboard. Use the **Major I & V** Keyboard Card. Line up DO with F and Eb.

LESSON 1.6
GENERALIZING NEW MAJOR TONIC PATTERNS

Now that we have learned to read three familiar tonic patterns in two DO-signatures, we will harness the power of **generalization** to read more tonic patterns. Some of the patterns will be familiar to you aurally from Part I, while others will be brand new.

GENERALIZATION

Generalization is the ability to figure out the unfamiliar on the basis of the familiar. For example, when you were young, your parent probably told you that fruit is sweet. If they handed you a mango, and you asked what it was, and your parents said, "It's a mango. A mango is a fruit," you should have been able to infer then, through generalization, that a mango is sweet. Using those same inference skills, you should be able to read many more patterns than just DMS, SMD and DSD.

GENERALIZING NEW PATTERNS

Look at the two patterns below.

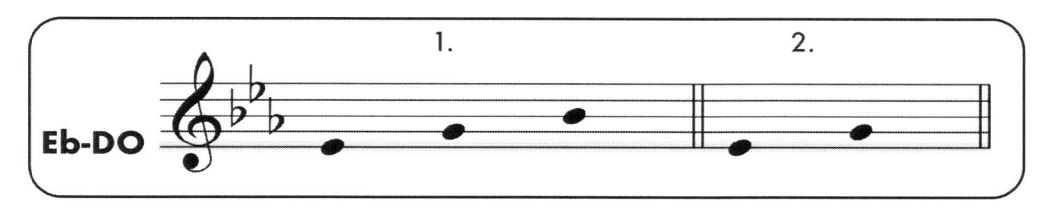

The first pattern (DO MI SO) is familiar to you. Using that knowledge, can you figure out the second pattern? Hopefully, you generalized that it was DO MI.

GENERALIZING TONIC PATTERNS IN Eb-DO

Use the skill of generalization to read these new patterns in Eb-DO.

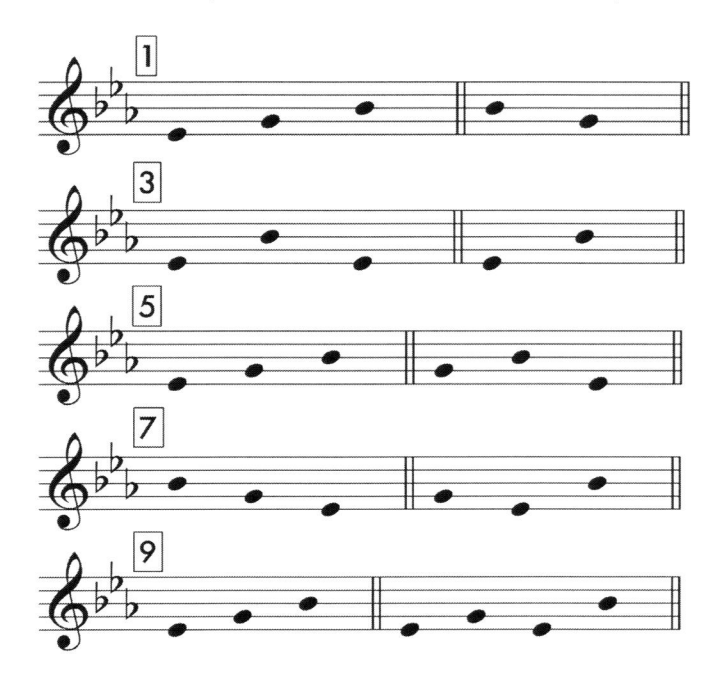

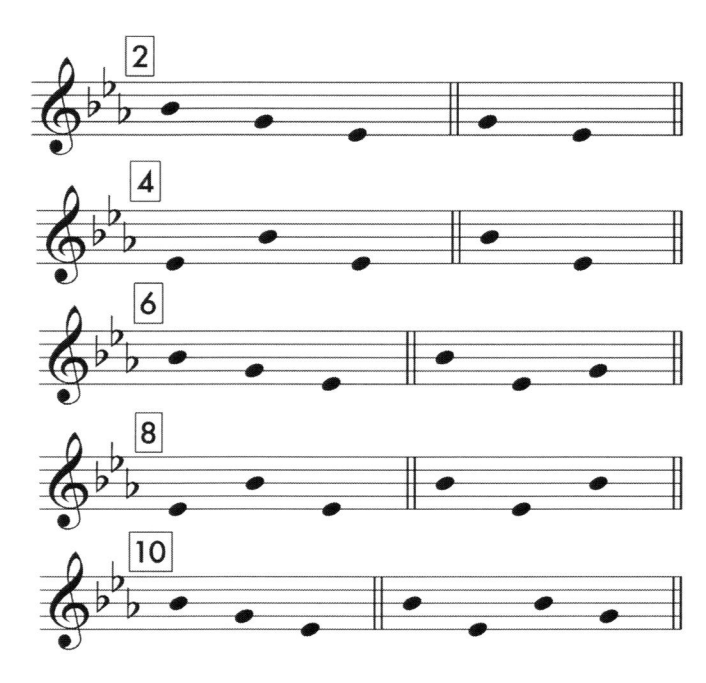

Use the skill of generalization to read these new patterns in F-DO.

GENERALIZING TONIC PATTERNS IN F-DO

At this point, for means of comparison, you may wish to **spiral** to Reading Sequence 6 and read minor tonic patterns. Remember: we learn what something is by what it's not.

READING BENCHMARKS
COMBINING TONAL PATTERNS AND RHYTHM PATTERNS

▶ Watch the video lesson **"Combining Tonal Patterns and Rhythm Patterns in 'Real' Music"** on The Improving Musician YouTube channel before you read this section.

INTRODUCTION

Up to this point, we have had an introduction to reading tonic and dominant patterns, learned to read macrobeats and microbeats in duple and triple meters, as well as tonic major tonic patterns in two DO-signatures.

Throughout the rest of this book, there will be **Reading Benchmarks**. Reading Benchmarks (usually) combine tonal patterns and rhythm patterns into "real" music. That is to say, tonal patterns and rhythm patterns are no longer isolated, but are combined as they would be when coming across music notation "out in the wild."

PROCEDURES

The steps I'm going to outline for you are merely actions you should probably take when you are **first** attempting to combine tonal patterns and rhythm patterns. After a while, these steps will be ingrained in the reading process, and you will do them subconsciously. Thankfully, we can read a lot quicker than we can perform, so many of these steps will also happen simultaneously as you are reading. In fact you will likely be performing one measure while reading another.

Let's begin with a very simple example of combining tonal patterns with rhythm patterns. As you can see, we have both tonal patterns and rhythm patterns to contend with.

Combining Tonal and Rhythm Example

We will use a three step process to break the song apart, and put it back together again.

3 STEP PROCESS FOR READING TONAL AND RHYTHM TOGETHER

Step 1: Analyze the song rhythmically.
Step 2: Analyze the song tonally.
Step 3: Put the parts together, and read the song in its entirety.

STEP 1: RHYTHM ANALYSIS

First, **identify the meter.**
- Is it duple or triple? Are you seeing DU DEs or DU DA DIs?
- If you are seeing DU DEs, the music is in duple meter. If you are seeing DU DA DIs, the music is in triple meter.

In the example on the previous page, we are seeing DU DEs, so it's a pretty good bet that this song is in duple meter. If we look at the time signature, our suspicions are confirmed, and it is indeed in duple meter.

Next, **remind yourself of the rhythm solfege** representing macrobeats and microbeats in the meter of the piece of music.
- **Macrobeats** in duple meter are "DU, DU, DU, DU."
- **Microbeats** in duple meter are "DU DE, DU DE, DU DE, DU DE."

Then, look at the notation, and confirm **what notes** represent the macrobeats and microbeats. In these early examples, there is no variation, but when you read in different time signatures, different notes will represent macrobeats and microbeats.

Scan the entire piece for **familiar rhythm patterns**. All of the rhythm patterns will be based on previously learned rhythm cells. Isolate any difficult rhythm pattern, and "sound out" the word.

Next, **chant the rhythm** of the entire song with a neutral syllable.
- Set a reasonable tempo for yourself. Use the neutral syllable "BAA."

Finally, chant the rhythm of the song **using rhythm solfege**.

STEP 2: TONAL ANALYSIS

First, **identify where DO is** on the staff. In the early examples, that will be quite easy because each piece will always start and end on DO. The key signature tells you where DO is.

Next, you'll need to **identify the tonality**. Since I've told you that it starts and ends on DO, you can assume it's likely major tonality. Play the resting tone for the key of the exercise using a keyboard, ukulele, or a Smartphone app.

Once you know what tonality you're in, **ground yourself in that tonality and key**. You can do this in a number of ways.
- A very easy way is to sing familiar tonal patterns. Try singing the first four harmonic patterns from Part I: DO MI, SO DO, TI RE, MI DO.
- Or, simply recite the tonal sequence for major tonality: SO LA SO FA MI RE TI DO. .

Then, **scan the melody**. Look for **familiar tonal patterns**. In Reading Benchmark 1, the only pitches you will see are pitches of the tonic chord, so most of the patterns will be familiar. If they are not, you will be able to figure them out through **generalization**! Later, we will need to do further analysis by circling and squaring chords, but not yet!

Next, **trace the entire melody** by audiating or humming the pitches to yourself.
- Don't concern yourself with rhythm; just notice the rise and fall of the melody. You should be **audiating** the solfege, but not singing it.
- If necessary, track the melody with your finger on your "hand staff" while you are reading.
- If you lose your sense of tonality, use the tonal sequence (SO LA SO FA MI RE TI DO) or the first four harmonic patterns as a problem-solving tool.

STEP 3: READ THE SONG

Now that you have done your preliminary tonal and rhythmic analysis, it's time to read the song. First, pause and **take a full audiation breath**.

Then, set yourself a reasonable tempo, and **sing the song** (pitches and rhythm) with a neutral syllable ("NOO" works well) in its entirety. Don't stop, even if you make a mistake!

When you are done, if you made a mistake, go back and do further tonal or rhythm analysis to isolate the troubled areas and do some problem-solving. Then, read it again.

Finally, your teacher may ask you to also sing the melody using tonal solfege while singing the correct rhythms or rhythm solfege while singing the correct pitches. When we are reading music out in the wild, we will usually either have words to sing, or be playing an instrument, but this step is a useful thing to do.

Try steps one, two and three on the example below.

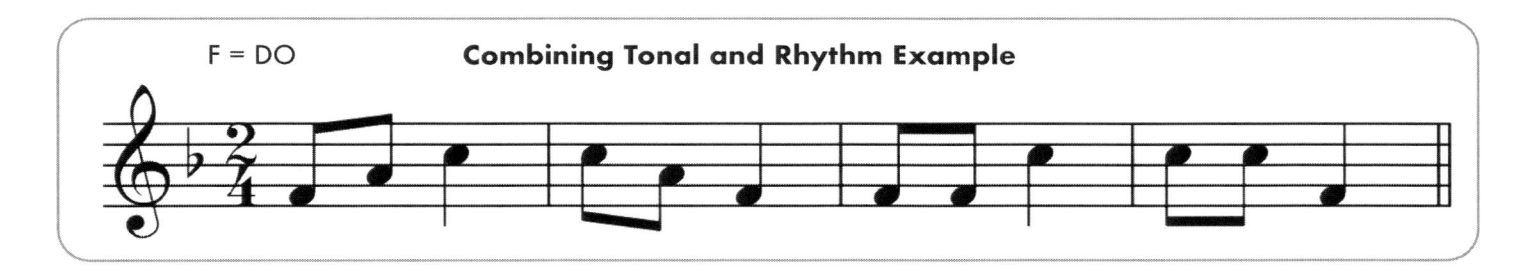

F = DO
Combining Tonal and Rhythm Example

READING BENCHMARKS

After each series of lessons on reading tonal patterns and rhythm patterns separately, there will be a **Reading Benchmark** in which all of the new material will be presented in new musical examples.

There will be written hints and prompts in the examples which remind you of new concepts.

As you read the early examples, try to hold true to the **3 Step Reading Process**. As you get better and better at reading, these steps will happen subconsciously just as they do when you read familiar words in English.

Often times, the first 10 exercises will be on the easier side while the second 10 exercises will be more challenging.

READING BENCHMARK 1

Tonality = Major
Pitches = Tonic chord only
Keys = F, Eb

Meters = Duple and Triple
Time Signatures = 2/4, 6/8
Functions = Macrobeat/Microbeat

More Difficult Exercises

READING SEQUENCE 2

SEQUENCE 2 AT A GLANCE

Reading Content	
TONAL	**RHYTHM**
• Tonality: Major • Pitches: tDRM • Keys: G-DO, F-DO, Eb-DO	• Meters: Duple and Triple • Functions: Macrobeats and Microbeats • Time Signatures: 2/4, 4/4; 6/8, 3/4

Lesson Sequence	
2.1 Tonal	Introduction to Reading Stepwise Patterns, Major Tonality
2.2 Tonal	Stepwise Patterns (DRM, MRD, DTD), Major Tonality (F-DO, Eb-DO)
2.3 Tonal	A New DO: DRM, MRD, DTD in **G-DO**
2.4 Tonal	Generalizing New Stepwise Patterns

Reading Benchmark 2A
- Major (G, F & Eb); Stepwise (DO, RE, MI and TI); Starts and ends on DO
- Macro/micro; Duple & Triple; 2/4; 6/8

2.5 Rhythm	Enrhythmic Patterns in Duple Meter (4/4)
2.6 Rhythm	Enrhythmic Patterns in Triple Meter (3/4)

Reading Benchmark 2B
- Major (G, F & Eb); Stepwise (DO, RE, MI and TI); Starts and ends on DO
- Macro/micro; Duple & Triple; 2/4, 4/4; 6/8, 3/4

LESSON 2.1
INTRODUCTION TO READING STEPWISE PATTERNS
MAJOR TONALITY

Up to this point, we have learned to audiate and perform both harmonic patterns and stepwise acculturation patterns. We learned harmonic patterns first because they set up the tonal context for stepwise patterns. Let's begin our journey reading stepwise patterns in the same way we did with harmonic patterns: by reading familiar patterns in their familiar order.

STAIRS VS ELEVATOR ANALOGY

To continue with our building metaphor, think about the pitches in each tonality as steps that you climb in succession. When learning to read stepwise patterns, we will take the stairs up one step at a time. When learning to read harmony, we will need to skip steps. (We might even take the elevator!)

FAMILIAR PATTERNS IN FAMILIAR ORDER

Below are the familiar stepwise acculturation patterns in their familiar order (FPIFO) in major tonality with F and G as DO. This will give you a sense of the whole scale before we read patterns within the scale. Engage with these patterns in the following ways.

- Watch the **Patterns Only** video from Part I, and as you echo each pattern, point to the notation.
- Watch the **Tonal Pattern Recital** video from Part I, and point to each pattern as you sing.

F-DO, Stepwise Patterns, FPIFO

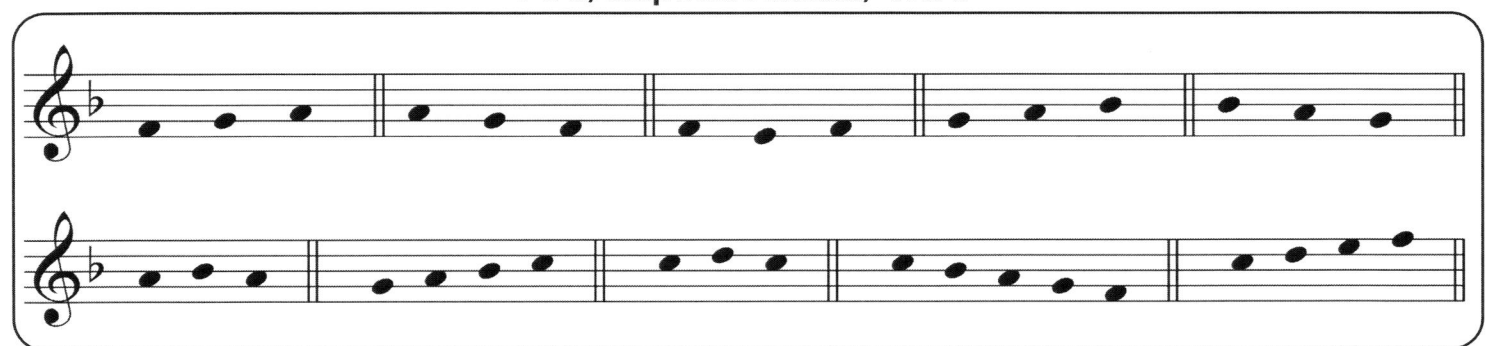

Eb-DO, Stepwise Patterns, FPIFO

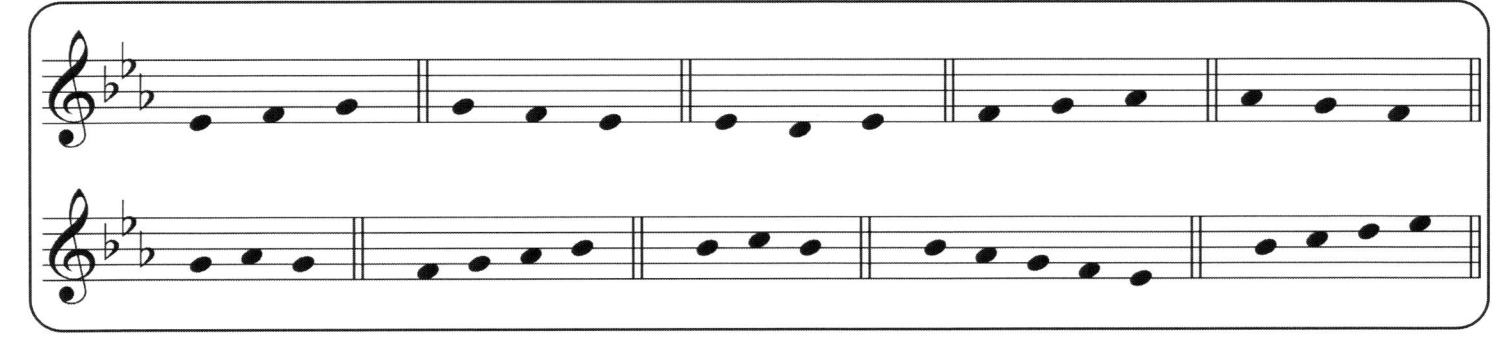

LESSON 2.2
STEPWISE PATTERNS IN MAJOR TONALITY
DRM, MRD, DTD IN F-DO AND Eb-DO

Just as we did in Reading Sequence 1, we will first learn to read stepwise patterns that are **already familiar** to us as the verbal association level. We wouldn't want to learn to read English beginning with the word "antidisestablishmentarianism," would we? No, we would start with words that already represent something in our minds: our name, cat, dog.

We will learn to read a few pitches at a time until all of the pitches of major tonality are learned. The visual representation of our stepwise reading trajectory appears below:

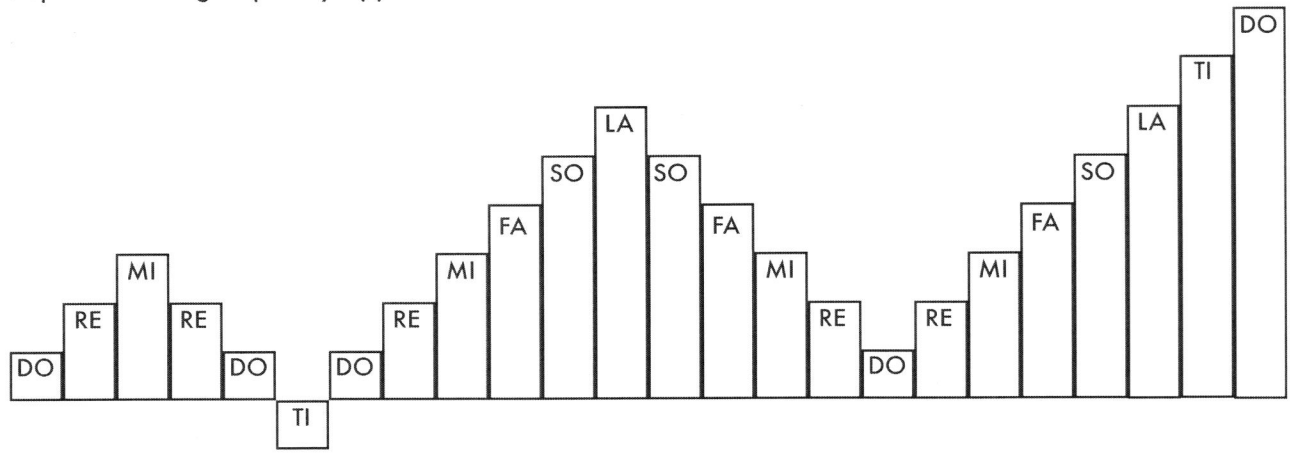

We will begin very simply with our first three stepwise patterns: DO RE MI, MI RE DO, DO TI DO.

FIRST THREE PATTERNS: DRM, MRD, DTD

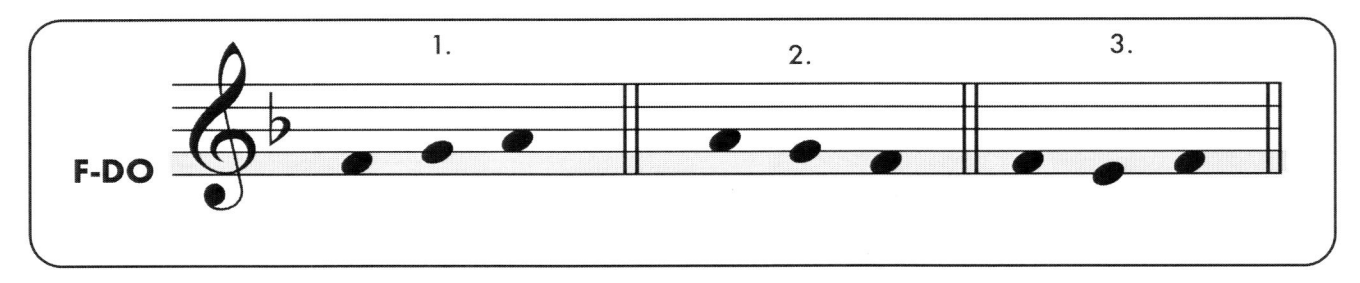

The first pattern is **DO RE MI**. Look at the notation, take a breath and sing **DO RE MI**. Just as you did when you echoed the patterns, keep the pitches separated. The second pattern is **MI RE DO**. Look at the notation, take a breath and sing **MI RE DO**. The third pattern is **DO TI DO**. Look at the notation, take a breath and sing **DO TI DO**.

Finally, read these three patterns one after the other with a short pause in-between. These are **familiar patterns in a familiar order**.

> ! If you need an aural reminder of these three patterns, review them in the companion course videos. Remember: we are learning to read **familiar patterns**. !

Lesson 2.2

FAMILIAR PATTERNS, UNFAMILIAR ORDER (FPIUFO)

Read the same three familiar patterns, but this time, read them in an unfamiliar order. Remember to keep the pitches separated, and to make a short pause in-between each pattern.

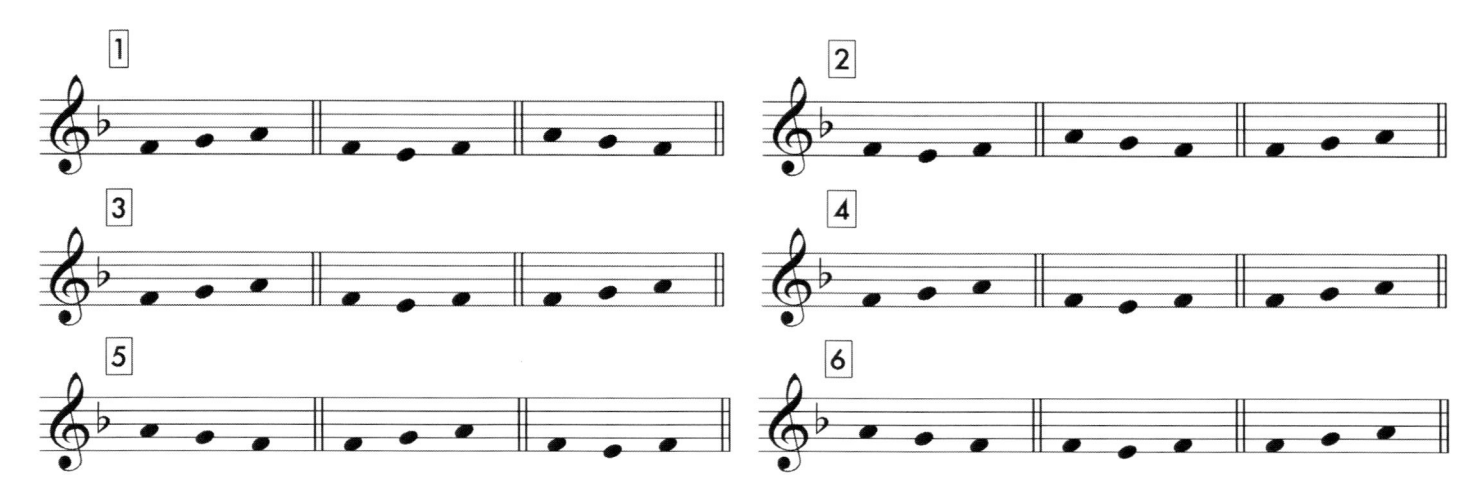

SAME PATTERNS IN Eb-DO

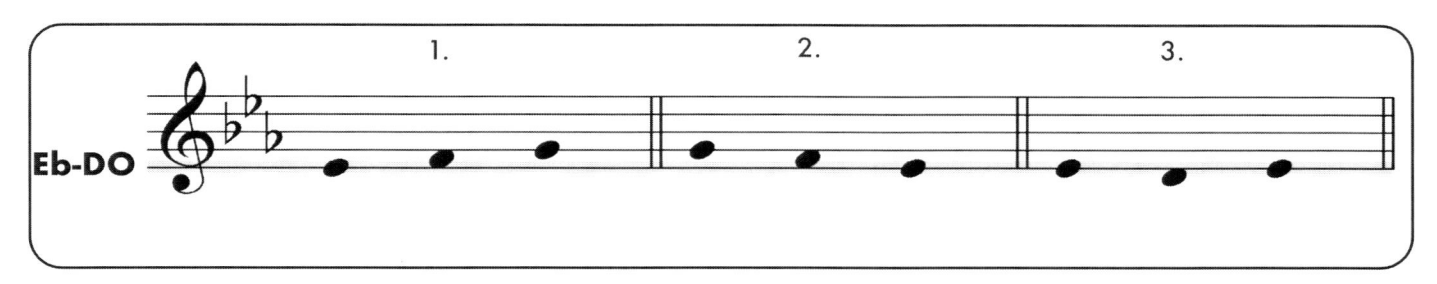

Read the same three familiar patterns in both their familiar and unfamiliar orders in Eb-DO.

Try writing these patterns.

Create **new tonal patterns** that only have the pitches DO RE MI and TI.

LESSON 2.3: A NEW DO
STEPWISE PATTERNS IN MAJOR TONALITY
DRM, MRD, DTD IN G-DO

We have already learned how to read three stepwise patterns with F and Eb as DO. Now, let's learn to read those same patterns with a new DO: **G-DO**. Here are the 10 familiar patterns in familiar order in G-DO.

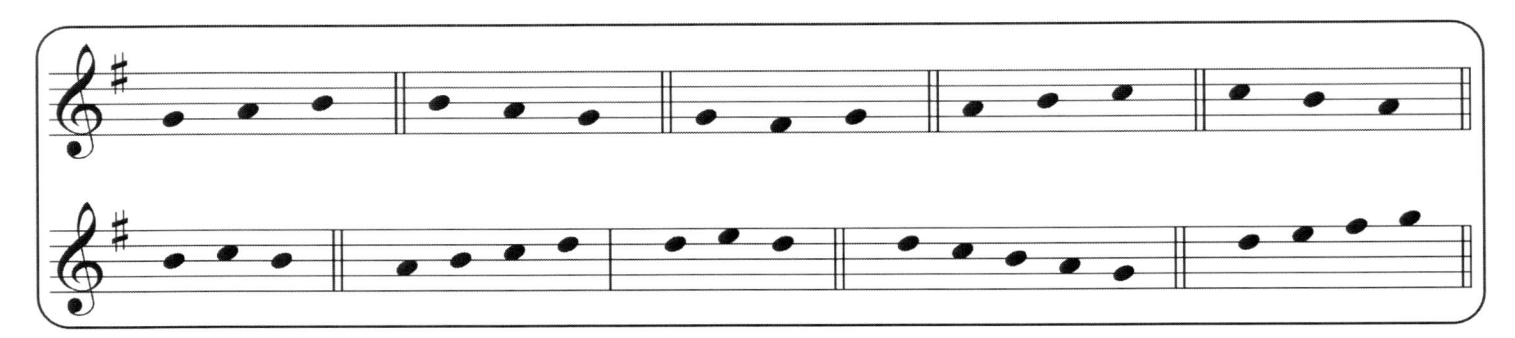

DRM, MRD, DTD IN G-DO

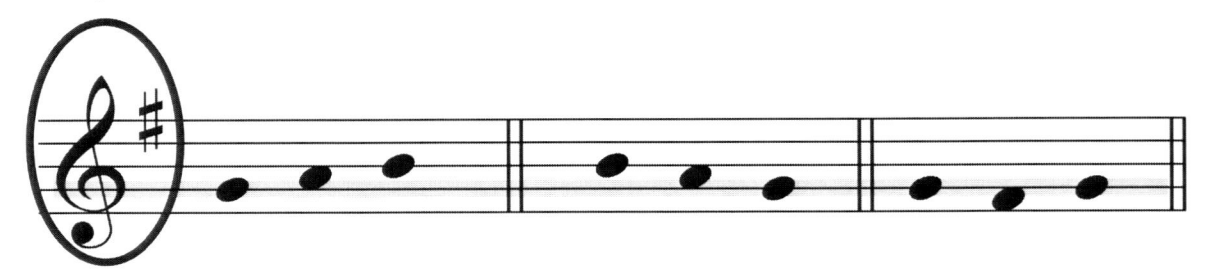

This DO-signature tells us that DO is on the second line from the bottom. It is also named G, so we will call this G-DO. Notice that the patterns look the same as they did in F-DO and Eb-DO, only they simply start in a different place.

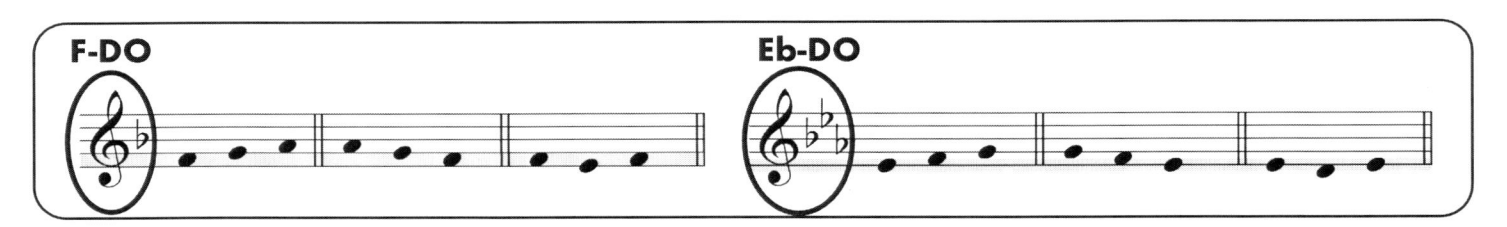

F-DO   **Eb-DO**

Read the same three familiar patterns in both their familiar and unfamiliar orders in G-DO.

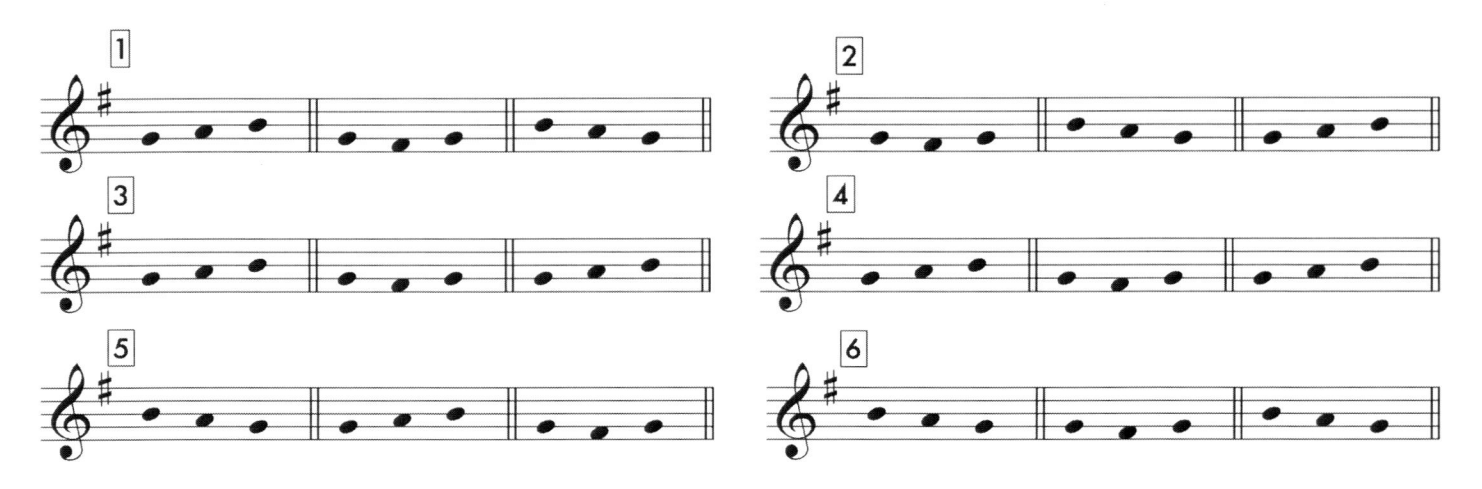

LESSON 2.4
GENERALIZING NEW STEPWISE PATTERNS
DO, RE, MI & TI

So far, we have learned to read three stepwise patterns (DRM, MRD, DTD) in three different DO-signatures (F-DO, Eb-DO and G-DO). Using that knowledge and a bit of persistence, we can teach ourselves to read **new patterns** with the pitches DO, RE, MI and TI if we harness the power of **generalization**.

GENERALIZATION

Generalization, an inference skill, is the ability to figure out the unfamiliar on the basis of the familiar. Using those inference skills, you should be able to read many more patterns than just DRM, MRD and DTD.

Here are our three familiar patterns in their familiar order in G-DO (DO RE MI, MI RE DO, DO TI DO).

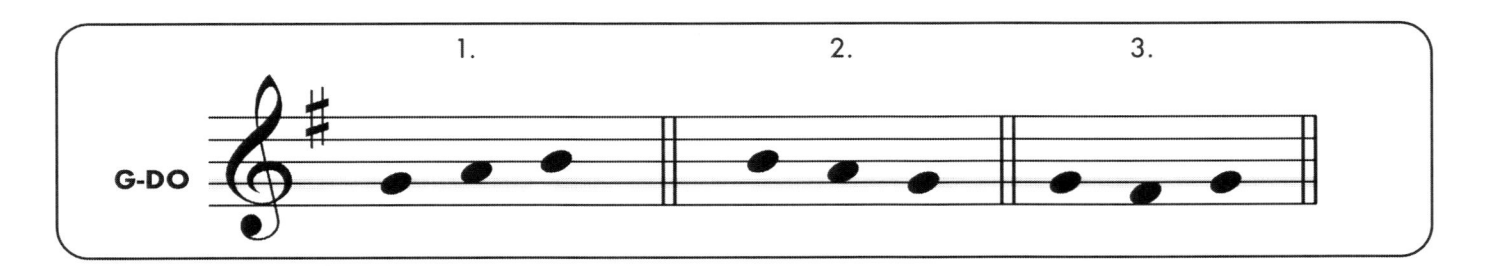

GENERALIZATION IN ACTION

By knowing how to read these three patterns, we know how to read four pitches: DO, RE, MI and TI.

Look at this new pattern set below.

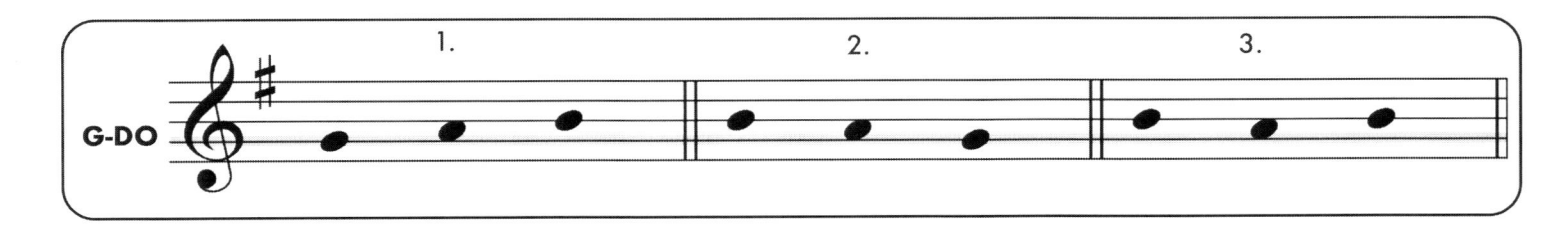

The first pattern is familiar. (DO RE MI) The second pattern is also familiar (MI RE DO). On the basis of that information, can you figure out the third pattern? Hopefully, you can infer that it's MI RE MI.

GENERALIZATION EXERCISES IN G-DO

Continue to use the new skill of generalization to read more unfamiliar patterns. The final pattern in each of the pattern sets below is unfamiliar. If you are struggling: remember that generalization is an **inference** skill. Struggling while making inferences is a good thing. It means you are working new parts of your brain. The struggle is real; the struggle is good!

TRACING MELODY IN G-DO

Trace the pitches in the below exercises. They all start and end on DO. The beams have been removed so you do not concern yourself with rhythm. Do these all in one breath. Follow along with your finger, as necessary.

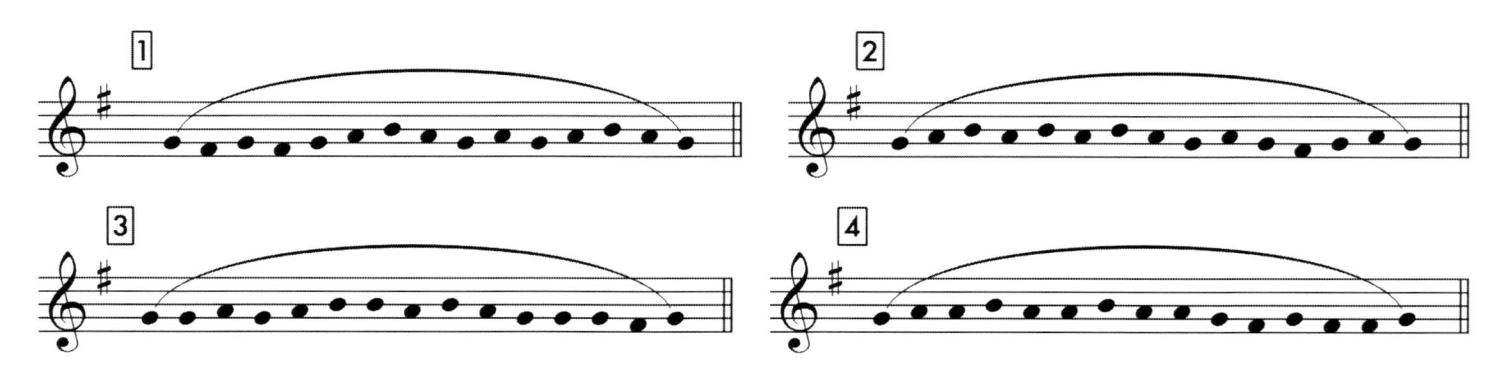

GENERALIZATION EXERCISES IN F-DO

Read these pattern sets in F-DO. Again, the final pattern will be unfamiliar, and will require generalization.

TRACING MELODY IN F-DO

Trace the pitches in the below exercises. They all start and end on DO. The beams have been removed so you do not concern yourself with rhythm. Do these all in one breath. Follow along with your finger, as necessary.

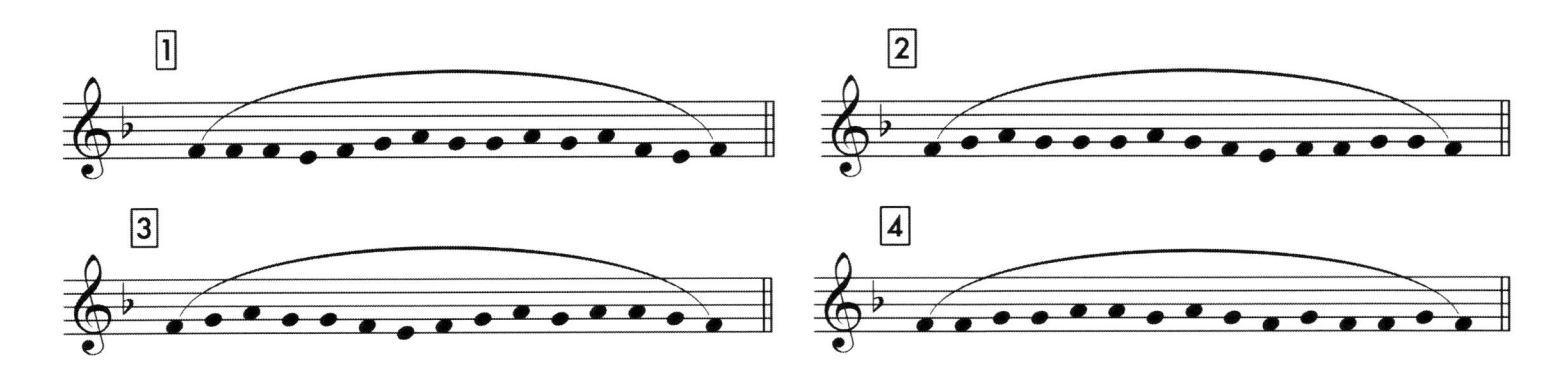

GENERALIZATION EXERCISES IN Eb-DO

Read these pattern sets in Eb-DO. Again, the final pattern will be unfamiliar, and will require generalization.

TRACING MELODY IN Eb-DO

Trace the pitches in the below exercises. They all start and end on DO. The beams have been removed so you do not concern yourself with rhythm. Do these all in one breath. Follow along with your finger, as necessary.

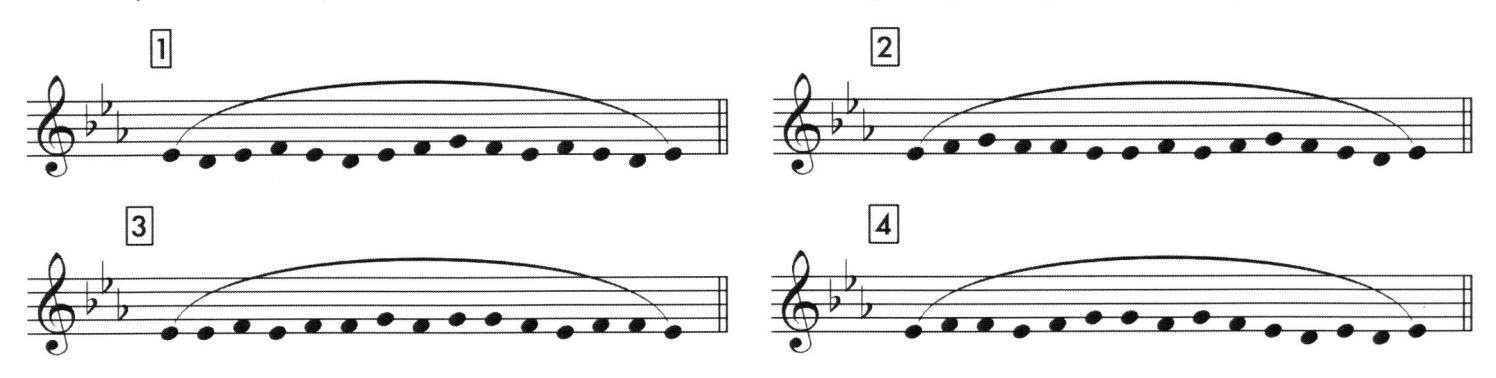

You may wish to **spiral** to Reading Sequence 7 and read the parallel patterns in minor tonality.

READING BENCHMARK 2A

Tonality = Major
Pitches = tDRM, Stepwise
Keys = G, F, Eb

Meters = Duple and Triple
Time Signatures = 2/4, 6/8
Functions = Macrobeat/Microbeat

More Difficult Exercises

LESSON 2.5
ENRHYTHMIC PATTERNS IN DUPLE METER
4/4

ENRHYTHMIC DEFINED

Rhythm can be notated in a number of ways. That may seem confusing at first, but the same can be said about language. I have been teaching for a long time, and have had many students named Cameron. I have seen the same name spelled many ways! I have seen it spelled Cameron, Camron, Camryn, Camren, Kameron, Kamron, and Kamryn. It's spelled differently, but it is still the same name.

George Bernard Shaw quipped that you could spell the word "fish" like this: ghoti. If you take the "gh" from the word "rough," the "o" from the word "women" and the "ti" from the word "nation," he is absolutely right. Written English is filled with all manner of inconsistencies. Written music is no exception.

If two patterns are **enrhythmic**, they sound the same, but are notated differently. The first way we are going to see patterns notated differently is by **how many macrobeats are in a measure**.

NEW TIME SIGNATURE

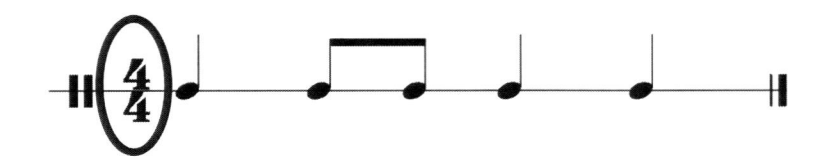

Just like 2/4, the time signature 4/4 usually (but not always!) tells us that the macrobeats (DU) will be represented by a quarter note, and that microbeats (DU DE) will be represented by paired eighth notes.

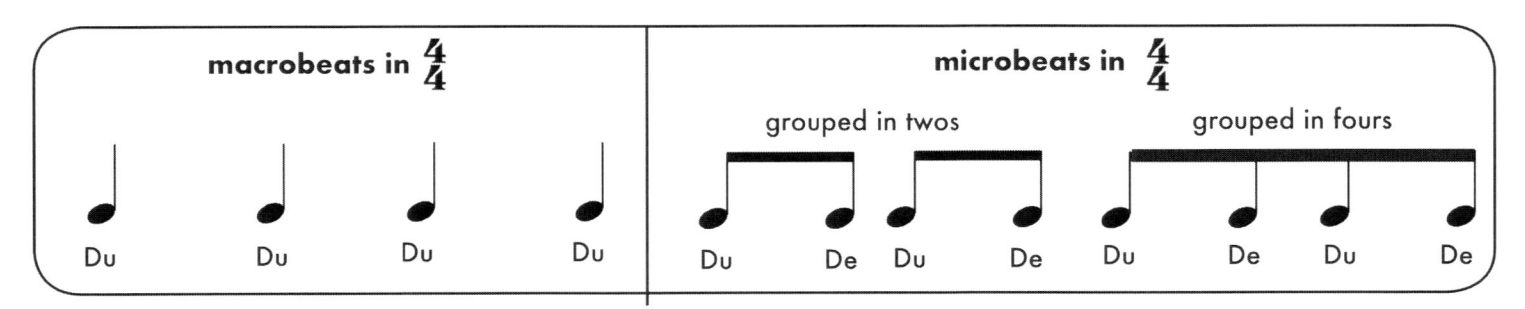

macrobeats in 4/4	microbeats in 4/4
Du Du Du Du	grouped in twos: Du De Du De grouped in fours: Du De Du De

We can read the exact same patterns from Lesson 1.1, except this time, we will notate them in 4/4. This is as simple as removing the bar line, and reading four macrobeats in a measure instead of two. Sometimes, if there are two pairs of microbeats, all four microbeats are beamed together.

Look at the two example on the next page. They are exactly the same, but the 2/4 pattern has a bar line.

Enrhythmic Rhythm Patterns

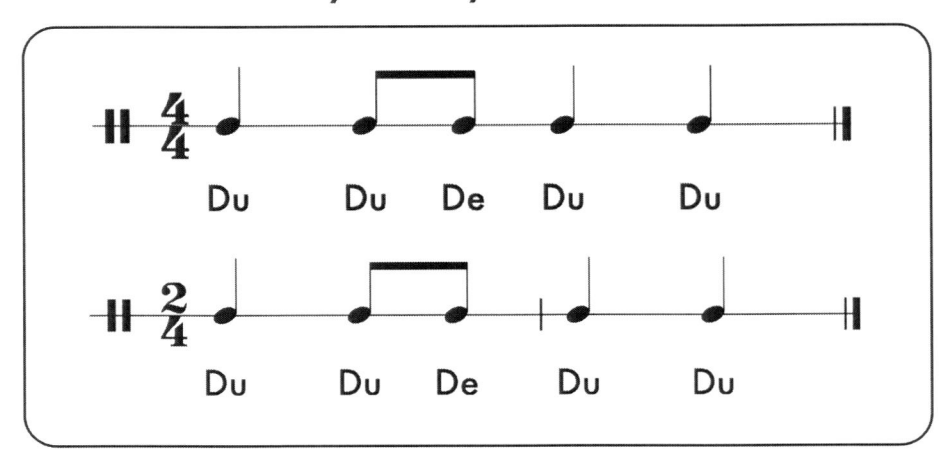

	Du	Du	De	Du	Du

	Du	Du	De	Du	Du

RHYTHM PATTERNS IN 4/4

Here are the same eight rhythm patterns that you already read in 2/4. Can you read them in 4/4? (Notice that the pairs of microbeats are beamed together in patterns 2 and 6.)

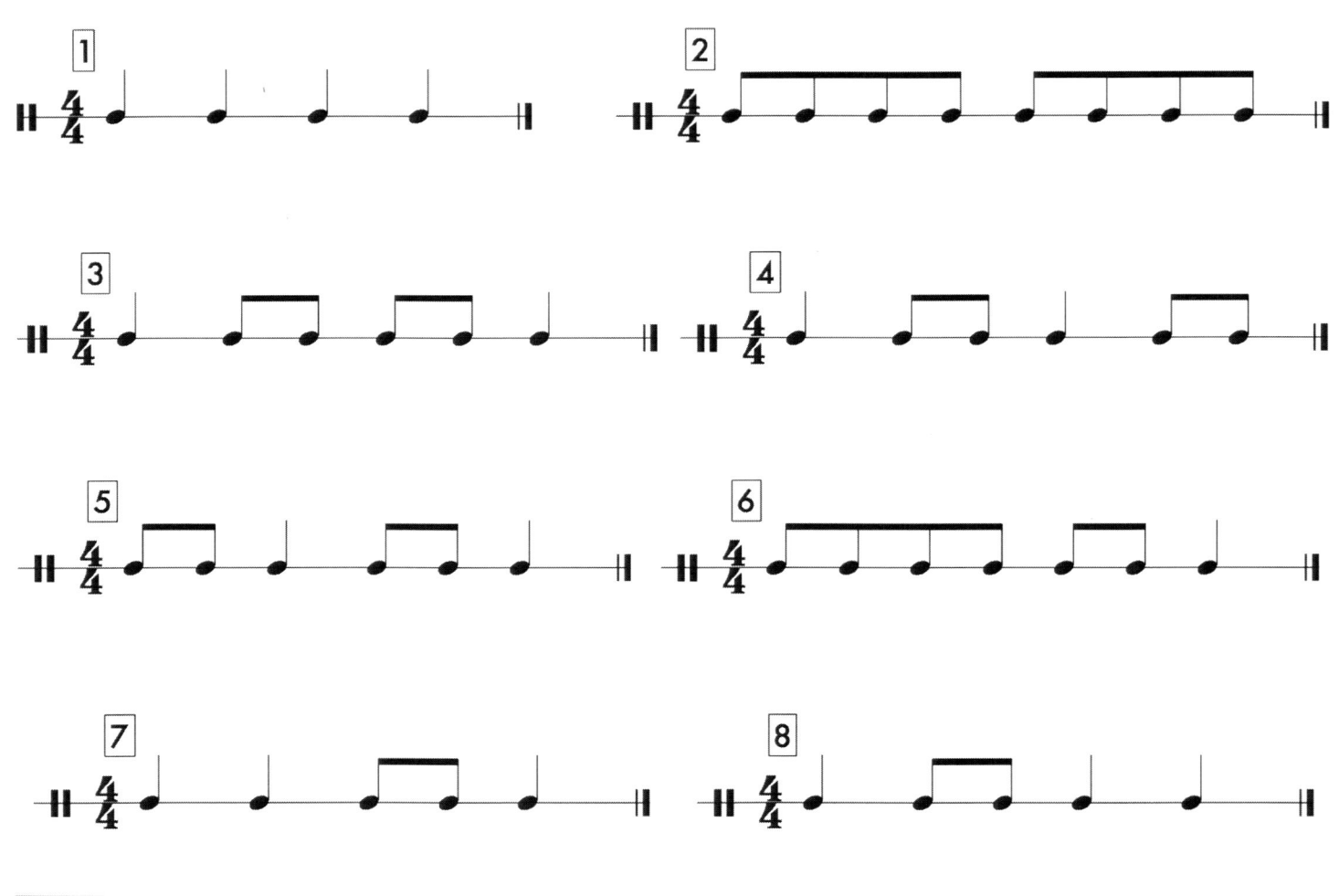

Try writing these patterns.

LESSON 2.6
ENRHYTHMIC PATTERNS IN TRIPLE METER
3/4

In Lesson 2.5, we learned that we can have an **enrhythmic** rhythm pattern by including more macrobeats in one measure. In this lesson, we are going to learn that **different notes can represent the same rhythmic function**.

NEW TIME SIGNATURE

The time signature $\frac{3}{4}$ tells us that the music is in **triple meter**. Additionally, it tells us that macrobeats will be represented by a dotted half note, and microbeats will be represented by quarter notes. Note that there is only one macrobeat in each measure.

macrobeats in 3/4	microbeats in 3/4
𝅗𝅥.	♩ ♩ ♩
Du	Du Da Di

! Interestingly, we will use the same solfege for macrobeats and microbeats that we used in the time signature 6/8. The sound itself is exactly the same, however the sound is represented by different notes. All triple meter time signatures use the same solfege.

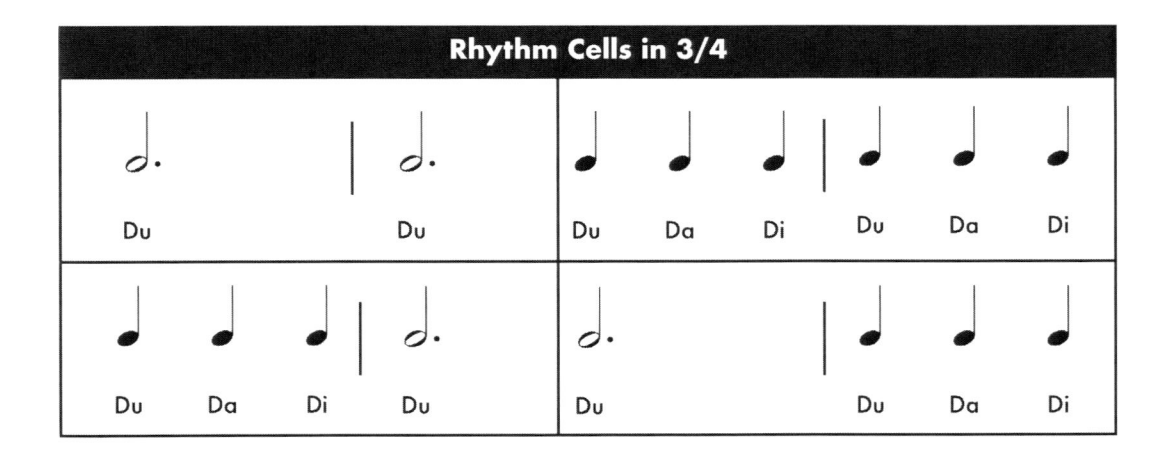

Rhythm Cells in 3/4

𝅗𝅥.	𝅗𝅥.	♩ ♩ ♩	♩ ♩ ♩
Du	Du	Du Da Di	Du Da Di

♩ ♩ ♩	𝅗𝅥.	𝅗𝅥.	♩ ♩ ♩
Du Da Di	Du	Du	Du Da Di

115

These two rhythm patterns sound the same, but are notated differently.

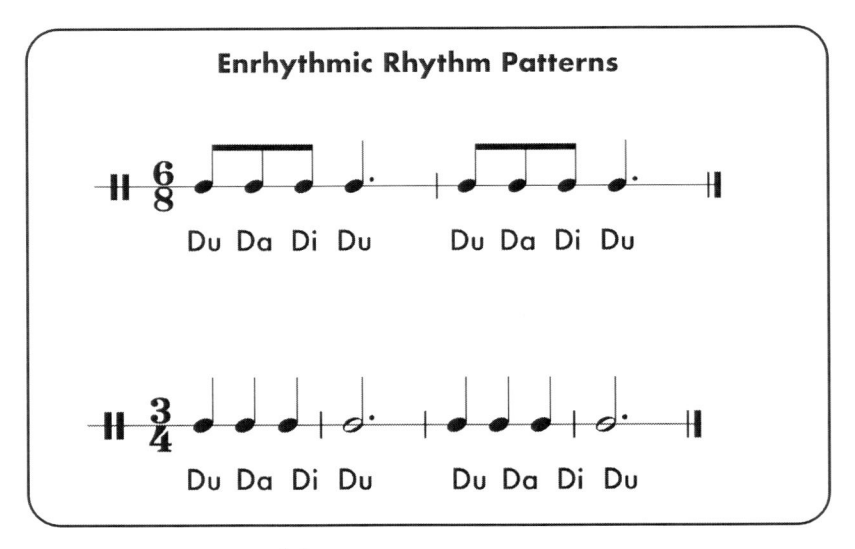

Enrhythmic Rhythm Patterns

Du Da Di Du Du Da Di Du

Du Da Di Du Du Da Di Du

RHYTHM PATTERNS IN 3/4

Here are the same eight rhythm patterns that you already read in 6/8. Can you read them in 3/4?

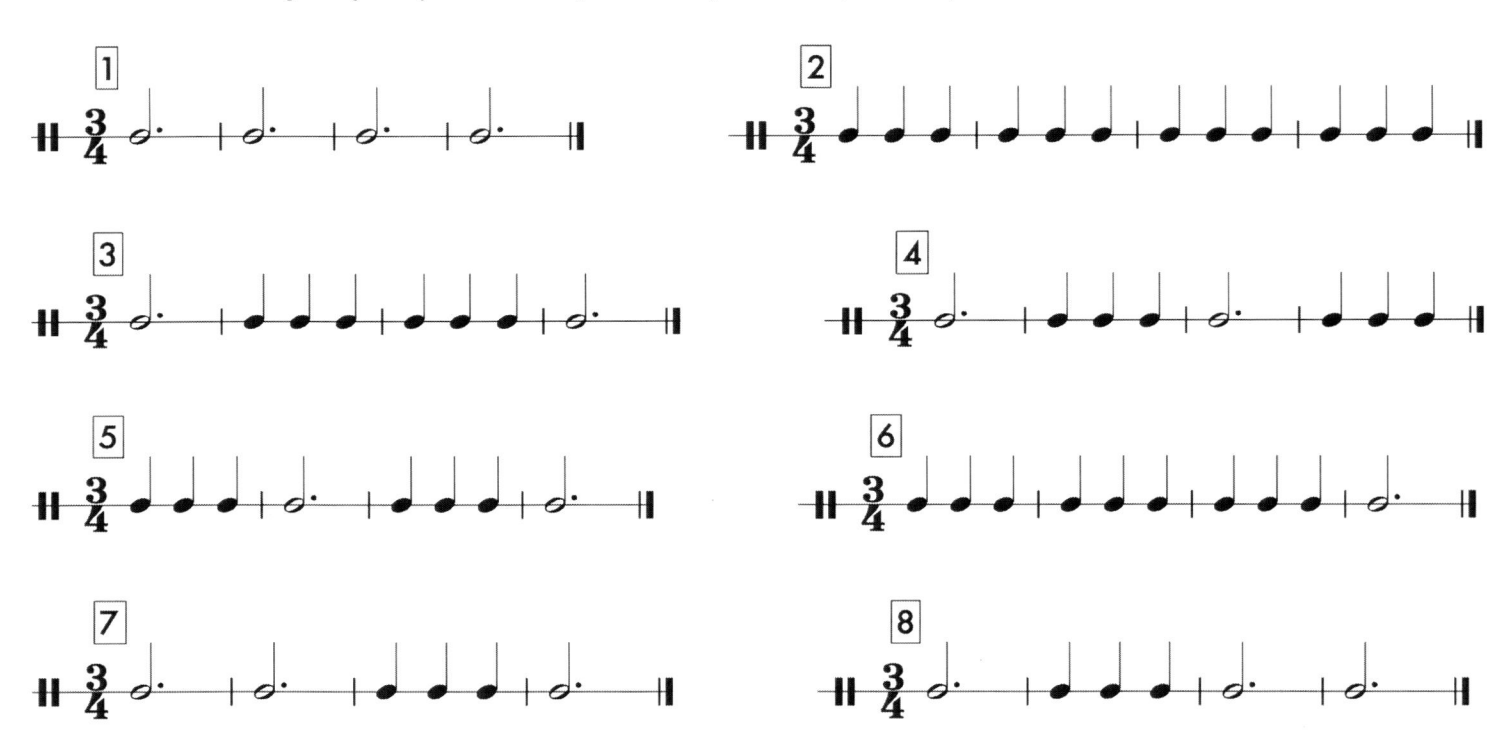

IMPORTANT CONCEPTS TO REMEMBER!
- Macrobeats and microbeats can be represented by different notes.
- The solfege stays the same for each meter, regardless of the time signature because the **sound of the pattern does not change**, only the way it is notated.
- You will find varying numbers of macrobeats per measure (3/4 = 1; 6/8 = 2; 2/4 = 2; 4/4 = 4).

Try writing these patterns.

LESSON 2.7
LONGER RHYTHM PATTERNS
DUPLE & TRIPLE

Just as we did in Lesson 1.3, identify the meter and read these longer rhythm patterns.

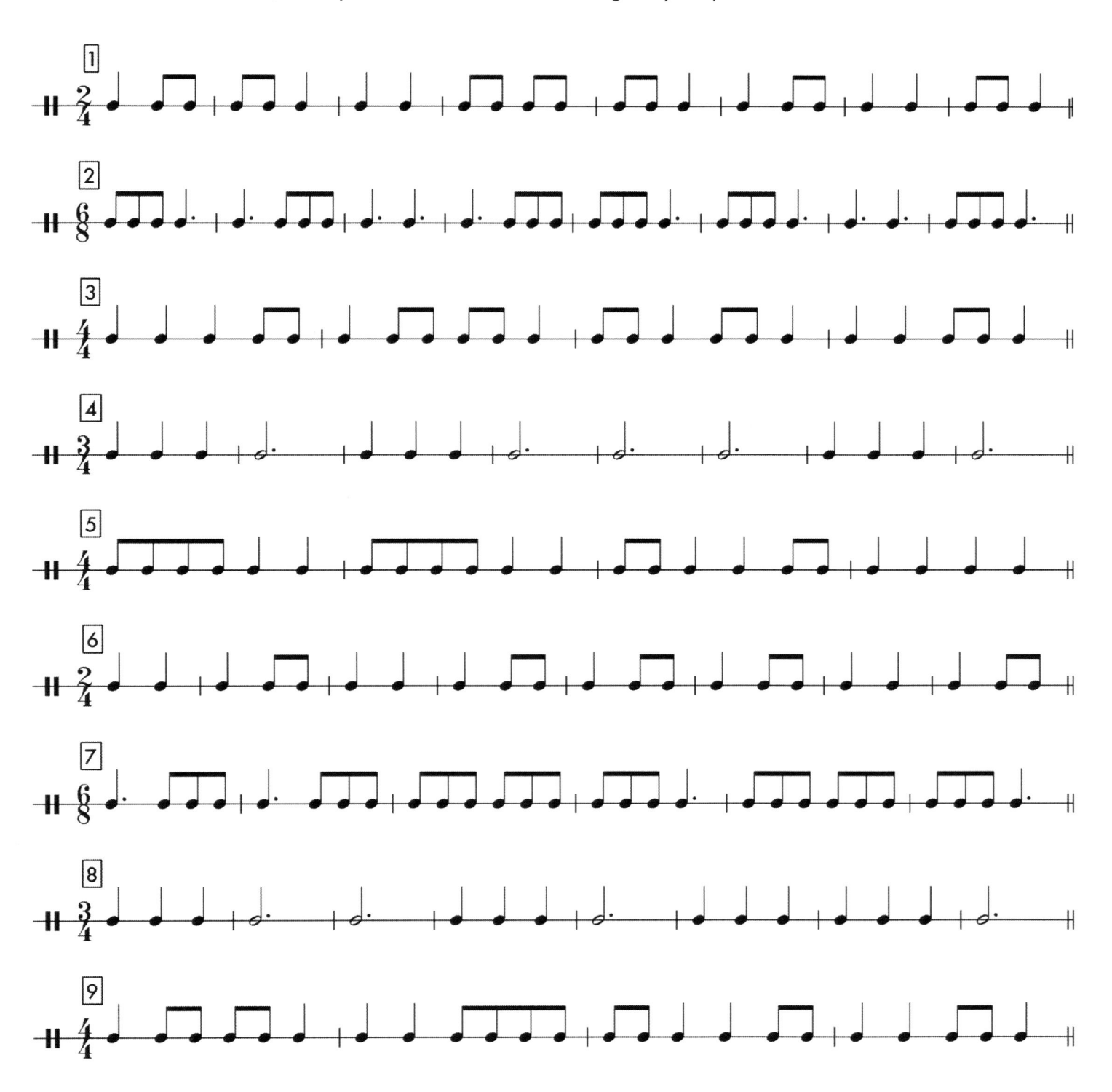

Add pitches to these longer rhythmic sentences and turn into a composition.

READING BENCHMARK 2B

Tonality = Major
Pitches = tDRM, Stepwise
Keys = G, F, Eb

Meters = Duple and Triple
Time Signatures = 2/4, 4/4, 6/8, 3/4
Functions = Macrobeat/Microbeat

More Difficult Exercises

READING BENCHMARK 2C

Tonality = Major
Pitches = Tonic chord only
Keys = G, F, Eb

Meters = Duple and Triple
Time Signatures = 2/4, 4/4, 6/8, 3/4
Functions = Macrobeat/Microbeat

READING SEQUENCE 3

SEQUENCE 3 AT A GLANCE

Reading Content	
TONAL	**RHYTHM**
• Tonality: Major • Pitches: tDRMFSL and Tonic • Keys: C, D, Eb, F, G	• Meters: Duple and Triple • Functions: Macro/Microbeats and Divisions • Time Signatures: 2/4, 4/4, 6/8, 3/4

Lesson Sequence	
3.1 Tonal	How to Find DO & Two New DO-Signatures (D-DO and C-DO)
3.2 Tonal	Combining Harmonic and Stepwise Patterns
Reading Benchmark 3A • Major; Tonic chord and tDRM; Keys = C, D, Eb, F, G • Macro/micro; Duple & Triple; 2/4; 6/8	
3.3 Rhythm	Divisions in Duple Meter (2/4 and 4/4)
Reading Benchmark 3B • Major; Tonic chord and tDRM; Keys = C, D, Eb, F, G • Duple; Macro/micro **and Divisions**; 2/4, 4/4	
3.4 Tonal	New Stepwise Patterns in Major Tonality (MFM, RMFS, SLS)
3.5 Tonal	Generalization in Major Tonality (tDRMFSL)
Reading Benchmark 3C • Major; tDRMFSL, Stepwise; Keys = C, D, Eb, F, G • Duple & Triple; Macro/micro; 2/4, 4/4; 6/8, 3/4	
Reading Benchmark 3D • Major; tDRMFSL, Stepwise; Keys = C, D, Eb, F, G • Duple; Macro/micro **and Divisions**; 2/4, 4/4	
3.6 Tonal	Combining Stepwise and Harmonic Patterns
Reading Benchmark 3E • Major; Tonic and tDRMFSL; Keys = C, D, Eb, F, G • Duple & Triple; Macro/micro and Divisions; 2/4, 4/4; 6/8, 3/4	

LESSON 3.1
HOW TO FIND "DO" & TWO NEW DO-SIGNATURES (D & C)

So far, we have learned to read our familiar patterns in F-DO, Eb-DO and G-DO, and experienced the skill of generalization. Let's learn how to figure out where DO is if Mr. Mullen isn't around to tell you.

FINDING DO

Throughout the course of this book, we will be reading in several different DO (and LA!) signatures. There is a trick to figuring out where DO is, regardless of the key signature (or the tonality!).

HOW TO FIND DO

♭ When the key signature has FLATS, **the last flat is FA**. Count down or up to get to DO.

♯ When the key signature has SHARPS, **the last sharp is TI**. Count up or down to get to DO.

Below is a familiar key signature, Eb-DO. It has FLATS, so the last flat will be FA.

Or, count **up** to get to DO using stepwise patterns.

Count **down** to get to DO using stepwise patterns.

Below is a familiar key signature, G-DO. It has SHARPS, so the last sharp will be TI.

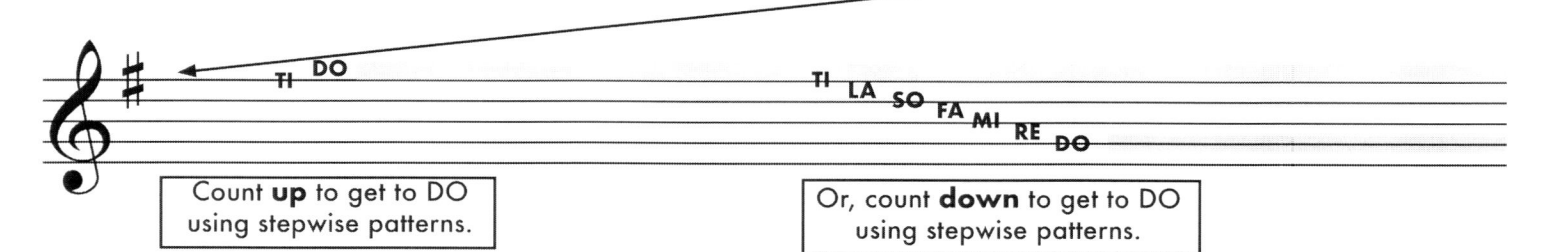

Count **up** to get to DO using stepwise patterns.

Or, count **down** to get to DO using stepwise patterns.

TRANSFERRING KNOWLEDGE TO NEW DO-SIGNATURES

You will be able to transfer the knowledge and skills that you acquired in other DO-signatures to new DO-signatures with just a little bit of guidance. Once you begin to see the visual patterns repeating themselves, you will make rapid generalizations from one DO-signature to the next. Remember: the spatial relationships between notes will remain consistent from one DO-signature to another. **The only thing that will change is where DO is.**

D-DO

Let's learn how to read in a new DO-signature: **D-DO**. Use the skill we just learned to find out where DO is on the staff.

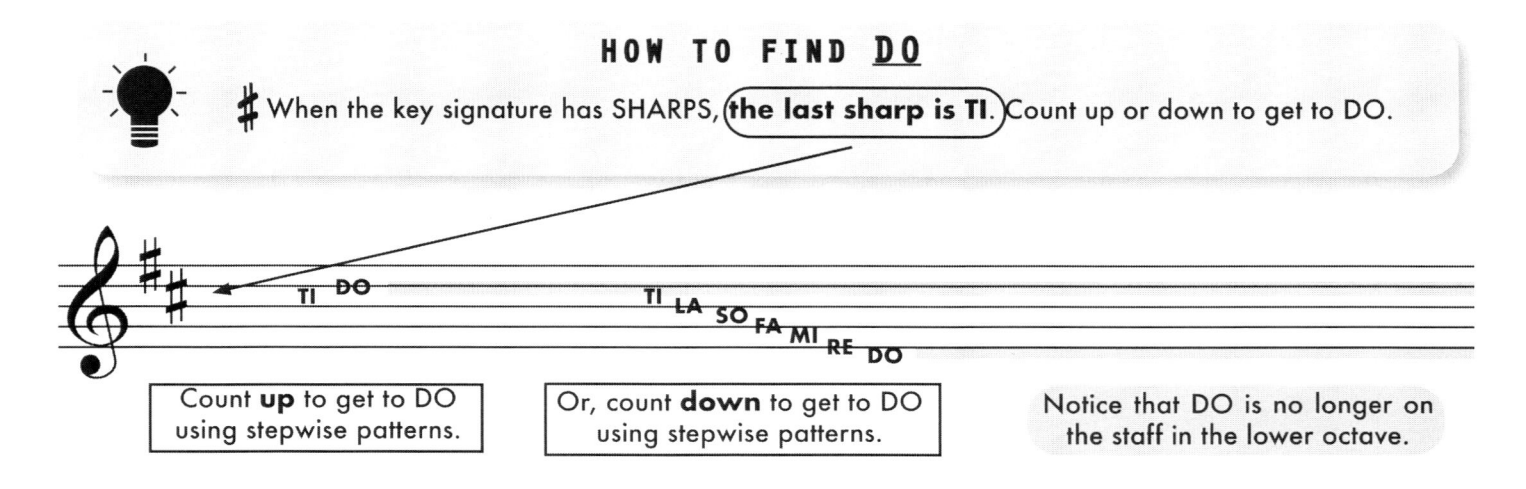

HOW TO FIND DO

♯ When the key signature has SHARPS, **the last sharp is TI**. Count up or down to get to DO.

Count **up** to get to DO using stepwise patterns.

Or, count **down** to get to DO using stepwise patterns.

Notice that DO is no longer on the staff in the lower octave.

FAMILIAR PATTERNS IN D-DO

Here are the six familiar patterns we learned to read in G-DO, F-DO and Eb-DO. Read them in their familiar orders.

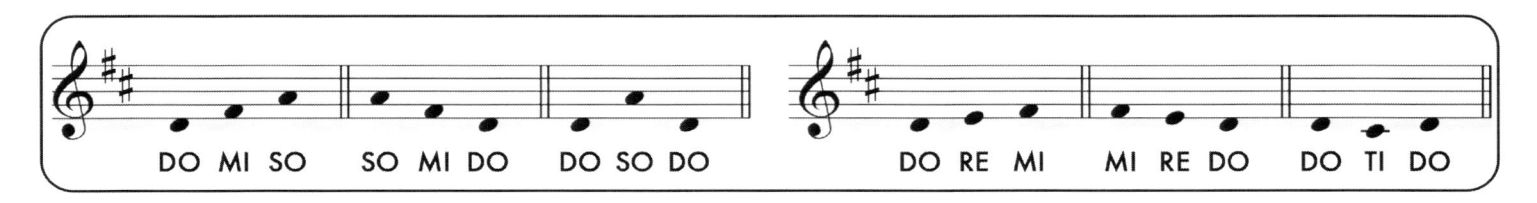

DO MI SO   SO MI DO   DO SO DO   DO RE MI   MI RE DO   DO TI DO

Read these familiar harmonic patterns in unfamiliar order in D-DO:

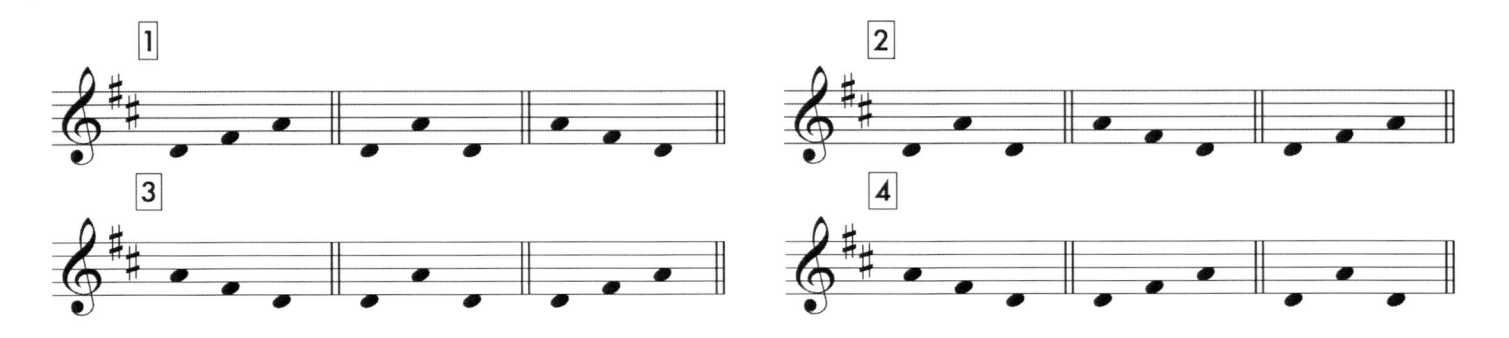

1

2

3

4

Read these familiar stepwise patterns in unfamiliar order in D-DO:

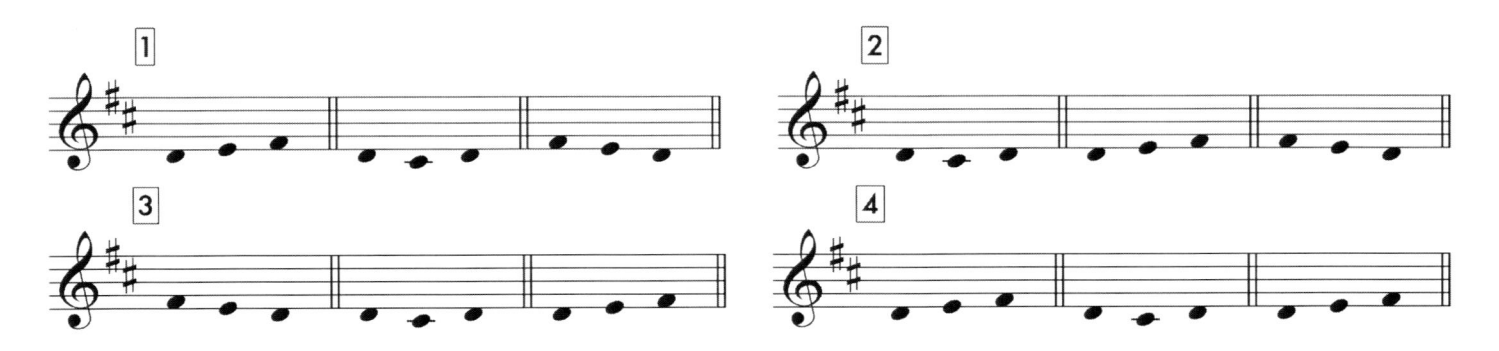

1

2

3

4

C-DO

Let's learn how to read in a new DO-signature: **C-DO**.

HOW TO FIND C-DO

Since there are no sharps or flats, there is no trick to finding DO. You simply have to memorize this one.

We can find DO in two places. First, DO is in the third space. Second, DO appears below the staff on a ledger line.

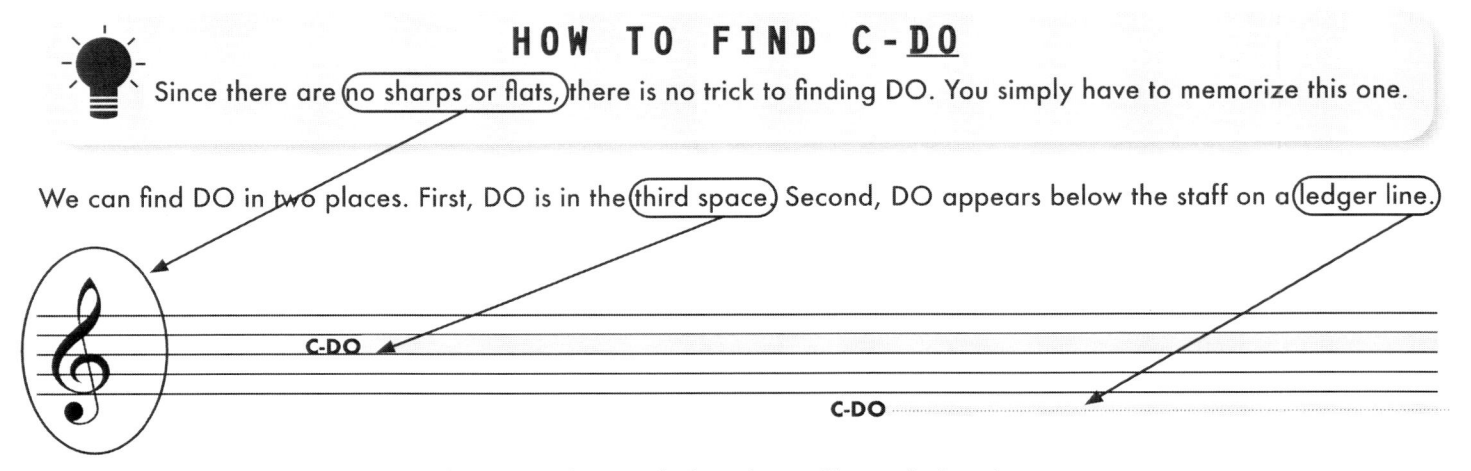

For ease of singing range, we will begin on the DO below the staff on a ledger line.

FAMILIAR PATTERNS IN C-DO

Here are the six familiar patterns in C-DO. Read them in their familiar order.

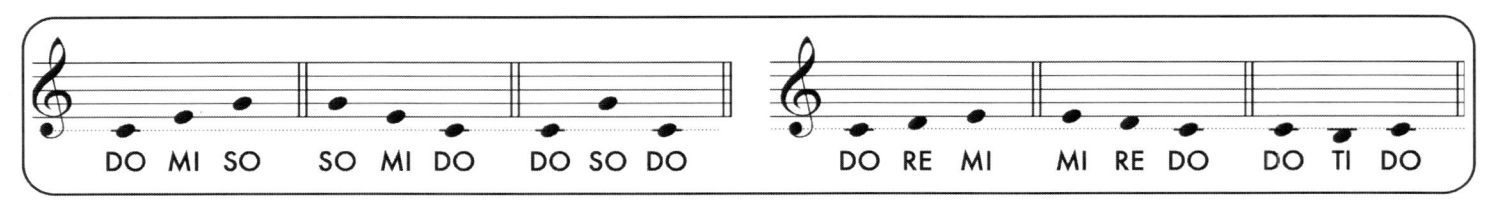

DO MI SO   SO MI DO   DO SO DO   DO RE MI   MI RE DO   DO TI DO

Read these familiar harmonic patterns in unfamiliar order in C-DO:

1

2

3

4

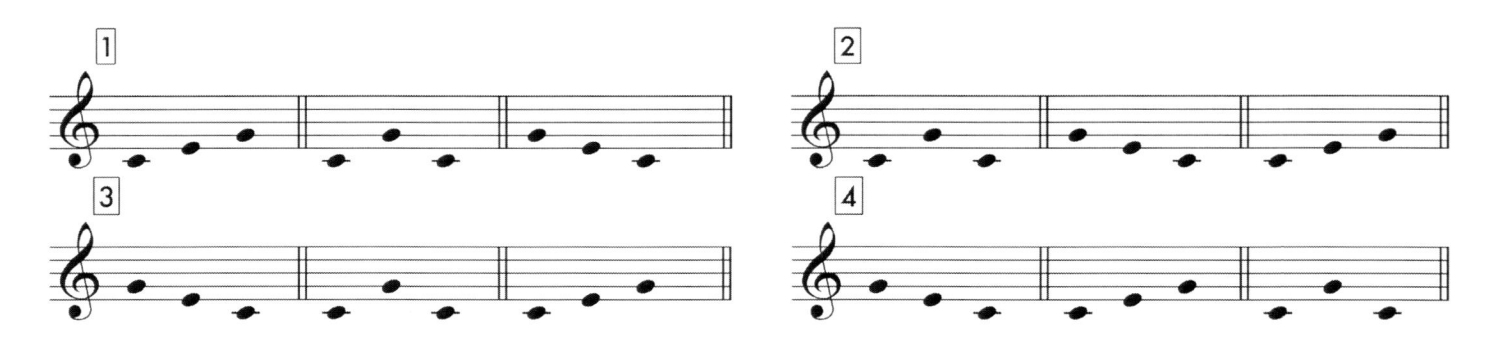

Read these familiar stepwise patterns in unfamiliar order in C-DO:

1

2

3

4

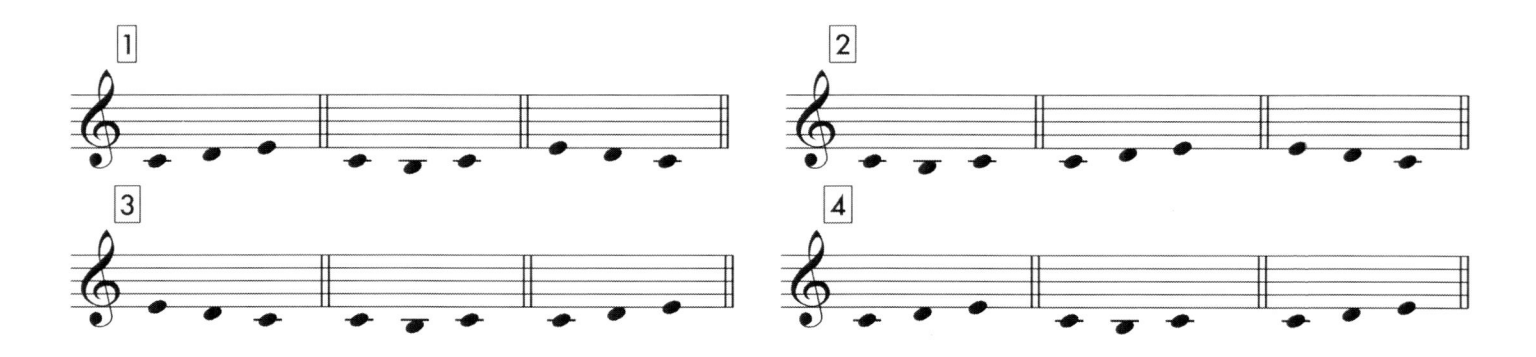

LESSON 3.2
COMBINING HARMONIC AND STEPWISE PATTERNS

Before we combine rhythm patterns **and unfamiliar** stepwise patterns and harmonic patterns in **Reading Benchmark 3A**, we will first combine **familiar** stepwise and harmonic patterns.

STEPS VS. LEAPS

One item to take note of before we proceed to the exercises is the visual difference between reading patterns by **step** and by **leap**. When you read by step, the notes are right next to each other (on a line, and then on a space, or on a space and then on a line). When you read by leap, you will skip either a line or a space.

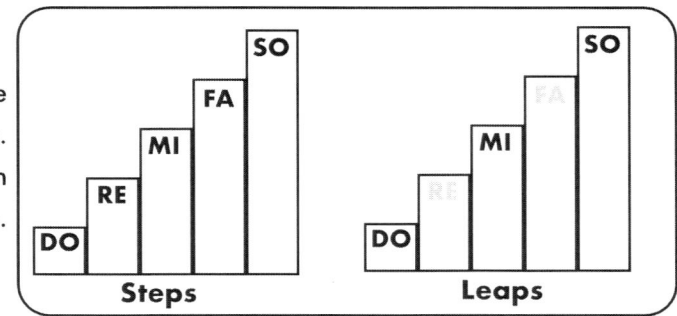

Moving by Step — Line Space Line — DO RE MI
Moving by Leap — Line Line Line — DO MI SO
Moving by Step — Line Space Line — MI RE DO
Moving by Leap — Line Line Line — SO MI DO

Moving by Step — Space Line Space — DO RE MI
Moving by Leap — Space Space Space — DO MI SO
Moving by Step — Space Line Space — MI RE DO
Moving by Leap — Space Space Space — SO MI DO

Read these familiar harmonic and stepwise patterns in all of our familiar DO-signatures.

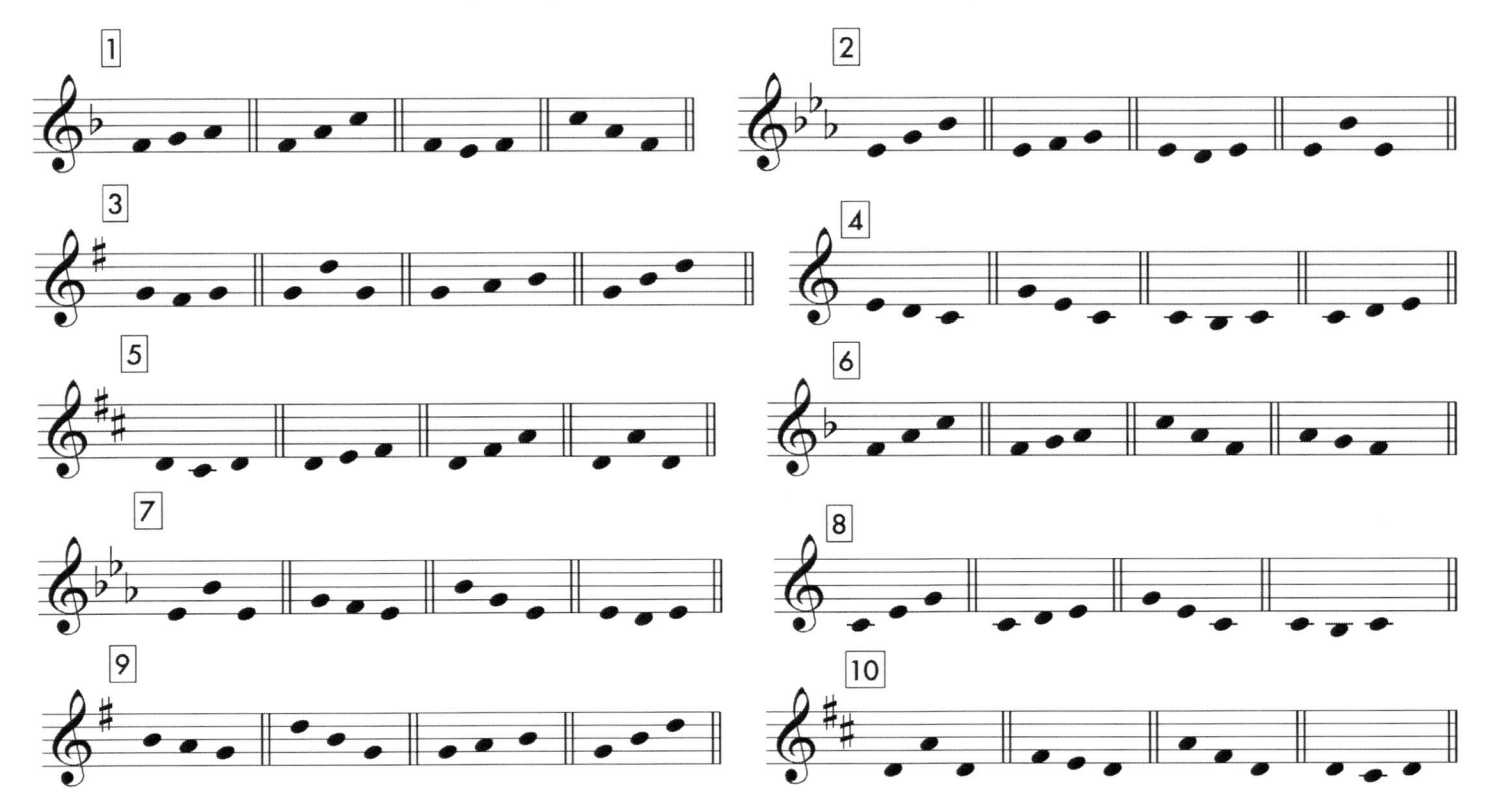

Read these familiar **and unfamiliar** harmonic and stepwise patterns in all of our familiar DO-signatures.

PREPARING FOR BENCHMARK 3A

As you approach the upcoming Reading Benchmarks, it may be a useful technique to include some annotations in your tonal analysis. As you scan the pitches of the melody, be on the lookout for familiar and unfamiliar tonic patterns. You may wish to **circle** them. That way, you will know that everything else is merely a stepwise pattern. Look at the example below.

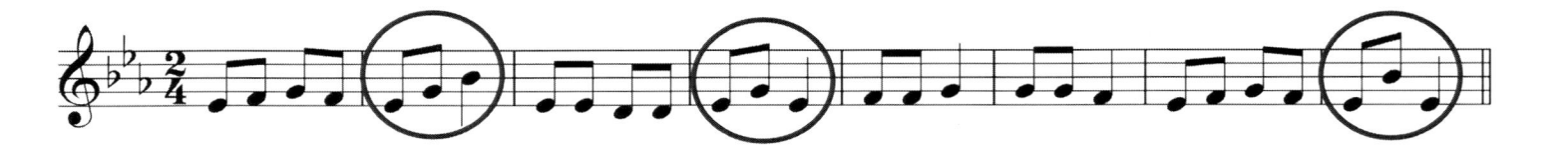

READING BENCHMARK 3A

Tonality = Major
Pitches = tDRM and Tonic
Keys = C, D, Eb, F, G

Meters = Duple and Triple
Time Signatures = 2/4, 4/4, 6/8, 3/4
Functions = Macrobeat/Microbeat

LESSON 3.3
DIVISIONS IN DUPLE METER
TIME SIGNATURES: 2/4 & 4/4

REVIEW

Take a moment to review macrobeats, microbeats and divisions in duple meter. Review p. 44 if necessary. Say the following chant to yourself:

"**Macrobeats** in duple meter are DU DU DU DU.
Microbeats in duple meter are DU DE, DU DE, DU DE, DU DE.
Divisions in duple meter are DU TA DE TA, DU TA DE TA, DU TA DE TA, DU TA DE TA."

READING MACROBEATS, MICROBEATS & DIVISIONS
2/4 & 4/4

In the time signatures 2/4 and 4/4, macrobeats (DU) will be represented by a quarter note, microbeats (DU DE) will be represented by paired eighth notes, and divisions (DU TA DE TA) will be represented by sixteenth notes.

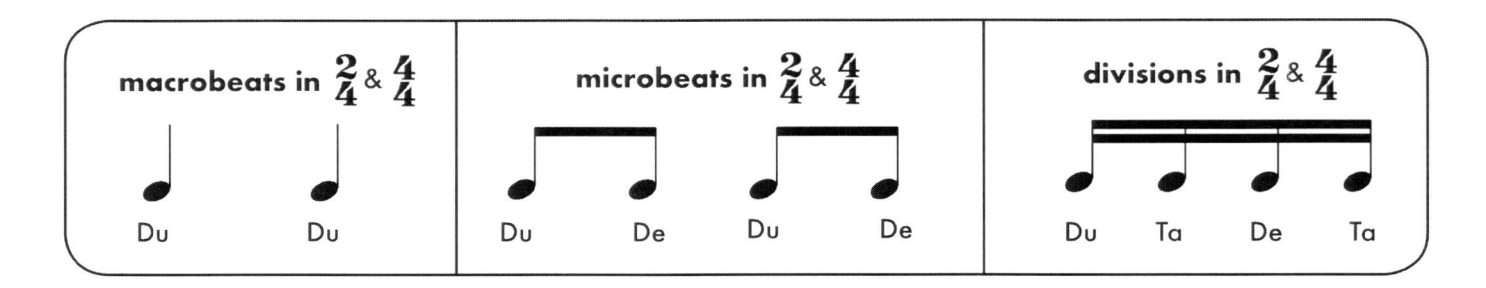

DIVISION RHYTHM CELLS

There are three division rhythm cells to learn in 2/4 and 4/4. Look at the notation, and chant these to yourself.

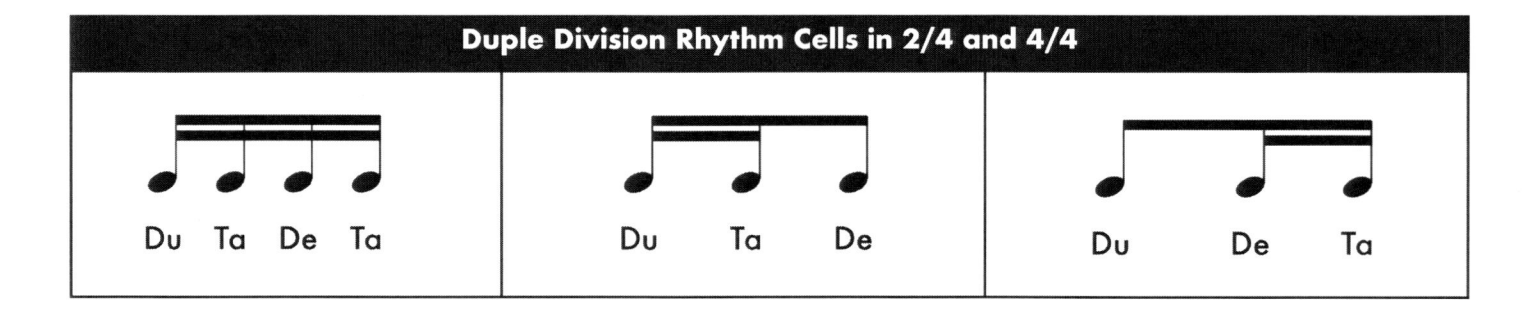

Duple Division Rhythm Cells in 2/4 and 4/4

| Du Ta De Ta | Du Ta De | Du De Ta |

Try writing these rhythm cells. Take particular note of the beams. You may also wish to try writing some of the longer rhythm patterns on the following pages.

READING RHYTHM PATTERNS

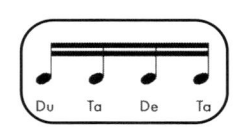

Read these rhythm patterns with macrobeats, microbeats and the first division rhythm cell: *Du Ta De Ta*

Read these rhythm patterns with macrobeats, microbeats and the third division rhythm cell:

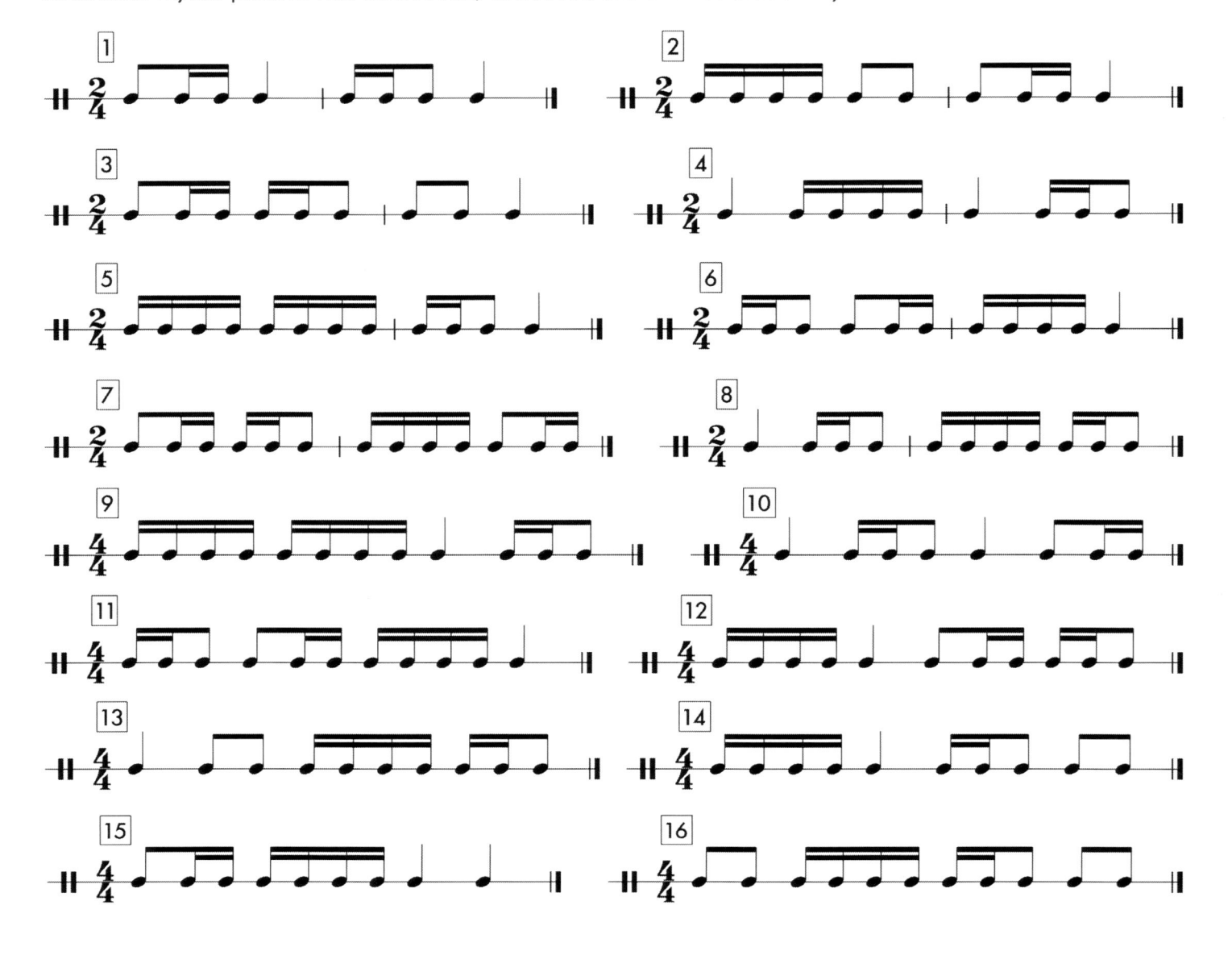

Du De Ta

READING BENCHMARK 3B

Tonality = Major	**Meters** = Duple
Pitches = tDRM and Tonic	**Time Signatures** = 2/4, 4/4
Keys = C, D, Eb, F, G	**Functions** = Macro/microbeat and divisions

As before, you may wish to circle the tonic patterns as part of your tonal analysis.

1

2

3

4

5

6

7

8

9

10

LESSON 3.4
NEW STEPWISE PATTERNS IN MAJOR TONALITY
MI FA MI, RE MI FA SO, SO LA SO

We will be learning to read two new pitches: FA and LA. We will learn them in the context of three familiar patterns that we previously learned in Part 1: MFM, RMFS, and SLS. Let's begin in the familiar key of Eb-DO.

THREE NEW PATTERNS: MFM, RMFS, SLS

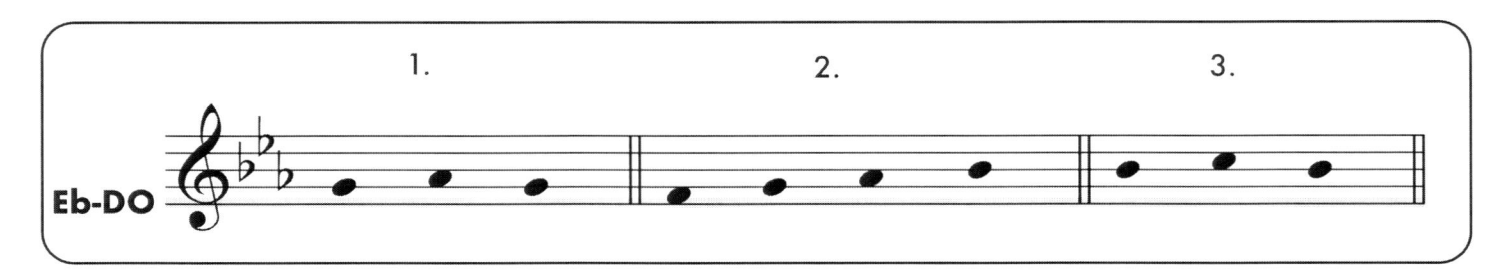

Since none of these patterns contains DO, the resting tone, ground yourself in major tonality by singing the Tonal Sequence (SO LA SO FA MI RE TI DO) and/or the first four harmonic patterns (DO MI, SO DO, TI RE, MI DO).

The first pattern is **MI FA MI**. Look at the notation, take a breath and sing **MI FA MI**. Just as you did when you echoed the patterns, keep the pitches separated. The second pattern is **RE MI FA SO**. Look at the notation, take a breath and sing **RE MI FA SO**. The third pattern is **SO LA SO**. Look at the notation, take a breath and sing **SO LA SO**.

Look at each of the patterns individually, and take note of where the first pitch of each pattern is **in relation to DO**. Visually recall the tonic chord, which will tell you where DO MI and SO are. If you ever get lost, you can always use the tonic chord as a visual problem-solving tool.

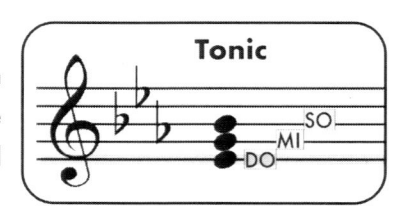

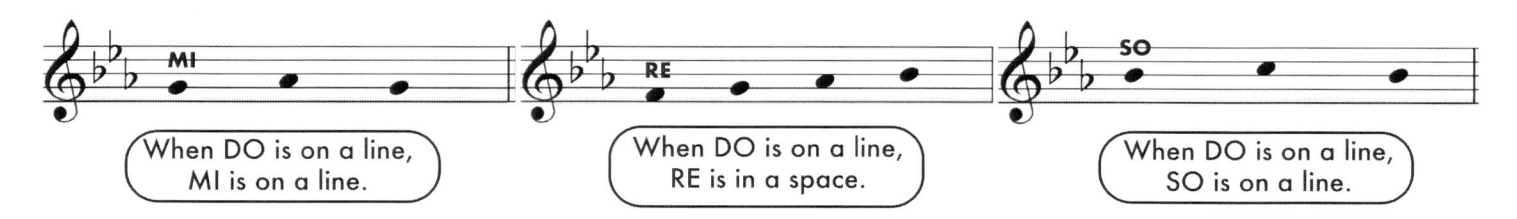

When DO is on a line, MI is on a line.

When DO is on a line, RE is in a space.

When DO is on a line, SO is on a line.

Read these three patterns, one after the other with a short pause in-between. These are **familiar patterns in a familiar order**. Also read them in **unfamiliar order** (3 2 1; 1 3 2; 2 3 1; 2 1 3; 3 1 2). Establishing tonality each time will help you maintain DO in your audiation.

> ❗ If you need an aural reminder of these three patterns, review them in the companion course videos. Remember: we are learning to read **familiar patterns**. ❗

Lesson 3.4 **133**

COMBINING DRM, MRD, DTD & MFM, RMFS, SLS IN Eb-DO

Since none of our three new patterns contains DO, the resting tone, if we were to read them in isolation, we would lose our sense of major tonality. Each of the pattern sets below establishes tonality with a DRM, MRD, DTD pattern, and then includes one or more MFM, RMFS, SLS patterns. Be sure to put a space between both the pitches and the patterns.

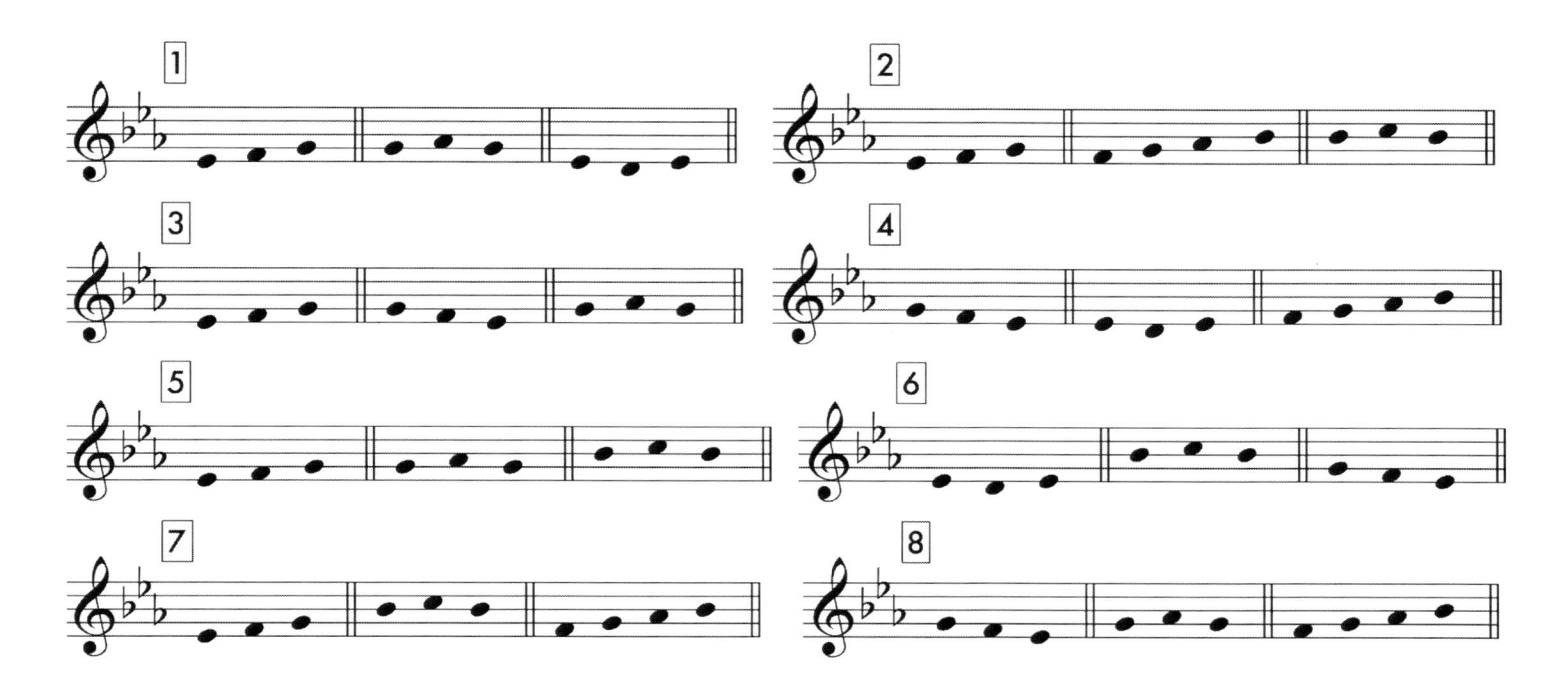

SAME PATTERNS IN OTHER KEYS

Let's look at our three new patterns in our other familiar keys. Let's begin with F-DO. Look at each of the patterns individually, and take note of where the **first pitch** of each pattern is **in relation to DO**. It will be different in F-DO since F is on a space.

F-DO

When DO is in a space, MI is in a space.

When DO is in a space, RE is on a line.

When DO is in a space, SO is in a space.

Sing these patterns in both their familiar order and as many unfamiliar orders as you can. Establish tonality each time to keep DO in your audiation. Then, read the patterns on the following page which combine DRM, MRD, DTD and MFM, RMFS, SLS in F-DO.

COMBINING DRM, MRD, DTD & MFM, RMFS, SLS IN F-DO

Since you have seen one key with DO on a line and one key with DO on a space, you should be able to make generalizations to the other keys below.

COMBINING DRM, MRD, DTD & MFM, RMFS, SLS IN G-DO

Here are our three familiar patterns in G-DO.

COMBINING DRM, MRD, DTD & MFM, RMFS, SLS IN C-DO

Here are our three familiar patterns in C-DO.

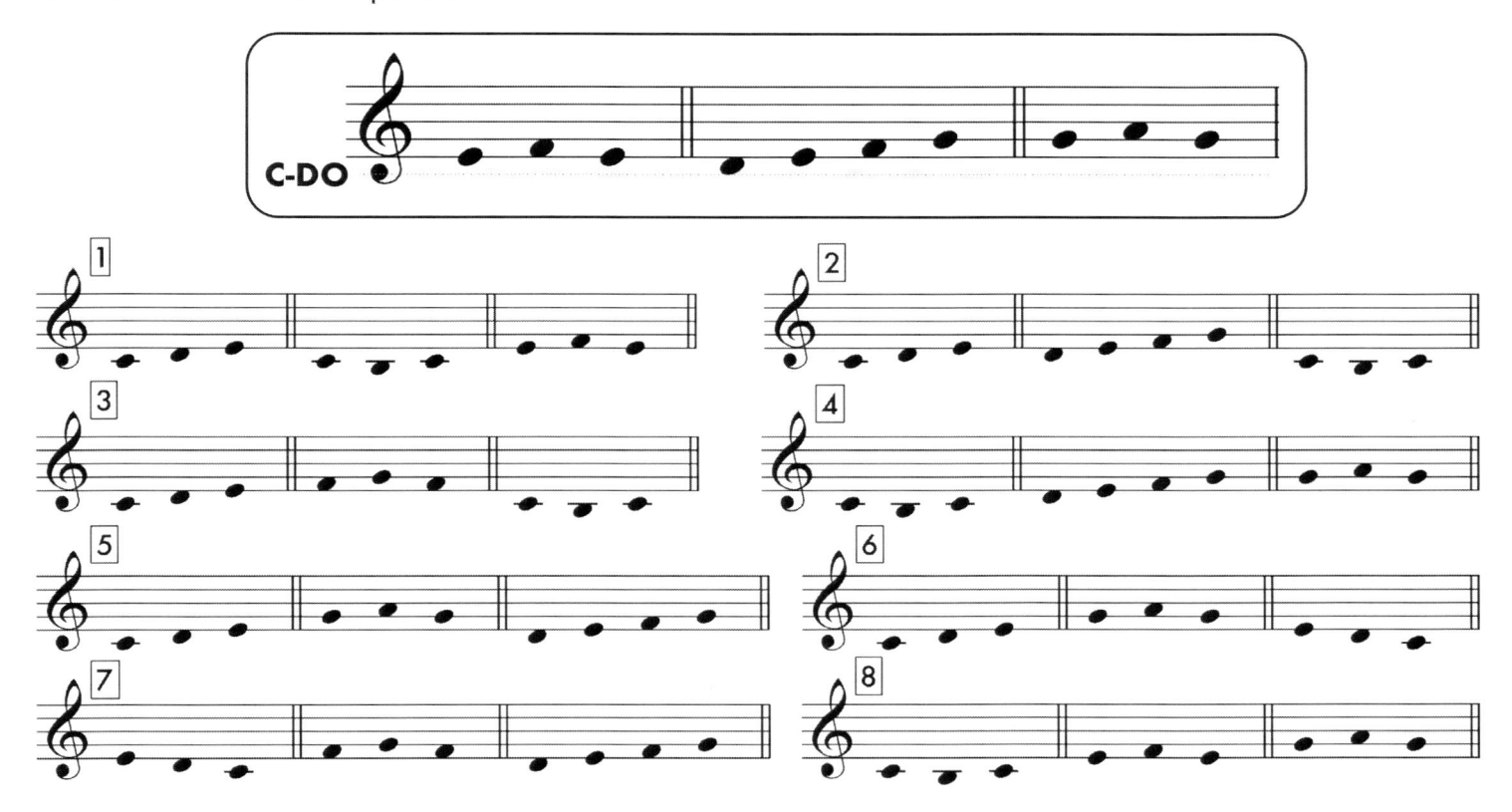

COMBINING DRM, MRD, DTD & MFM, RMFS, SLS IN D-DO

Here are our three familiar patterns in D-DO.

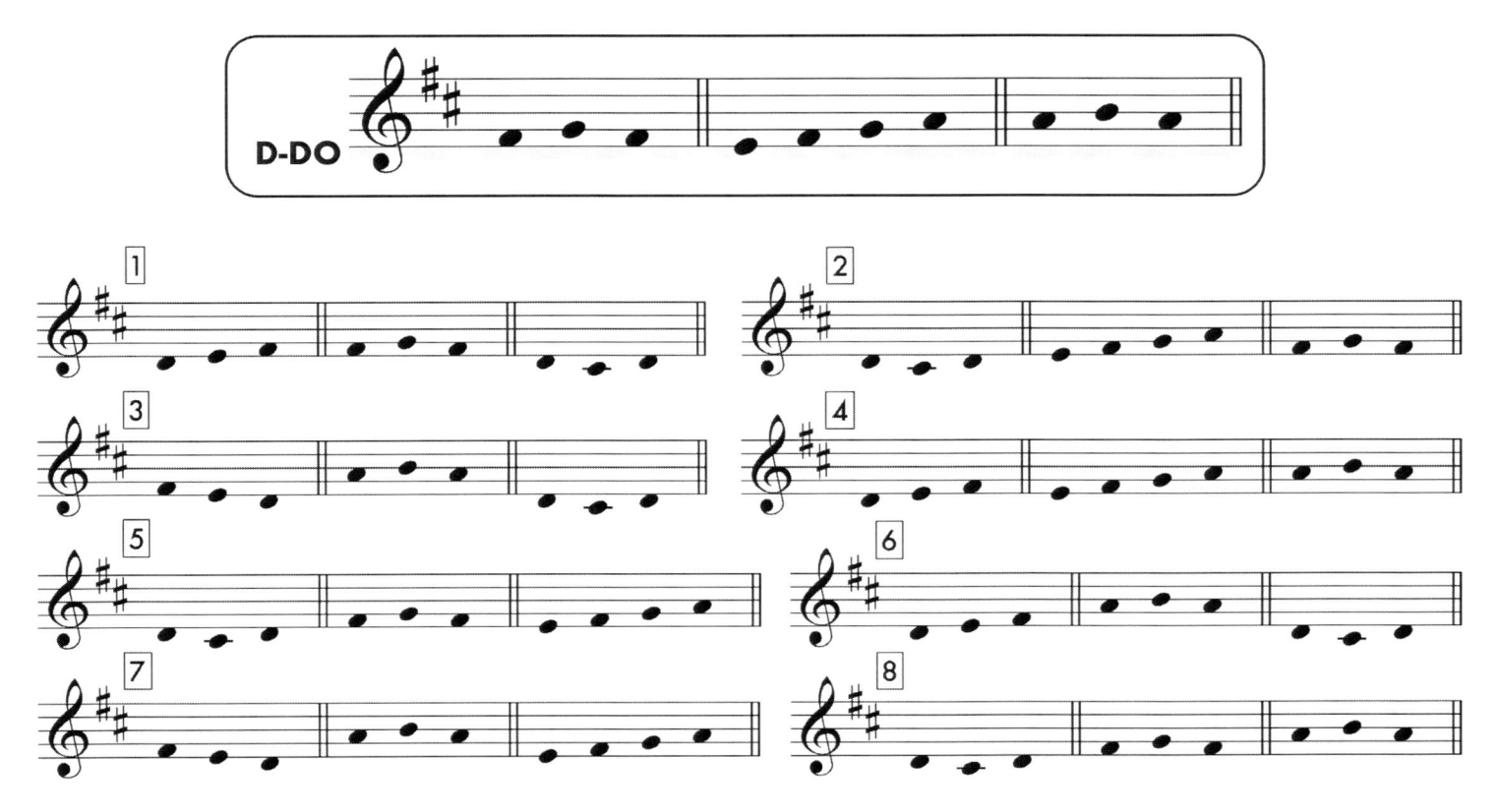

LESSON 3.5
GENERALIZATION IN MAJOR TONALITY
tDRMFSL

GET READY FOR NOTATIONAL GENERALIZATION

Before you generalize patterns **notationally**, be sure that you can generalize **audiationally**. Have you matched the syllable to the sound? Additionally, improvisation - being able to speak the language of music - is readiness for being able to read. **There is never any shame in reviewing content both at the Verbal Association and Aural/Oral levels.**

Read these familiar **and unfamiliar** stepwise patterns in major tonality. The final pattern will be unfamiliar and will require generalization.

GENERALIZATION IN D-DO

GENERALIZATION IN C-DO

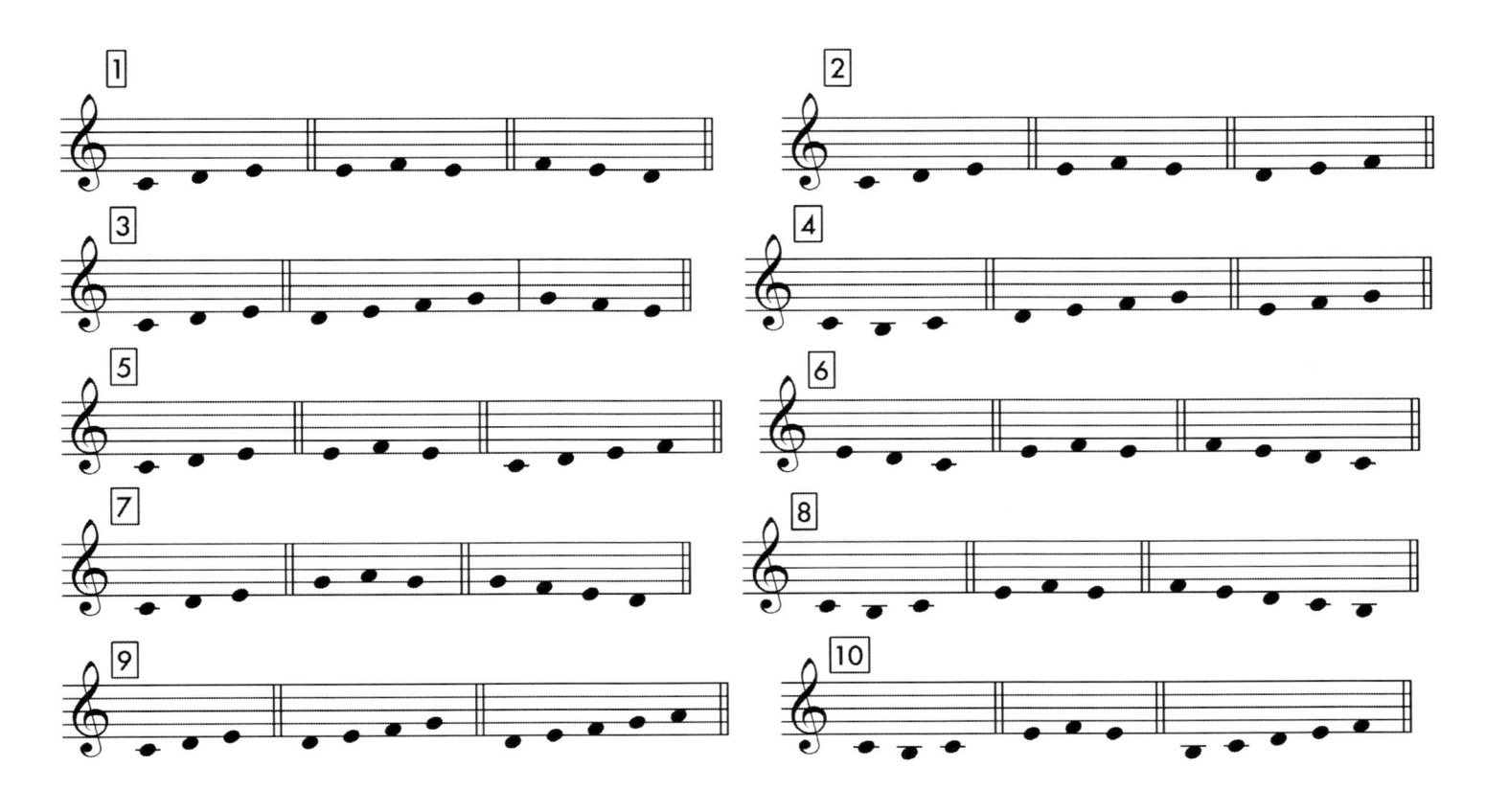

GENERALIZATION IN Eb-DO

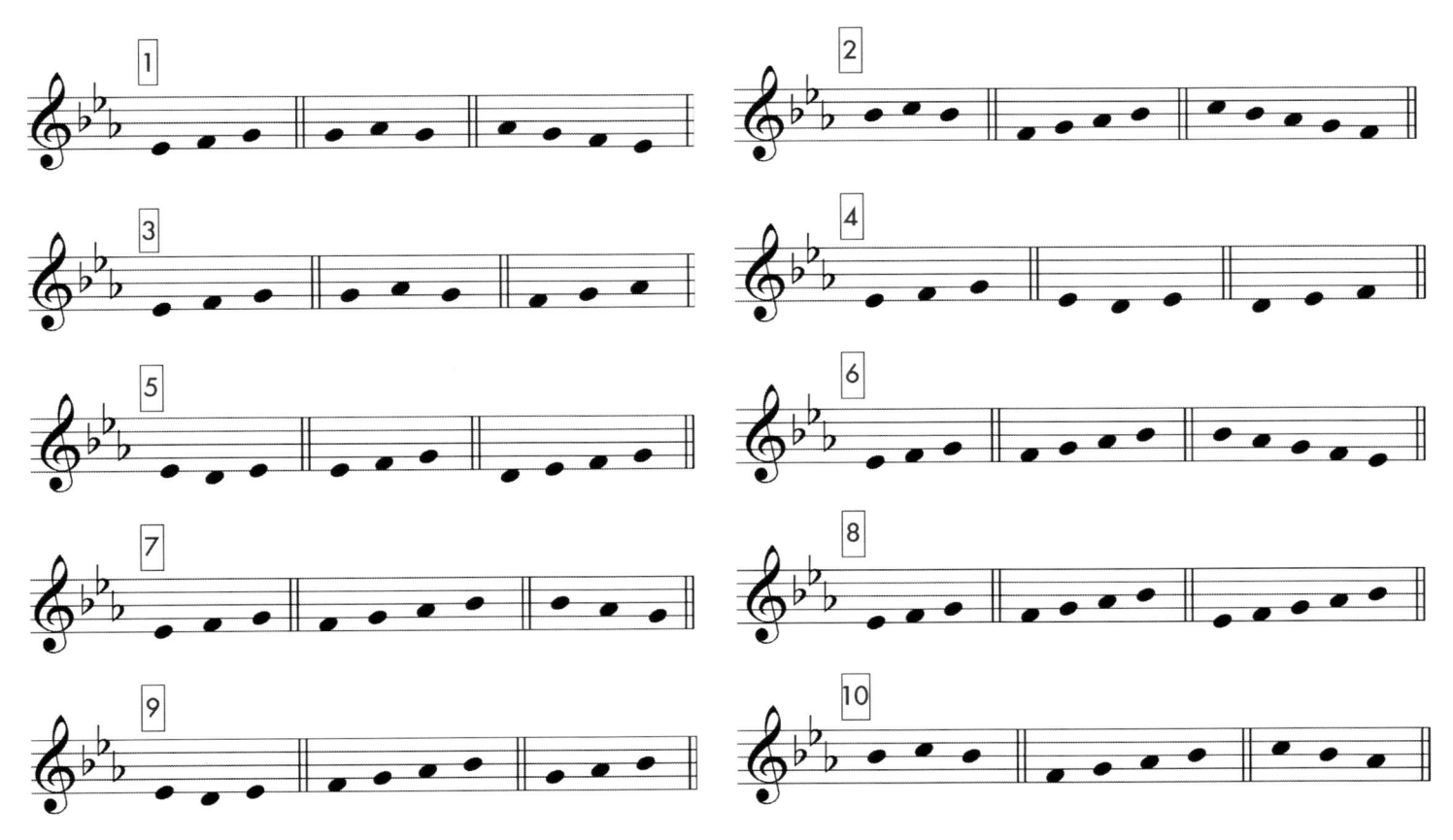

GENERALIZATION IN F-DO

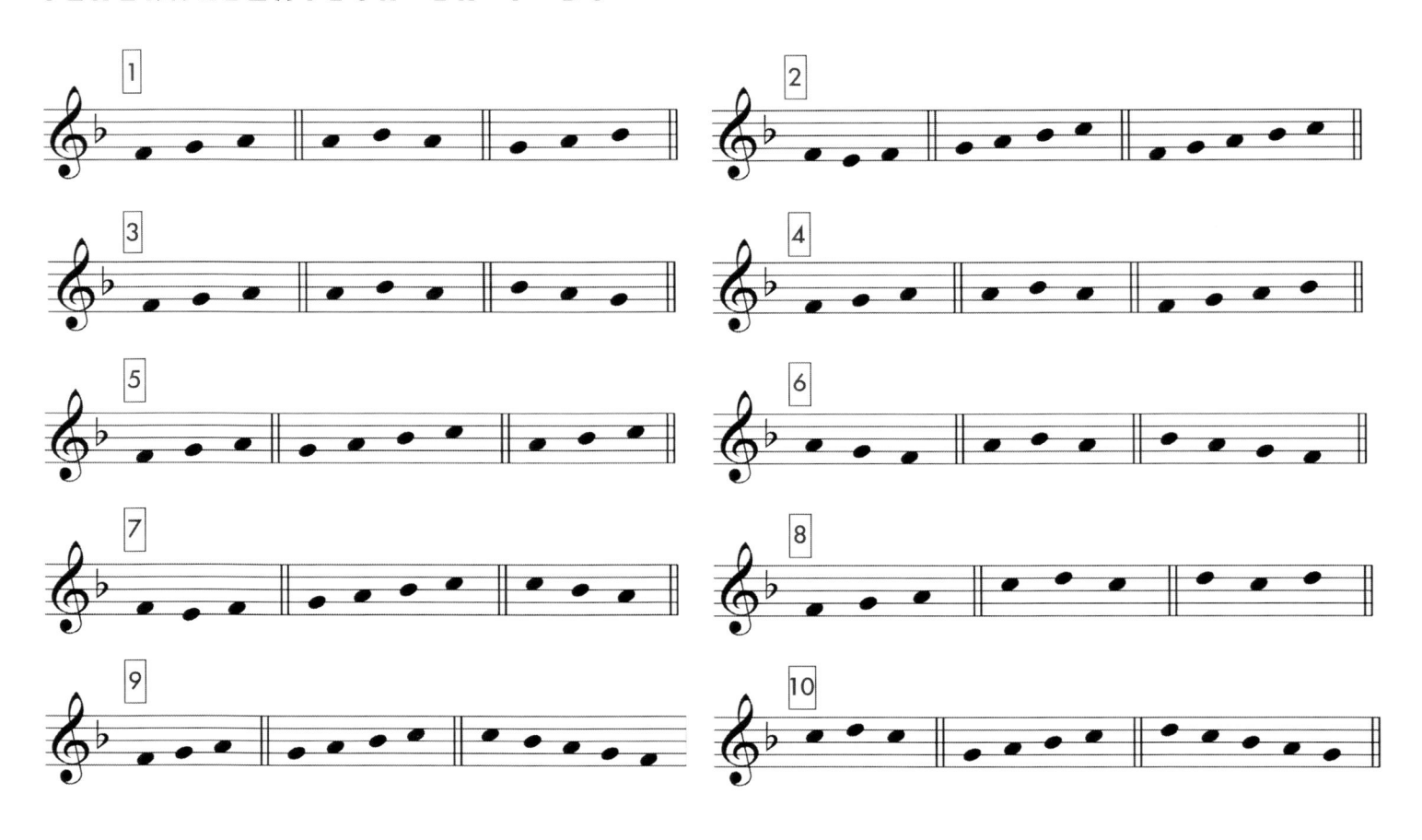

GENERALIZATION IN G-DO

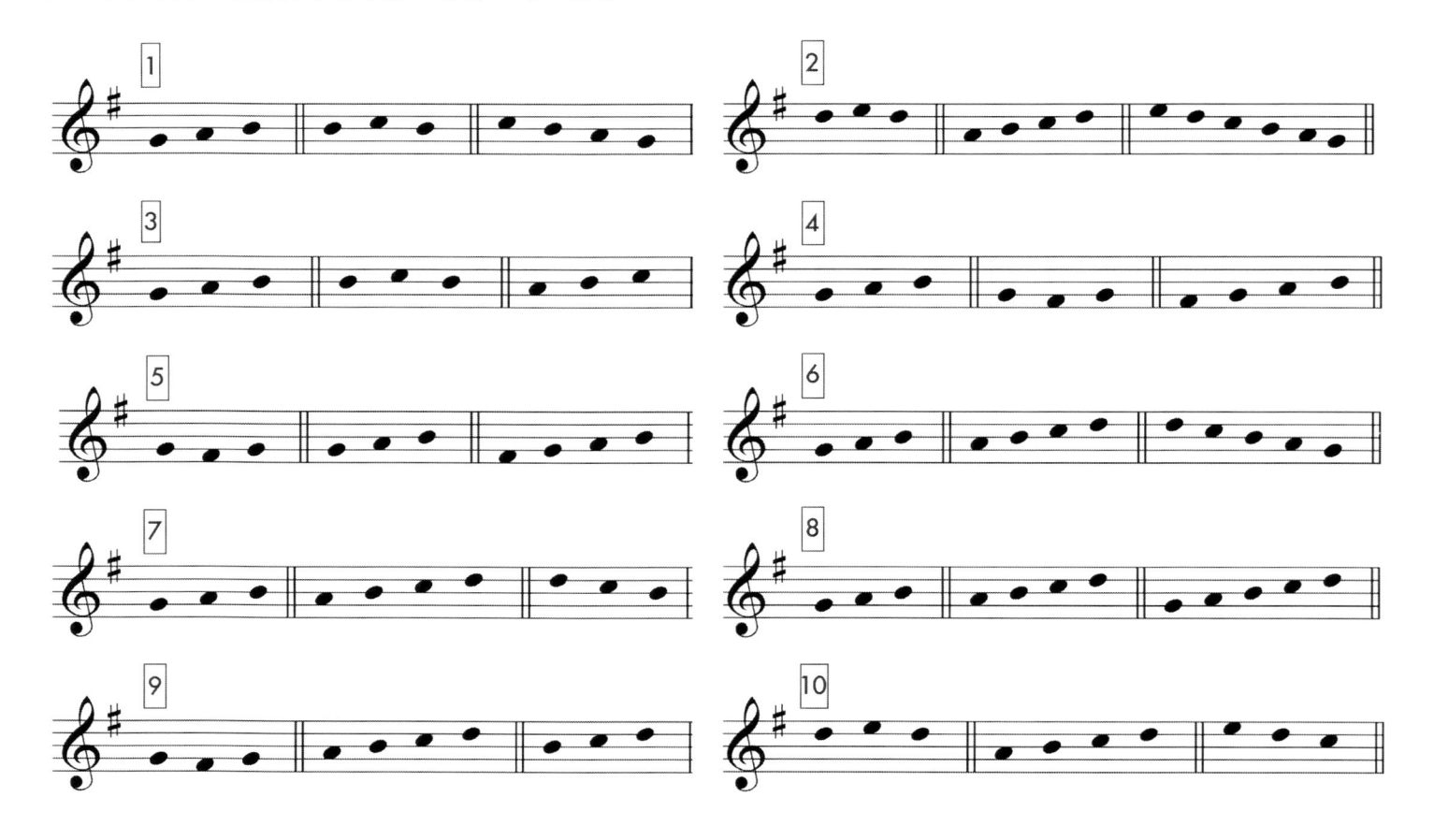

TRACING MELODIES

Trace the pitches in the below exercises. They all start and end on DO. The beams have been removed so you do not concern yourself with rhythm. Do these all in one breath. Follow along with your finger, as necessary.

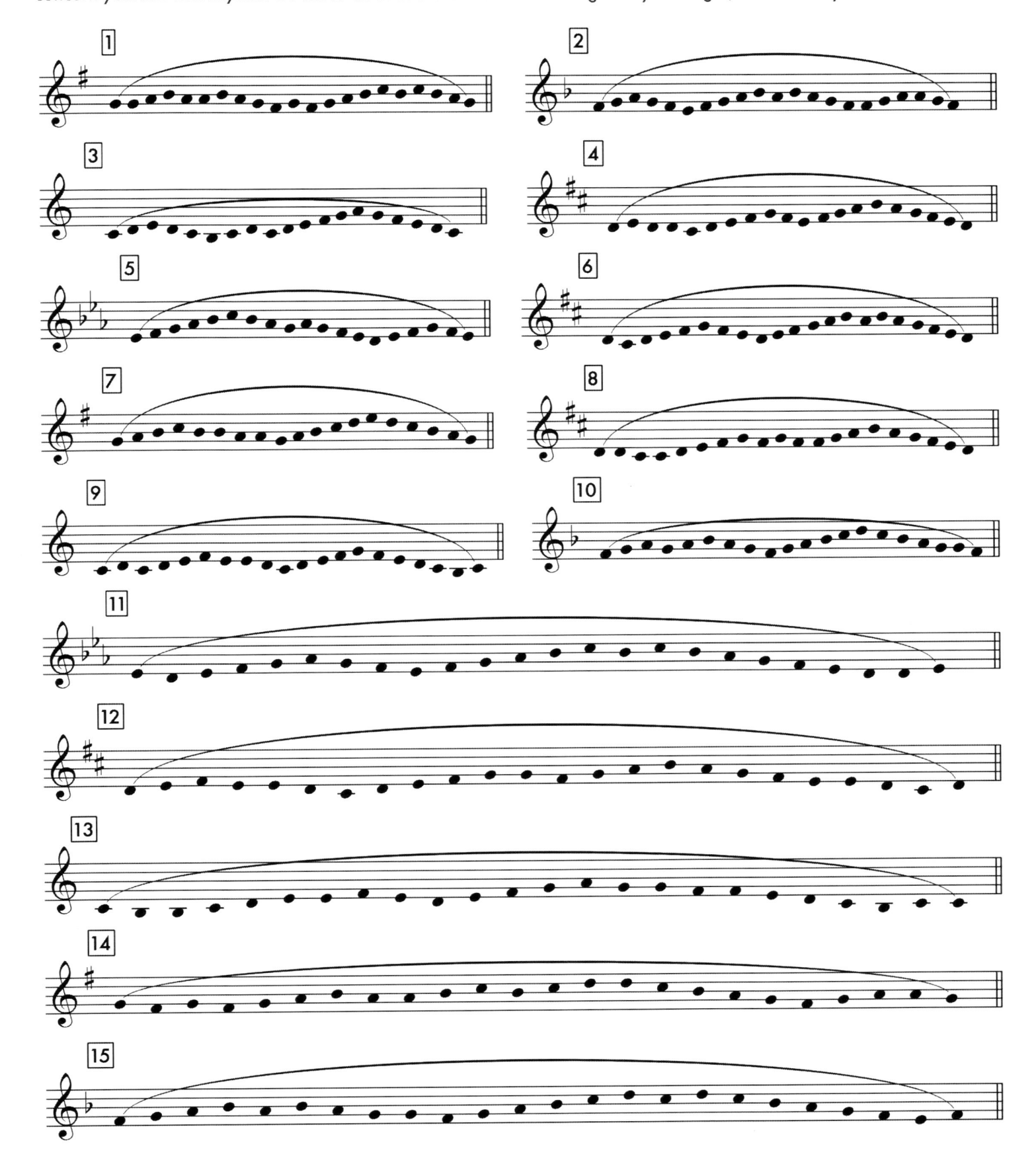

READING BENCHMARK 3C

Tonality = Major
Pitches = tDRMFSL, Stepwise
Keys = C, D, Eb, F, G

Meters = Duple and Triple
Time Signatures = 2/4, 4/4, 6/8, 3/4
Functions = Macrobeat/Microbeat

11

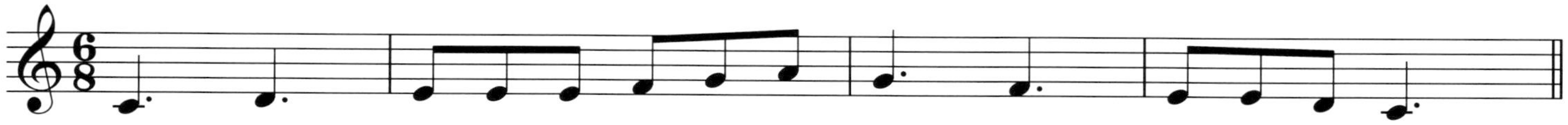

12

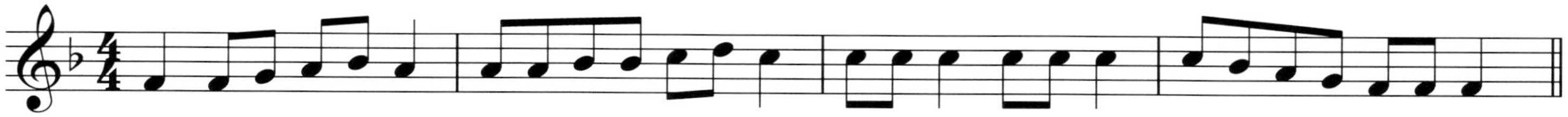

13

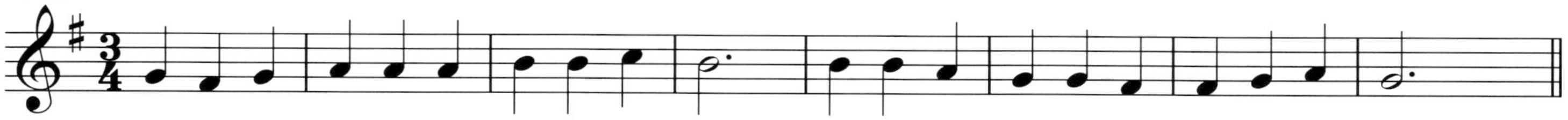

14

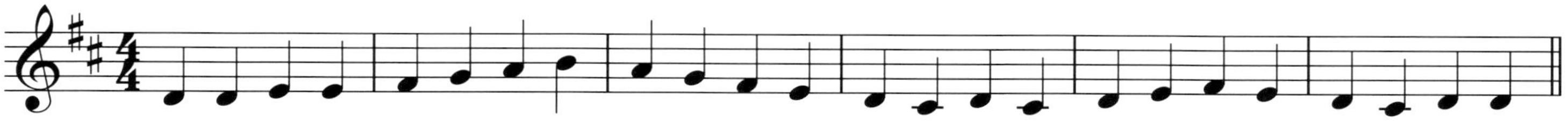

15

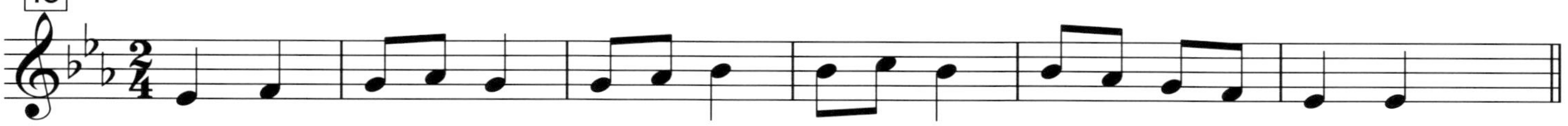

16

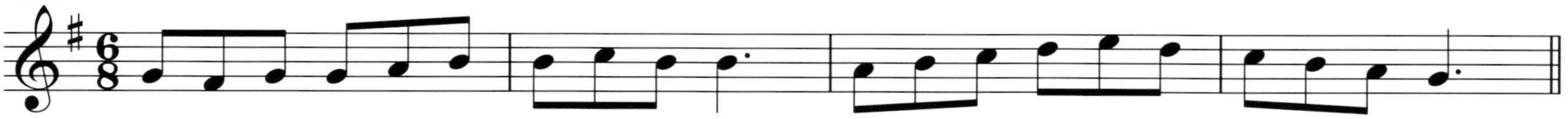

17

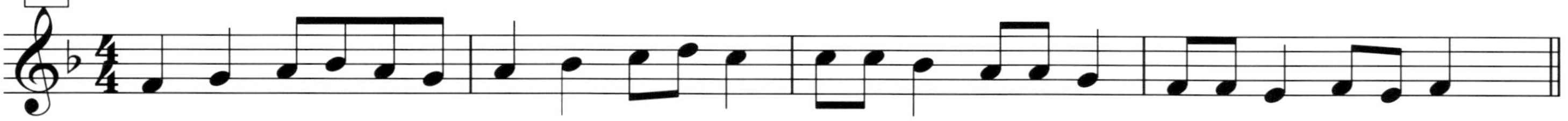

18

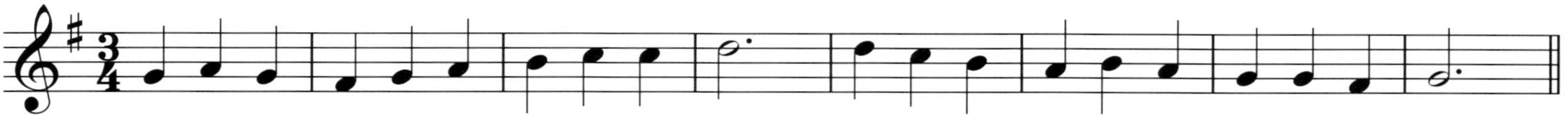

19

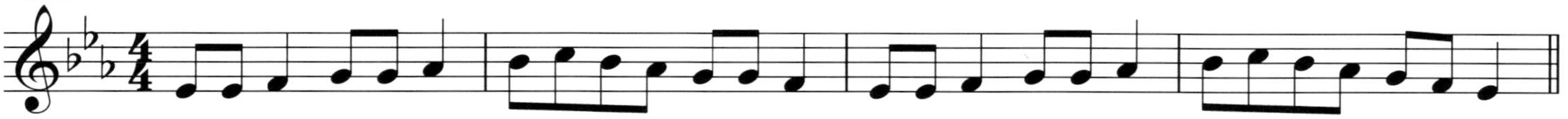

20

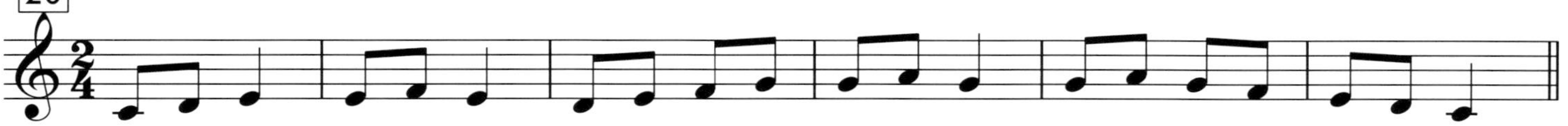

READING BENCHMARK 3D

Tonality = Major
Pitches = tDRMFSL, Stepwise
Keys = C, D, Eb, F, G

Meters = Duple
Time Signatures = 2/4, 4/4
Functions = Macro/microbeat and divisions

LESSON 3.6
COMBINING STEPWISE AND HARMONIC PATTERNS

Read these **familiar** stepwise and harmonic patterns.

Read these familiar **and unfamiliar** stepwise and harmonic patterns.

READING BENCHMARK 3E

Tonality = Major
Pitches = Tonic and tDRMFSL
Keys = C, D, Eb, F, G

Meters = Duple and Triple
Time Signatures = 2/4, 4/4; 6/8, 3/4
Functions = Macro/microbeat and divisions

As before, you may wish to circle the tonic patterns as part of your tonal analysis.

1

C = DO

2

G = DO

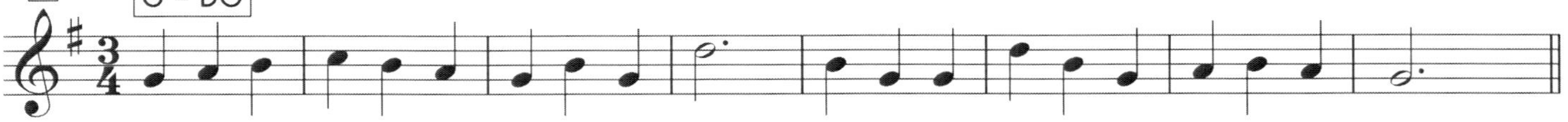

3

Eb = DO

4

F = DO

5

6

D = DO

7

8

9

10

More Difficult Exercises

READING SEQUENCE 4

SEQUENCE 4 AT A GLANCE

Reading Content	
TONAL	**RHYTHM**
• Tonality: Major • Pitches: Tonic and Dominant; tDRMFSL • Keys: Bb, C, D, Eb, F, G, A	• Meters: Duple and Triple • Functions: Macro/Microbeats and Divisions • Time Signatures: 2/4, 4/4, Cut Time; 6/8, 3/4

Lesson Sequence	
4.1 Rhythm	New Duple Time Signature: Cut Time
Reading Benchmark 4A • Major; Tonic chord and tDRMFSL; Keys = C, D, Eb, F, G • Duple; **Cut Time**; Macro/Micro and Divisions	
4.2 Rhythm	Divisions in Triple Meter (6/8 and 3/4)
Reading Benchmark 4B • Major; Tonic chord and tDRMFSL; Keys = C, D, Eb, F, G • Triple; 6/8 and 3/4; Macro/Micro **and Divisions**	
4.3 Rhythm	Longer Rhythm Patterns in Duple and Triple
Reading Benchmark 4C • Major;Tonic chord and tDRMFSL; Keys = C, D, Eb, F, G • Duple & Triple; Macro/micro **and Divisions**; 2/4, 4/4; 6/8, 3/4	
4.4 Tonal	Two New DO-Signatures (Bb and A)
4.5 Tonal	Dominant Patterns, Major Tonality
4.6 Tonal	Generalizing New Dominant Patterns, Major Tonality
4.7 Tonal	Combining Familiar and Unfamiliar Tonic and Dominant Patterns
Reading Benchmark 4D • Major; Tonic **and Dominant** only; Keys = Bb, C, D, Eb, F, G, A • Duple & Triple; Macro/micro and Divisions; 2/4, 4/4; 6/8, 3/4	

LESSON 4.1
NEW DUPLE TIME SIGNATURE: CUT TIME

In Reading Lesson 2.6, we learned that we can have an enrhythmic rhythm pattern by representing macrobeats, microbeats and divisions with different notes. In this lesson, we will do the same thing in duple meter with a new time signature: **Cut Time**.

NEW TIME SIGNATURE: CUT TIME

The time signature ₵ tells us the music is in **duple meter**. Additionally, it tells us that macrobeats will be represented by a half note, microbeats will be represented by quarter notes, and divisions will be represented by eighth notes. There are two macrobeats in each measure. Note: sometimes you will see Cut Time notated as 2/2.

macrobeats in ₵	microbeats in ₵	divisions in ₵
Du Du	Du De Du De	Du Ta De Ta

! We will use the same solfege for macrobeats, microbeats and divisions that we used in the time signatures 2/4 and 4/4. The sound itself is exactly the same, however the sound is represented by different notes. All duple meters use the same solfege.

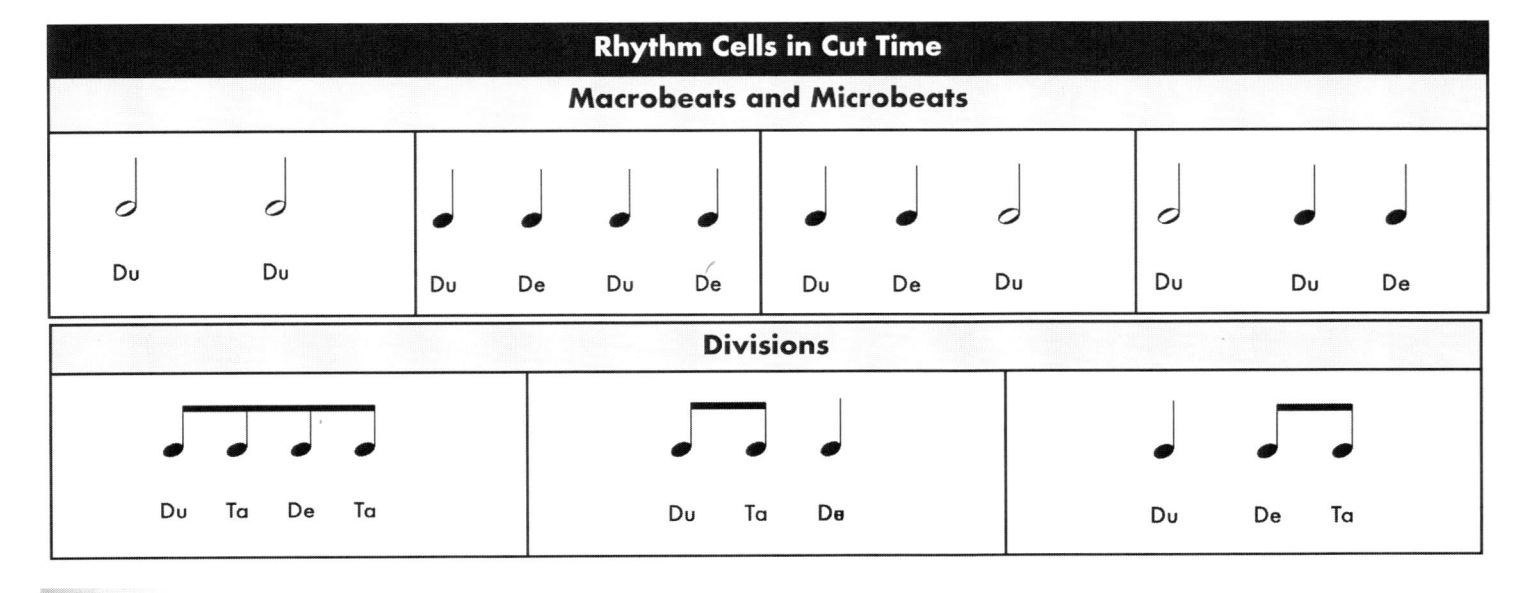

Rhythm Cells in Cut Time

Macrobeats and Microbeats

| Du Du | Du De Du De | Du De Du | Du Du De |

Divisions

| Du Ta De Ta | Du Ta De | Du De Ta |

📝 Try writing these rhythm cells. You may also wish to try writing some of the longer rhythm patterns on the following pages.

148 The Literate Musician

ENRHYTHMIC RHYTHM PATTERNS

Now, we can notate the exact same sounding pattern in three different time signatures.

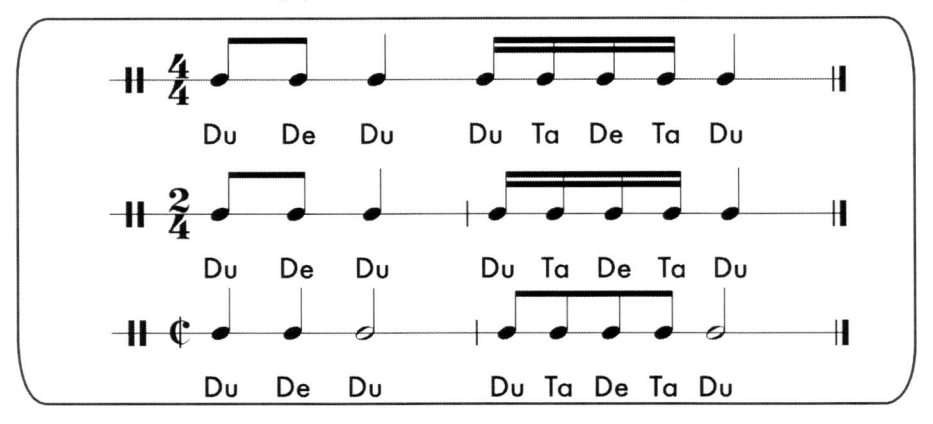

Du De Du   Du Ta De Ta Du
Du De Du   Du Ta De Ta Du
Du De Du   Du Ta De Ta Du

Here are the same eight macro/microbeat patterns that you already read in 2/4 and 4/4. Can you read them in Cut Time?

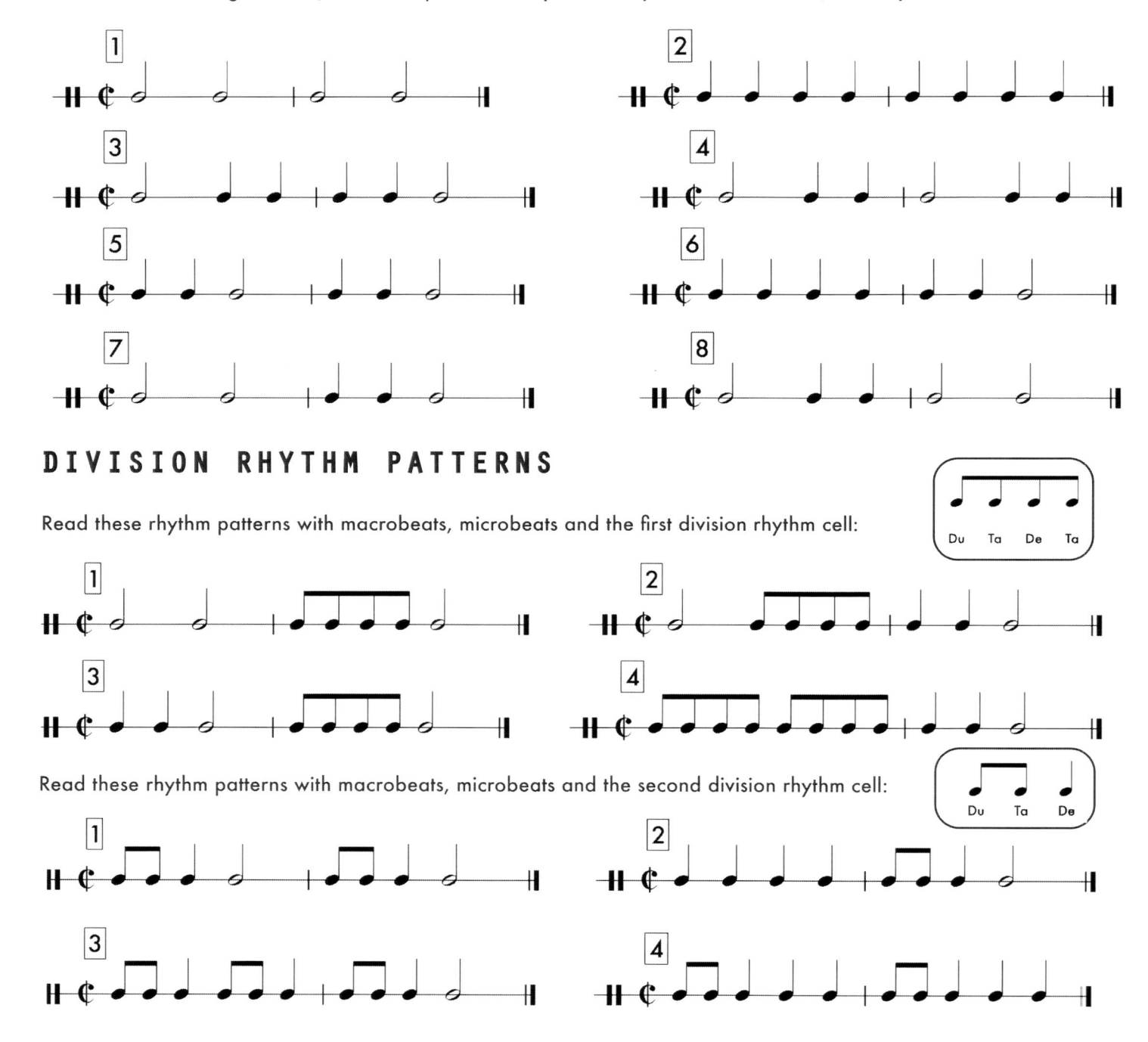

DIVISION RHYTHM PATTERNS

Read these rhythm patterns with macrobeats, microbeats and the first division rhythm cell:

Du Ta De Ta

Read these rhythm patterns with macrobeats, microbeats and the second division rhythm cell:

Du Ta De

Lesson 4.1

Read these rhythm patterns with macrobeats, microbeats and the third division rhythm cell:

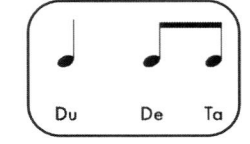

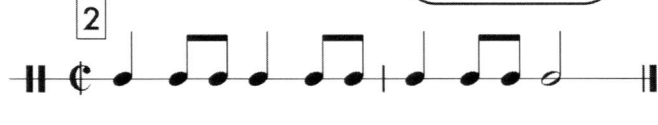

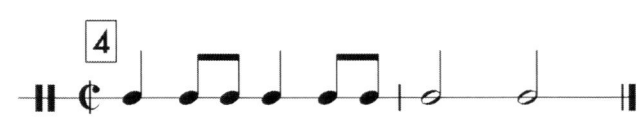

(Du De Ta)

Read these rhythm patterns with macrobeats, microbeats and all three division rhythm cells:

Read these longer rhythm patterns with macrobeats, microbeats and all three division rhythm cells:

Do a rhythmic composition in Cut Time.

READING BENCHMARK 4A

Tonality = Major
Pitches = Tonic and tDRMFSL
Keys = C, D, Eb, F, G

Meters = Duple
Time Signatures = Cut Time
Functions = Macro/microbeat and divisions

1

2

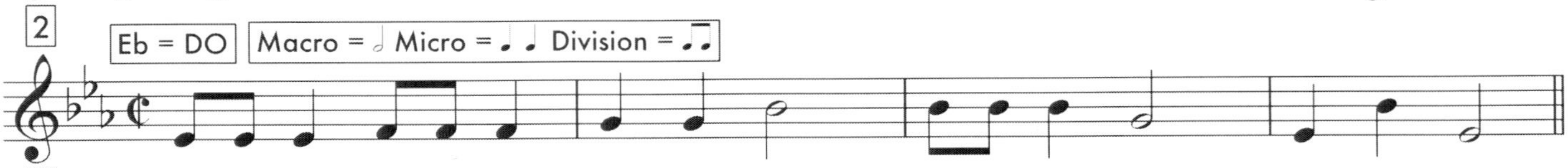

3

4

5

6

7

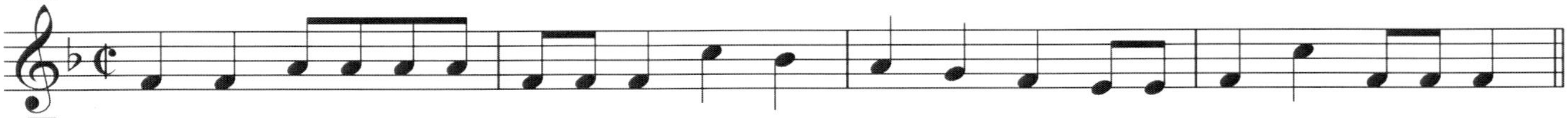

8

9

10

LESSON 4.2
READING DIVISIONS IN TRIPLE METER
TIME SIGNATURES: 6/8 & 3/4

REVIEW

Take a moment to review macrobeats, microbeats and divisions in triple meter. Review p. 46 if necessary. Say the following chant to yourself:

"**Macrobeats** in triple meter are DU DU DU DU.
Microbeats in triple meter are DU DA DI, DU DA DI, DU DA DI, DU DA DI.
Divisions in triple meter are DU-Ta DA-Ta DI-Ta, DU-Ta DA-Ta DI-Ta, DU-Ta DA-Ta DI-Ta, DU-Ta DA-Ta DI-Ta."

READING MACROBEATS, MICROBEATS & DIVISIONS IN 6/8

In the time signatures 6/8, macrobeats (DU) will be represented by a dotted quarter note, microbeats (DU DA DI) will be represented by three paired eighth notes, and divisions (DU-Ta DA-Ta DI-Ta) will be represented by sixteenth notes.

macrobeats in 6/8	microbeats in 6/8	divisions in 6/8
♩.	♪ ♪ ♪	♬ ♬ ♬
Du	Du Da Di	Du Ta Da Ta Di Ta

DIVISION RHYTHM CELLS

There are seven division rhythm cells to learn in 6/8. For this lesson, however, we will focus on only four. Look at the notation, and chant these four rhythm cells to yourself.

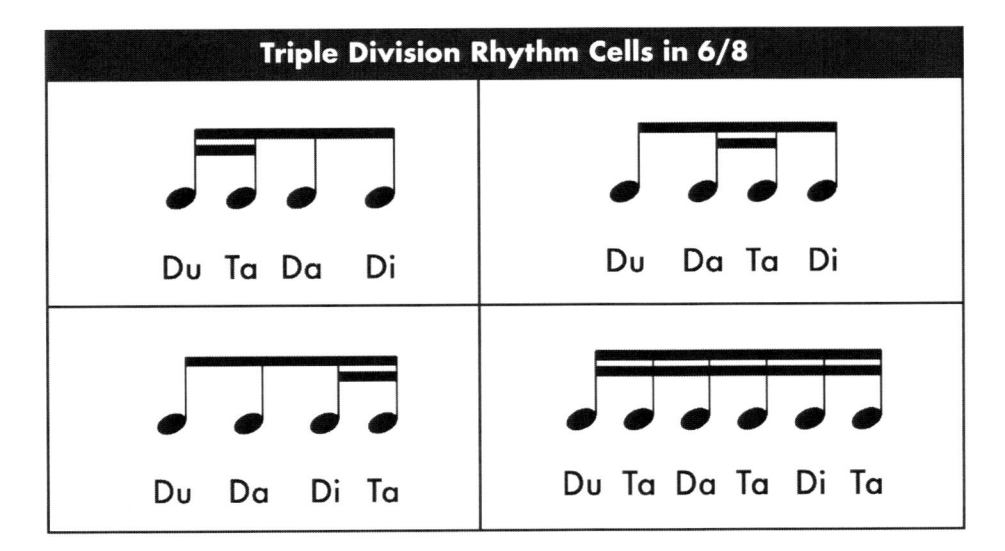

Triple Division Rhythm Cells in 6/8

Du Ta Da Di	Du Da Ta Di
Du Da Di Ta	Du Ta Da Ta Di Ta

Try writing these rhythm cells, paying particular attention to the beams. You may also wish to try writing some of the longer rhythm patterns on the following pages.

READING RHYTHM PATTERNS

Read these rhythm patterns with macrobeats, microbeats and the first division rhythm cell:

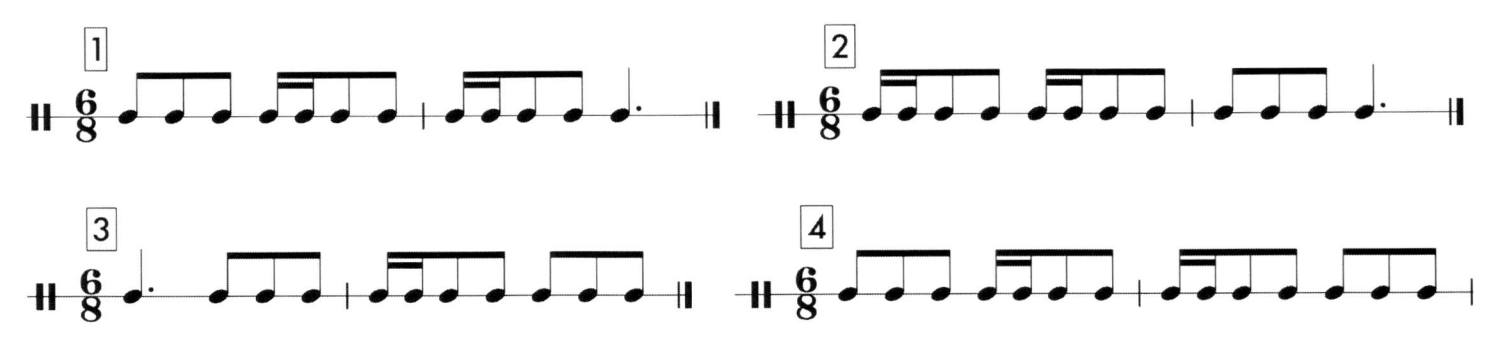

Du Ta Da Di

Read these rhythm patterns with macrobeats, microbeats and the second division rhythm cell:

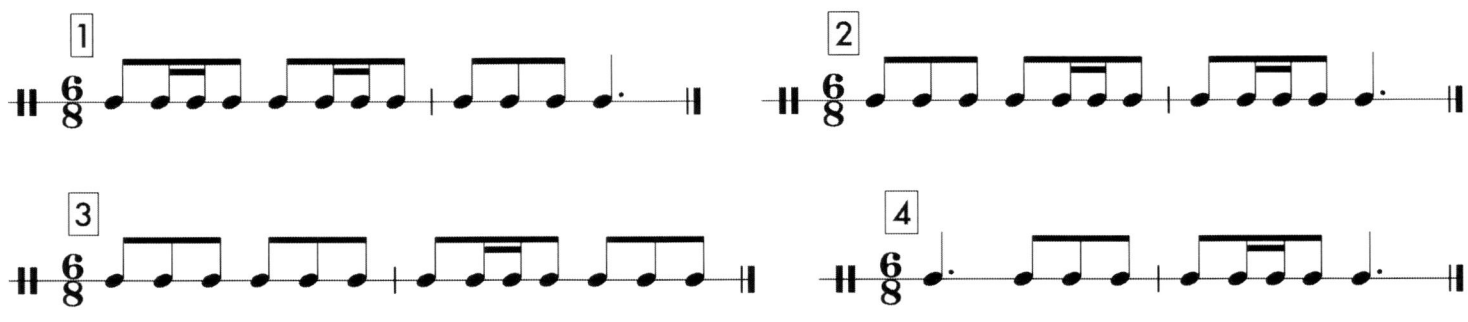

Du Da Ta Di

Read these rhythm patterns with macrobeats, microbeats and the third division rhythm cell:

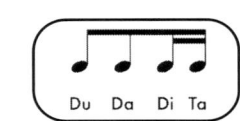

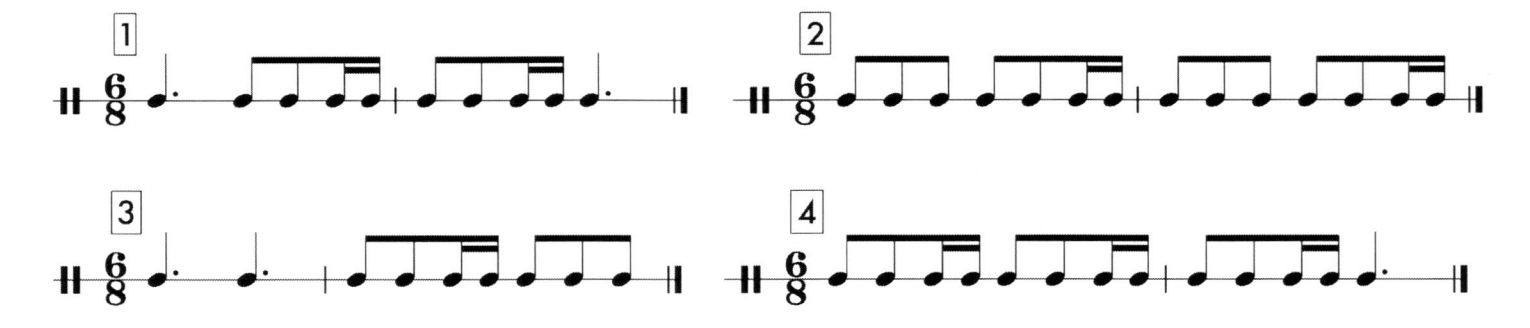

Du Da Di Ta

Read these rhythm patterns with macrobeats, microbeats and the fourth division rhythm cell:

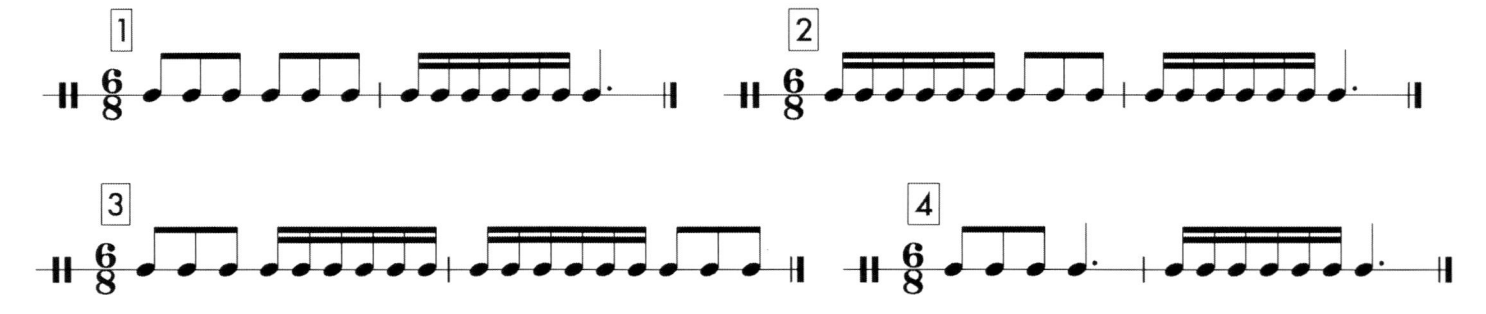

Du Ta Da Ta Di Ta

Read these rhythm patterns with macrobeats, microbeats and all four triple division rhythm cells in 6/8.

READING MACROBEATS, MICROBEATS & DIVISIONS IN 3/4

In the time signatures 3/4, macrobeats (DU) will be represented by a dotted half note, microbeats (DU DA DI) will be represented by three quarter, and divisions (DU-Ta DA-Ta DI-Ta) will be represented by eighth notes.

macrobeats in 3/4	microbeats in 3/4	divisions in 3/4
𝅗𝅥.	♩ ♩ ♩	♫ ♫ ♫
Du	Du Da Di	Du Ta Da Ta Di Ta

DIVISION RHYTHM CELLS

There are seven division rhythm cells to learn in 3/4. For this lesson, however, we will focus on only four. Look at the notation, and chant these four rhythm cells to yourself.

Triple Division Rhythm Cells in 3/4

Du Ta Da Di	Du Da Di Ta
Du Da Ta Di	Du Ta Da Ta Di Ta

READING RHYTHM PATTERNS

Read these rhythm patterns with macrobeats, microbeats and the first division rhythm cell:

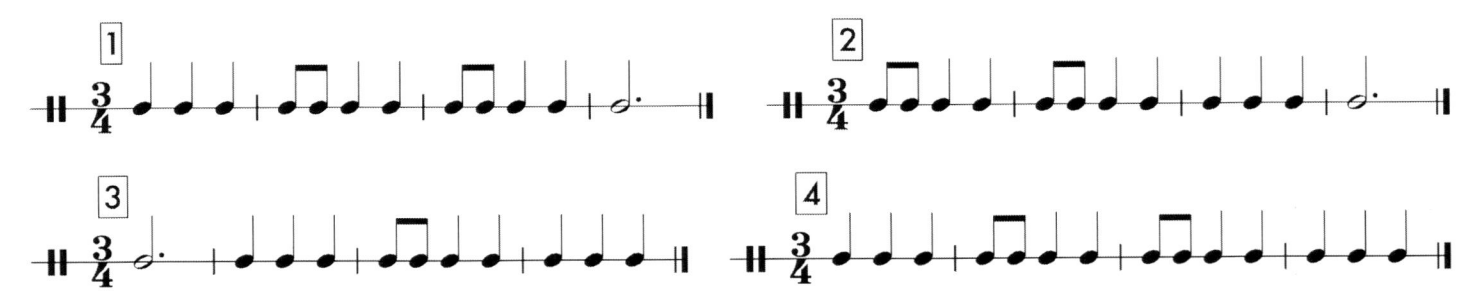

Du Ta Da Di

Read these rhythm patterns with macrobeats, microbeats and the second division rhythm cell:

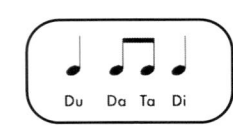

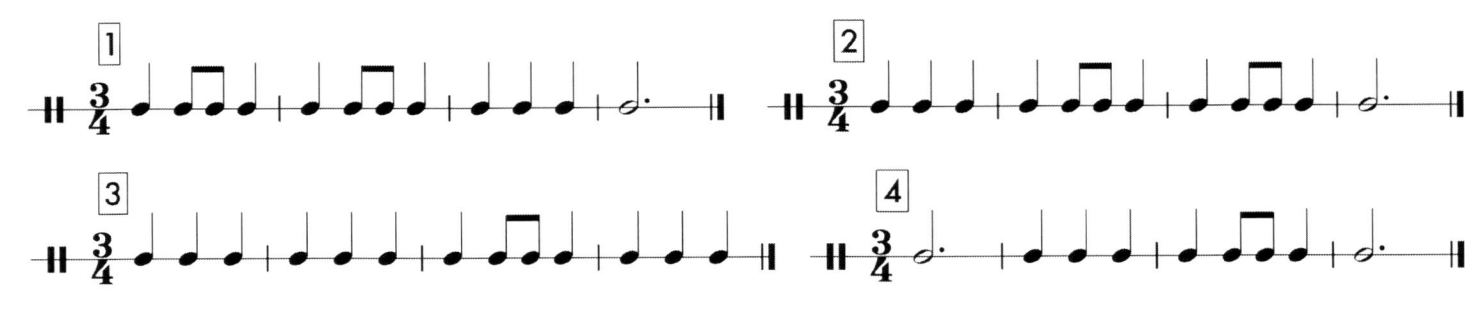

Du Da Ta Di

Read these rhythm patterns with macrobeats, microbeats and the third division rhythm cell:

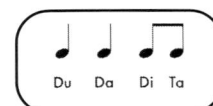

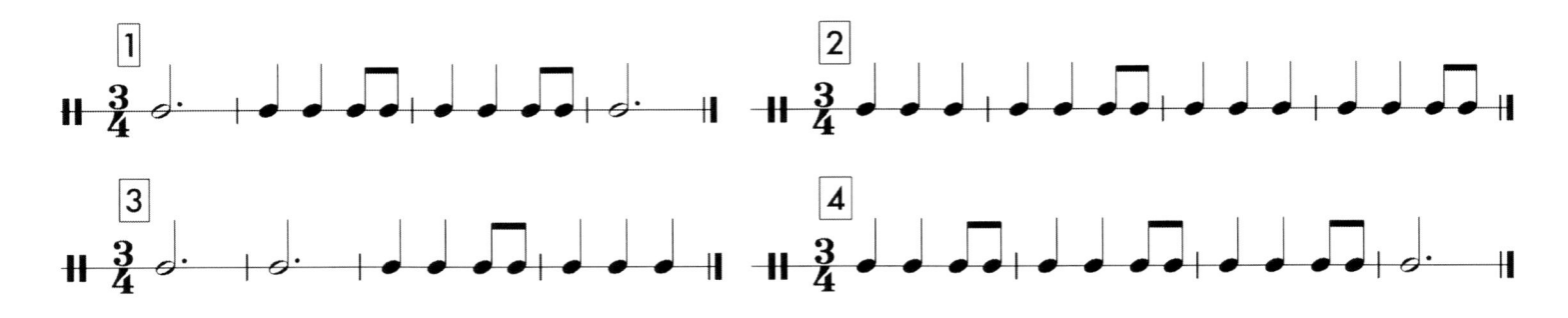

Du Da Di Ta

Read these rhythm patterns with macrobeats, microbeats and the fourth division rhythm cell:

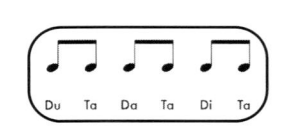

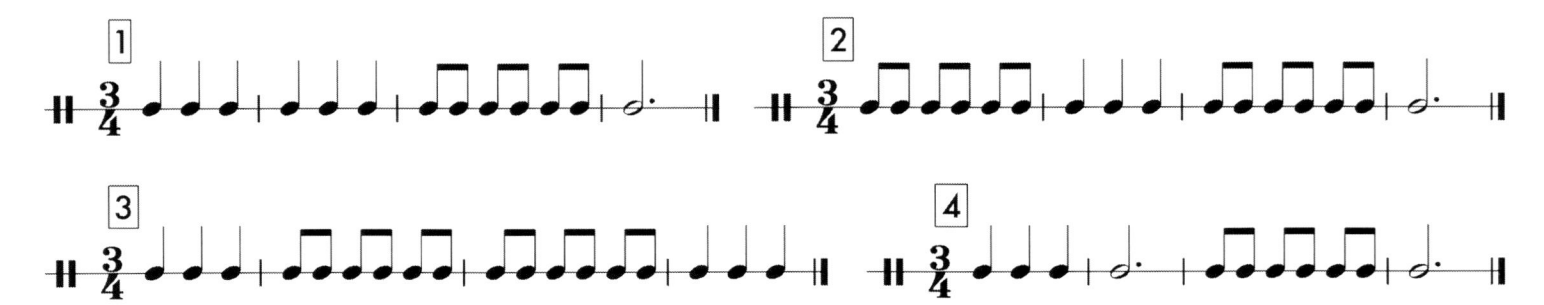

Du Ta Da Ta Di Ta

Read these rhythm patterns with macrobeats, microbeats and all four triple division rhythm cells in 3/4.

CHALLENGE

Can you use the skill of generalization to figure out the remaining three triple division patterns? Use the same logic skills that you used tonally to figure out one pitch on the basis of another.

Try writing these rhythm patterns, as well. For an additional challenge, try writing two patterns at a time.

READING BENCHMARK 4B

Tonality = Major
Pitches = Tonic and tDRMFSL
Keys = C, D, Eb, F, G
Meters = Triple
Time Signatures = 6/8, 3/4
Functions = Macro/microbeat and divisions

LESSON 4.3
LONGER RHYTHM PATTERNS IN DUPLE & TRIPLE TIME SIGNATURES: 2/4, 4/4, 2/2, 6/8 & 3/4

Before we combine tonal patterns and rhythms in **Reading Benchmark 4C**, it is a good idea to review all of the new rhythm patterns and time signatures we have learned so far.

Up to this point, all of the rhythm patterns we have looked at have been 2-4 measures long. You can think of these as short sentences (For example, "I like ice cream."). In the upcoming benchmarks, you will be reading longer, more complicated sentences. (For example, "Considering that chocolate is my favorite ice cream, I made sure to order it for dessert at the new restaurant on Cabbot Street.") This skill is called **Composite Synthesis**.

Since we have introduced new content (divisions), the steps to rhythmic analysis bear repeating.

First, **identify the meter.**
- Look at the time signature and the rhythm patterns. Are you audiating DU DE or DU DA DI as the microbeats?
- If you are audiating DU DE, you are in duple meter. If you are audiating DU DA DI, you are in triple meter.

Next, **remind yourself of the rhythm solfege** representing macrobeats, microbeats and divisions. Chant them to yourself.

Then, look at the notation, and confirm **what notes** represent the macrobeats and microbeats in that time signature.

Scan the entire piece for **familiar rhythm patterns**. All of the rhythm patterns will be based on previously learned rhythm cells. Isolate any difficult rhythm pattern, and "sound out" the musical word.

Next, **chant the rhythm** of the entire song with a neutral syllable.
- Set a reasonable tempo for yourself.
- Use the neutral syllable "BAA."

Finally, chant the rhythm of the song **using rhythm solfege**.

READING LONGER RHYTHM PATTERNS

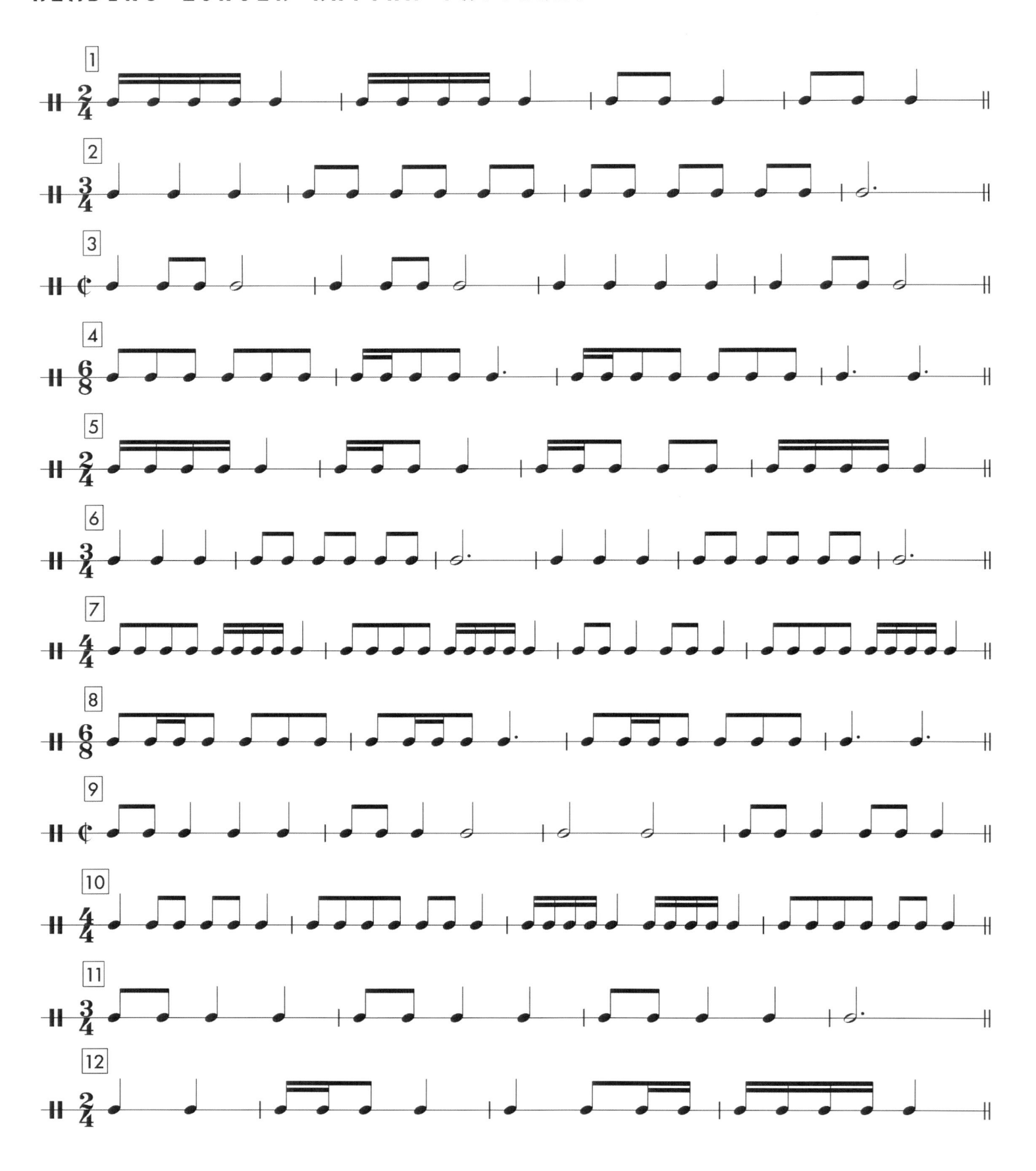

Lesson 4.3

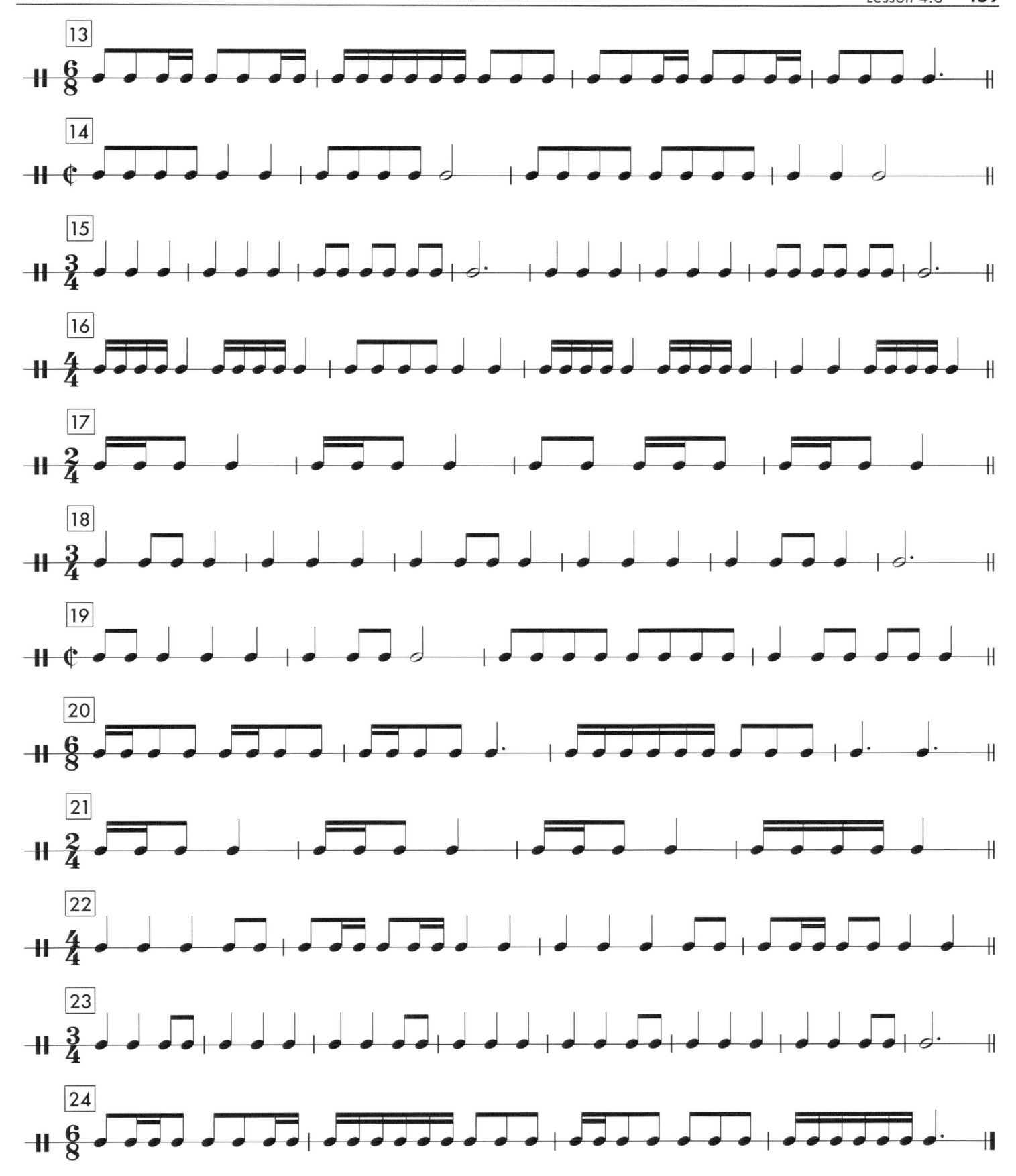

Add pitches to one or more of these longer rhythmic sentences and turn them into a piano composition.

READING BENCHMARK 4C

Tonality = Major **Pitches** = Tonic and tDRMFSL **Keys** = C, D, Eb, F, G	**Meters** = Duple and Triple **Time Signatures** = 2/4, 4/4; 6/8, 3/4 **Functions** = Macro/microbeat and divisions

1

C = DO | Macro = 𝅗𝅥; Micro = ♩♩; Division = ♫

2

G = DO | Macro = 𝅗𝅥.; Micro = ♩; Division = ♫

3

Eb = DO

4

F = DO | Macro = ♩.; Micro = ♫♪; Division = ♬

5

Macro = ♩; Micro = ♫; Division = ♬

6

7

8

9

10

11

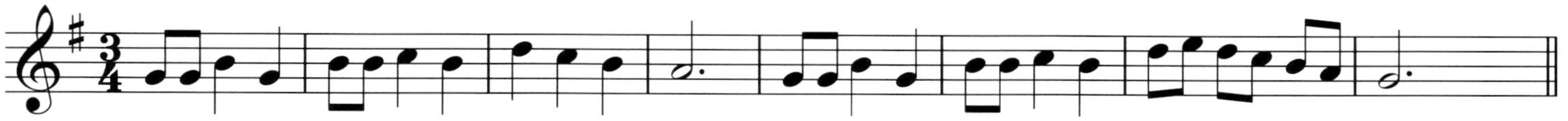

12

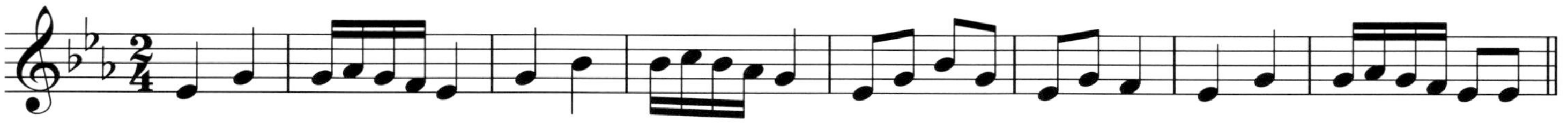

13

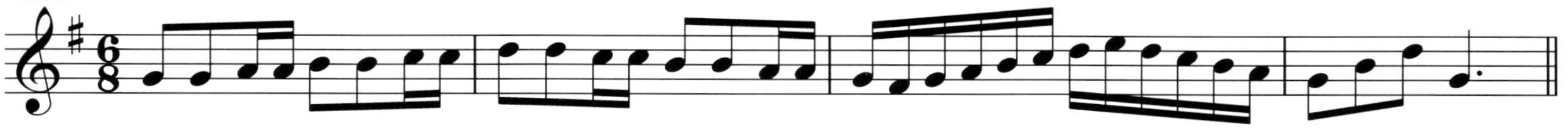

14

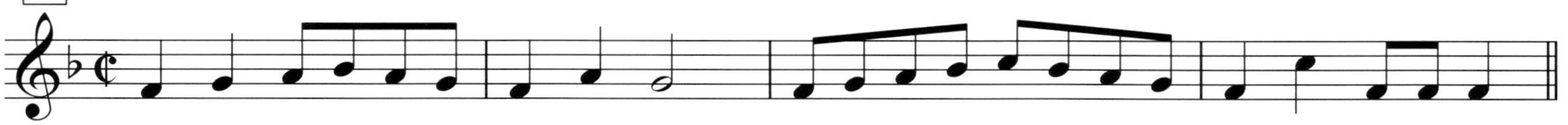

15

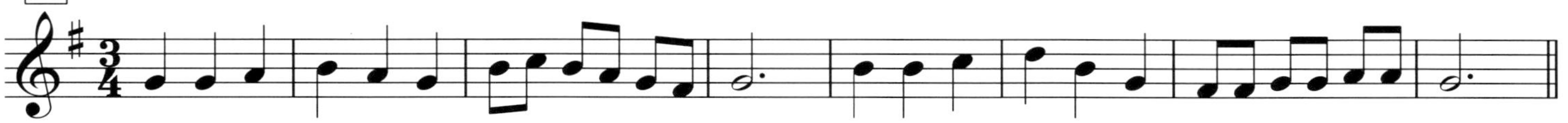

16

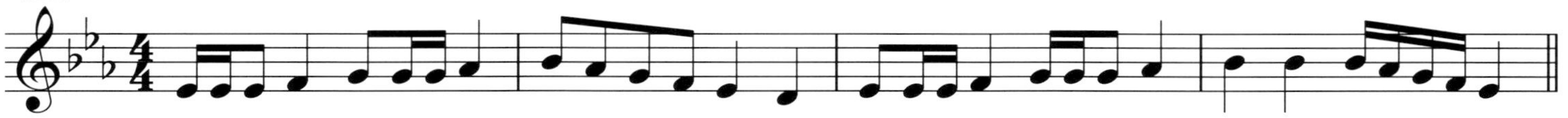

17

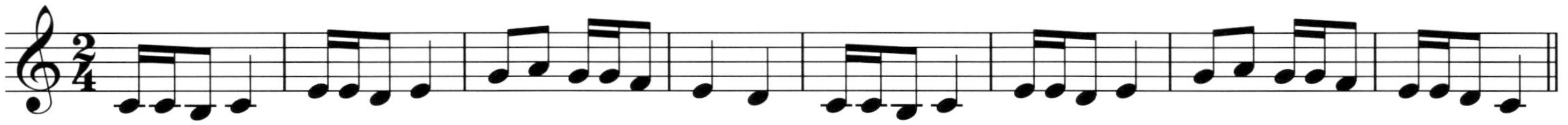

18

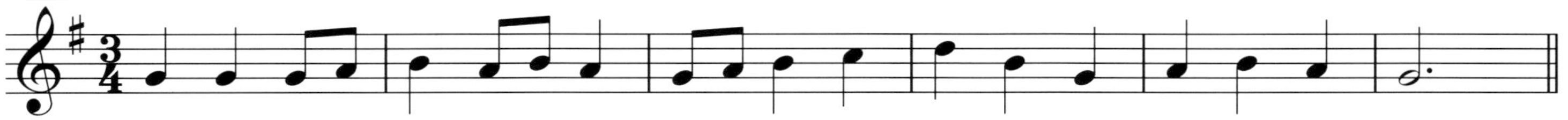

19

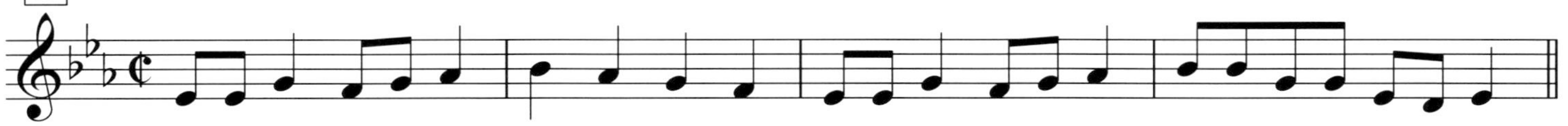

20

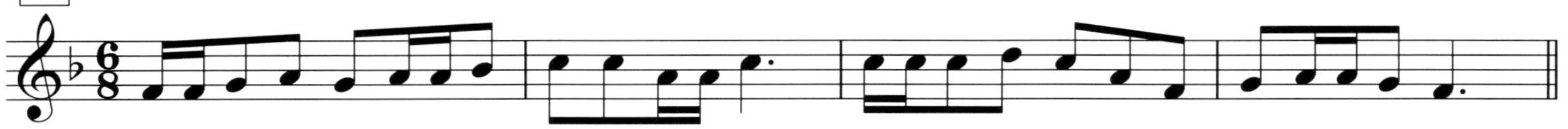

LESSON 4.4
TWO NEW DO SIGNATURES

Bb-DO

HOW TO FIND DO
When the key signature has FLATS, **the last flat is FA**. Count up or down to get to DO.

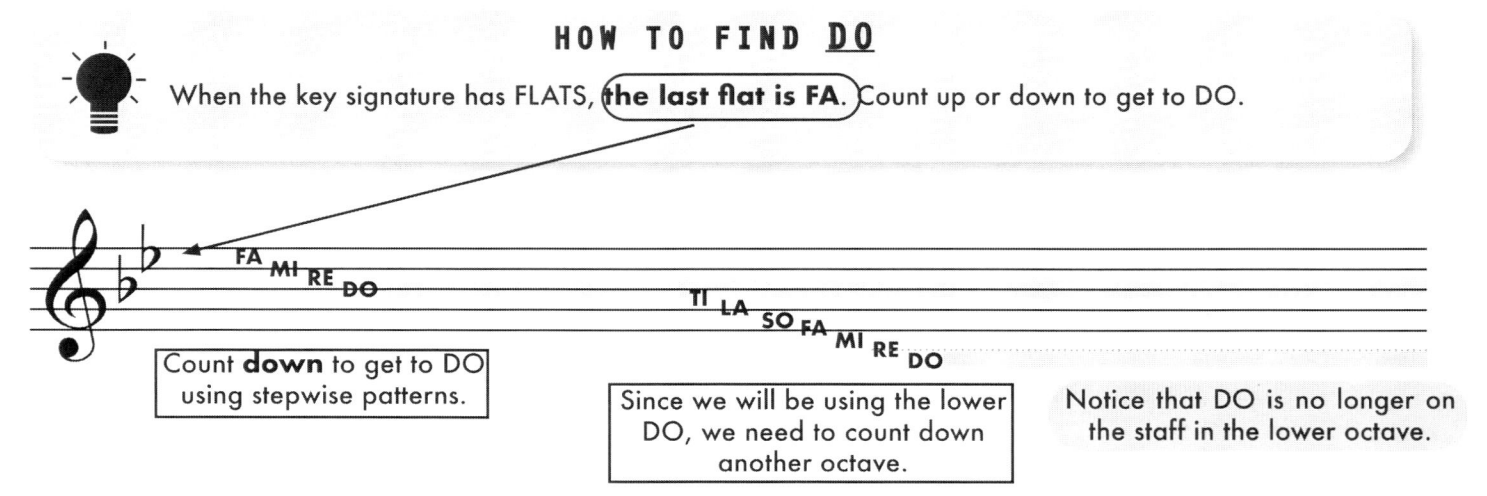

Count **down** to get to DO using stepwise patterns.

Since we will be using the lower DO, we need to count down another octave.

Notice that DO is no longer on the staff in the lower octave.

Trace the pitches below in Bb-DO using solfege.

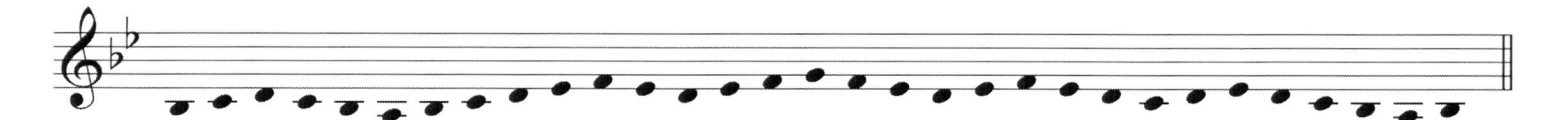

Read these familiar stepwise patterns in unfamiliar order in **Bb-DO**.

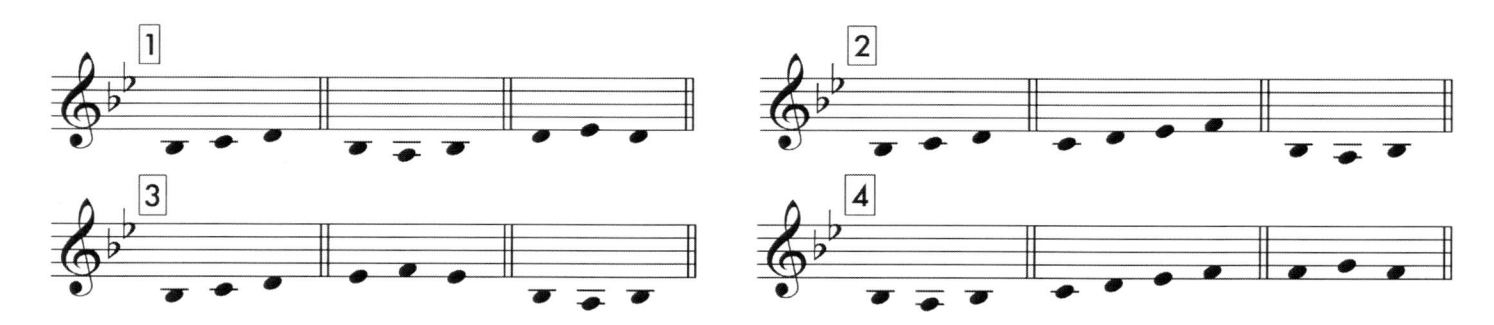

Read these familiar harmonic patterns in unfamiliar order in **Bb-DO**

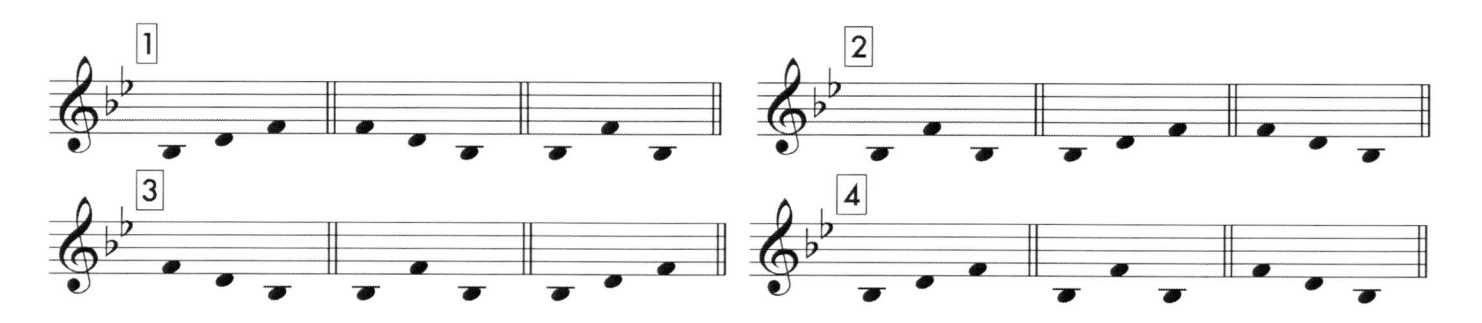

A-DO

HOW TO FIND DO

💡 When the key signature has SHARPS, **the last sharp is TI**. Count up or down to get to DO.

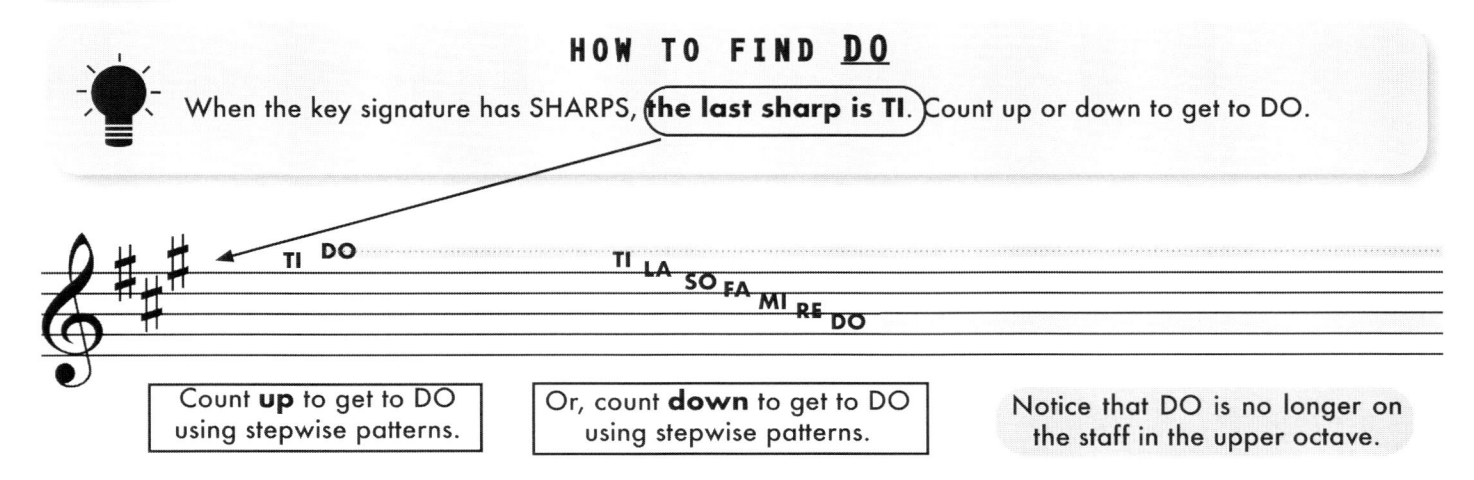

| Count **up** to get to DO using stepwise patterns. | Or, count **down** to get to DO using stepwise patterns. | Notice that DO is no longer on the staff in the upper octave. |

Trace the pitches below in A-DO using solfege.

Read these familiar stepwise patterns in unfamiliar order in **A-DO**.

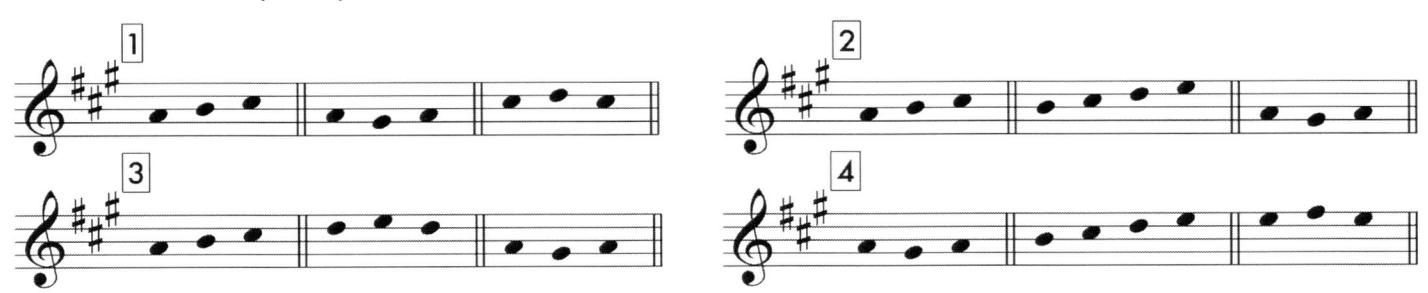

1 2 3 4

Read these familiar harmonic patterns in unfamiliar order in **A-DO**

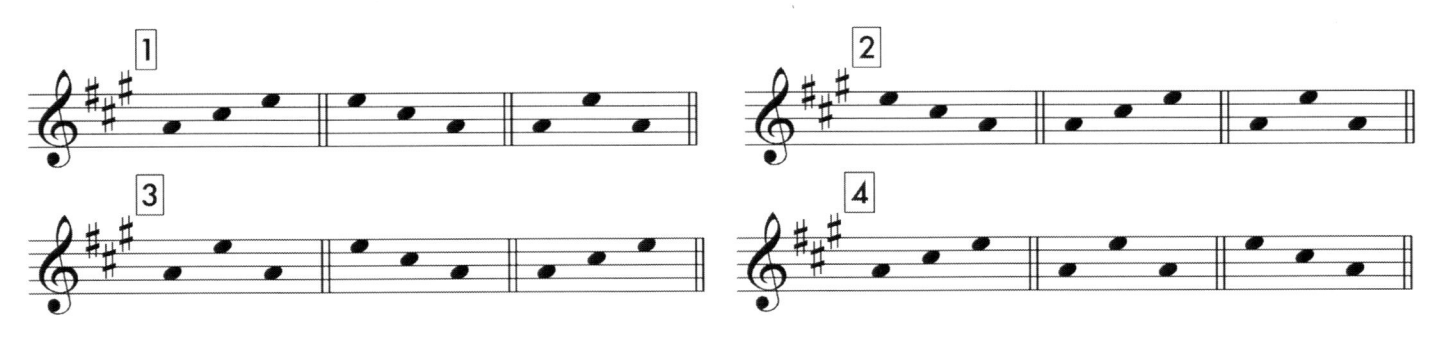

1 2 3 4

🎹 Try playing these patterns on the keyboard. Use the **Major I & V** & **Solfege** Keyboard Card. Line up DO with Bb and A.

LESSON 4.5
DOMINANT PATTERNS, MAJOR TONALITY

INTRODUCTION

Just as we did with tonic patterns, we can conceive of dominant patterns in two different ways. First, we can think about them happening **vertically**, all at once, underneath the melody. Second, we can think of them moving **horizontally**, as if they were melody.

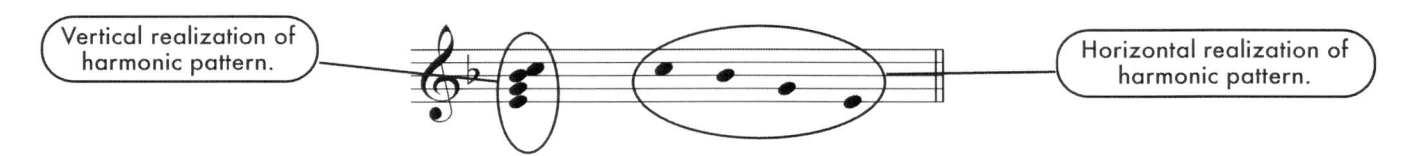

Vertical realization of harmonic pattern.

Horizontal realization of harmonic pattern.

THREE FAMILIAR DOMINANT PATTERNS: SRT, TRS, SFRT

We will learn dominant patterns in a very similar way that we learned tonic patterns. However, since dominant patterns feel unresolved, we will learn them in conjunction with familiar tonic patterns. We will begin by learning 3 familiar dominant patterns: SO RE TI, TI RE SO, SO FA RE TI. Begin by establishing major tonality (SO LA SO FA MI RE TI DO).

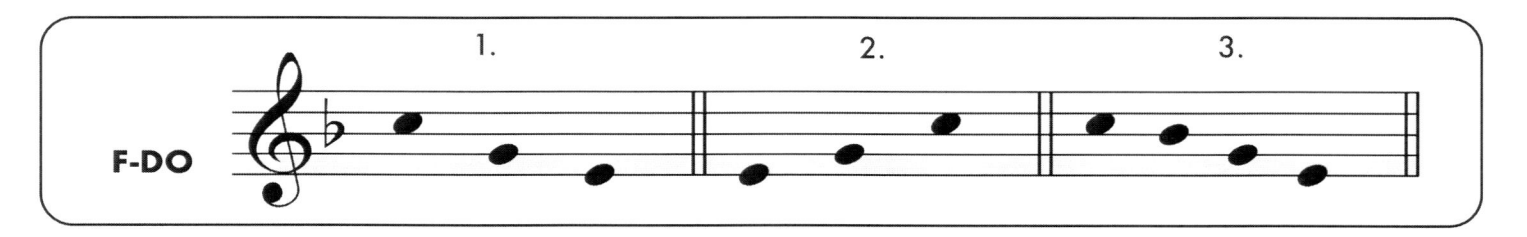

The first pattern is **SO RE TI**. Look at the notation, take a breath and sing **SO RE TI**. Just as you did when you echoed the patterns, keep the pitches separated. The second pattern is **TI RE SO**. Look at the notation, take a breath and sing **TI RE SO**. The third pattern is **SO FA RE TI**. Look at the notation, take a breath and sing **SO FA RE TI**.

! If you need an aural reminder of these three patterns, review them in the companion course !
videos. Remember: we are learning to read **familiar patterns**.

When you read a dominant pattern, take note of where each pitch is on the staff **in relation to DO**. You may want to review the first three stepwise patterns for a visual refresher of where RE and TI are in relation to DO.

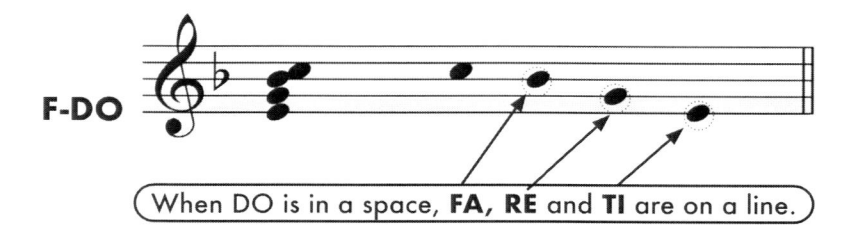

When DO is in a space, **FA, RE** and **TI** are on a line.

Lesson 4.5 **165**

FAMILIAR I-V-I PATTERNS, UNFAMILIAR ORDER

Read the same three familiar dominant patterns, but this time, read them in an unfamiliar order in conjunction with familiar tonic chords. The first pattern will be a tonic chord, the second pattern will be one of our three familiar dominant chords, and the third chord will be another tonic chord.

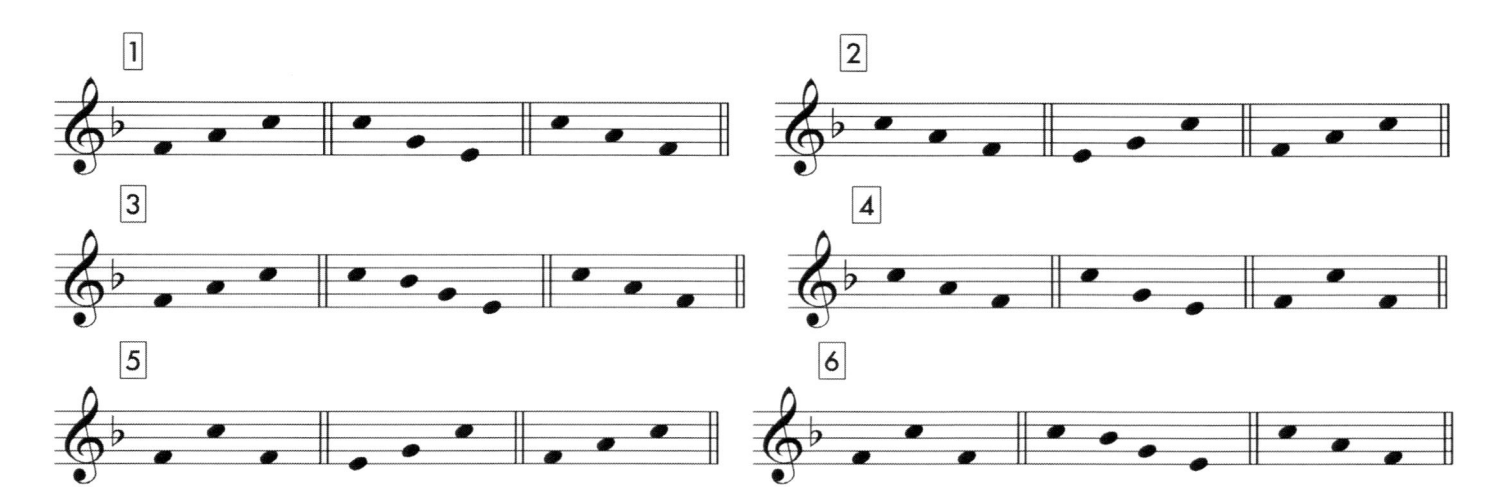

SAME PATTERNS IN DIFFERENT DO-SIGNATURES

Let's learn to read those same three dominant patterns in our familiar DO-signatures.

G-DO

Dominant Chord in G-DO

When DO is on a line, **FA, RE** and **TI** are in a space.

3 Familiar Dominant Chords in G-DO

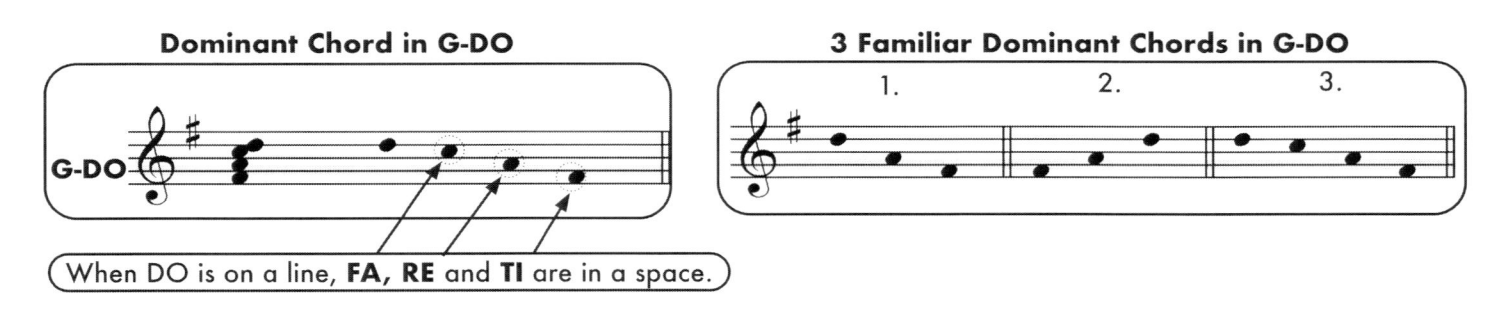

Read these familiar I-V-I harmonic patterns in unfamiliar order in **G-DO**

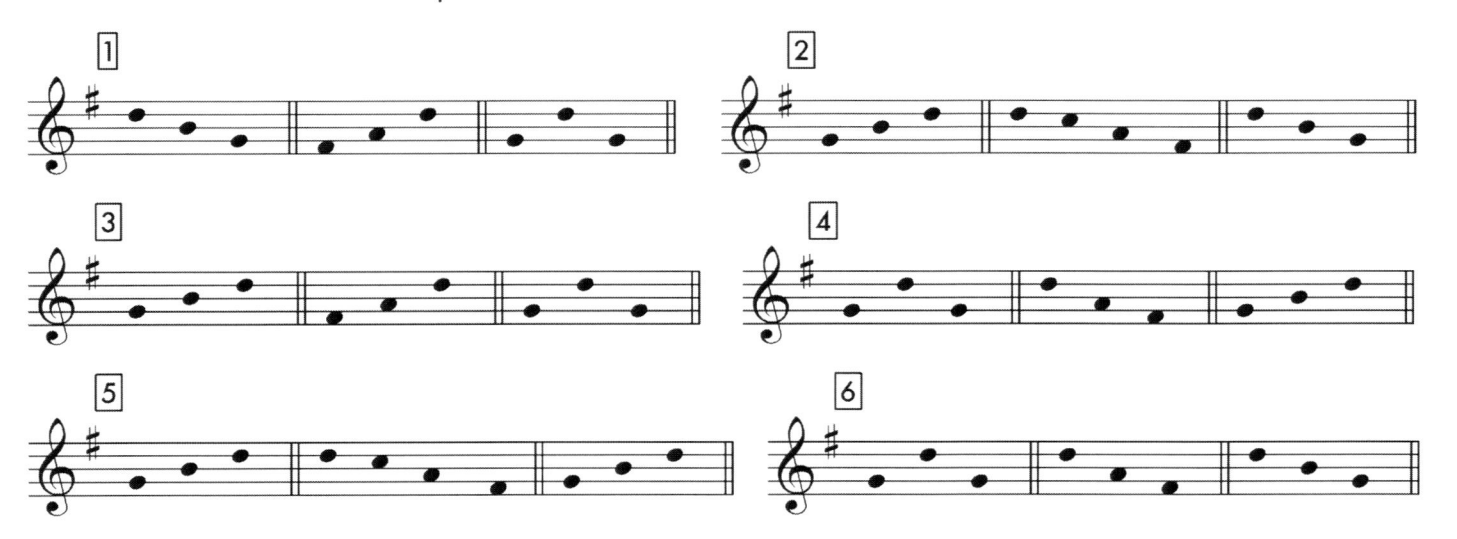

A - DO

Dominant Chord in A-DO

3 Familiar Dominant Patterns in A-DO

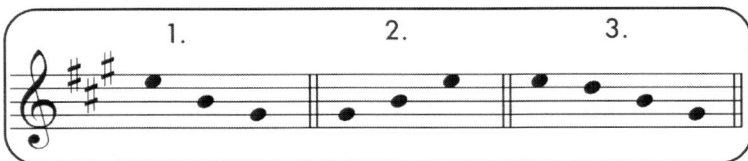

Read these familiar I-V-I harmonic patterns in unfamiliar order in **A-DO**

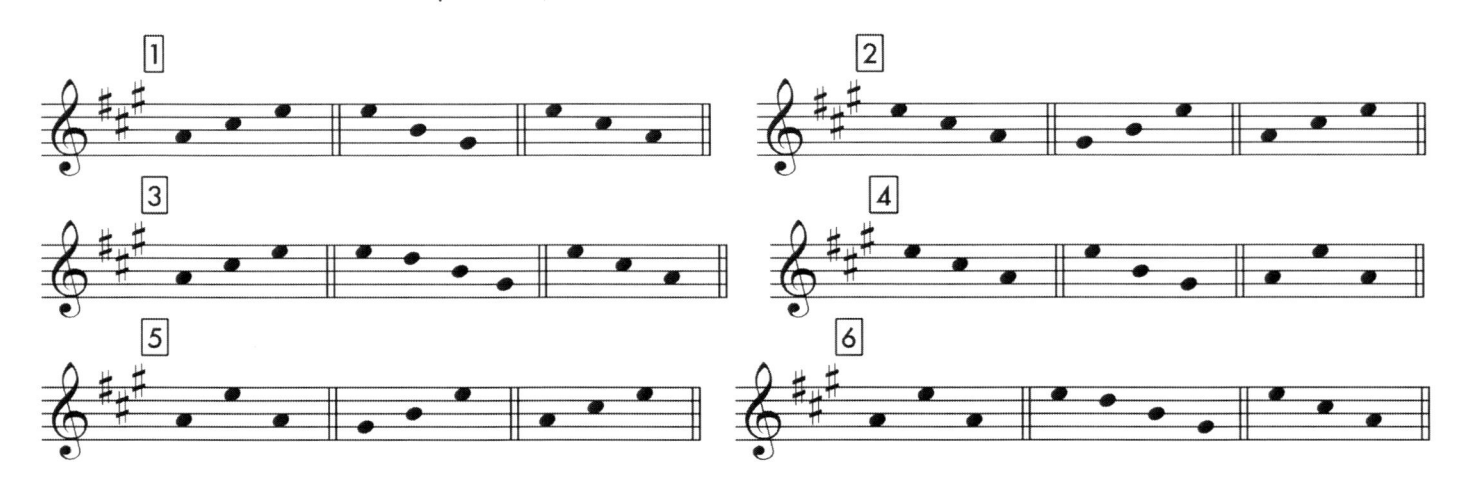

Bb - DO

Dominant Chord in Bb-DO

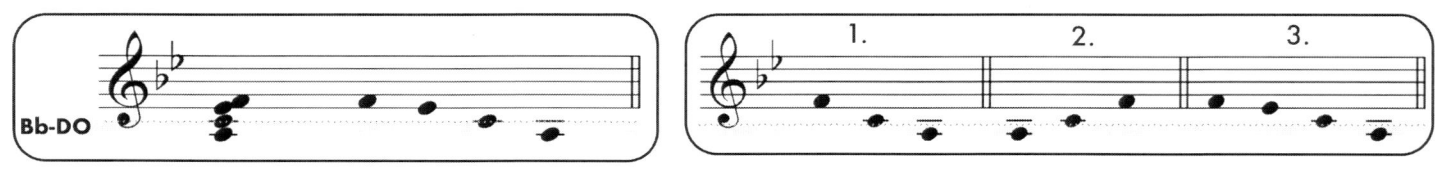

3 Familiar Dominant Patterns in Bb-DO

Read these familiar I-V-I harmonic patterns in unfamiliar order in **Bb-DO**

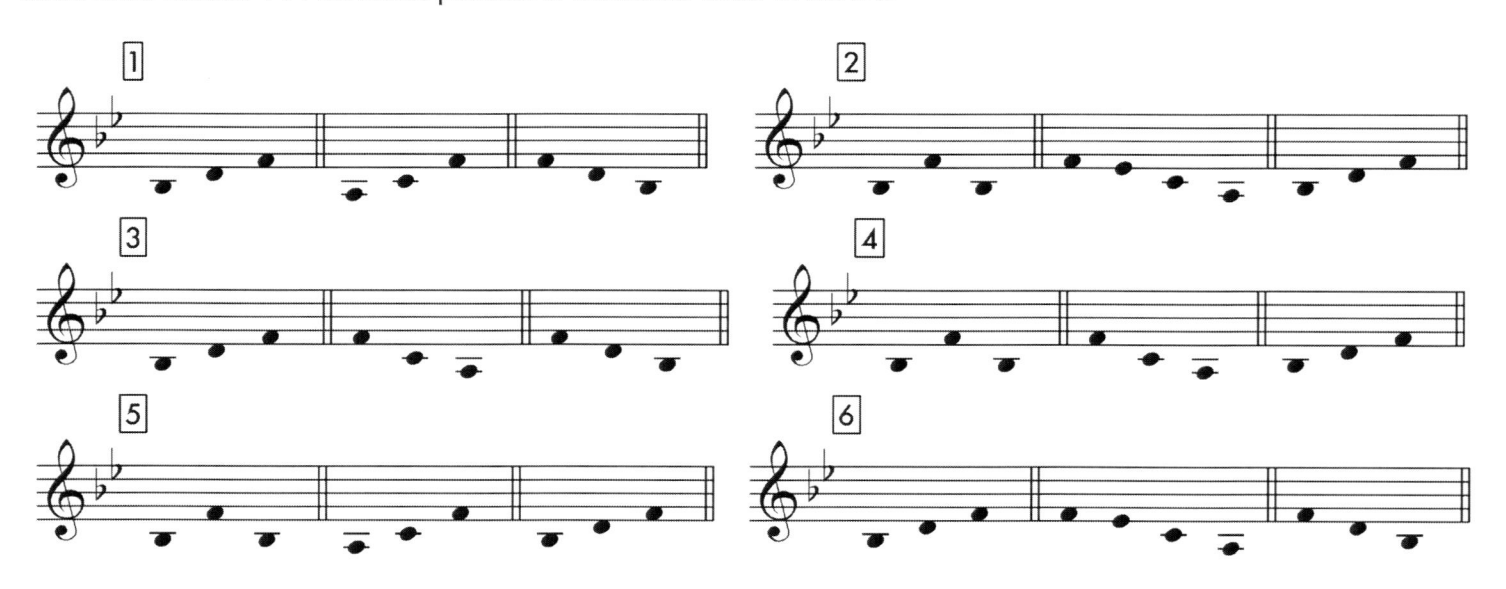

C - DO

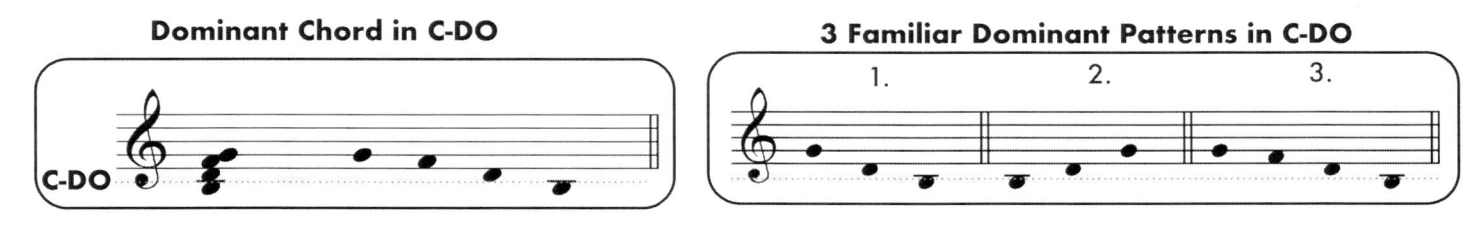

Dominant Chord in C-DO

3 Familiar Dominant Patterns in C-DO

Read these familiar I-V-I harmonic patterns in unfamiliar order in **C-DO**

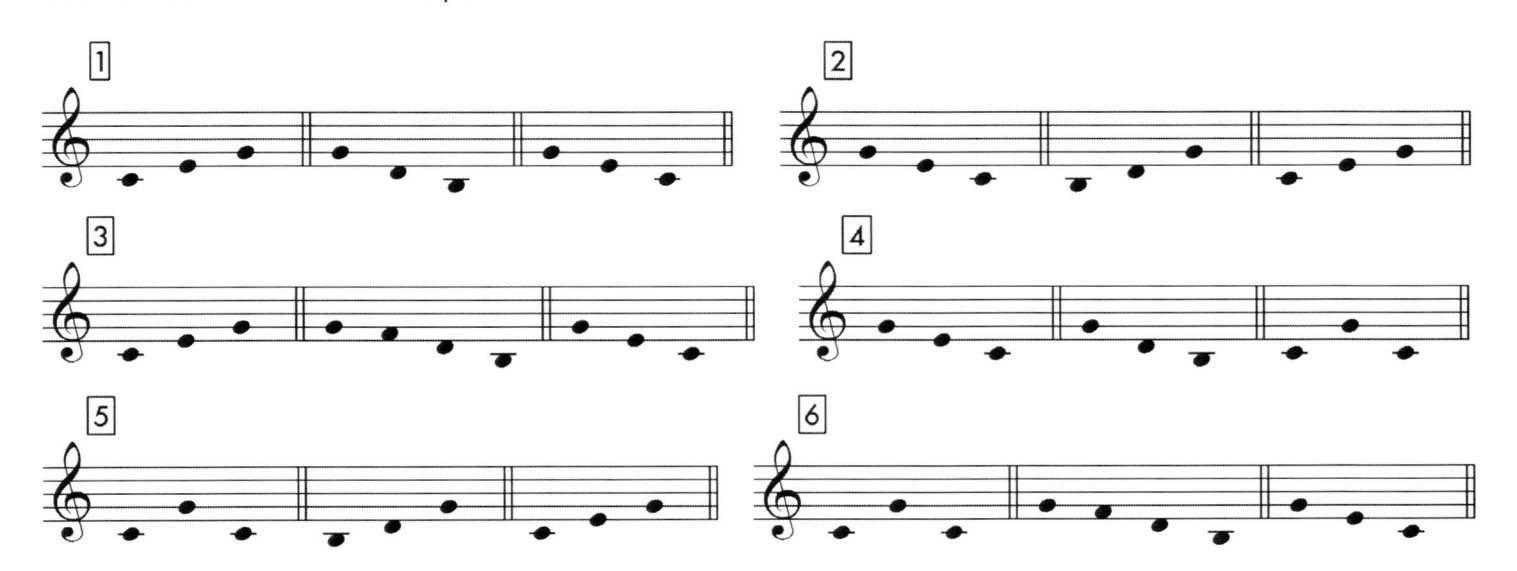

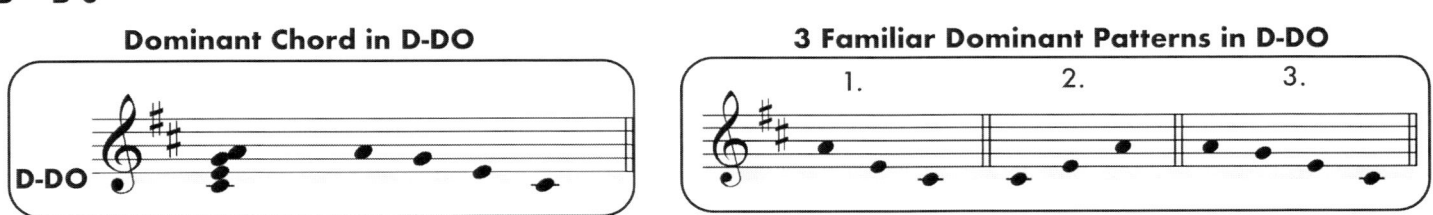

D - DO

Dominant Chord in D-DO

3 Familiar Dominant Patterns in D-DO

Read these familiar I-V-I harmonic patterns in unfamiliar order in **D-DO**

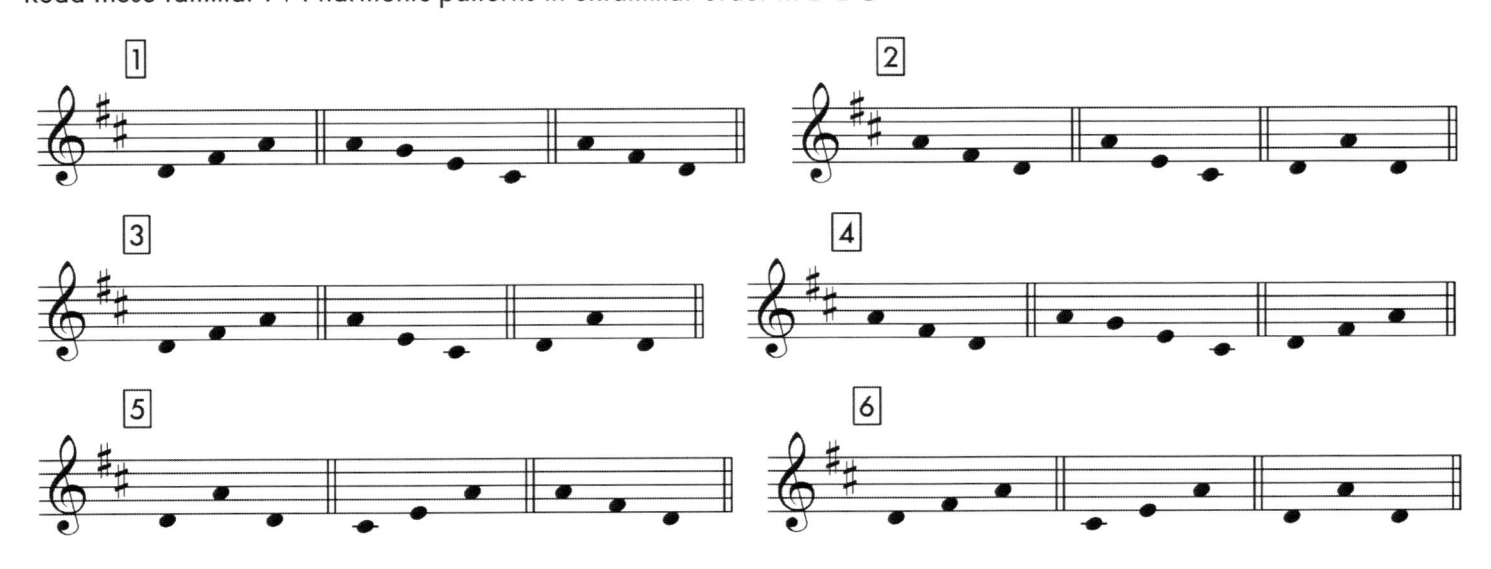

168 The Literate Musician

Eb-DO

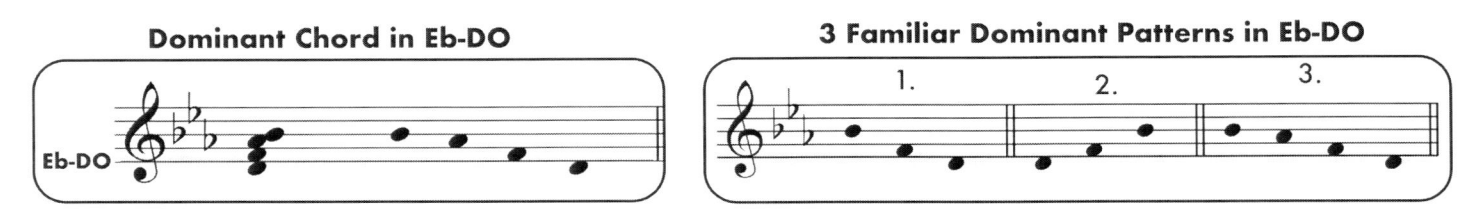

Dominant Chord in Eb-DO

3 Familiar Dominant Patterns in Eb-DO

Read these familiar I-V-I harmonic patterns in unfamiliar order in **Eb-DO**

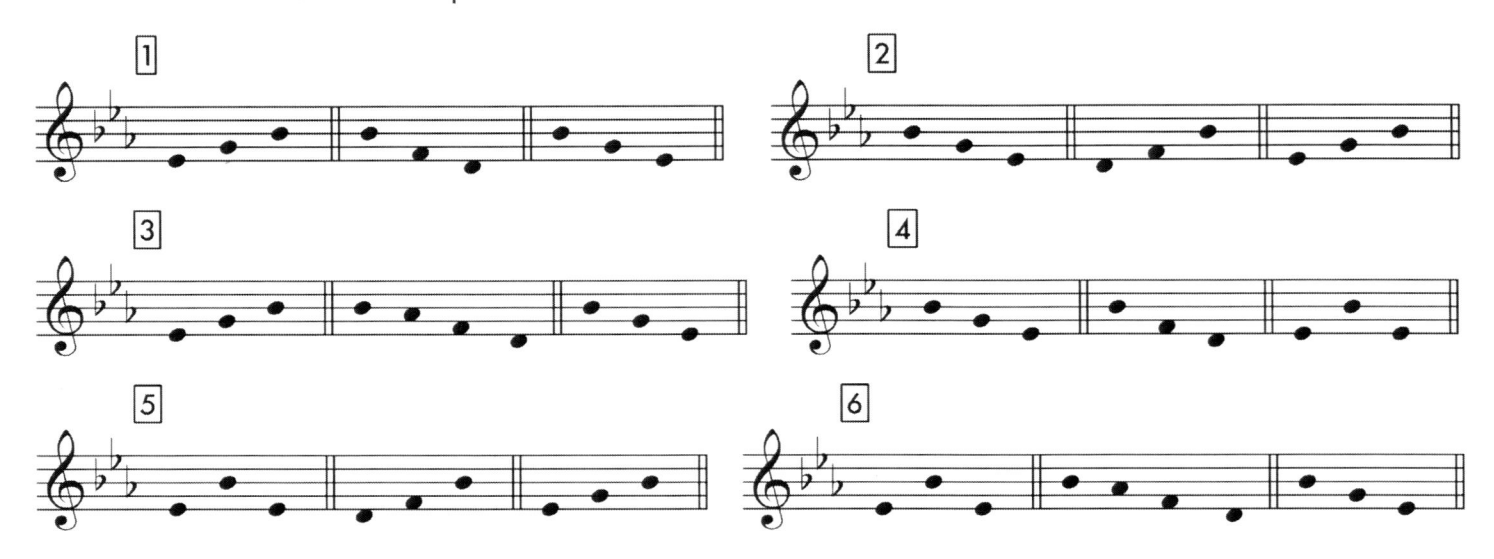

[1] [2]

[3] [4]

[5] [6]

- Try writing these three pattern sequences in several different DO-signatures.

- This would be a perfect time to get the sound of a new function, **Subdominant**, in your audiation. **Spiral** to Lesson 10.1 for an aural introduction to the IV chord.

- You may also wish to **spiral** to Reading Sequence 9 and read dominant patterns in minor tonality.

- Try reading these exercises at the keyboard. Use the **Major I & V** Keyboard Card.

LESSON 4.6
GENERALIZING NEW DOMINANT PATTERNS
MAJOR TONALITY

INTRODUCTION

Now that we have learned to read three familiar dominant patterns, we will harness the power of **generalization** to read more dominant patterns. Some of the patterns will be familiar to you aurally from Part 1, while others will be brand new. **As we did in previous lessons, review translating patterns before you generalize notationally.**

GENERALIZING NEW PATTERNS

Look at the two patterns below in F-DO.

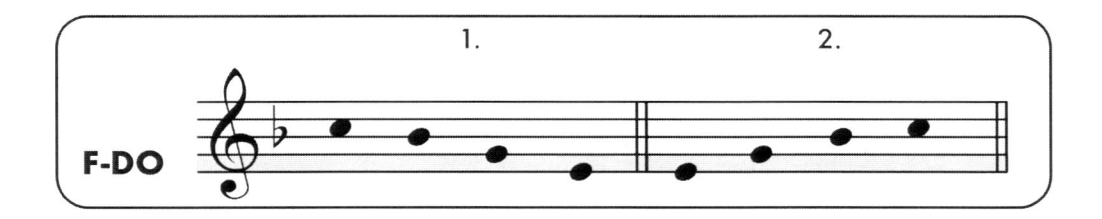

The first pattern (SO FA RE TI) is familiar to you. Using that knowledge, can you figure out the second pattern? Hopefully, you generalized that it was TI RE FA SO.

GENERALIZING DOMINANT PATTERNS IN F-DO

Use the skill of generalization to read these patterns. The final pattern in each example below will be unfamiliar. Familiar tonic patterns are included to help you maintain a sense of tonality.

On the following pages, you will have the opportunity to generalize in all of our familiar keys. Be sure to establish tonality in each new key before you read the patterns. You can simply play a I-V-I in the new key. **If the notes are out of your vocal range, you may sing these in any comfortable octave.**

GENERALIZING DOMINANT PATTERNS IN G-DO

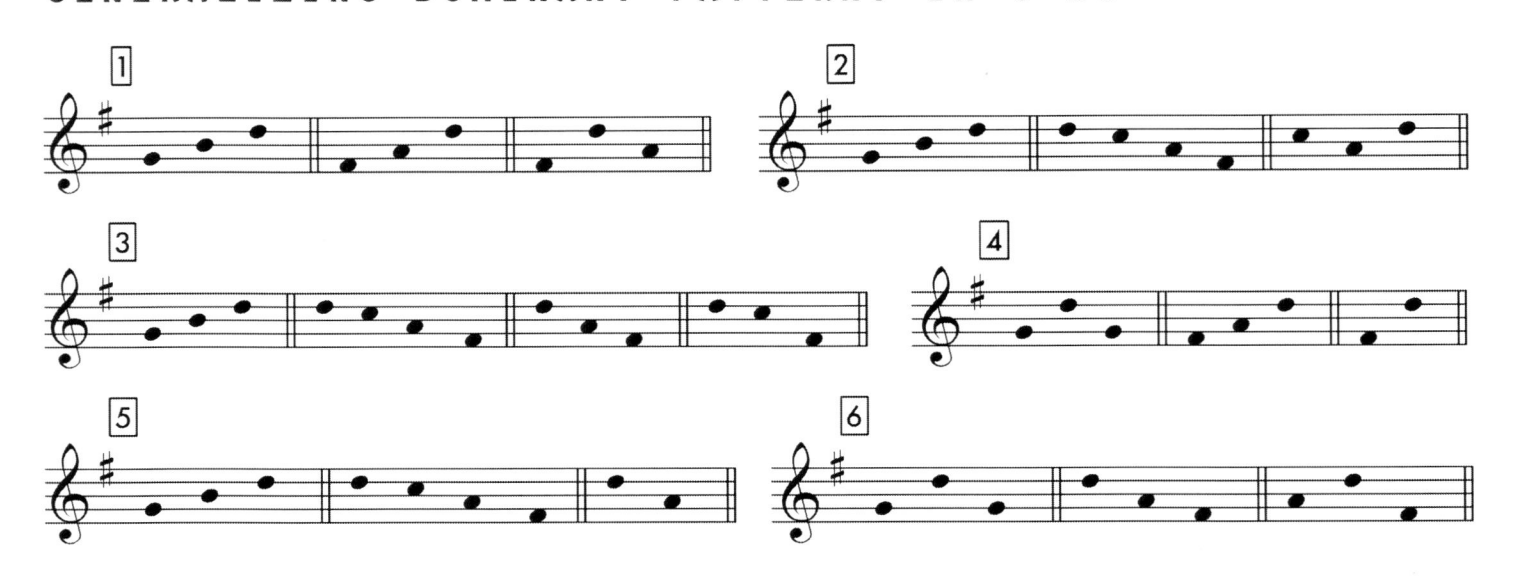

GENERALIZING DOMINANT PATTERNS IN A-DO

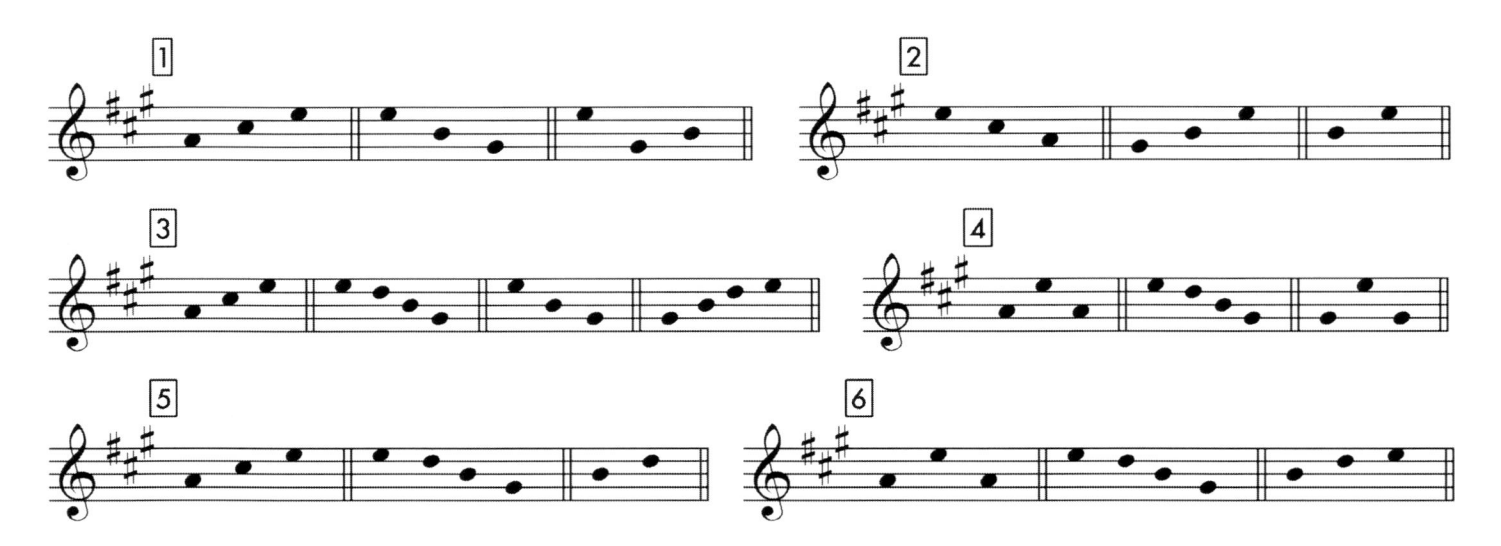

GENERALIZING DOMINANT PATTERNS IN Bb-DO

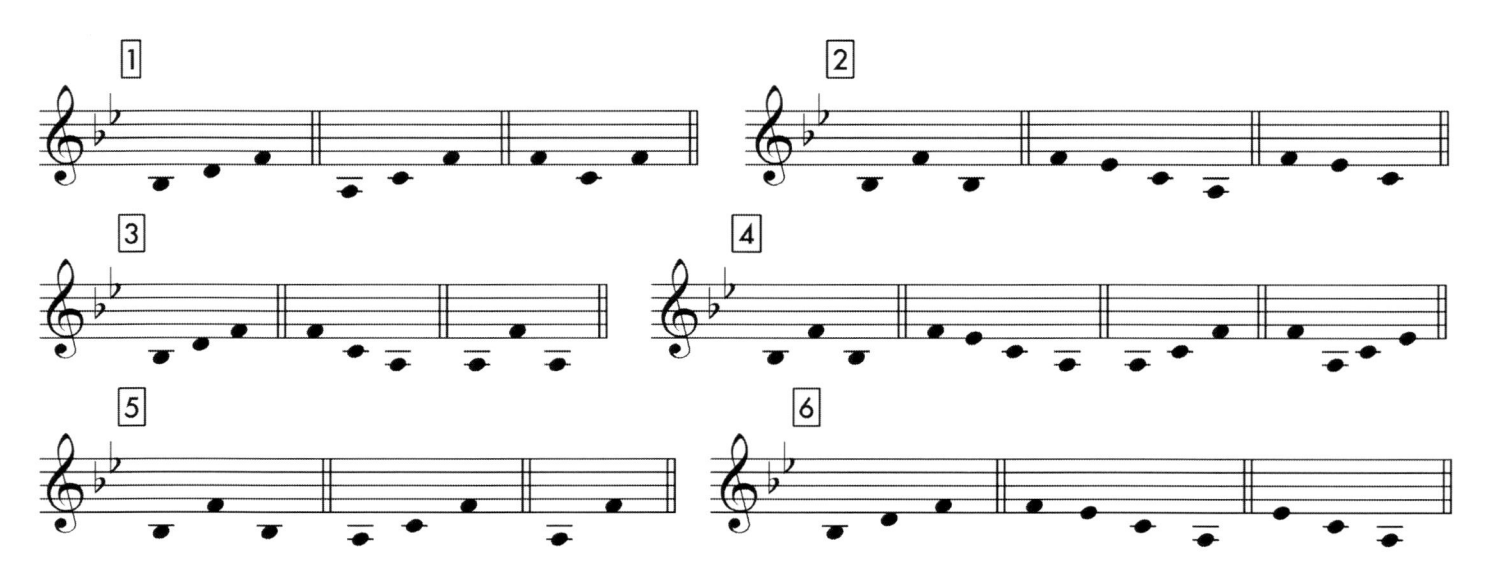

GENERALIZING DOMINANT PATTERNS IN C-DO

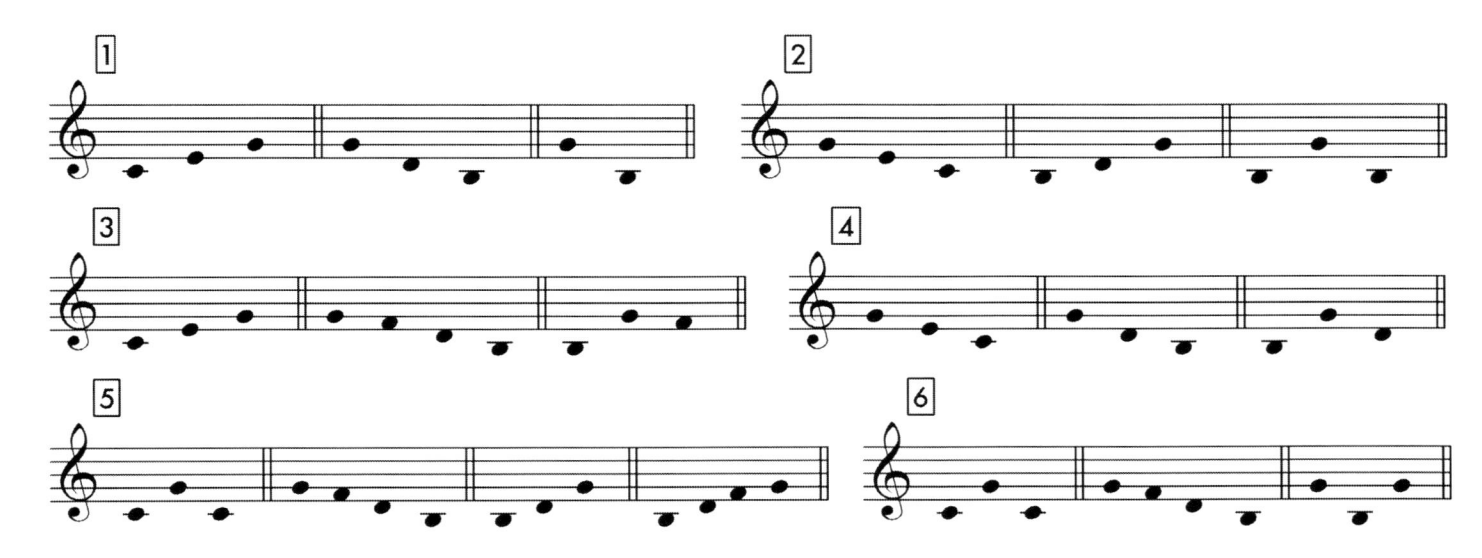

GENERALIZING DOMINANT PATTERNS IN D-DO

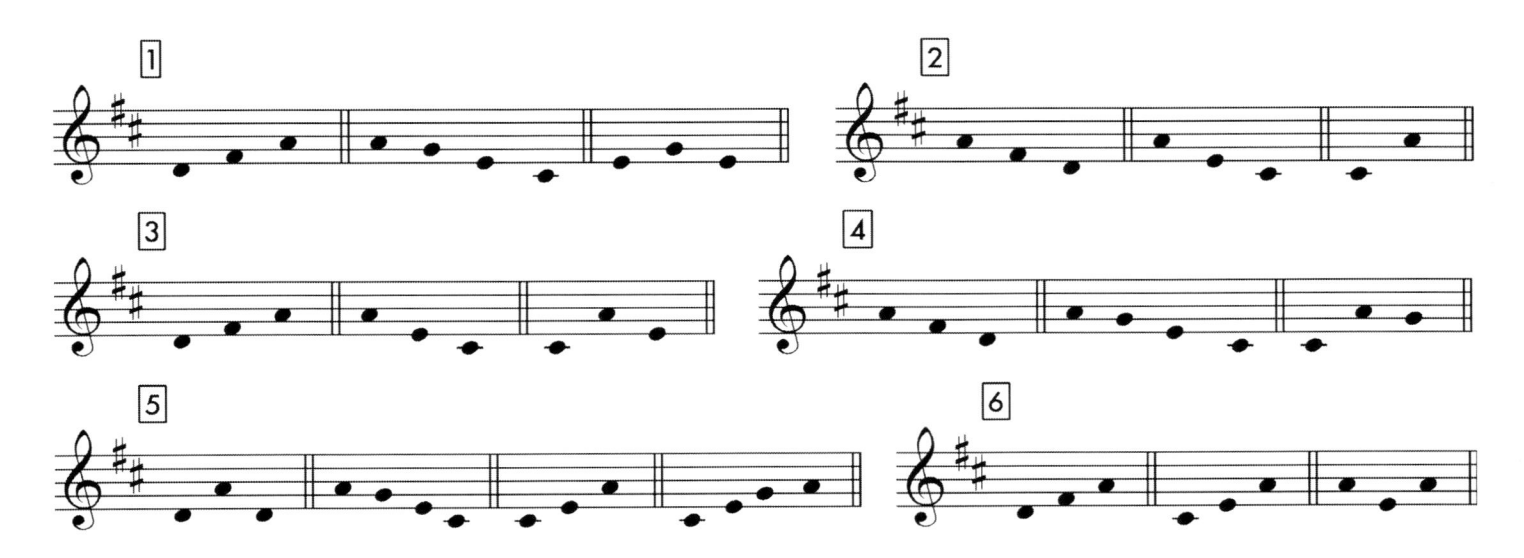

GENERALIZING DOMINANT PATTERNS IN Eb-DO

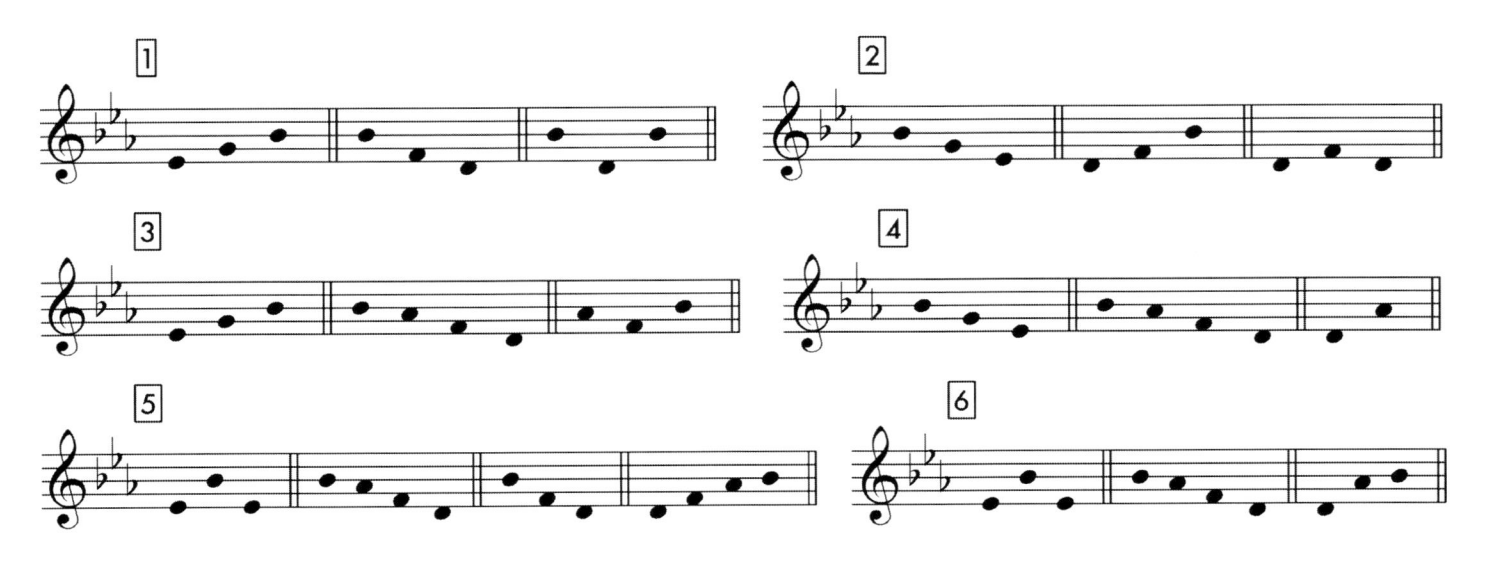

LESSON 4.7
COMBINING FAMILIAR AND UNFAMILIAR TONIC AND DOMINANT PATTERNS

FAMILIAR I & V PATTERNS, UNFAMILIAR ORDER

In preparation for **Reading Benchmark 4D**, read these **familiar** tonic and dominant patterns in all of our familiar key signatures in an unfamiliar order. Be sure to ground yourself in the key and tonality by playing a I-V-I on the keyboard before you read.

Try writing these four pattern sequences in several different DO-signatures. Remember: audiate, read, remove them from your view, and then write **from your audiation**.

FAMILIAR AND UNFAMILIAR I&V PATTERNS

Read these familiar **and unfamiliar** tonic and dominant patterns in all of our familiar keys. At least one pattern in each set will require generalization. Be patient, and remember that generalization is an inference skill, and will need persistence on your part.

PREPARING FOR BENCHMARK 4D

As you approach the upcoming Reading Benchmark, it may be a useful technique to include some annotations in your tonal analysis. As you scan the pitches of the melody, be on the lookout for familiar and unfamiliar tonic and dominant patterns. You may wish to **circle tonic patterns**, and **square dominant patterns** as in the example below.

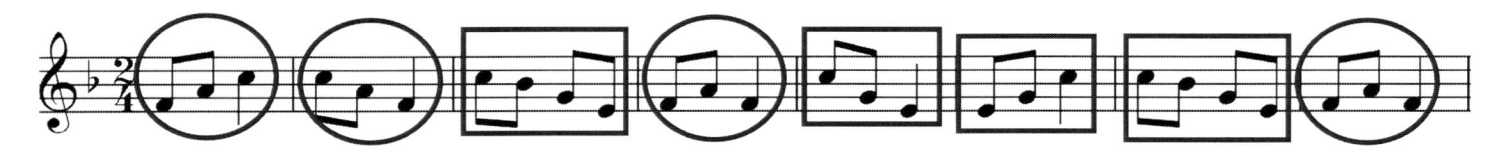

READING BENCHMARK 4D

Tonality = Major
Pitches = Tonic and Dominant Only
Keys = Bb, C, D, Eb, F, G, A

Meters = Duple and Triple
Time Signatures = 2/4, 4/4; 6/8, 3/4
Functions = Macro/microbeat and divisions

More Difficult Exercises

READING SEQUENCE 5

SEQUENCE 5 AT A GLANCE

Reading Content	
TONAL	**RHYTHM**
• Tonality: Major • Pitches: Tonic and Dominant; tDRMFSL • Keys: Bb, C, D, Eb, F, G, A	• Meters: Duple and Triple • Functions: Macro/Microbeats, Divisions and Elongations • Time Signatures: 2/4, 4/4, Cut Time; 6/8, 3/4

Lesson Sequence	
5.1 Tonal	The Letter System
5.2 Rhythm	The Math of Rhythm
5.3 Tonal	Combining Stepwise and Harmonic Patterns, Major Tonality
Reading Benchmark 5A • Major; Tonic/Dominant and tDRMFSL; Keys = C, D, Eb, F, G • Duple & Triple; Macro/micro and Divisions; 2/4, 4/4; 6/8, 3/4	
5.4 Rhythm	Elongations in Duple Meter; 2/4, 4/4, Cut Time
Reading Benchmark 5B • Major; Tonic chord and tDRMFSL; Keys = Bb, C, D, Eb, F, G, A • Duple; 2/4, 4/4 and Cut Time; Macro/Micro **and Elongations**	
5.5 Rhythm	Elongations in Triple Meter; 6/8, 3/4
Reading Benchmark 5C • Major; Tonic chord and tDRMFSL; Keys = Bb, C, D, Eb, F, G, A • Triple; 6/8 and 3/4; Macro/Micro **and Elongations**	
5.6 Rhythm	Longer Rhythm Patterns
Reading Benchmark 5D • Major; Tonic/Dominant and tDRMFSL; Keys = C, D, Eb, F, G • Duple & Triple; Macro/Micro, Divisions **and Elongations**; 2/4, 4/4, Cut Time; 6/8, 3/4	

LESSON 5.1
THE LETTER SYSTEM

Up to this point, we have been focused on using solfege (DO RE MI) as the main tonal system for communicating pitches and patterns, and using letters (A B C) only to indicate which DO is which. At some point, if you learn to play an instrument, you will also want to learn the **letter system** so you can communicate in a multitude of ways with other musicians who only know this system.

COMPARING THE TWO SYSTEMS

TONAL SOLFEGE
Solfege is a **movable system**, and represents pitches **in your audiation** within the context of a tonality. We can superimpose this audiation-based system into any key. As you have seen, we have C-DO, G-DO, F-DO, and so on.

THE LETTER SYSTEM
The letter system is a **fixed system** that connects to pitches on the staff (A B C D E F G, along with sharps and flats) and/or specific notes on an instrument. "A" will always be "A," regardless of the tonality.

CLEFS, LINES, SPACES AND LEDGER LINES

A **clef** will tell you where to place the letter system. Specifically, it will tell you what notes (A B C D E F, and in turn solfege) will fall on which **line** or **space**. **Ledger lines** extend the alphabet outside the confines of the **staff**.

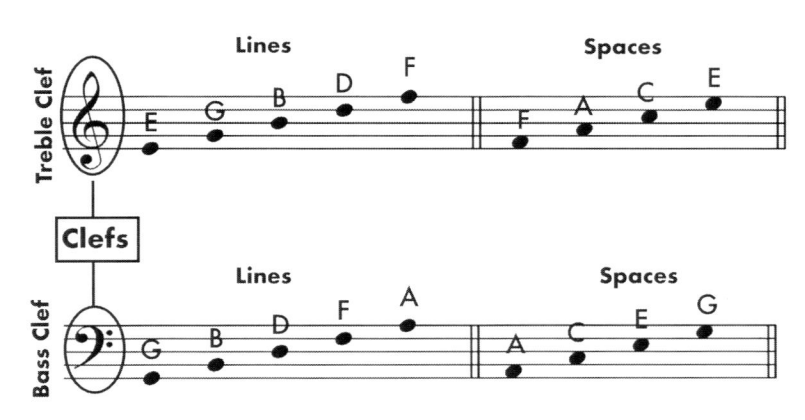

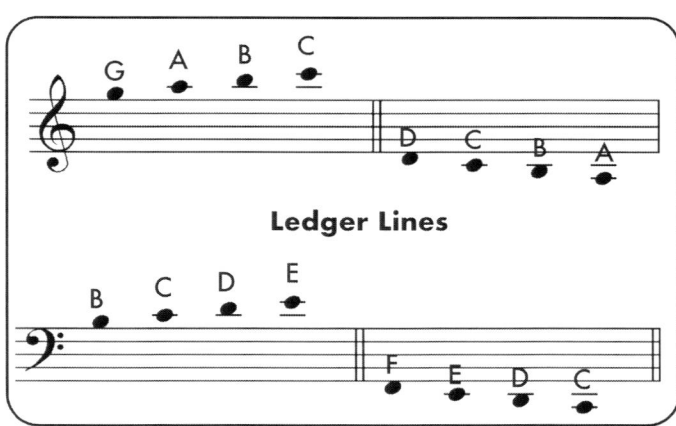

Below are the letters on the staff in four different octaves, and how they connect to the white keys of a piano keyboard. This **instrumental association** helps to organize pitches linearly.

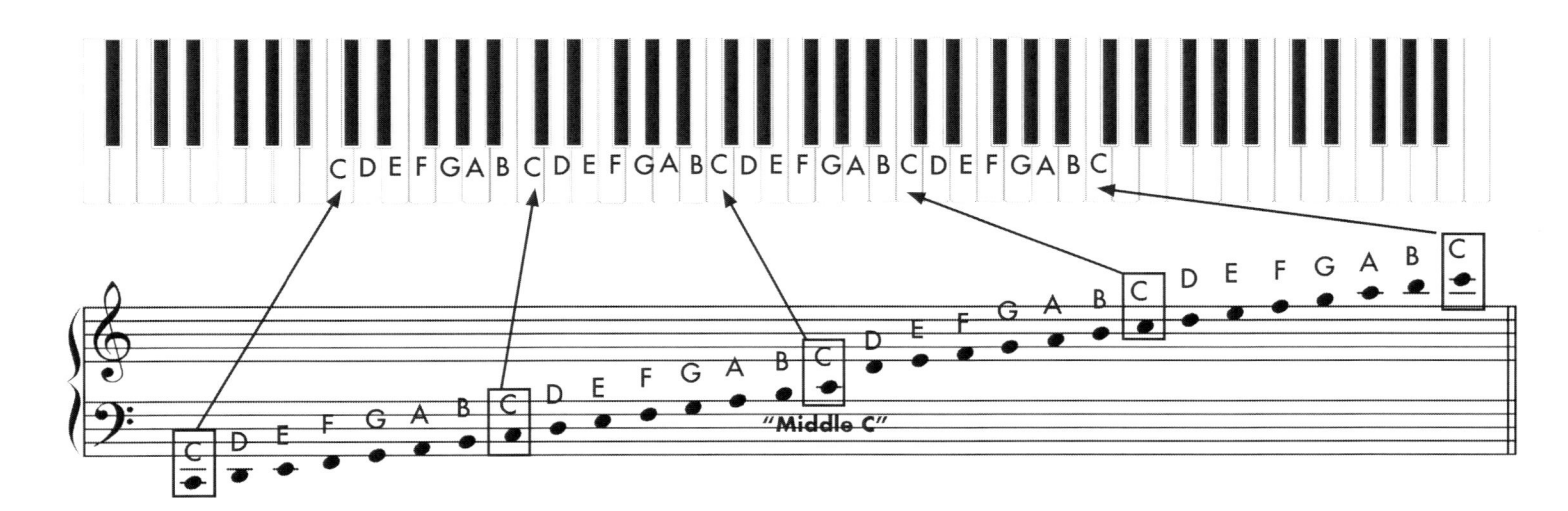

CHROMATIC NOTES

In addition to the note letters, you can add a sharp (#) or a flat (♭) after a note. A sharp **raises** a note by one half step and a flat **lowers** a note by one half step. A half step can be represented on a piano by moving from a white key to an adjacent black key, or a black key to an adjacent white key (or from the white keys B to C, or E to F).

! Notice that the same note could be called by two different names (Ab=G#, C#=Db, etc.).

CONNECTING THE TWO SYSTEMS

Eventually in your training as a musician, the **movable** solfege-based audiation system will come into contact with the letter-based **fixed** system. This will give you the freedom to navigate musical instruments (which can function on both the fixed and movable systems) with ease because you are **bringing audiation to the instrument**. As Dr. Gordon says, "An instrument is only an extension of your audiation."

For example, if you want to bring the pattern DO MI SO to an instrument, you will need to figure out **which** DO MI SO. Are you in C-DO? Bb-DO? Where do those pitches lie on the instrument? What fingerings will you use? What letters are represented by the pitches DO MI SO in each particular key? This is something that comes with practice and experience. But remember: **the learning of the movable audiation-based system should precede the learning of the fixed letter system.**

SOLFEGE TO LETTER CHARTS

Use these handy charts to help translate solfege into letter names in all keys.

Major Tonality

Solfege Key	DO	RE	MI	FA	SO	LA	TI	DO
C	C	D	E	F	G	A	B	C
C#	C#	D#	E#	F#	G#	A#	B#	C#
D	D	E	F#	G	A	B	C#	D
Eb	Eb	F	G	Ab	Bb	C	D	Eb
E	E	F#	G#	A	B	C#	D#	E
F	F	G	A	Bb	C	D	E	F
F#	F#	G#	A#	B	C#	D#	E#	F#
G	G	A	B	C	D	E	F#	G
Ab	Ab	Bb	C	Db	Eb	F	G	Ab
A	A	B	C#	D	E	F#	G#	A
Bb	Bb	C	D	Eb	F	G	A	Bb
B	B	C#	D#	E	F#	G#	A#	B

Minor Tonality

Solfege Key	LA	TI	DO	RE	MI	FA	SI	LA
Cm	C	D	Eb	F	G	Ab	B♮	C
C#m	C#	D#	E	F#	G#	A	B#	C#
Dm	D	E	F	G	A	Bb	C#	D
Ebm	Eb	F	Gb	Ab	Bb	C	D♮	Eb
Em	E	F#	G	A	B	C	D#	E
Fm	F	G	Ab	Bb	C	Db	E♮	F
F#m	F#	G#	A	B	C#	D	E#	F#
Gm	G	A	Bb	C	D	Eb	F#	G
G#m	G#	A#	B	C#	D#	E	F#	G#
Am	A	B	C	D	E	F	G#	A
Bbm	Bb	C	Db	Eb	F	Gb	A♮	Bb
Bm	B	C#	D	E	F#	G	A#	B

LESSON 5.2
THE MATH OF RHYTHM

Just as there was a movable tonal audiation system and a fixed system of letters, there is a movable rhythm audiational system (the rhythm solfege system that we have been learning throughout this book) and a fixed time-value system. It is useful to know both systems so that you can speak to other musicians who might only know one system, and so that you can understand the "why" of what you have been audiating.

THE TIME VALUE SYSTEM

Rhythm notes are given their names by their mathematical relationship to a whole note. A half note is called a half note because its mathematical value in the time continuum is half of a whole note. A quarter note is a quarter of a whole note, and so on. Depending upon the meter, any of the below notes can represent a macrobeat or a microbeat as long as the mathematical relationship is consistent. The diagram below shows the mathematical relationship between notes.

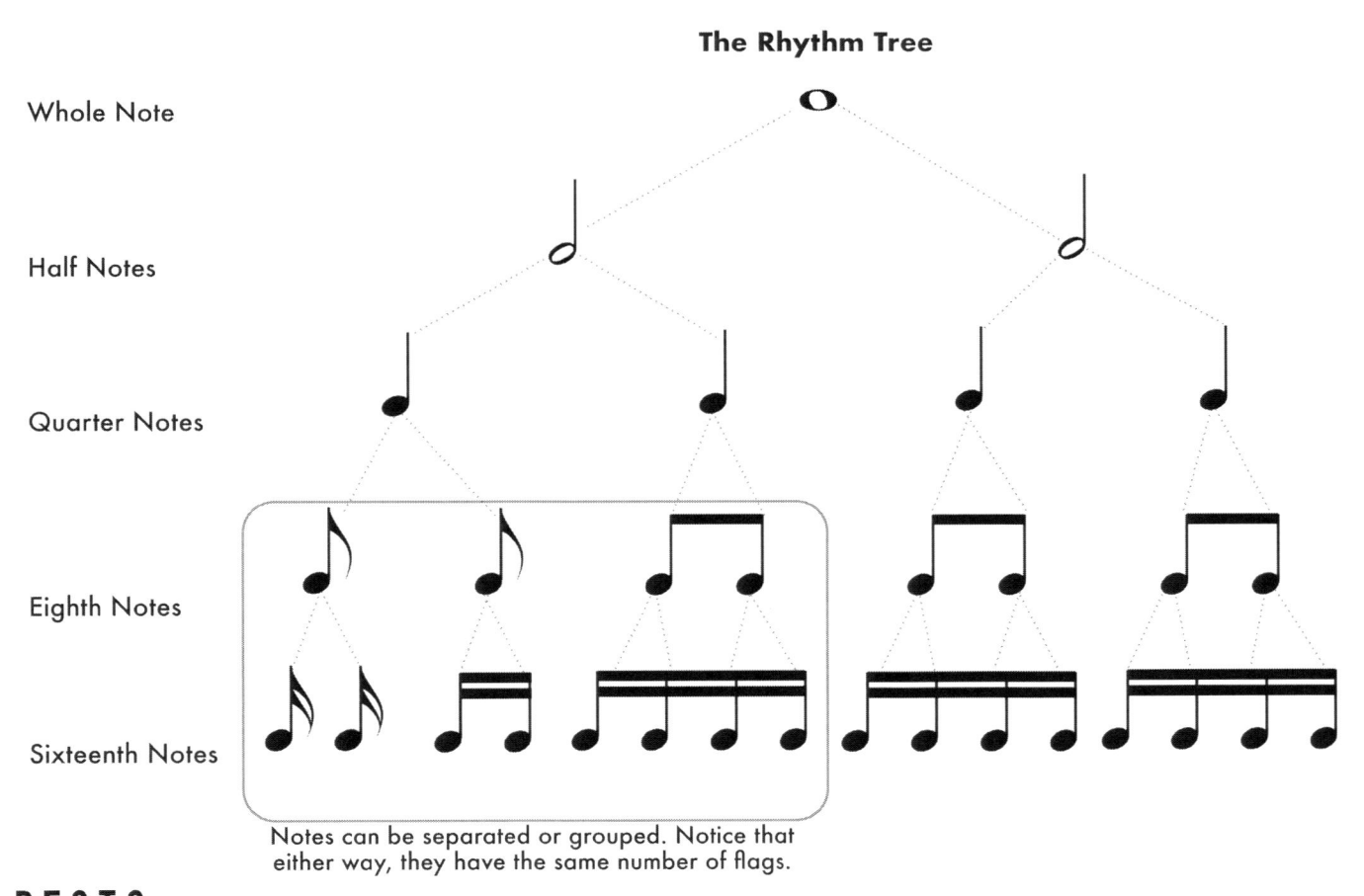

The Rhythm Tree

Whole Note

Half Notes

Quarter Notes

Eighth Notes

Sixteenth Notes

Notes can be separated or grouped. Notice that either way, they have the same number of flags.

RESTS

Although not covered extensively in this book, this what the equivalent rests for each note look like:

Time Value Names and Their Rests				
Whole Note	Half Note	Quarter Note	Eighth Note	Sixteenth Note
𝅝	𝅗𝅥	♩	♪	♬
Whole Note Rest	Half Note Rest	Quarter Note Rest	Eighth Note Rest	Sixteenth Note Rest
𝄻	𝄼	𝄽	𝄾	𝄿

LESSON 5.3
COMBINING STEPWISE AND HARMONIC PATTERNS
MAJOR TONALITY

FAMILIAR PATTERNS

Before we combine rhythm patterns and unfamiliar stepwise patterns and harmonic patterns in **Reading Benchmark 5A**, we will first combine **familiar** stepwise and harmonic patterns in the exercises below.

Try writing these four pattern sequences in several different DO-signatures. Remember: audiate, read, remove them from your view, and then write **from your audiation**.

Lesson 5.3 **181**

FAMILIAR AND UNFAMILIAR PATTERNS

Use the skill of generalization to read the patterns below. These examples will contain familiar **and unfamiliar** harmonic patterns, as well as familiar and unfamiliar stepwise patterns.

PREPARING FOR BENCHMARK 5A

As you did for Reading Benchmark 4D, you may wish to **circle tonic patterns**, and **square dominant patterns** like in the example below. If the melody is stepwise, leave it blank.

READING BENCHMARK 5A

Tonality = Major
Pitches = Tonic/Dominant and tDRMFSL
Keys = Bb, C, D, Eb, F, G, A
Meters = Duple and Triple
Time Signatures = 2/4, 4/4; 6/8, 3/4
Functions = Macro/microbeat and divisions

More Difficult Exercises

LESSON 5.4
ELONGATIONS IN DUPLE METER
TIME SIGNATURES: 2/4, 4/4, CUT TIME

REVIEW

Take a moment to review macrobeats and microbeats in duple meter. Say the following chant to yourself: "**Macrobeats** in duple meter are DU DU DU DU. **Microbeats** in duple meter are DU DE, DU DE, DU DE, DU DE." Then, review our 4 elongation patterns on p. 48.

READING ELONGATIONS IN 2/4 AND 4/4

Since we can elongate a macrobeat or a microbeat (or later, a division!), elongations can take on a different appearance. Let's see what our four elongation patterns in duple meter look like in the time signature 2/4 and 4/4. Look at the notation for each of these rhythm cells, and chant them along with the video as you are looking at the notation.

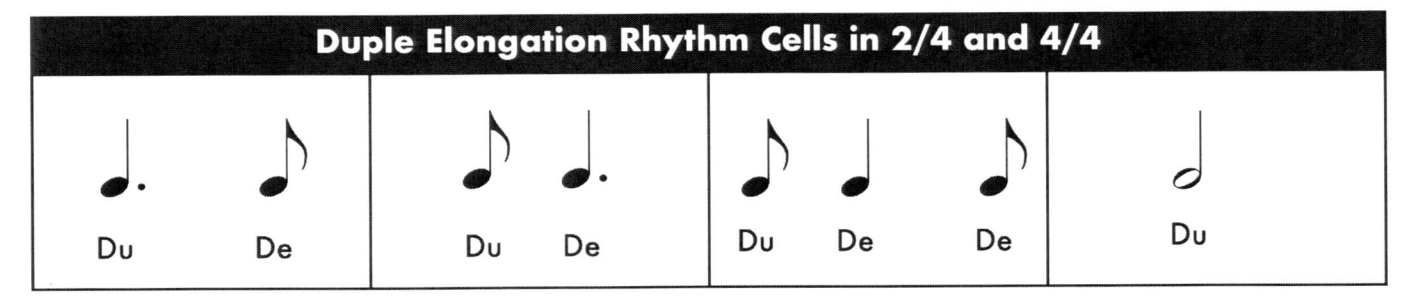

Duple Elongation Rhythm Cells in 2/4 and 4/4			
♩. ♪	♪ ♩.	♪ ♪ ♪	𝅗𝅥
Du De	Du De	Du De De	Du

MOVEMENT REMINDER

As you are chanting elongation patterns, it is particularly important that you **move**. The reason it is especially important to move is because you won't have the luxury of hearing every macrobeat and microbeat. You will need to **audiate** some. Moving is a great reminder that rhythm is **felt in the body** before it is understood by the brain.

Try some of the movement experiences from p. 35. In particular:
- Move to macrobeats and microbeats concurrently with your heels and hands.
- Try flowing your arms as if you were treading water in a pool. Your body will teach your brain the amount of **space** each elongation pattern takes.
- Then, try adding microbeat wrist flicks on top of your "flow."

THEORETICAL UNDERSTANDING OF A DOT

After you can read these patterns, it is sometimes useful to know the "why" behind certain concepts. In music theory terms, a dot represent the mathematical equivalent of half of the note. So, a dotted quarter note is the mathematical equivalent of a quarter note plus an eighth note. (See Lesson 5.2 for an explanation of the time value system.) Aren't you glad you know this?!

READING RHYTHM PATTERNS

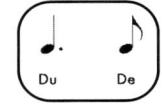

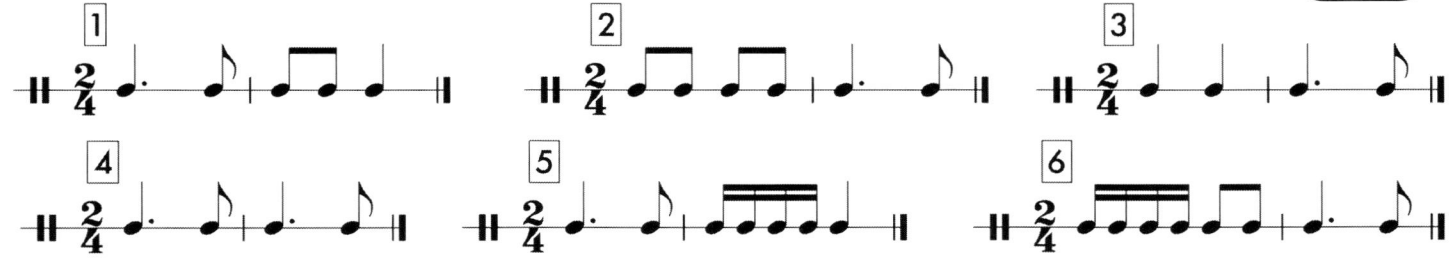

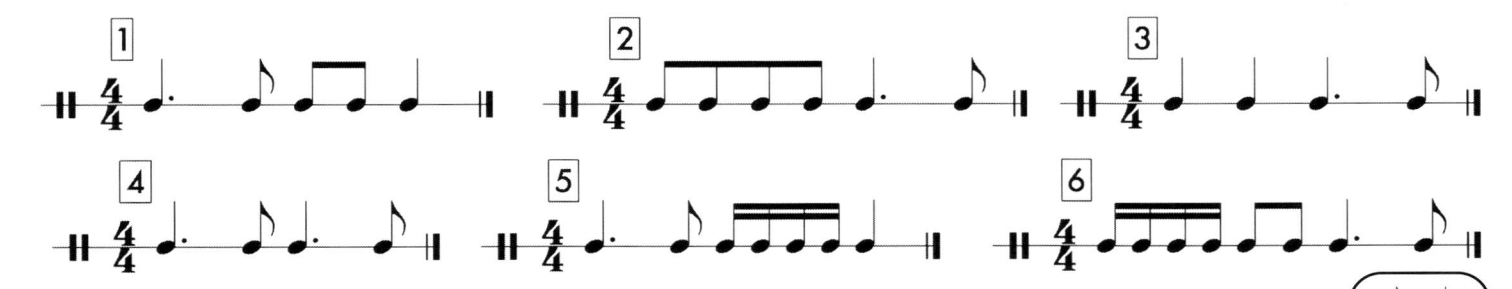

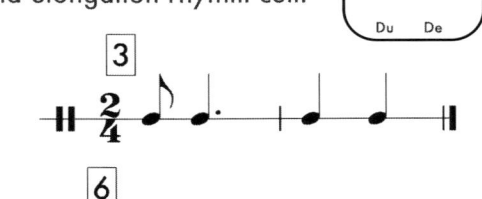

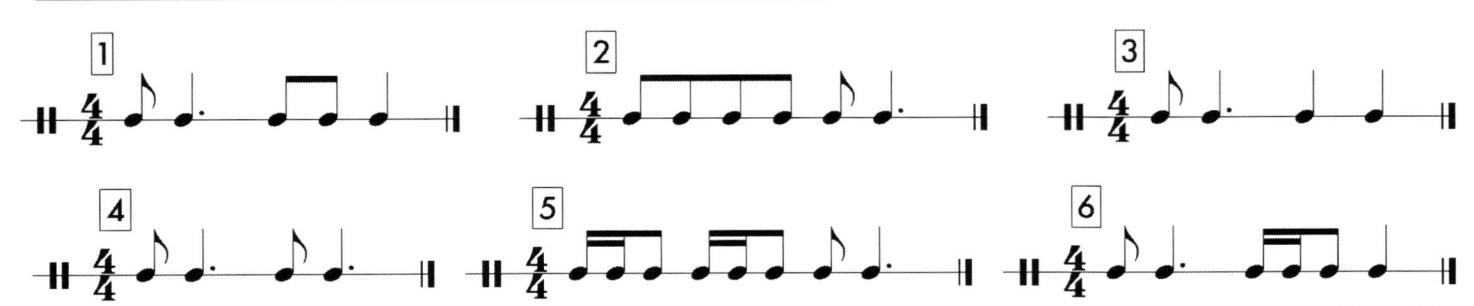

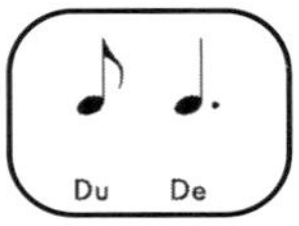

Read these rhythm patterns with macrobeats, microbeats, divisions and the first elongation rhythm cell:

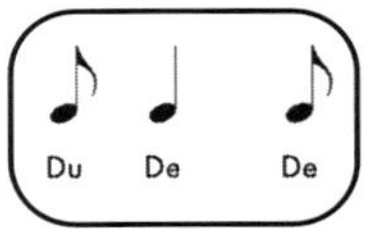

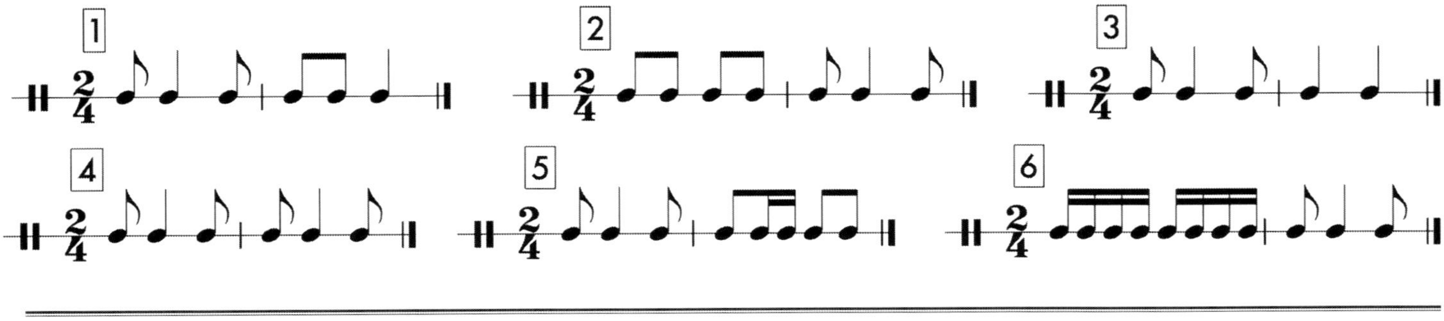

186 The Literate Musician

Read these rhythm patterns with macrobeats, microbeats, divisions and the fourth elongation rhythm cell:

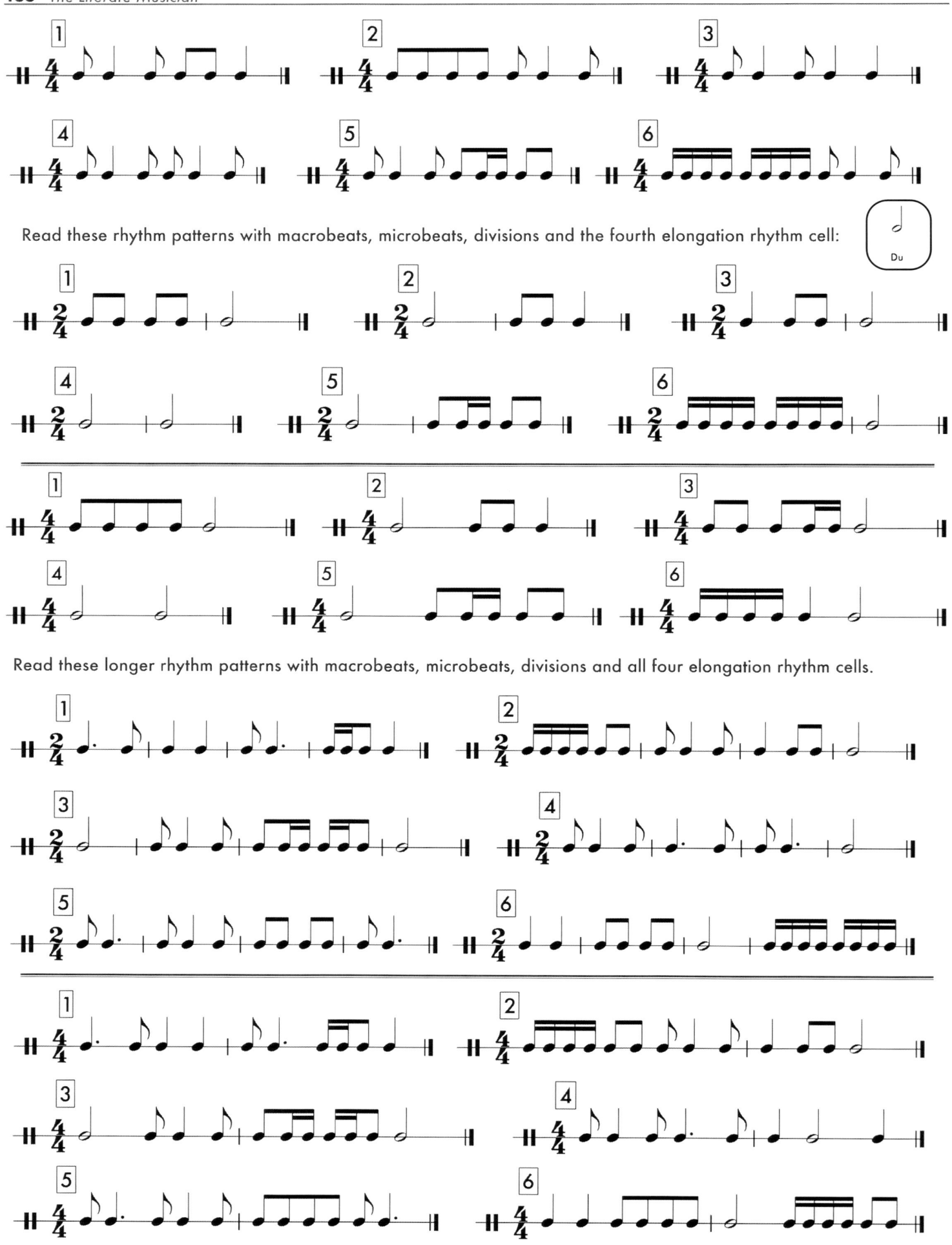

Read these longer rhythm patterns with macrobeats, microbeats, divisions and all four elongation rhythm cells.

Lesson 5.4 **187**

READING ELONGATIONS IN CUT TIME

These enrhythmic rhythm patterns will sound the same as the 2/4 and 4/4 patterns. However they will be notated differently. As a reminder, in cut time, the half note is our macrobeat; quarter notes are our microbeat; and eighth notes are our divisions. Here are the elongation rhythm cells in Cut Time:

Duple Elongation Rhythm Cells in Cut Time			
𝅗𝅥. 𝅘𝅥	𝅘𝅥 𝅗𝅥.	𝅘𝅥 𝅗𝅥 𝅘𝅥	𝅝
Du De	Du De	Du De De	Du

READING RHYTHM PATTERNS

Read these rhythm patterns with macrobeats, microbeats, divisions and the first elongation rhythm cell: [𝅗𝅥. 𝅘𝅥 / Du De]

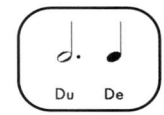

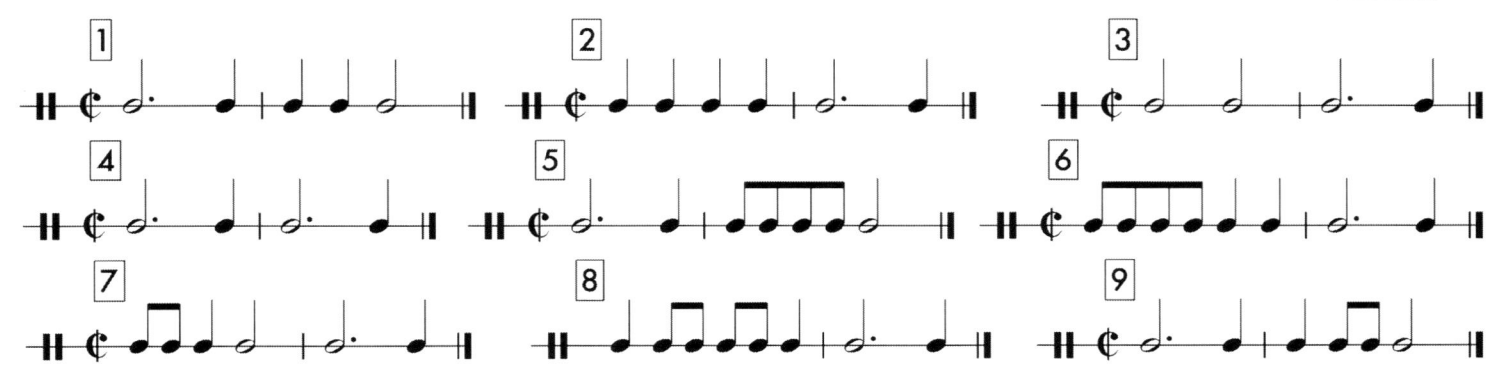

1.
2.
3.
4.
5.
6.
7.
8.
9.

Read these rhythm patterns with macrobeats, microbeats, divisions and the second elongation rhythm cell: [𝅘𝅥 𝅗𝅥. / Du De]

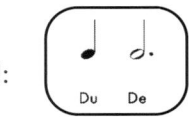

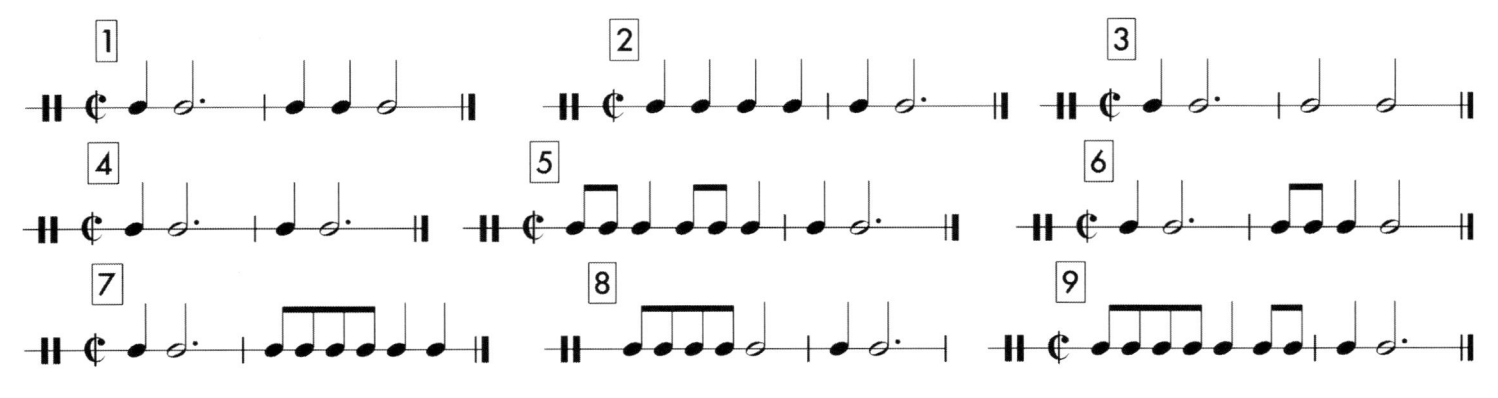

1.
2.
3.
4.
5.
6.
7.
8.
9.

188 *The Literate Musician*

Read these rhythm patterns with macrobeats, microbeats, divisions and the third elongation rhythm cell:

Read these rhythm patterns with macrobeats, microbeats, divisions and the fourth elongation rhythm cell:

Read these longer rhythm patterns with macrobeats, microbeats, divisions and all four elongation rhythm cells.

As usual, any time you learn to read a new rhythmic function, try writing both the individual rhythm cells and rhythm patterns **from your audiation**.

READING BENCHMARK 5B

Tonality = Major
Pitches = Tonic/Dominant and tDRMFSL
Keys = Bb, C, D, Eb, F, G, A
Meters = Duple
Time Signatures = 2/4, 4/4, Cut Time
Functions = Macro/microbeat and elongations

LESSON 5.5
ELONGATIONS IN TRIPLE METER
TIME SIGNATURES: 6/8 & 3/4

REVIEW

Take a moment to review macrobeats and microbeats in triple meter. Say the following chant to yourself: "**Macrobeats** in triple meter are DU DU DU DU. **Microbeats** in triple meter are DU DA DI, DU DA DI, DU DA DI, DU DA DI." Then, review our 3 elongation patterns on p. 49.

READING ELONGATIONS IN 6/8

Just as we did in duple meter, we can elongate a macrobeat or a microbeat (or later, a division!). Therefore, elongations can take on a different appearance. Let's see what our 3 elongation patterns in triple meter look like in the time signature 6/8. Look at the notation for each of these rhythm cells, and chant them along with the video as you are looking at the notation.

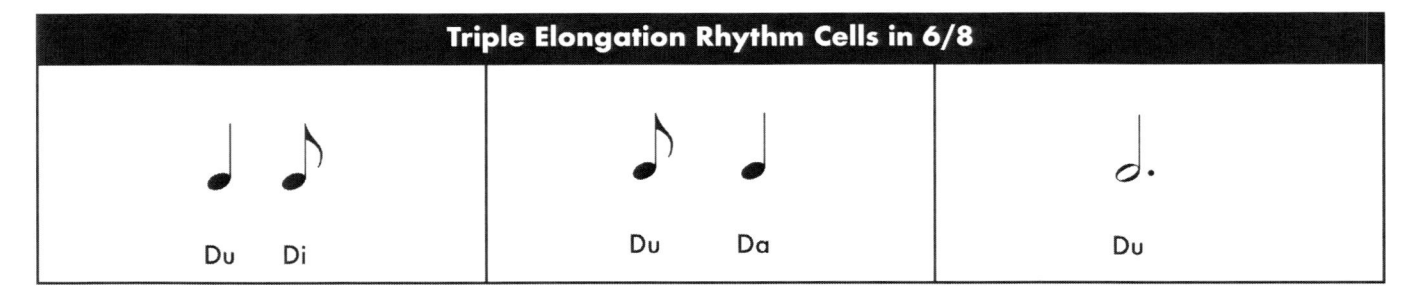

Triple Elongation Rhythm Cells in 6/8
♩ ♪   ♪ ♩   ♩.
Du Di   Du Da   Du

MOVEMENT REMINDER

Just as you did with duple elongations, as you are chanting triple patterns, it is particularly important that you **move**. There is a lot of space between notes with elongations, so movement helps as a timekeeper as you are learning to internalize macrobeats and microbeats in your audiation.

READING RHYTHM PATTERNS

Read these rhythm patterns with macrobeats, microbeats, divisions and the first elongation rhythm cell:

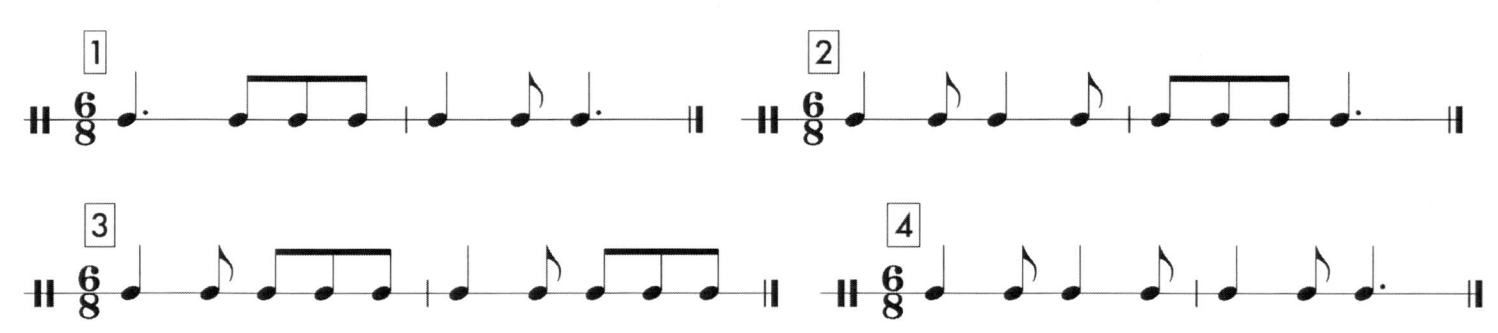

Read these rhythm patterns with macrobeats, microbeats and the second elongation rhythm cell:

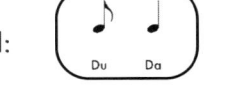

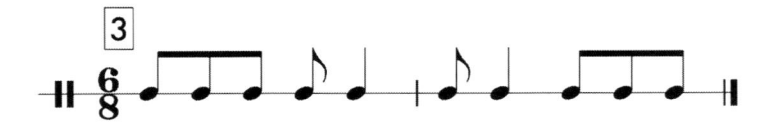

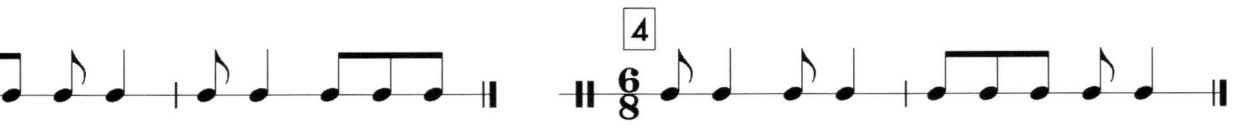

Read these rhythm patterns with macrobeats, microbeats and the third elongation rhythm cell:

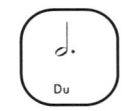

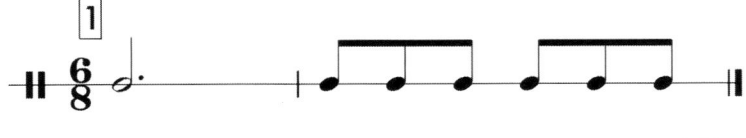

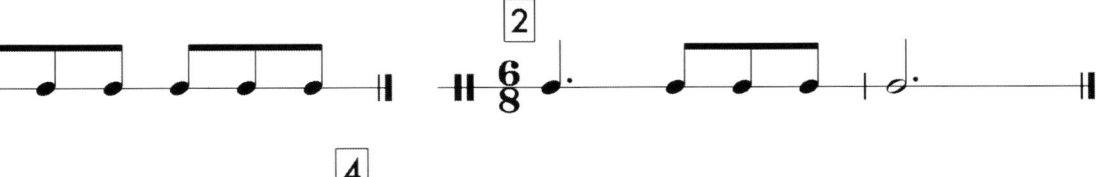

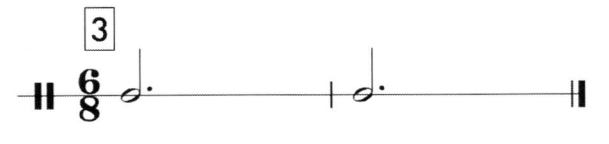

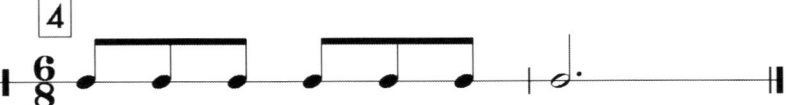

Read these rhythm patterns with macrobeats, microbeats and all three elongation rhythm cells:

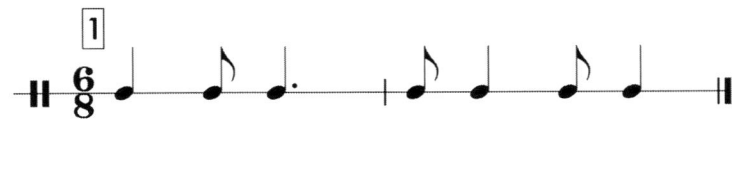

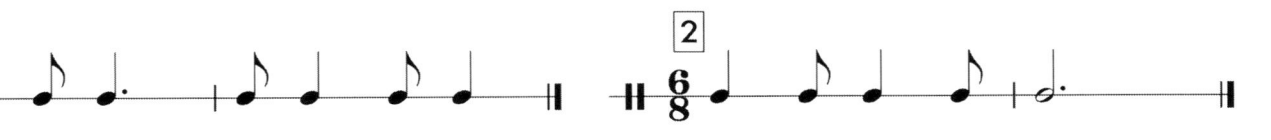

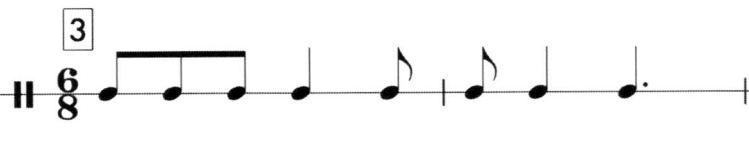

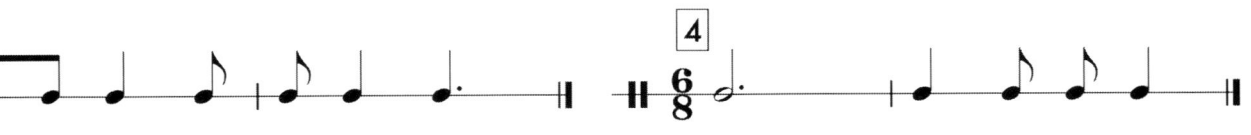

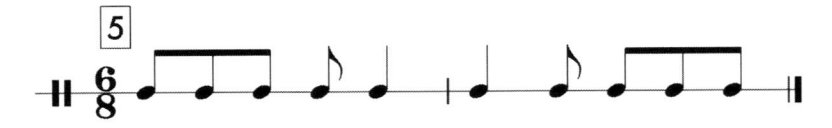

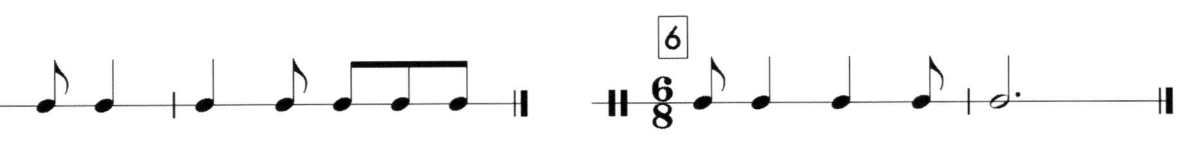

Read these rhythm patterns with macrobeats, microbeats, divisions and all three elongation rhythm cells:

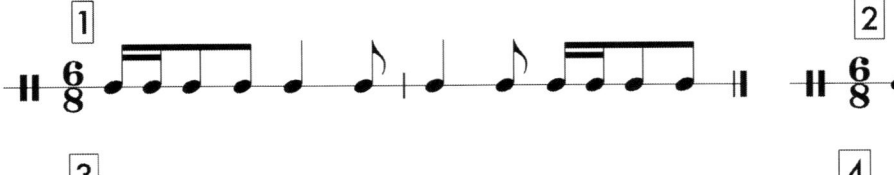

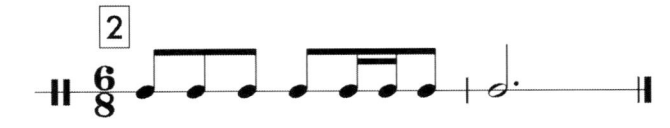

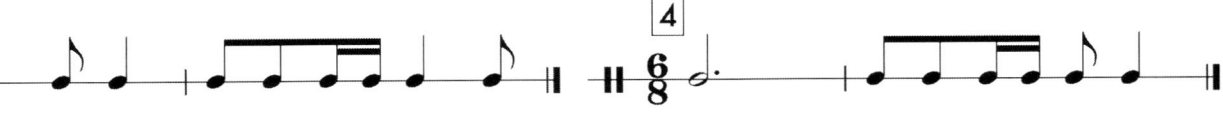

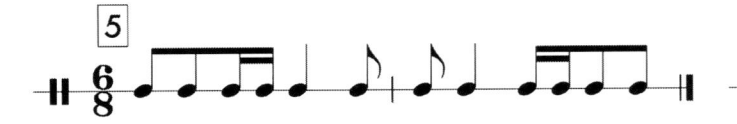

READING ELONGATIONS IN 3/4

These enrhythmic rhythm patterns will sound the same as the 6/8 patterns. However they will be notated differently. As a reminder, in 3/4 time, the dotted half note is the macrobeat; quarter notes are the microbeats; and eighth notes are the divisions.

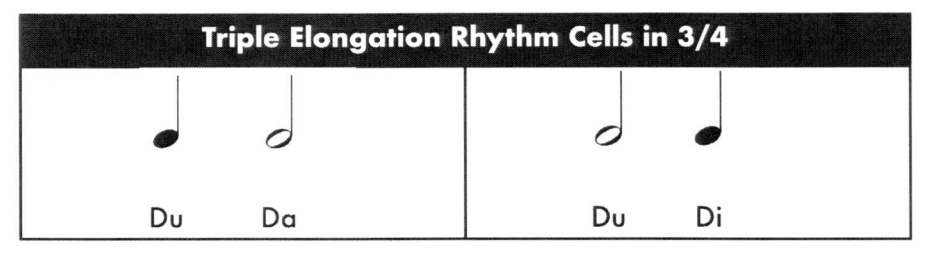

Triple Elongation Rhythm Cells in 3/4

Du Da

Du Di

Read these rhythm patterns with macrobeats, microbeats and the first elongation rhythm cell:

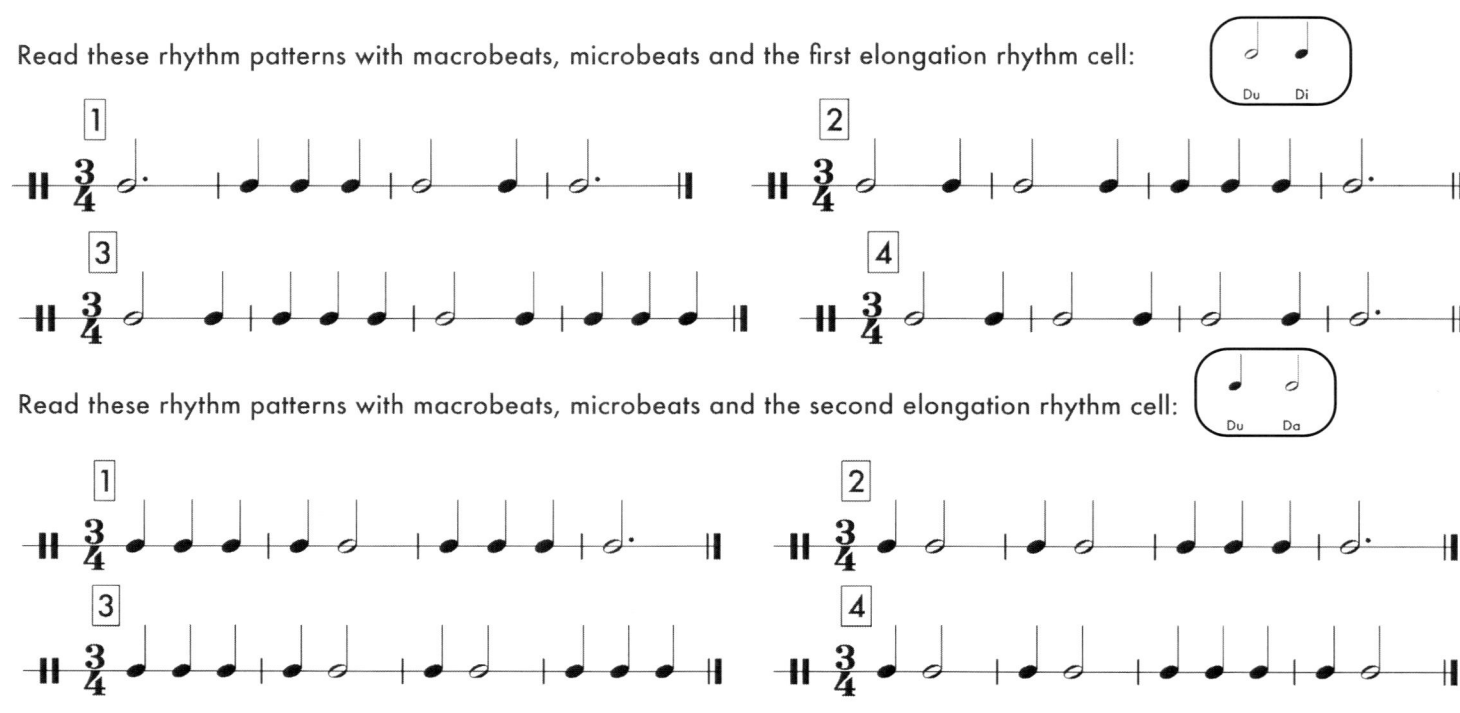

Read these rhythm patterns with macrobeats, microbeats and the second elongation rhythm cell:

Read these rhythm patterns with macrobeats, microbeats, divisions and both elongation rhythm cells:

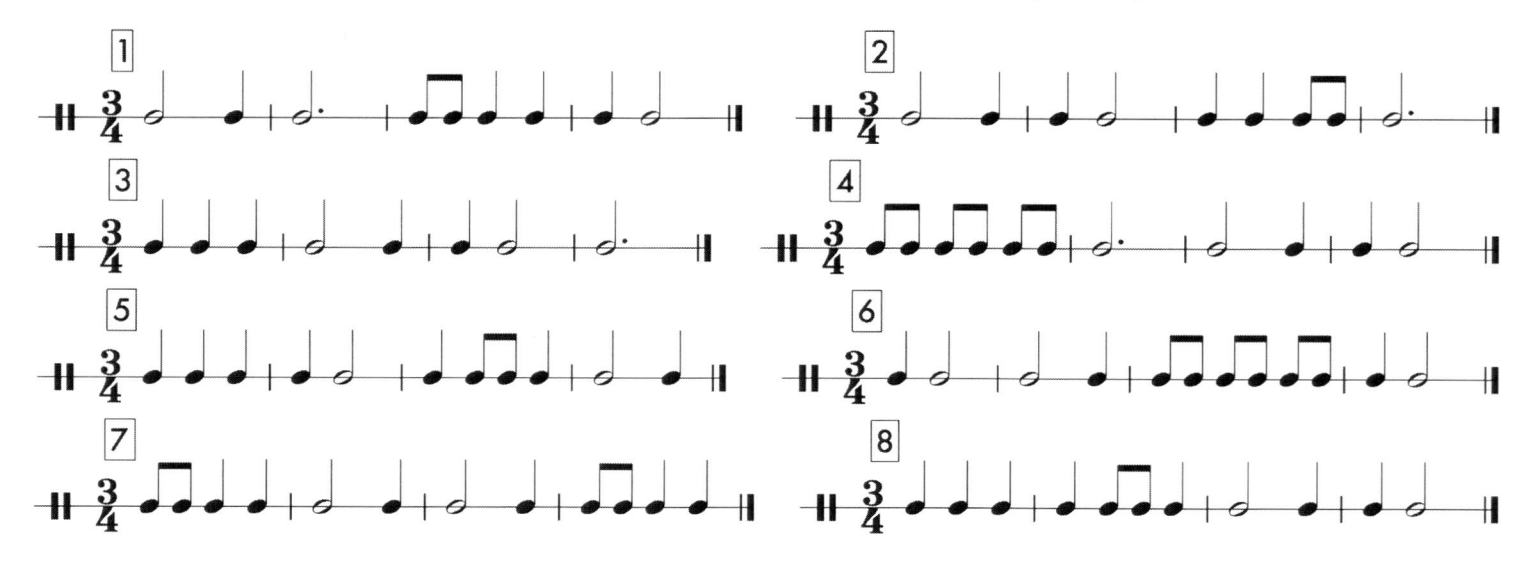

As usual, any time you learn to read a new rhythmic function, try writing both the individual rhythm cells and rhythm patterns **from your audiation**.

READING BENCHMARK 5C

Tonality = Major
Pitches = Tonic/Dominant and tDRMFSL
Keys = Bb, C, D, Eb, F, G, A
Meters = Triple
Time Signatures = 6/8, 3/4
Functions = Macro/microbeat and elongations

LESSON 5.6
LONGER RHYTHM PATTERNS
ALL PREVIOUS METERS AND FUNCTIONS

Before we combine tonal patterns and rhythms in **Reading Benchmark 5D**, it is a good idea to review all of the rhythm patterns and time signatures we have learned. Read these longer rhythm patterns in all of our previously learned meters, time signatures with macrobeats, microbeats, divisions and elongations.

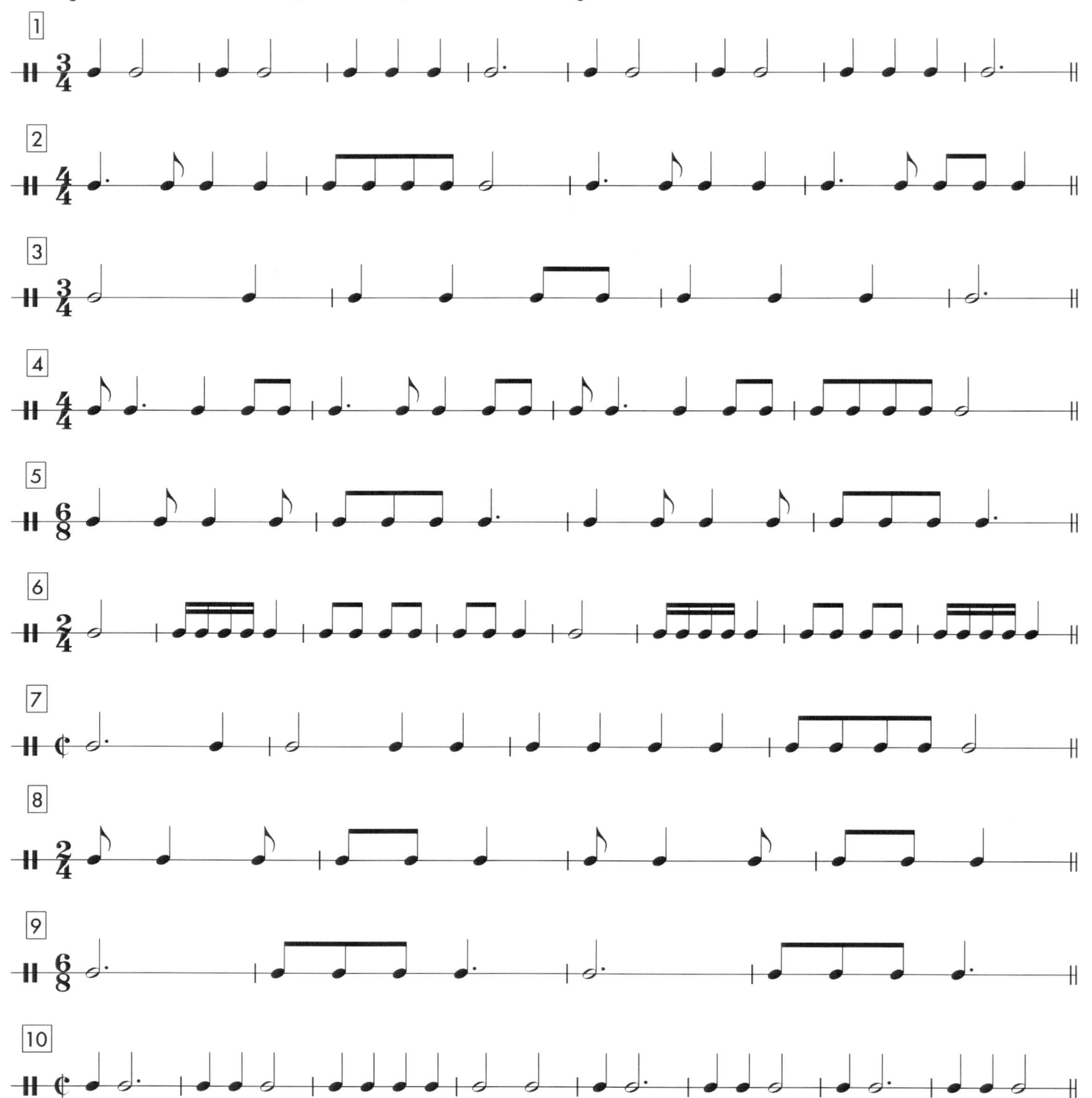

Lesson 5.6 **195**

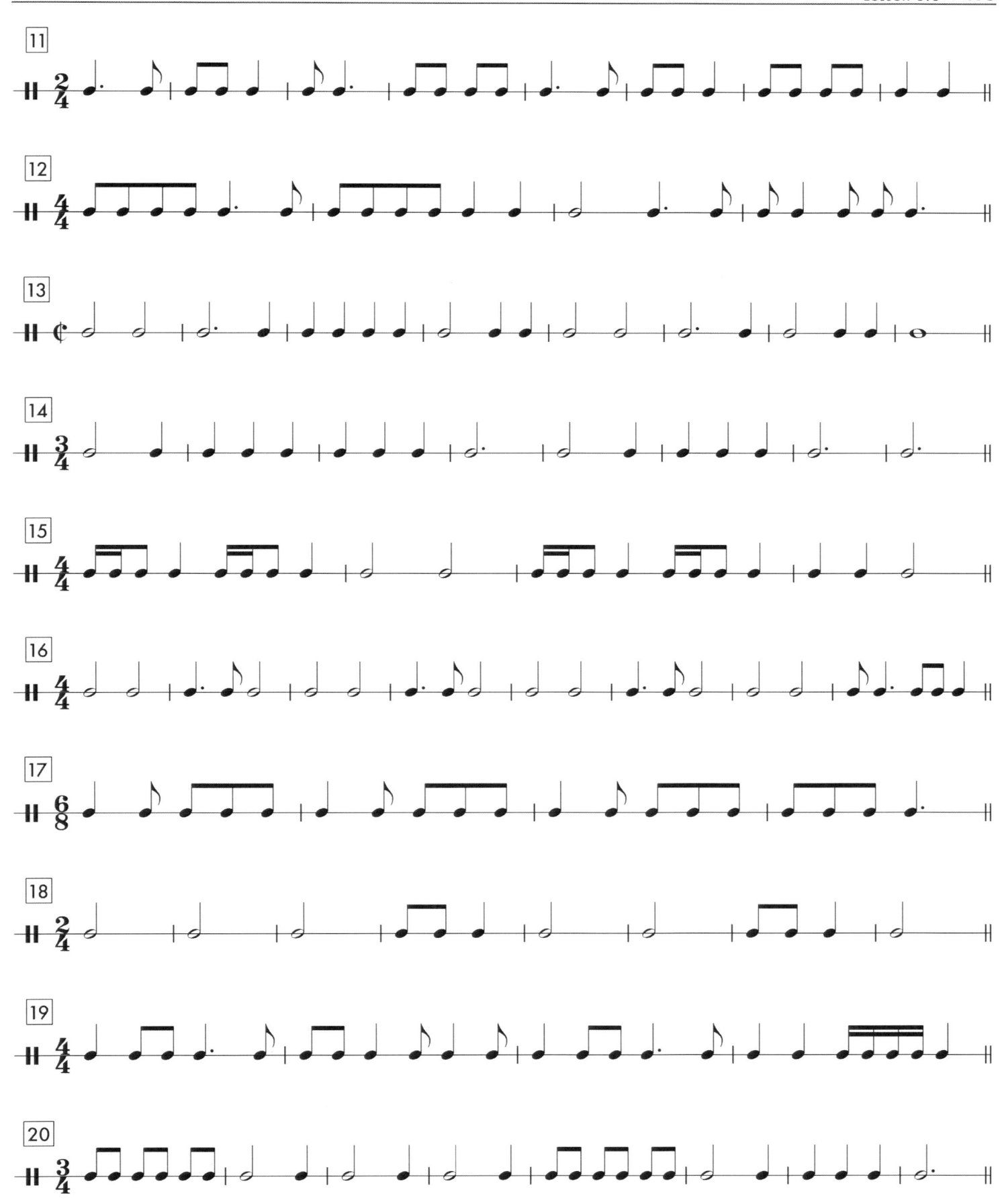

Add pitches to these longer rhythmic sentences and turn into composition.

READING BENCHMARK 5D

Tonality = Major
Pitches = Tonic/Dominant and tDRMFSL
Keys = Bb, C, D, Eb, F, G, A
Meters = Duple and Triple
Time Signatures = 2/4, 4/4; 6/8, 3/4
Functions = Macro/microbeat, divisions and elongations

Tonic and Dominant Only

tDRMFSL and Tonic

tDRMFSL and Tonic/Dominant

READING SEQUENCE 6

SEQUENCE 6 AT A GLANCE

Reading Content	
TONAL	**RHYTHM**
• Tonality: Minor • Pitches: Tonic • Keys: Em and Gm	• Meters: Duple and Triple • Functions: Macro/Microbeats, Divisions, Elongations and Division/Elongations • Time Signatures: 2/4, 4/4, Cut Time; 6/8, 3/4

Lesson Sequence	
6.1 Tonal	Minor Harmonic FPIFO
6.2 Tonal	Tonic Patterns, Minor Tonality
6.3 Tonal	Generalizing New Minor Tonic Patterns
Reading Benchmark 6A • Minor; Tonic Only; Keys = Em and Gm • Duple & Triple; Macro/micro; 2/4, 4/4; 6/8, 3/4	
6.4 Rhythm	Division/Elongations in Duple Meter; 2/4, 4/4, Cut Time
Reading Benchmark 6B • Duple; 2/4, 4/4 and Cut Time; Macro/Micro **and Elongations**	
6.5 Rhythm	Division/Elongations in Triple Meter; 6/8, 3/4
Reading Benchmark 6C • Triple; 6/8 and 3/4; Macro/Micro **and Elongations**	
6.6 Rhythm	Longer Rhythm Patterns
Reading Benchmark 6D • Major; Tonic/Dominant and tDRMFSL; Keys = C, D, Eb, F, G • Duple & Triple; Macro/Micro, Divisions, Elongations **and Division/Elongations**; 2/4, 4/4, Cut Time; 6/8, 3/4	
Reading Benchmark 6E • Minor; Tonic Only; Keys = Em and Gm • Duple & Triple; Macro/Micro, Divisions, Elongations **and Division/Elongations**; 2/4, 4/4, Cut Time; 6/8, 3/4	

LESSON 6.1
MINOR HARMONIC "FPIFO"

In Reading lesson 1.4, we read our familiar patterns in familiar order in major tonality. Let us proceed in a similar fashion in minor tonality.

DO-SIGNATURES IN MINOR TONALITY

Just as we used DO-signatures to tell us where DO is in major tonality, we will use them to tell us where LA (our resting tone) is in minor tonality. So theoretically, you could also consider them **LA-signatures**.

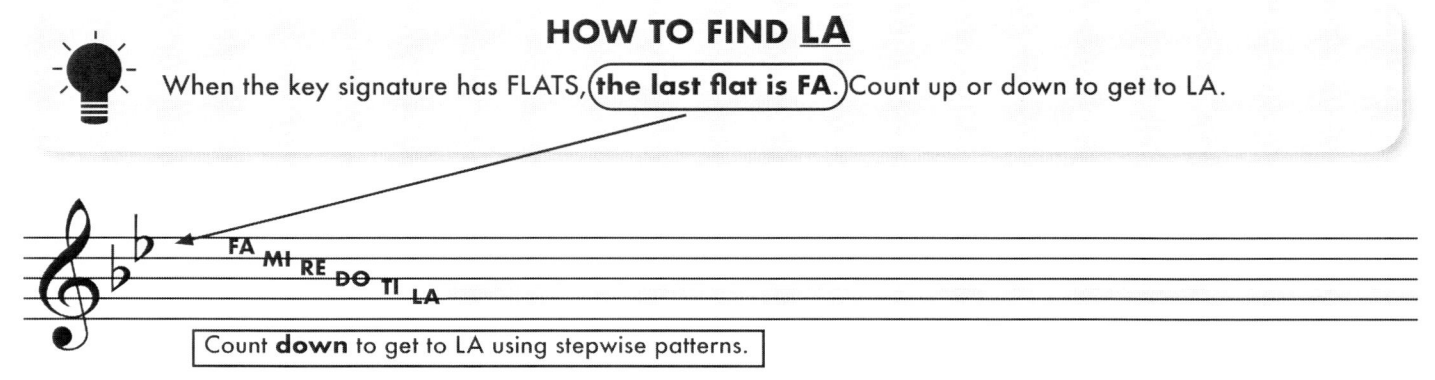

HOW TO FIND LA
When the key signature has FLATS, the last flat is FA. Count up or down to get to LA.

Count **down** to get to LA using stepwise patterns.

G-LA

Just as you did in major tonality, realize that you can think about harmonic patterns happening in two directions: **vertically and horizontally.** When you conceive of a harmonic function vertically, the individual pitches happen concurrently, and you have a chord (as if you strummed a chord on the ukulele). This is what our initial tonic and dominant chords look like when conceived **vertically** in G-LA.

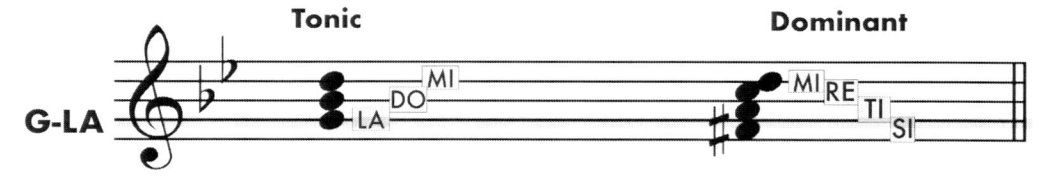

You can also conceive of the pitches of these patterns happening **horizontally**, one after the after, as when you echoed the patterns.

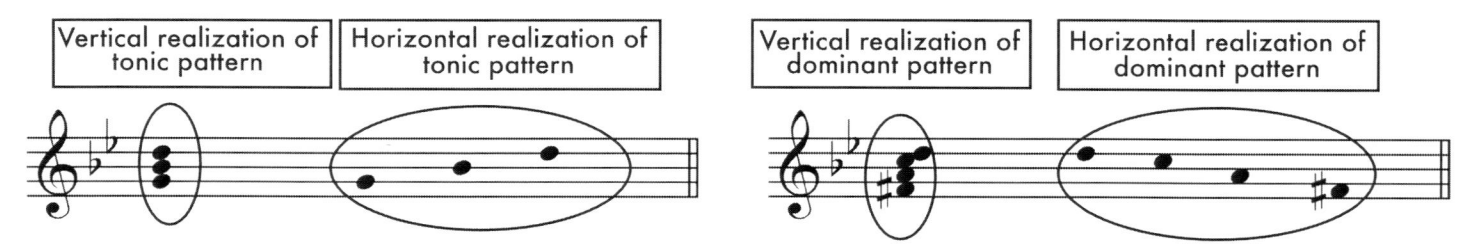

| Vertical realization of tonic pattern | Horizontal realization of tonic pattern | Vertical realization of dominant pattern | Horizontal realization of dominant pattern |

Regardless of whether they are played together (as in a chord strummed on a ukulele) or performed pitch by pitch, they should still be audiated as a gestalt, as one harmonic function.

Strum a Gm (tonic) and D7 (dominant) on the ukulele to hear the gestalt sound. Sing **LA DO MI** as you strum tonic, and **MI RE TI SI** as you strum dominant.

Lesson 6.1 **201**

FAMILIAR PATTERNS IN FAMILIAR ORDER (FPIFO)

Below are the familiar patterns in their familiar order (FPIFO) in minor tonality with G as LA. Engage with these patterns in the following ways.

- Watch the Patterns Only video from Part I, and as you echo each pattern, point to the notation.
- Watch the Tonal Pattern Recital video from Part I, and point to each pattern as you sing.

G-LA, Minor, i&V FPIFO

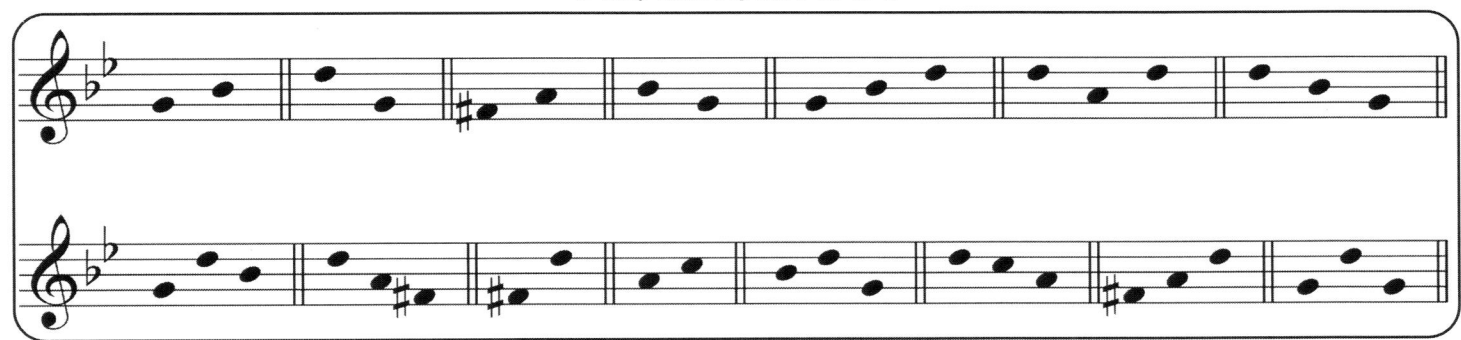

E-LA

Follow the same procedures in E-LA.

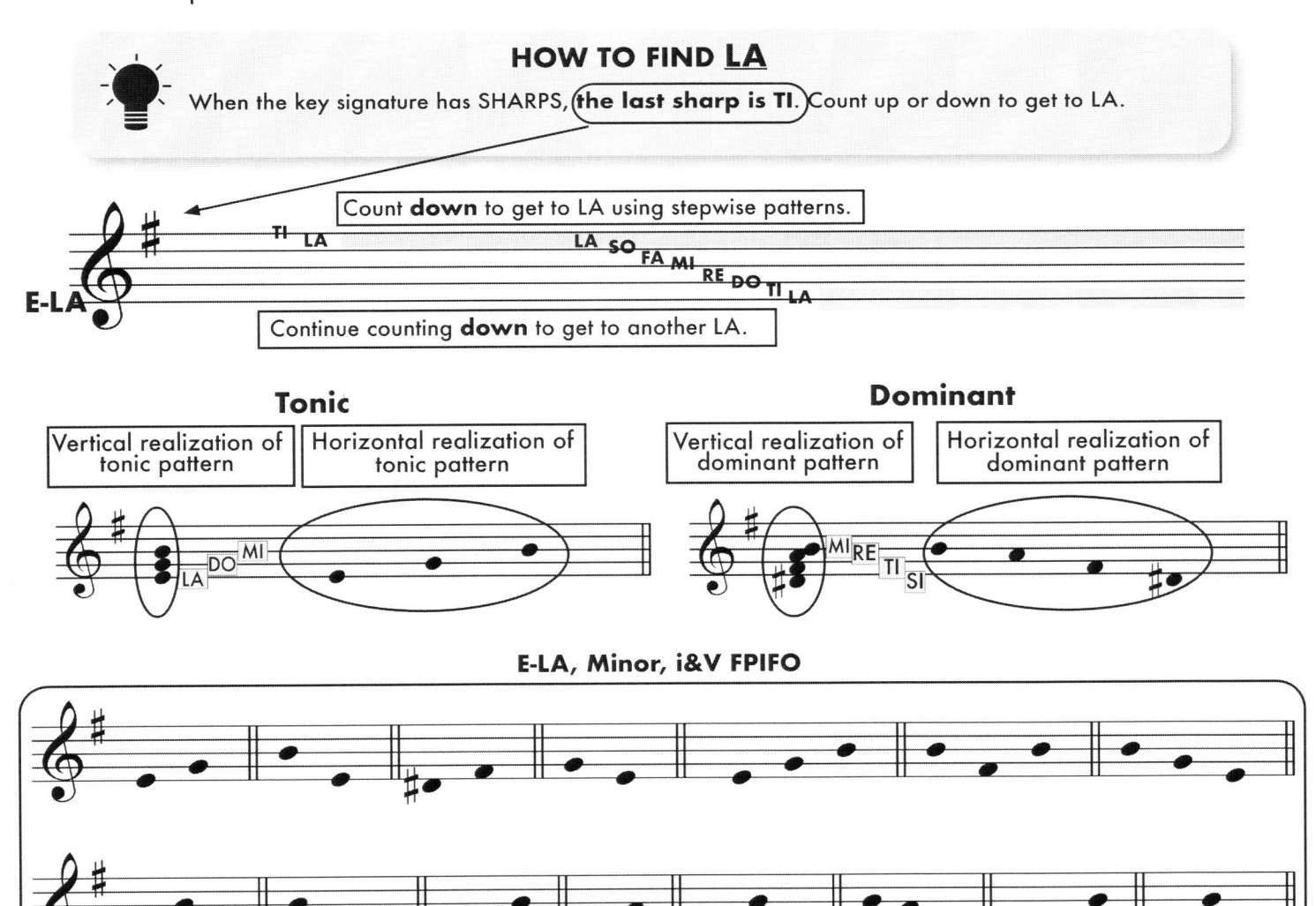

HOW TO FIND LA

When the key signature has SHARPS, **the last sharp is TI**. Count up or down to get to LA.

Count **down** to get to LA using stepwise patterns.

TI LA   LA SO FA MI RE DO TI LA

E-LA

Continue counting **down** to get to another LA.

Tonic

| Vertical realization of tonic pattern | Horizontal realization of tonic pattern |

LA DO MI

Dominant

| Vertical realization of dominant pattern | Horizontal realization of dominant pattern |

MI RE TI SI

E-LA, Minor, i&V FPIFO

LESSON 6.2
TONIC PATTERNS, MINOR TONALITY

We will learn to read harmony in minor tonality in a very similar way that we learned harmony in major tonality: First, we will learn tonic patterns by rote, and learn to generalize new ones. Then, we will do the same with dominant patterns, first learning by rote, and then through generalization. Then, we will combine tonic and dominant patterns.

THREE TONIC PATTERNS: LA DO MI, MI DO LA, LA MI LA

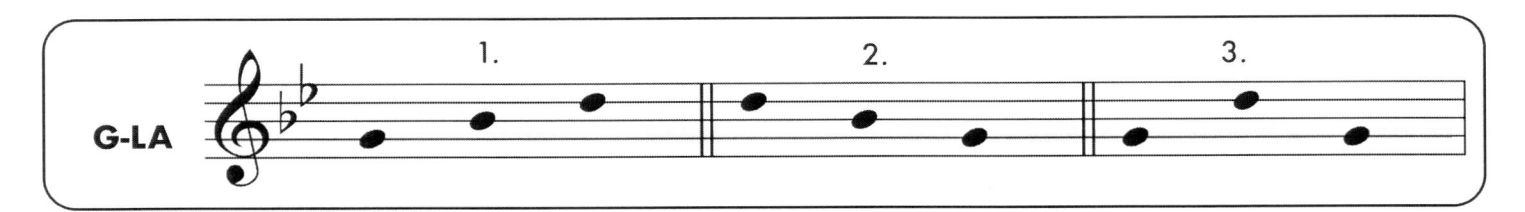

Establish minor tonality (MI FA MI RE DO TI SI LA) with **G as LA**. The first pattern is **LA DO MI**. Look at the notation, take a breath and sing **LA DO MI**. Just as you did when you echoed the patterns, keep the pitches separated. The second pattern is **MI DO LA**. Look at the notation, take a breath and sing **MI DO LA**. The third pattern is **LA MI LA**. Look at the notation, take a breath and sing **LA MI LA**.

! If you need an aural reminder of these 3 patterns, review them in the companion course ! videos. Remember: we are learning to read **familiar patterns**.

When you read a minor tonic pattern, take note of where each pitch is on the staff **in relation to LA**.

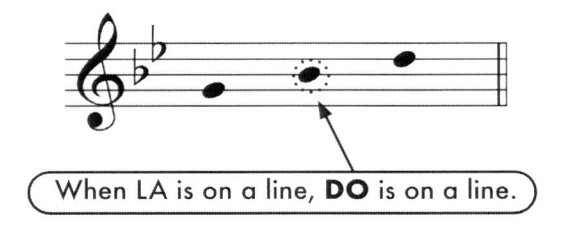

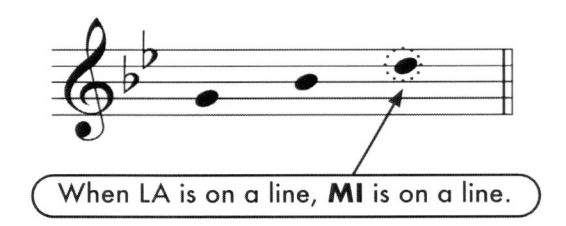

When LA is on a line, **DO** is on a line.

When LA is on a line, **MI** is on a line.

FAMILIAR PATTERNS, UNFAMILIAR ORDER

Read the same three familiar patterns in G-LA, but this time, read them in an unfamiliar order.

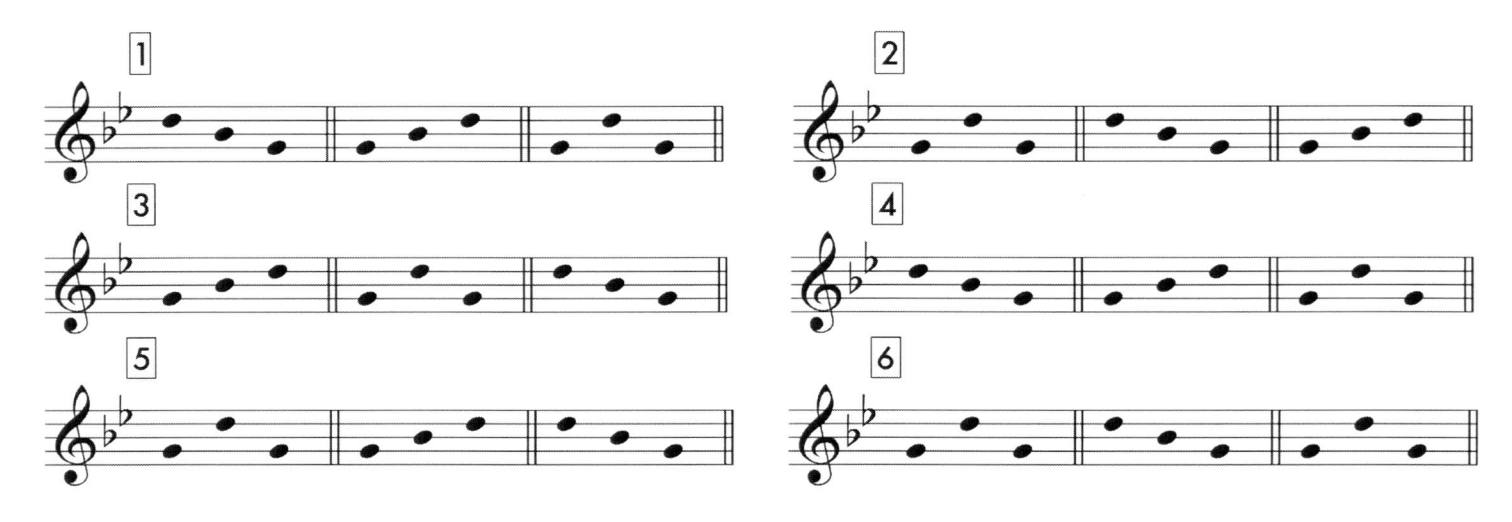

SAME PATTERNS IN E-LA

It bears repeating that when you read the same patterns in new LA-signatures, the patterns look the same in relation to themselves, however, they just start in different places on the staff. Let's learn to read those same 3 patterns in E-LA.

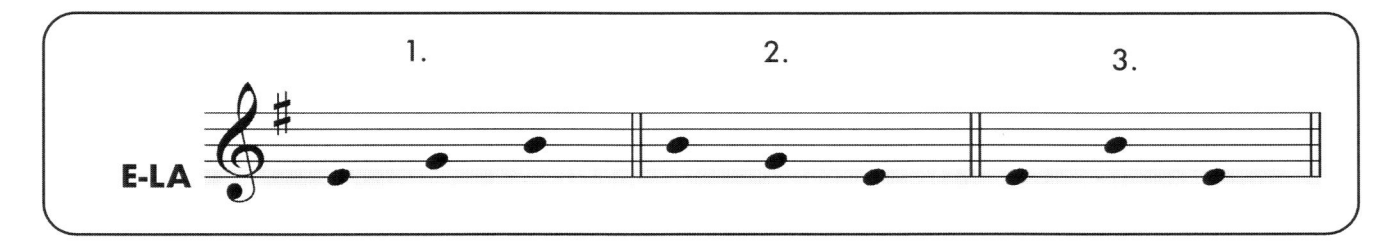

In E-LA, **LA,** the resting tone, is on a line. Take note of where each pitch is on the staff **in relation to LA**.

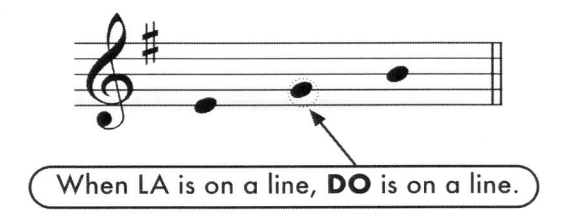

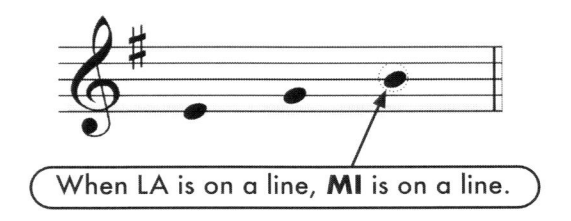

When LA is on a line, **DO** is on a line.

When LA is on a line, **MI** is on a line.

Read these familiar harmonic patterns in unfamiliar order in **E-LA.**

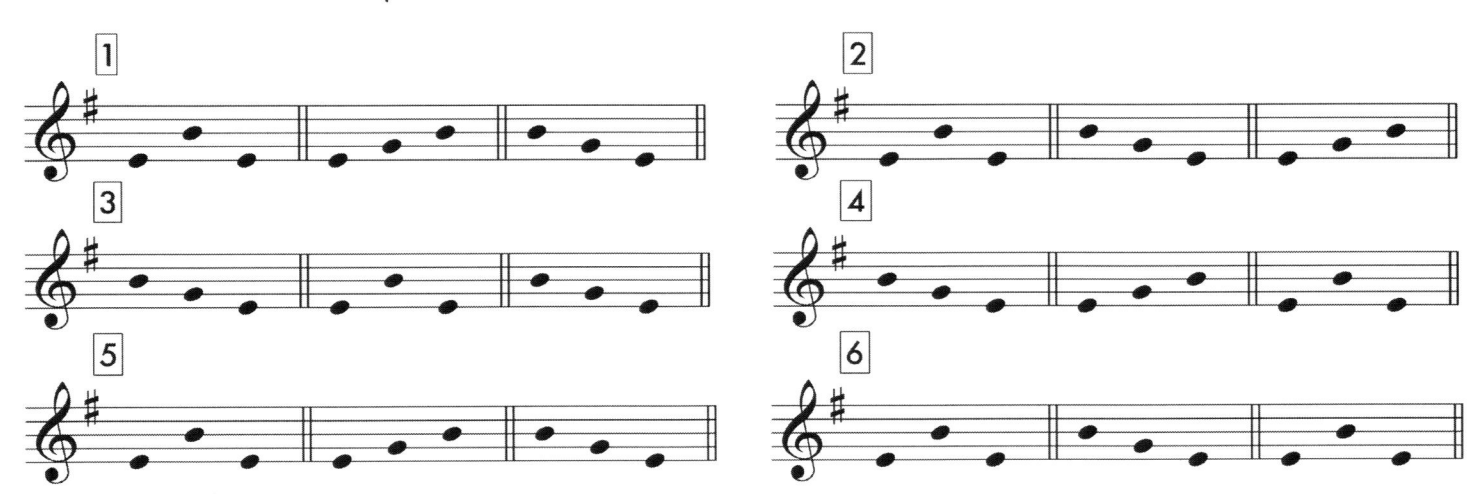

Try writing these three pattern sequences in G-LA and E-LA. Remember: audiate, read, remove them from your view, and then write **from your audiation**.

Also try reading these patterns keyboard. Use the **Minor i & V** Keyboard Card.

LESSON 6.3
GENERALIZING NEW MINOR TONIC PATTERNS

Now that we have learned to read three familiar tonic patterns, we will harness the power of **generalization** to read more tonic patterns. Some of the patterns will be familiar to you aurally from Part 1, while others will be brand new.

> **GET READY FOR NOTATIONAL GENERALIZATION**
> Before you generalize patterns notationally, be sure that you can translate patterns from a neutral syllable to the solfege.

GENERALIZING NEW PATTERNS IN NOTATION

Look at the two patterns below.

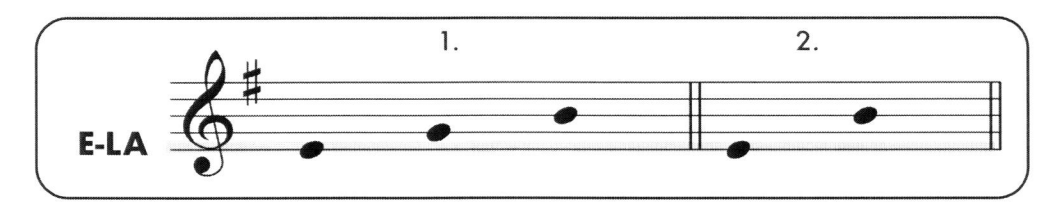

The first pattern (LA DO MI) is familiar to you. Using that knowledge, can you figure out the second pattern? Hopefully, you generalized that it was LA MI.

GENERALIZING TONIC PATTERNS IN E-LA

Use the skill of generalization to read these new patterns.

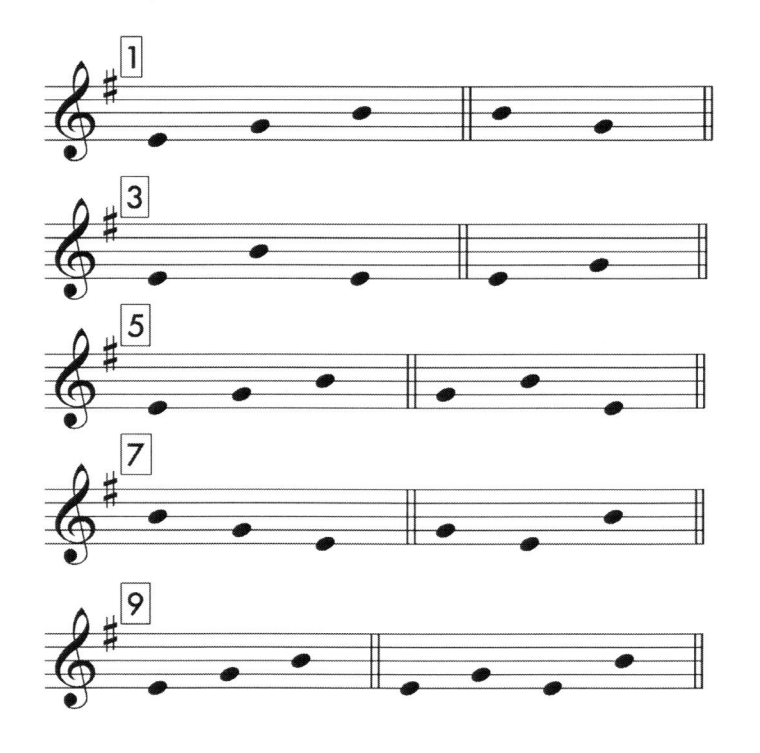

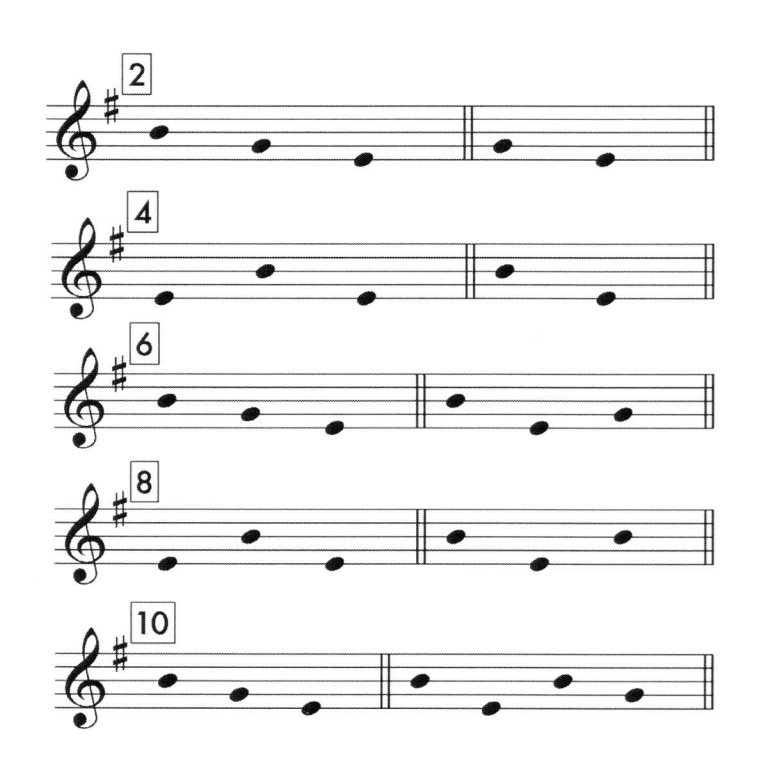

GENERALIZING TONIC PATTERNS IN G-LA

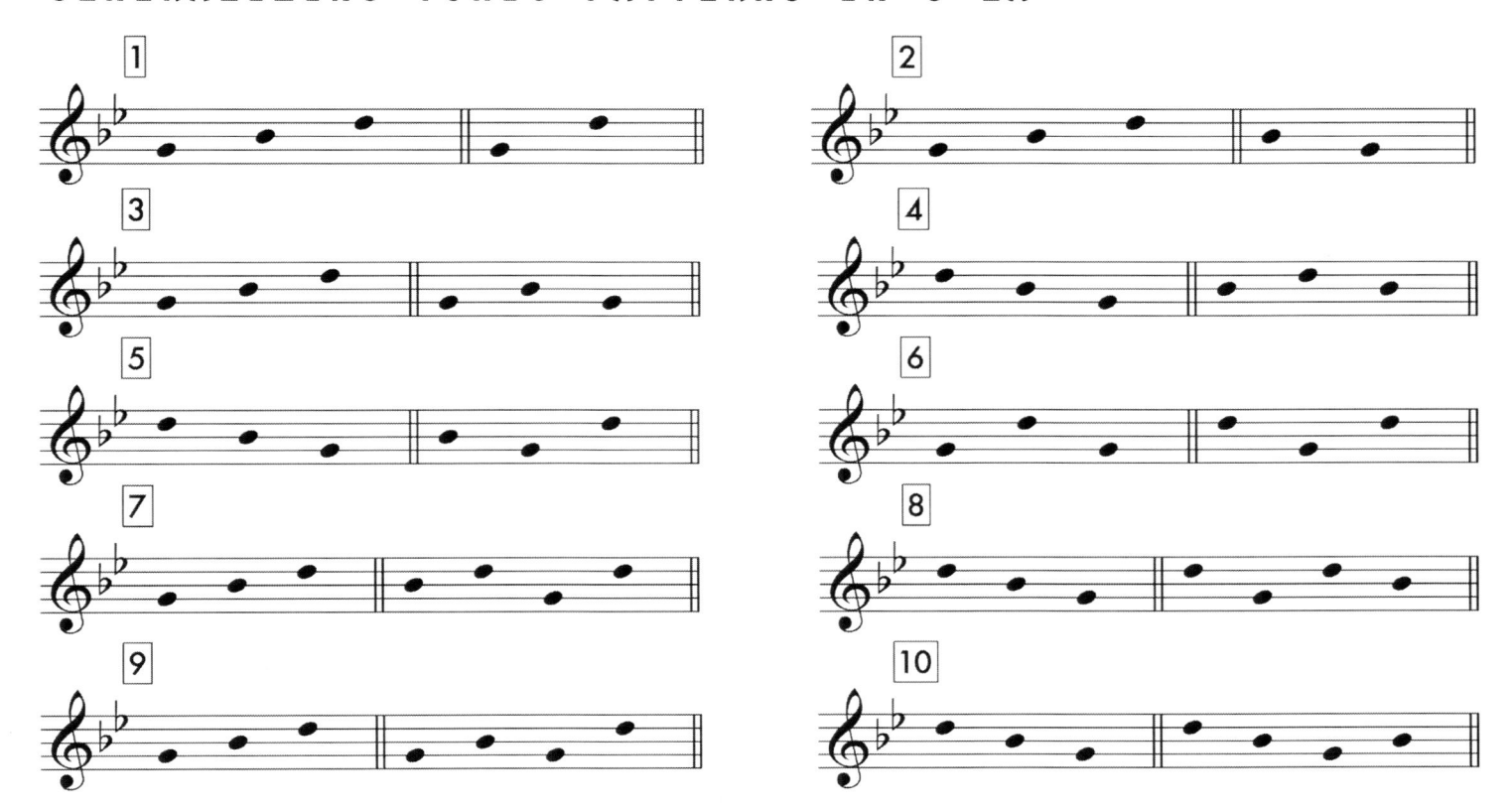

In addition to singing these a capella, you could try to accompany yourself by playing a minor tonic chord on the ukulele. See the ukulele chord chart in the appendix.

READING BENCHMARK 6A

Tonality = Minor
Pitches = Tonic only
Keys = Em, Gm

Meters = Duple and Triple
Time Signatures = 2/4, 4/4, 2/2; 6/8, 3/4
Functions = Macro/microbeat only

LESSON 6.4
DIVISION/ELONGATIONS IN DUPLE METER

A **division/elongation** is a new rhythmic function that contains a division **and** an elongation. Be sure to listen to and echo these patterns first at the Aural/Oral level (on BAH) and then with solfege at the Verbal Association level before you try to read them. Remember: we learn to read **familiar** words!

DIVISION/ELONGATIONS IN 2/4 AND 4/4

Division/Elongations in 2/4 and 4/4
♪. ♪   ♪ ♪.   ♪ ♪ ♪
Du   Ta   Du   Ta   Du   Ta   Ta

Read these rhythm patterns with macro/microbeats and the first division/elongation rhythm cell:

[rhythm exercises 1–6 in 2/4 and 4/4]

Read these rhythm patterns with macro/microbeats and the second division/elongation rhythm cell:

[rhythm exercises 1–6 in 2/4 and 4/4]

Read these rhythm patterns with macro/microbeats and the third division/elongation rhythm cell:

[rhythm exercises 1–6 in 2/4 and 4/4]

DIVISION/ELONGATIONS IN CUT TIME

Division/Elongations in Cut Time
♩. ♪ / ♪ ♩. / ♪ ♪ ♪
Du Ta / Du Ta / Du Ta Ta

Read these rhythm patterns with macro/microbeats and the first division/elongation rhythm cell: [♩. ♪]

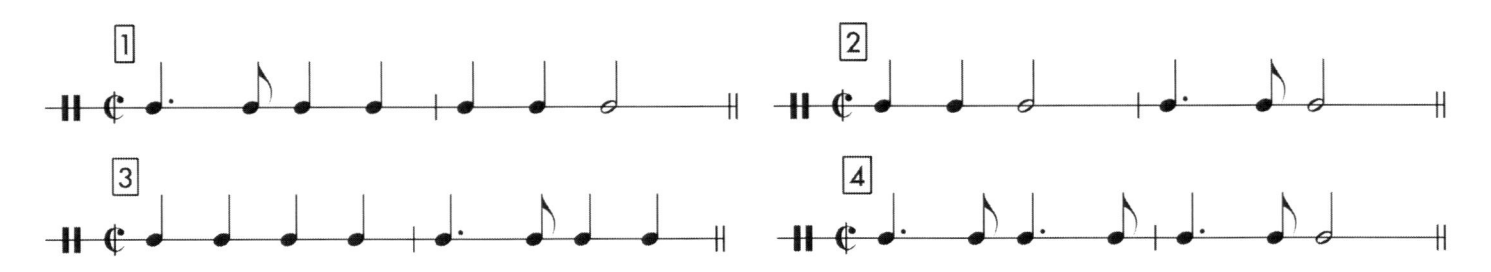

1.
2.
3.
4.

Read these rhythm patterns with macro/microbeats and the second division/elongation rhythm cell: [♪ ♩.]

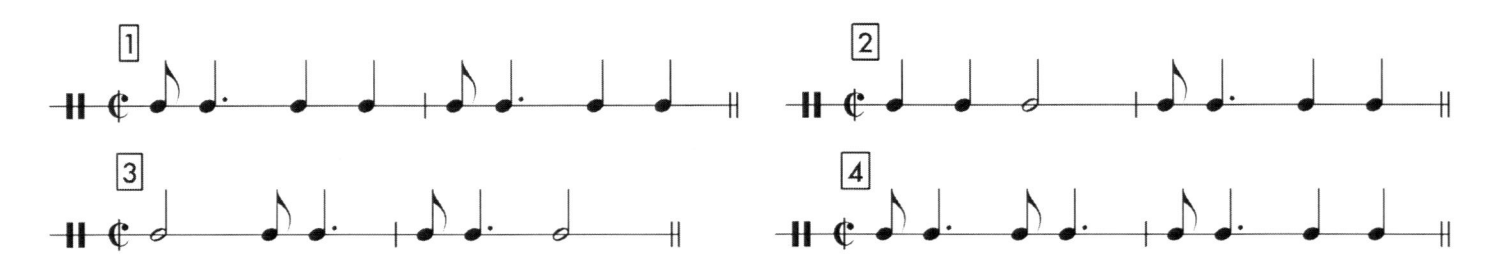

1.
2.
3.
4.

Read these rhythm patterns with macro/microbeats and the third division/elongation rhythm cell: [♪ ♪ ♪]

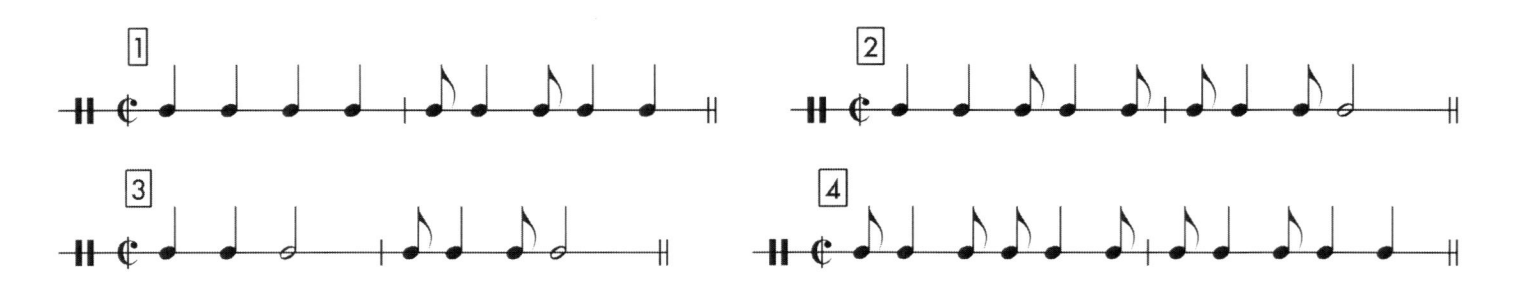

1.
2.
3.
4.

As usual, any time you learn to read a new rhythmic function, try writing both the individual rhythm cells and rhythm patterns **from your audiation**.

READING BENCHMARK 6B

Rhythm Only

Meters = Duple
Time Signatures = 2/4, 4/4, 2/2
Functions = Macro/microbeat, divisions, elongations and division/elongations

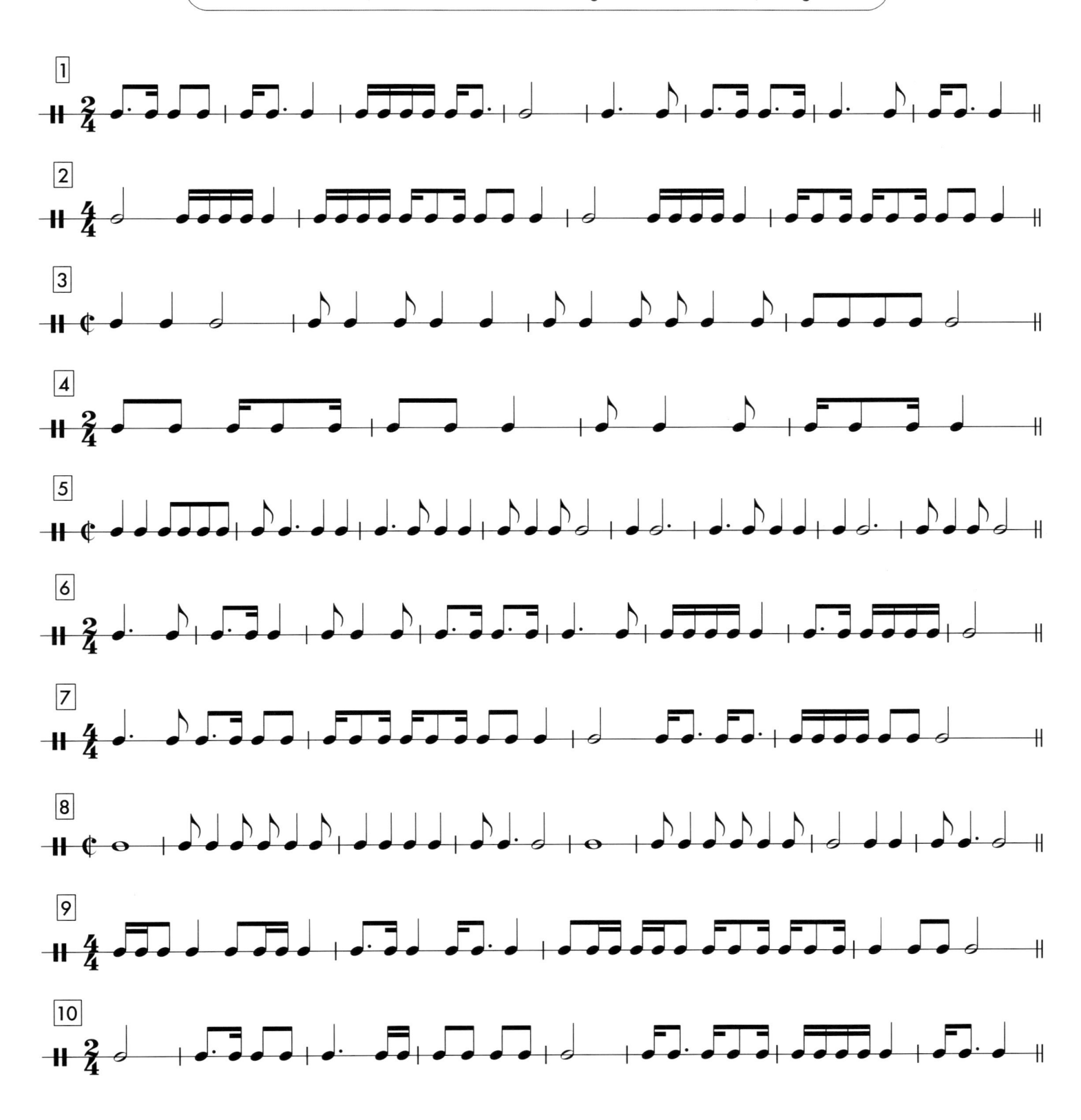

LESSON 6.5
DIVISION/ELONGATIONS IN TRIPLE METER

Follow the same procedures for Division/Elongations in triple meter.

Division/Elongations in 6/8

| Du Ta Di | Du Ta Di | Du Da Ta | Du Ta Ta Ta |

Read these rhythm patterns with macro/microbeats and the first division/elongation rhythm cell:

Read these rhythm patterns with macro/microbeats and the second division/elongation rhythm cell:

Read these rhythm patterns with macro/microbeats and the third division/elongation rhythm cell:

Read these rhythm patterns with macro/microbeats and the last division/elongation rhythm cell:

Division/Elongations in 3/4

♩. ♪ ♪	♪ ♩. ♪	♪ ♩. ♪	♪ ♪ ♪ ♪
Du Ta Di	Du Ta Di	Du Da Ta	Du Ta Ta Ta

Read these rhythm patterns with macro/microbeats and the first division/elongation rhythm cell:

Read these rhythm patterns with macro/microbeats and the second division/elongation rhythm cell:

Read these rhythm patterns with macro/microbeats and the third division/elongation rhythm cell:

Read these rhythm patterns with macro/microbeats and the last division/elongation rhythm cell:

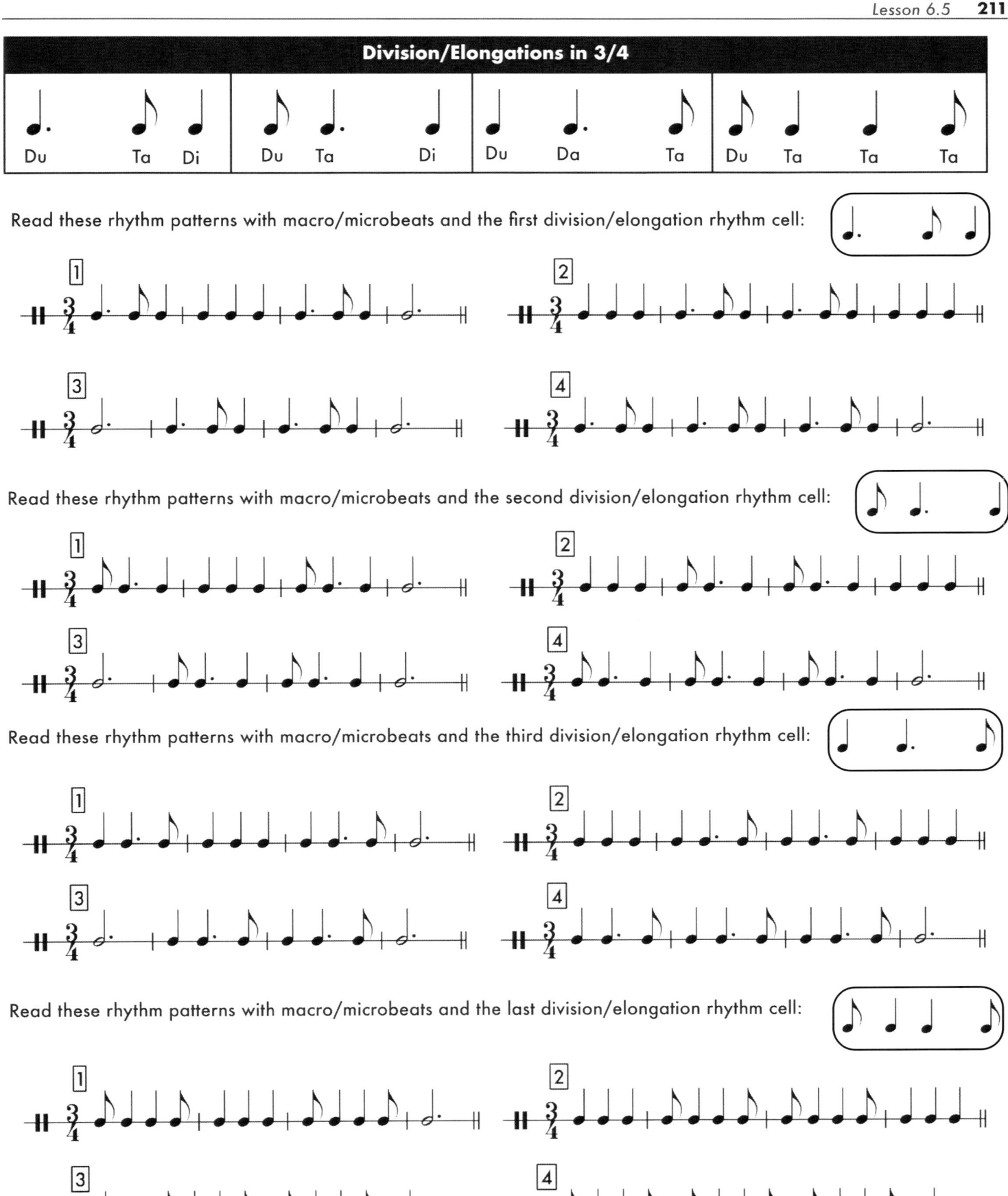

As usual, any time you learn to read a new rhythmic function, try writing both the individual rhythm cells and rhythm patterns **from your audiation**.

READING BENCHMARK 6C

Rhythm Only

Meters = Triple
Time Signatures = 6/8, 3/4
Functions = Macro/microbeat, divisions, elongations and division/elongations

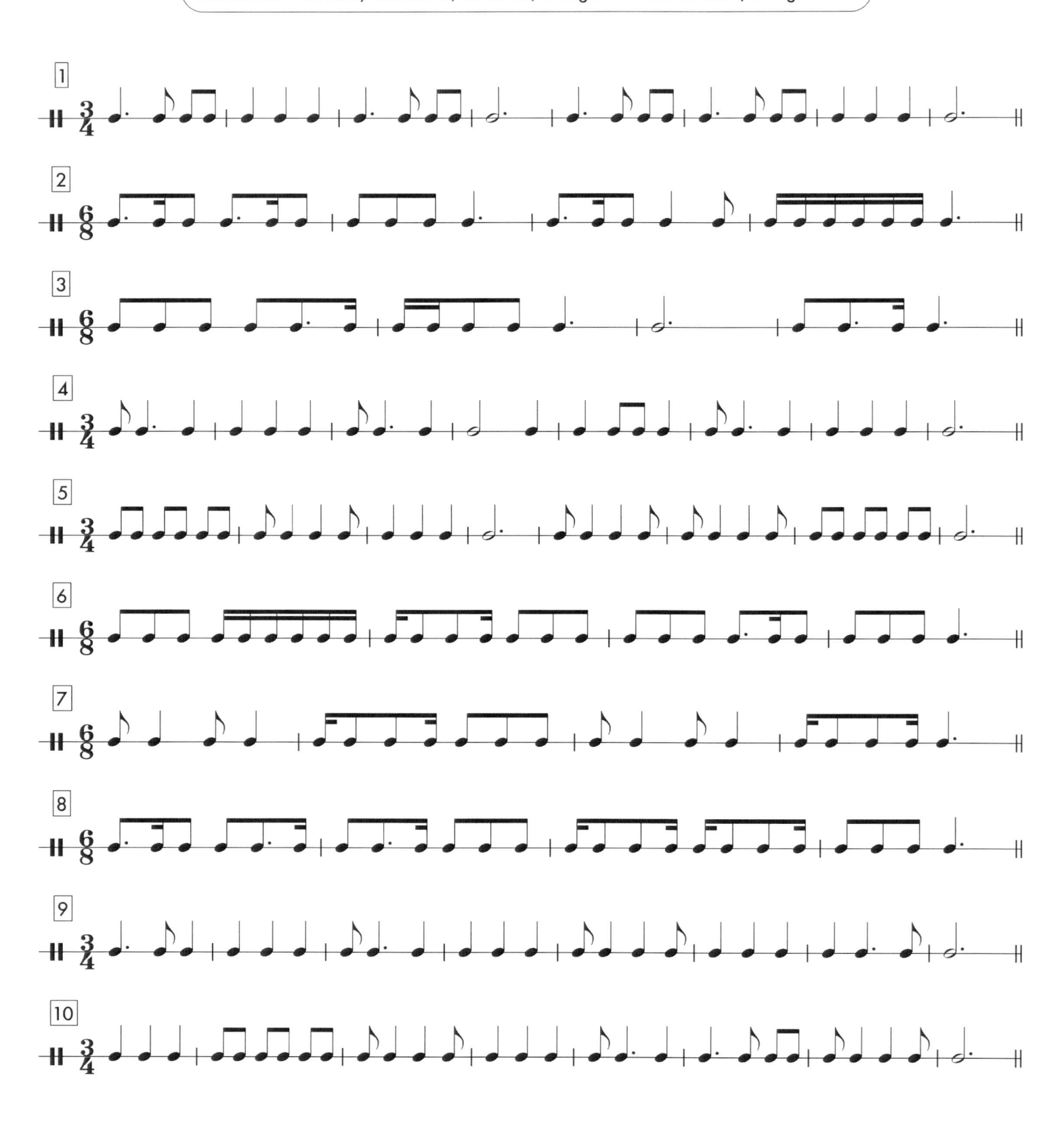

LESSON 6.6
LONGER RHYTHM PATTERNS
ALL PREVIOUS METERS AND FUNCTIONS

Before we combine tonal patterns and rhythms in **Reading Benchmark 6D**, it is a good idea to review all of the rhythm patterns and time signatures we have learned. Read these longer rhythm patterns in all of our previously learned meters, time signatures with macrobeats, microbeats, divisions, elongations **and division/elongations**.

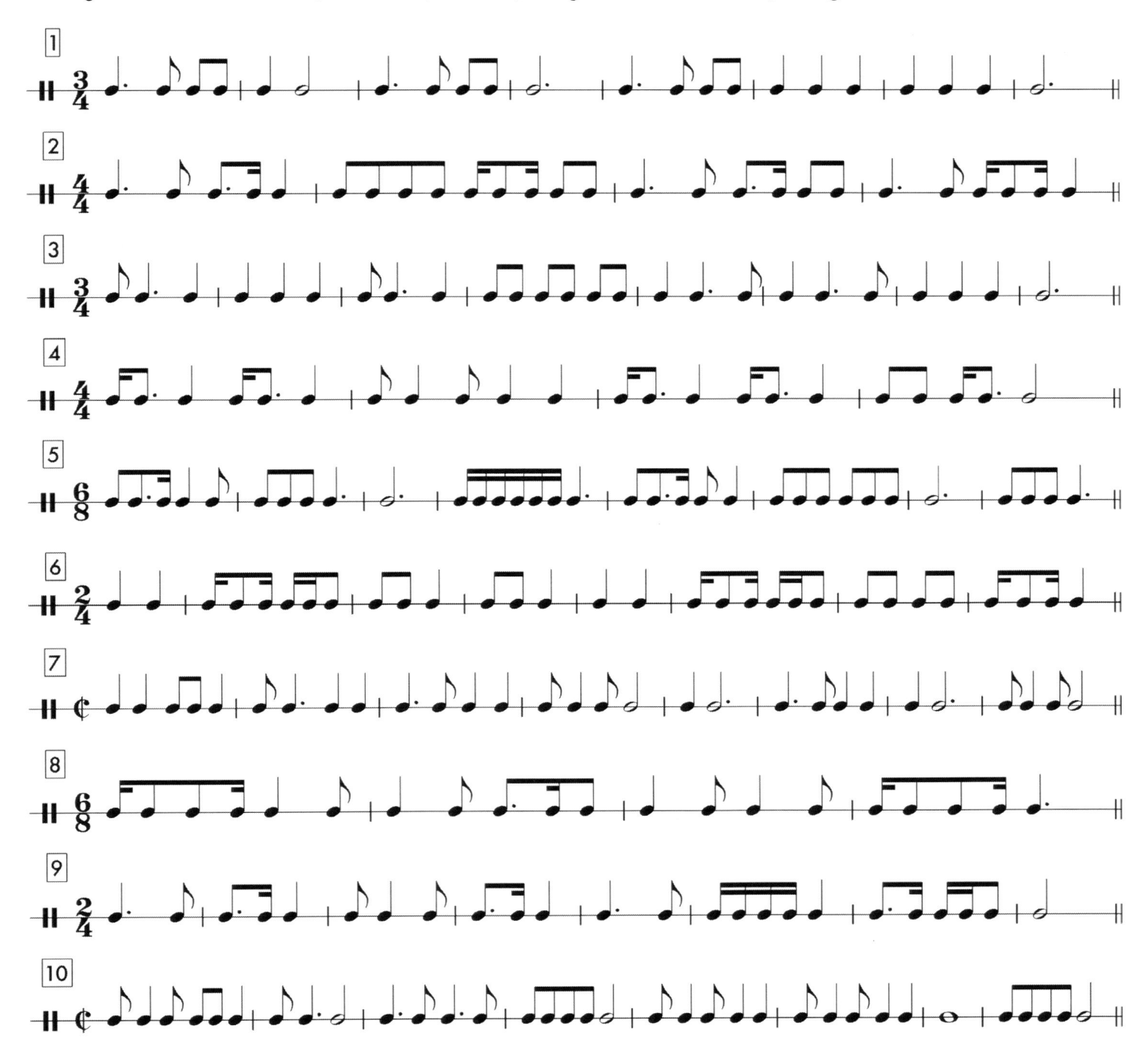

Add pitches to these longer rhythmic sentences and turn into composition. You could also try to strum these rhythms on a ukulele. Alternate between tonic and dominant chords.

READING BENCHMARK 6D

Tonality = Major
Pitches = Tonic/Dominant and tDRMFSL
Keys = Bb, C, D, Eb, F, G, A

Meters = Duple and Triple
Time Signatures = 2/4, 4/4; 6/8, 3/4
Functions = Macro/microbeat, divisions, elongations, and division/elongations

Tonic/Dominant Only

tDRMFSL and Tonic/Dominant

READING BENCHMARK 6E

Tonality = Minor
Pitches = Tonic only
Keys = Em, Gm

Meters = Duple and Triple
Time Signatures = 2/4, 4/4; 6/8, 3/4
Functions = Macro/microbeat, divisions, elongations, and division/elongations

READING SEQUENCE 7

SEQUENCE 7 AT A GLANCE

Reading Content	
TONAL	**RHYTHM**
• Tonality: Minor • Pitches: Tonic and siLTD • Keys: Cm, Dm, Em, Fm, Gm	• Meters: Duple and Triple • Functions: Macro/Microbeats, Divisions, Elongations, Division/Elongations and Macrobeat Rests • Time Signatures: 2/4, 4/4, Cut Time; 6/8, 3/4

Lesson Sequence	
7.1 Tonal	Introduction to Minor Stepwise Patterns; FPIFO in G-LA and E-LA
7.2 Tonal	Stepwise Patterns in Minor Tonality (LTD, DTL, LsiL)
7.3 Tonal	Generalizing New Minor Stepwise Patterns (LTD and si)
Reading Benchmark 7A • Minor; siLTD; Keys = Em and Gm • Duple & Triple; Macro/Micro, Divisions, Elongations and Division/Elongations; 2/4, 4/4, Cut Time; 6/8, 3/4	
7.4 Rhythm	Macrobeat Rests, Duple and Triple
Reading Benchmark 7B • Duple & Triple; Macro/Micro, Divisions, Elongations, Division/Elongations and **Macrobeat Rests**	
Reading Benchmark 7C • Major; Tonic/Dominant and tDRMFSL; Keys: C, D, Eb, F, G • Duple & Triple; Macro/Micro, Divisions, Elongations, Division/Elongations and **Macrobeat Rests**	
7.5 Tonal	Three New LA-Signatures (C-LA, D-LA and F-LA)
Reading Benchmark 7D • Minor; Tonic and siLTD; Keys: Cm, Dm, Em, Fm, Gm • Duple & Triple; Macro/Micro, Divisions, Elongations, Division/Elongations and Macrobeat Rests	

LESSON 7.1
INTRODUCTION TO MINOR STEPWISE PATTERNS FPIFO IN G-LA & E-LA

FAMILIAR PATTERNS IN FAMILIAR ORDER

Below are the familiar stepwise acculturation patterns in their familiar order (FPIFO) in minor tonality with G and E as LA. This will give you a sense of the whole scale before we read patterns within the scale. Engage with these patterns in the following ways.

- Watch the **Patterns Only** video from Part I, and as you echo each pattern, point to the notation.
- Watch the **Tonal Pattern Recital** video from Part I, and point to each pattern as you sing.

G-LA, Stepwise Patterns, FPIFO

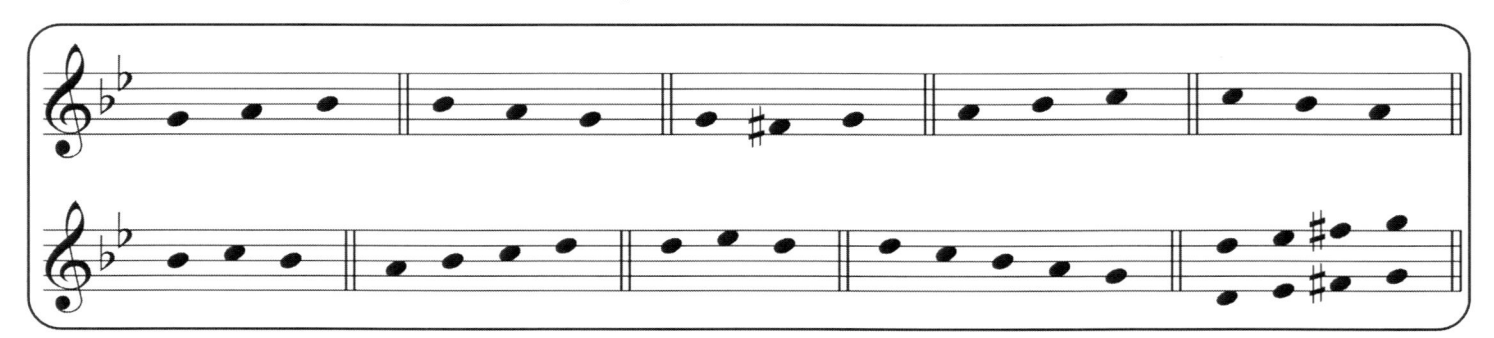

E-LA, Stepwise Patterns, FPIFO

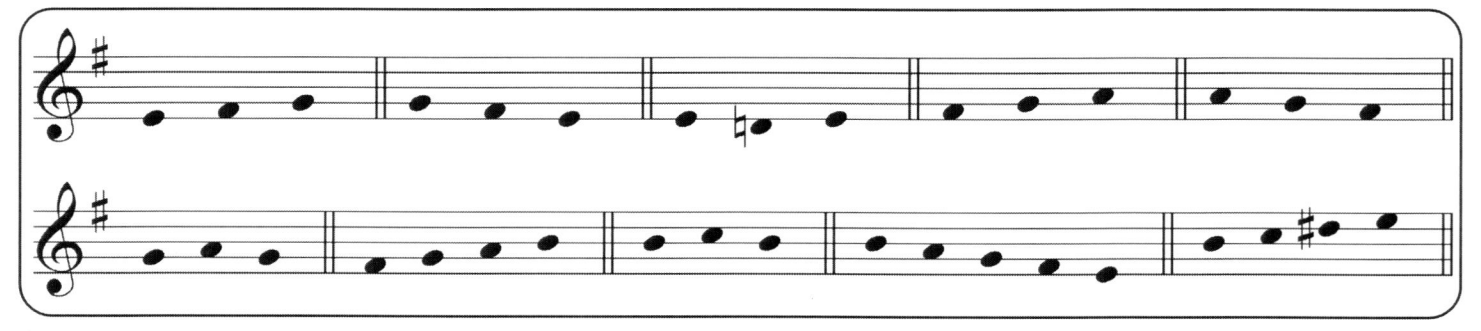

LESSON 7.2
STEPWISE PATTERNS IN MINOR TONALITY
LTD, DTL, LsiL IN G-LA & E-LA

LA TI DO, DO TI LA, LA SI LA IN G-LA

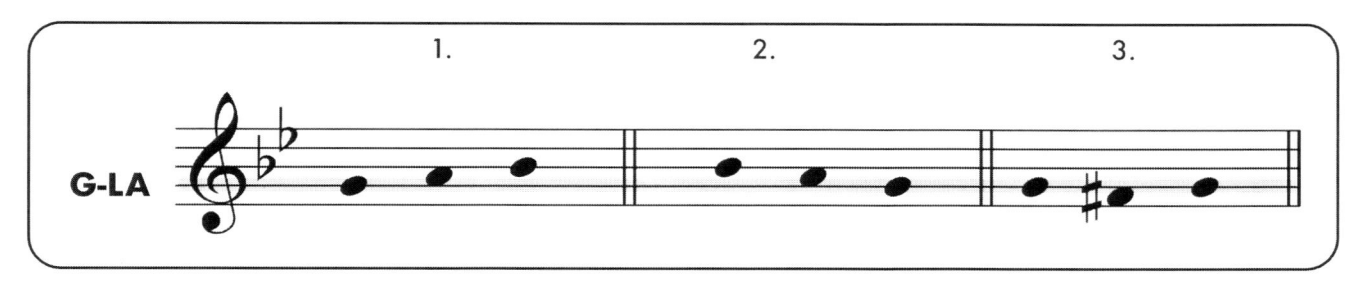

The first pattern is **LA TI DO**. Look at the notation, take a breath and sing **LA TI DO**. Just as you did when you echoed the patterns, keep the pitches separated. The second pattern is **DO TI LA**. Look at the notation, take a breath and sing **DO TI LA**. The third pattern is **LA SI LA**. Look at the notation, take a breath and sing **LA SI LA**. Finally, read these three patterns one after the other with a short pause in-between. These are **familiar patterns in a familiar order**.

> ! If you need an aural reminder of these three patterns, review them in the companion course videos. Remember: we are learning to read **familiar patterns**. !

FAMILIAR PATTERNS, UNFAMILIAR ORDER (FPIUFO)

Read the same three familiar patterns, but this time, read them in an unfamiliar order. Remember to keep the pitches separated, and to make a short pause in-between each pattern.

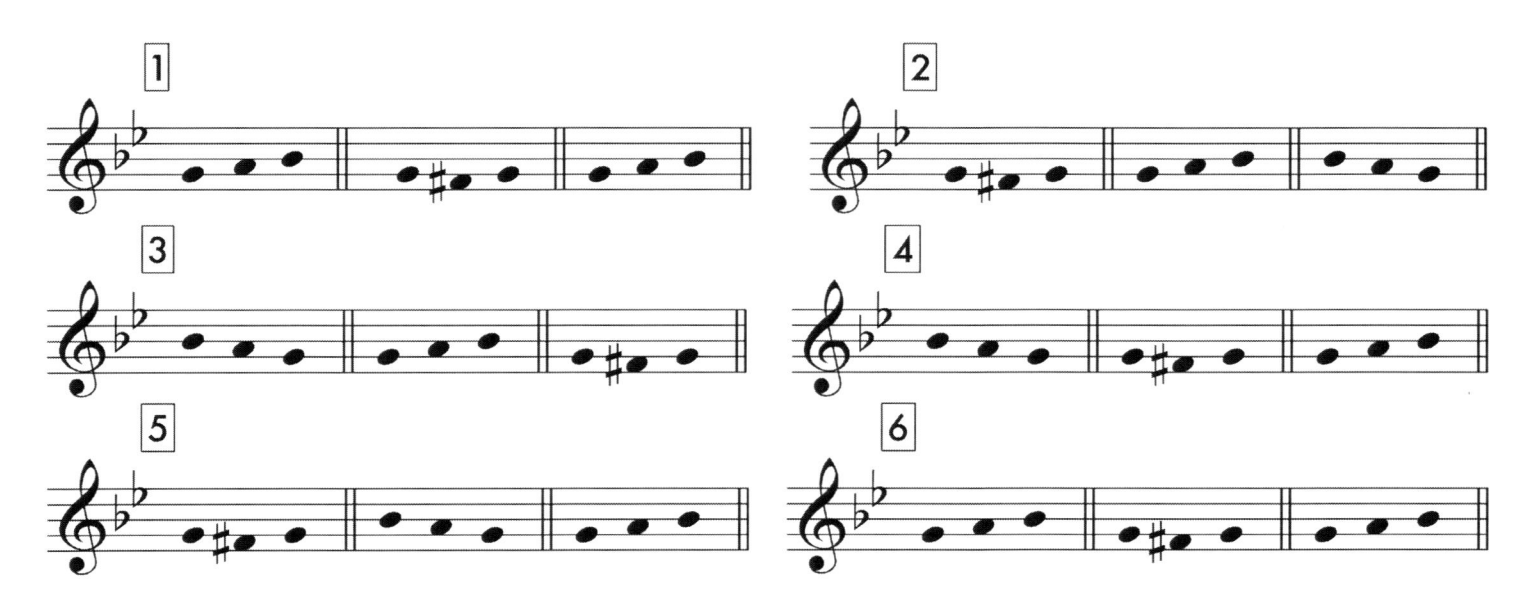

E-LA

Follow the same procedures in E-LA.

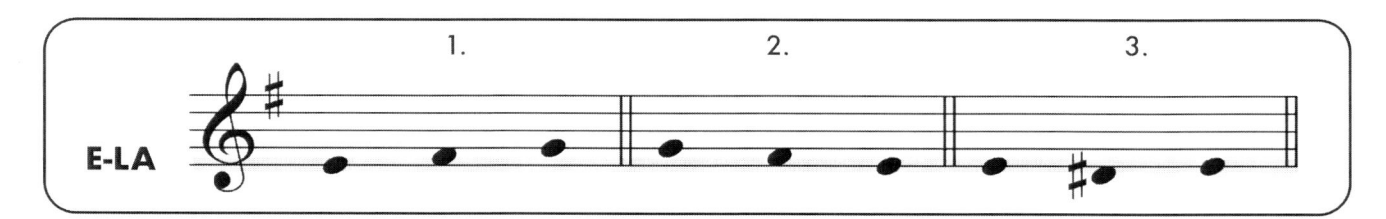

FAMILIAR PATTERNS, UNFAMILIAR ORDER

Read the same three familiar patterns, but this time, read them in an unfamiliar order. Remember to keep the pitches separated, and to make a short pause in-between each pattern.

GET READY FOR NOTATIONAL GENERALIZATION

Before you generalize patterns notationally, be sure that you can translate patterns from a neutral syllable to the solfege.

Try writing these patterns.

Create **new tonal patterns** that only have the pitches LA, TI, DO and SI.

Play these patterns on the keyboard. Use the **Solfege** Keyboard Card.

LESSON 7.3
GENERALIZING NEW MINOR STEPWISE PATTERNS
LTD&SI

Use generalization to read these unfamiliar patterns. The final pattern in each of the pattern sets below is unfamiliar. If you are struggling: remember that generalization is an **inference** skill, and requires patience and persistence.

GENERALIZATION EXERCISES IN G-LA

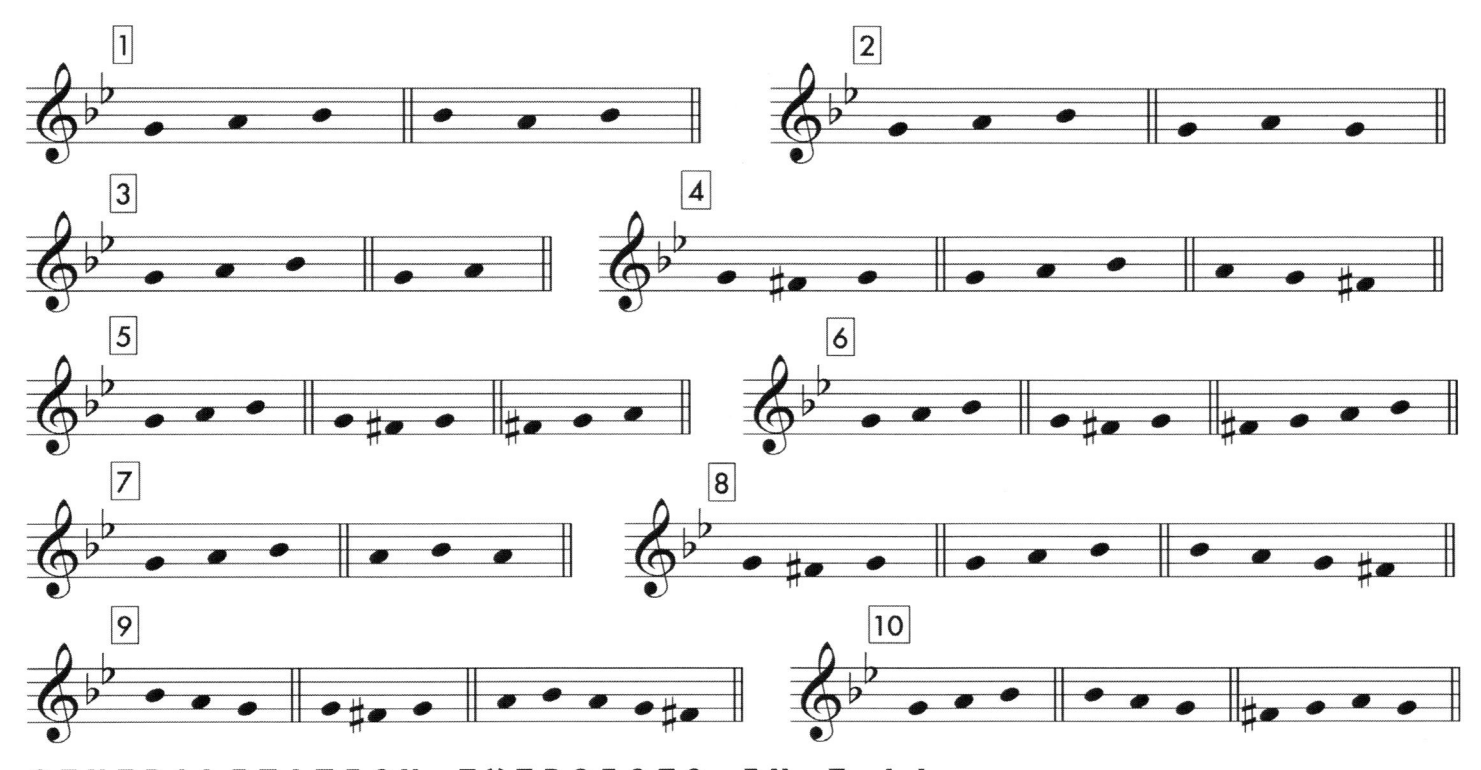

GENERALIZATION EXERCISES IN E-LA

READING BENCHMARK 7A

Tonality = Minor
Pitches = siLTD, Stepwise
Keys = Em, Gm

Meters = Duple and Triple
Time Signatures = 2/4, 4/4; 6/8, 3/4
Functions = Macro/microbeat, divisions, elongations, and division/elongations

1 E = LA

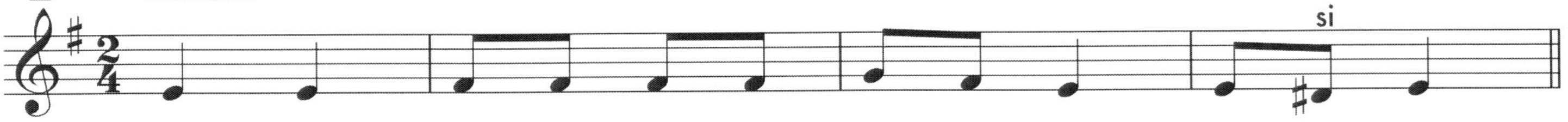

2 G = LA

3

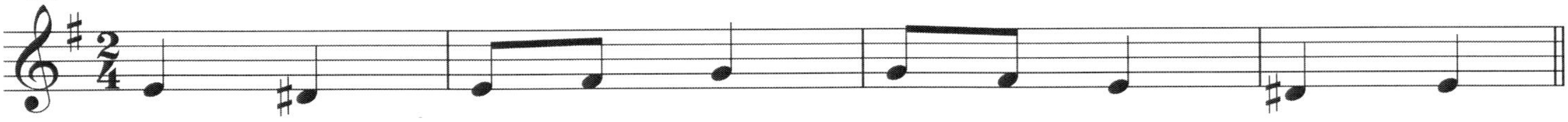

4

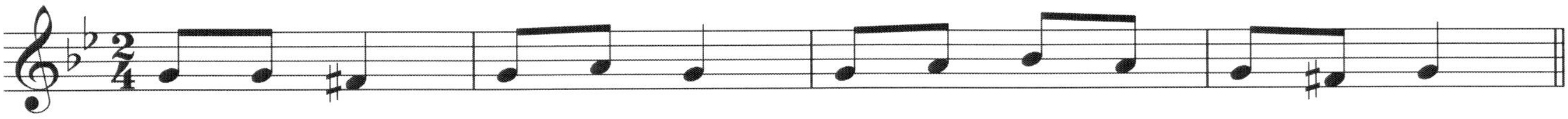

5

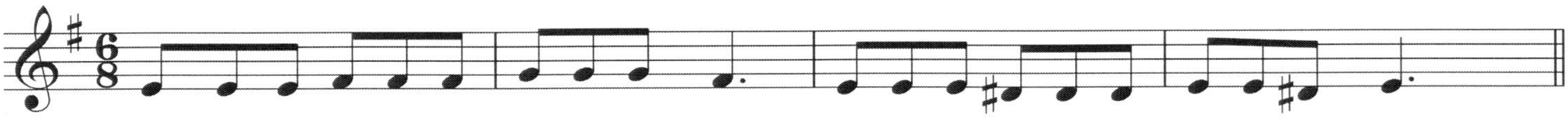

6

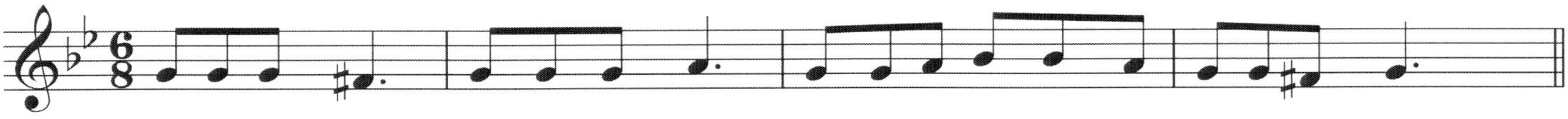

7

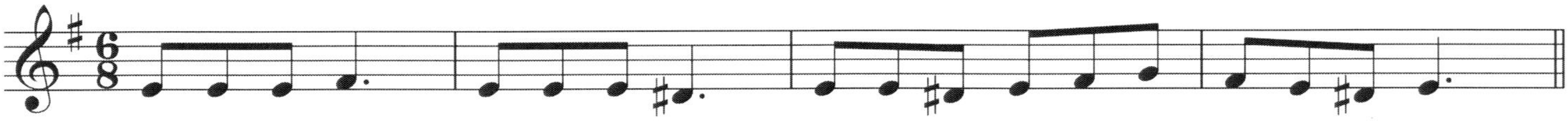

8

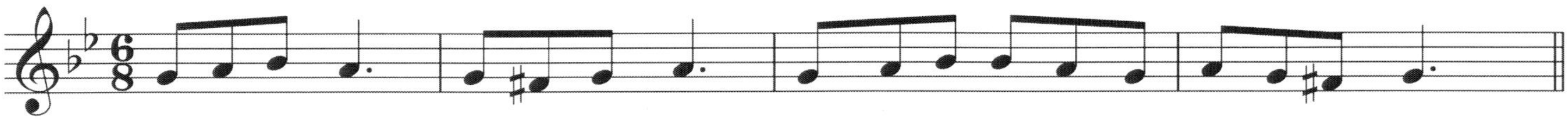

9

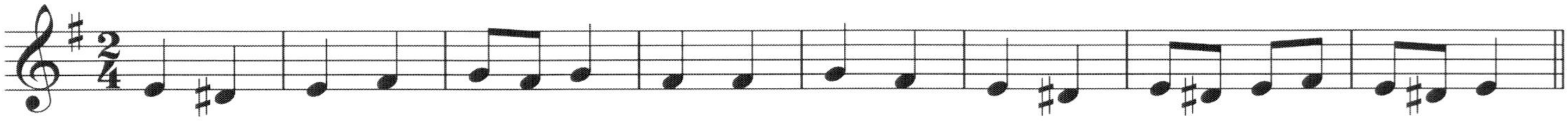

10

More Difficult Exercises

LESSON 7.4
MACROBEAT RESTS, DUPLE & TRIPLE

A **rest** is a new rhythmic function that indicates a lack of sound, but not a lack of audiation. In fact, rests are more difficult to audiate and perform with accuracy than all of the other rhythmic functions we have learned. Again, be sure to listen to and echo these patterns first at the Aural/Oral level (on BAH) and then with solfege at the Verbal Association level before you try to read them. Remember: we learn to read **familiar** words! Let's begin with macrobeat rests.

DUPLE MACROBEAT RESTS IN 2/4 AND 4/4

Read these patterns with macrobeats, microbeats and macrobeat rests in 2/4 and 4/4.

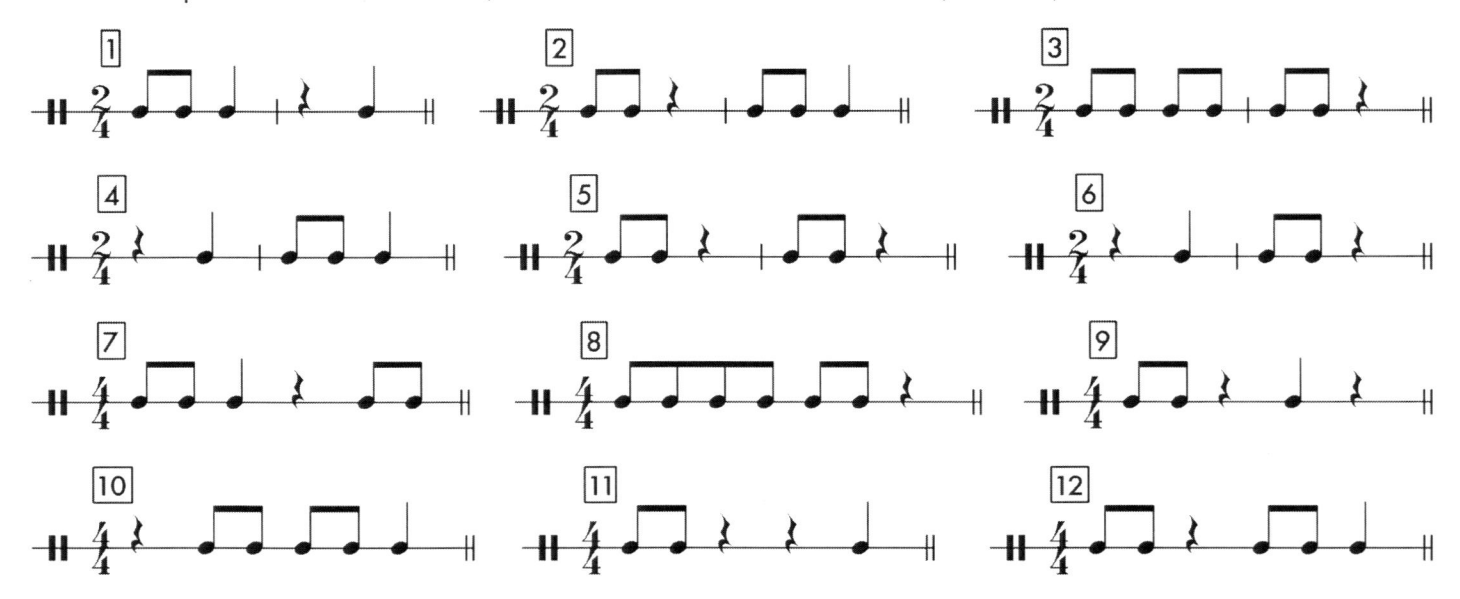

DUPLE MACROBEAT RESTS IN CUT TIME

Read these patterns with macrobeats, microbeats and macrobeat rests in Cut Time.

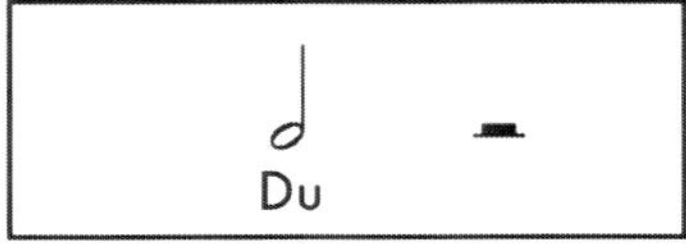

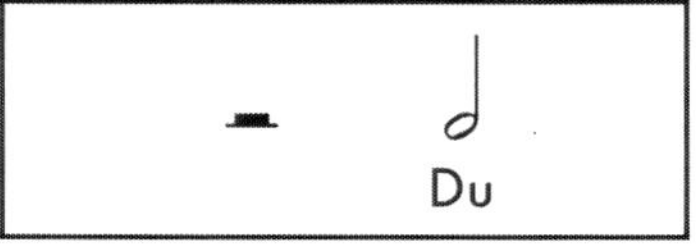

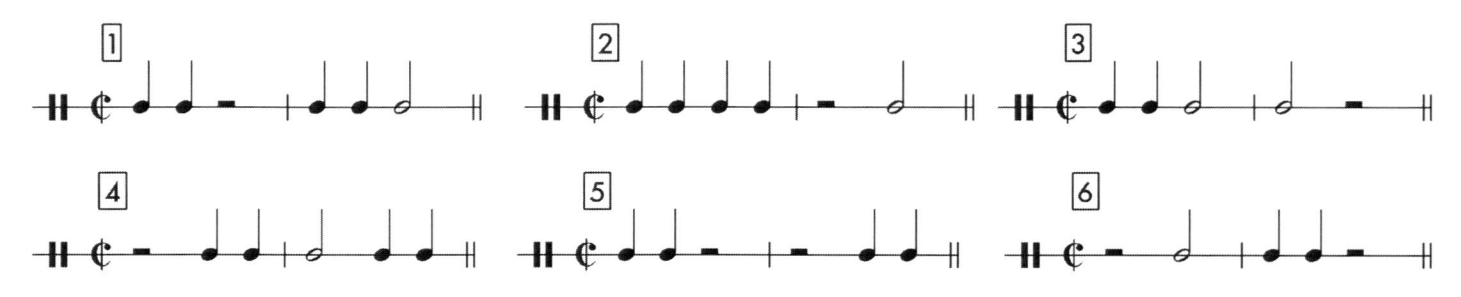

TRIPLE MACROBEAT RESTS IN 6/8

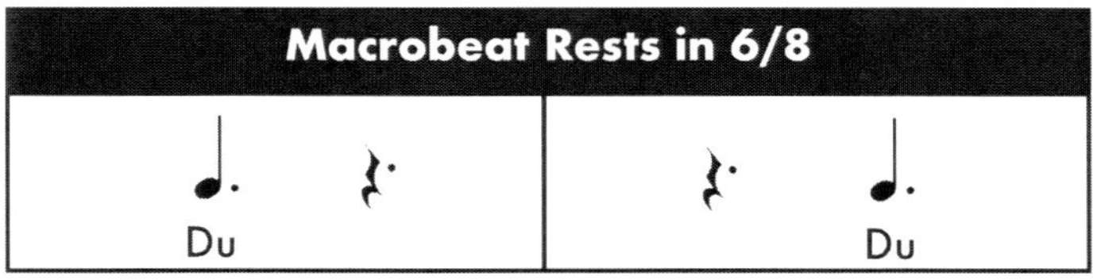

Macrobeat Rests in 6/8	
♩. 𝄽. Du	𝄽. ♩. Du

Read these patterns with macrobeats, microbeats and macrobeat rests in 6/8.

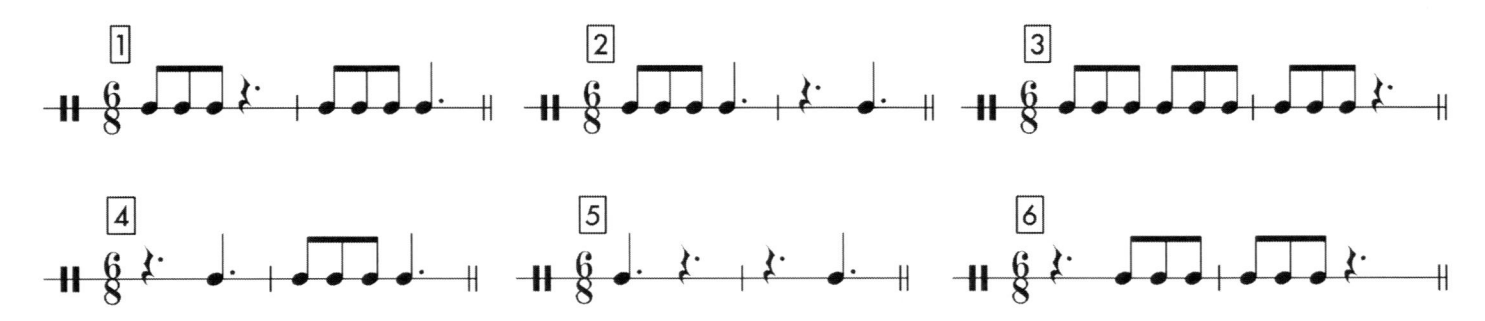

TRIPLE MACROBEAT RESTS IN 3/4

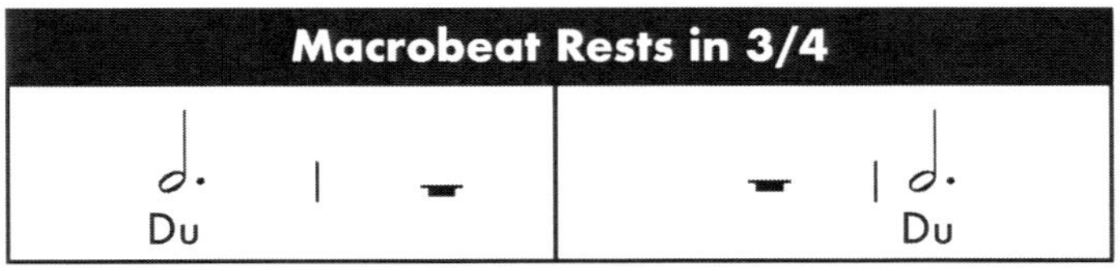

Macrobeat Rests in 3/4	
♩. | 𝄼 Du	𝄼 | ♩. Du

Read these patterns with macrobeats, microbeats and macrobeat rests in 3/4.

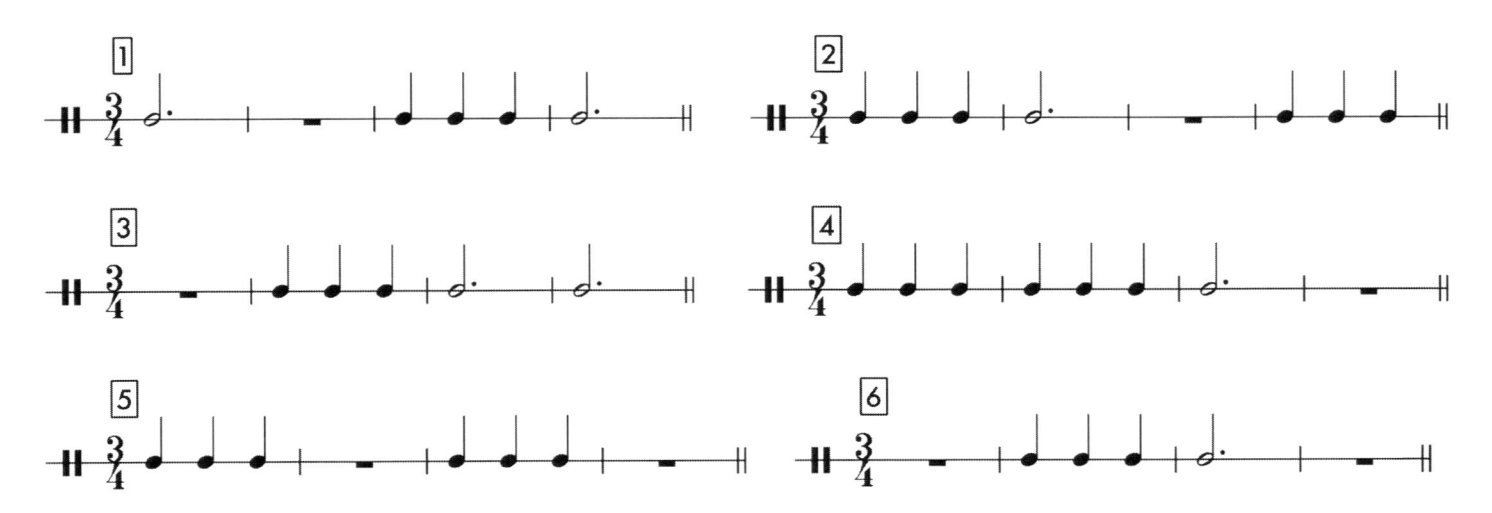

As usual, any time you learn to read a new rhythmic function, try writing both the individual rhythm cells and rhythm patterns **from your audiation**.

READING BENCHMARK 7B

Rhythm Only

Meters = Duple and Triple
Time Signatures = 2/4, 4/4, Cut Time, 6/8, 3/4
Functions = Macro/microbeat, divisions, elongations and division/elongations, macrobeat rests

More Difficult Exercises

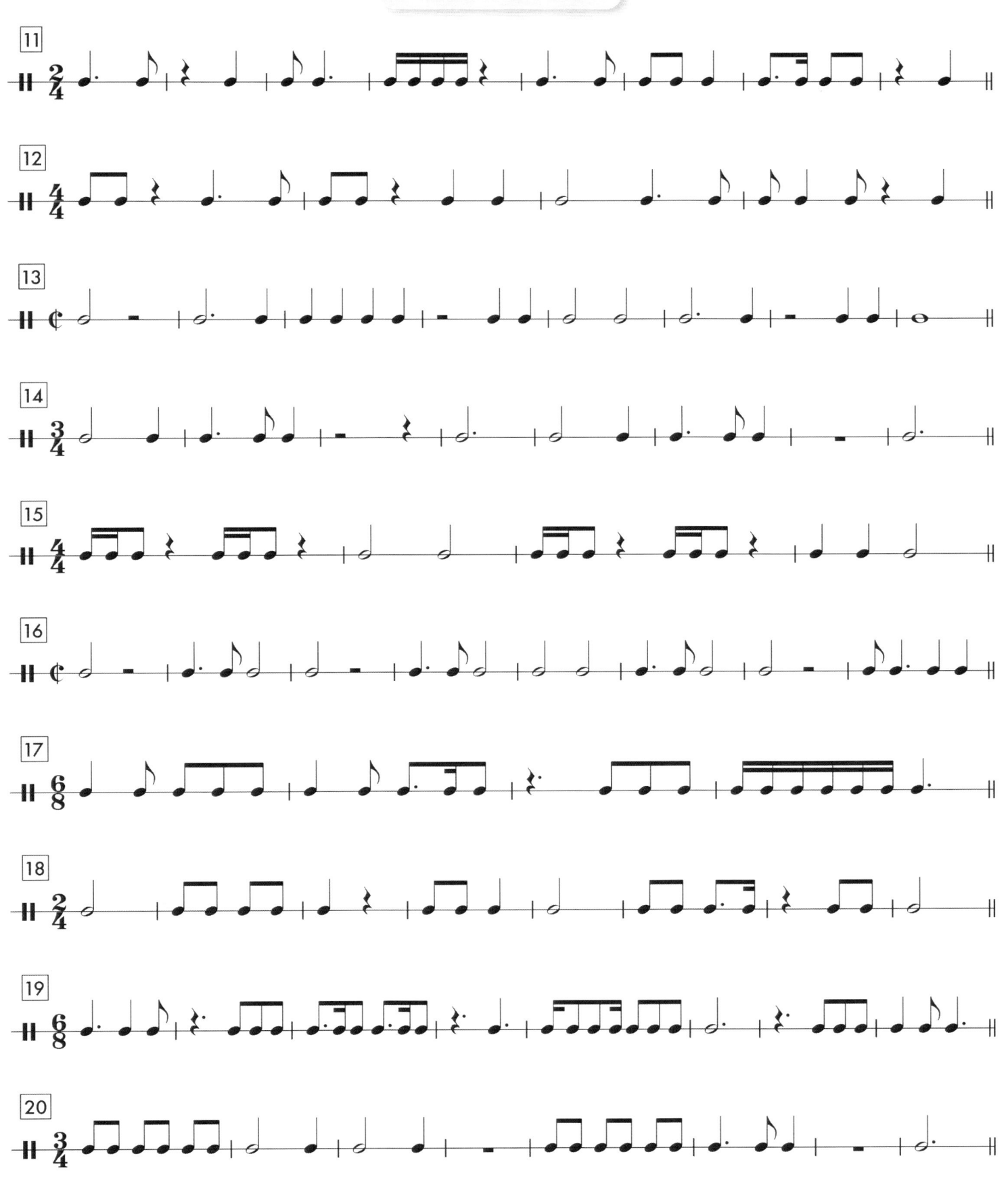

READING BENCHMARK 7C

Tonality = Major
Pitches = Tonic/Dominant and tDRMFSL
Keys = Bb, C, D, Eb, F, G, A

Meters = Duple and Triple
Time Signatures = 2/4, 4/4, 2/2; 6/8, 3/4
Functions = Macro/microbeat, divisions, elongations, division/elongations, macrobeat rests

LESSON 7.5
THREE NEW LA SIGNATURES: C-LA, D-LA & F-LA

C-LA

Let's read in a new LA-signature: **C-LA**. Use the skill we learned previously to find out where LA is on the staff.

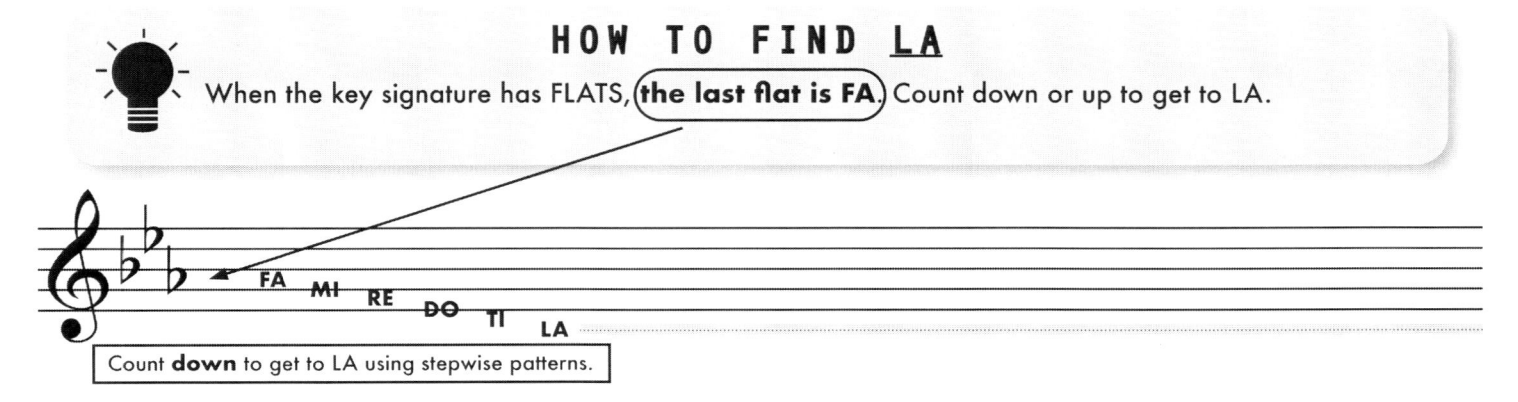

HOW TO FIND LA
When the key signature has FLATS, **the last flat is FA.** Count down or up to get to LA.

Count **down** to get to LA using stepwise patterns.

FAMILIAR PATTERNS IN C-LA

Here are the six familiar patterns in C-LA. Read them in their familiar order.

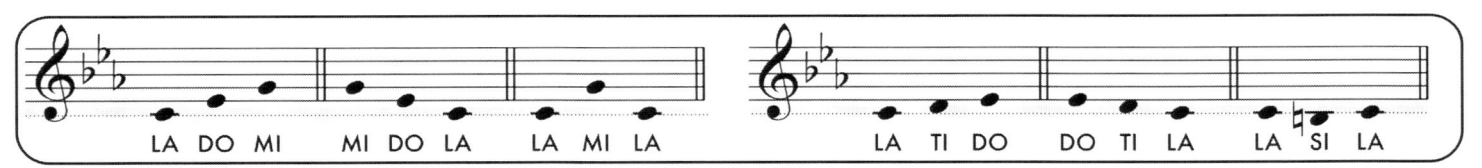

LA DO MI   MI DO LA   LA MI LA   LA TI DO   DO TI LA   LA SI LA

Read these familiar harmonic patterns in unfamiliar order in C-LA:

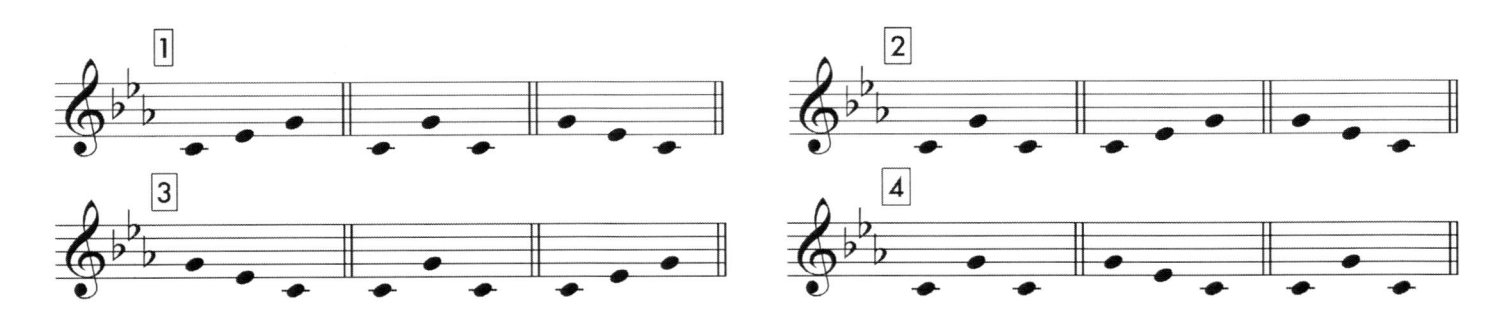

Read these familiar stepwise patterns in unfamiliar order in C-LA:

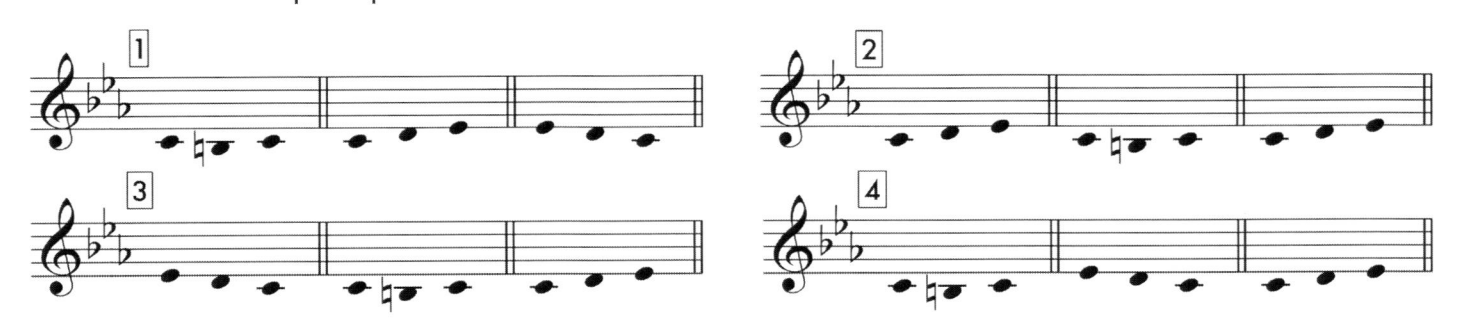

D-LA

Let's read in a new LA-signature: **D-LA**.

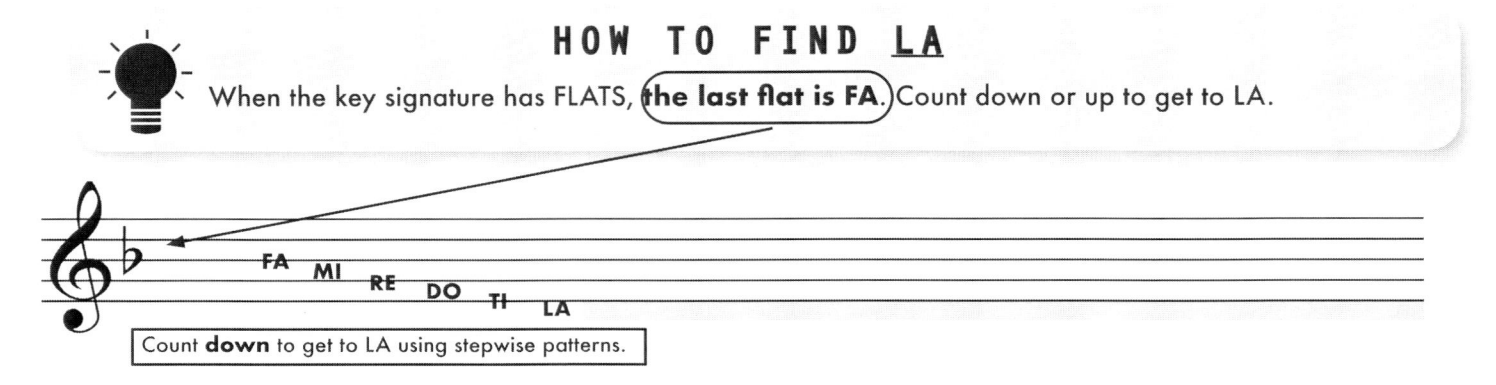

HOW TO FIND LA

When the key signature has FLATS, **the last flat is FA**. Count down or up to get to LA.

Count **down** to get to LA using stepwise patterns.

FAMILIAR PATTERNS IN D-LA

Here are the six familiar patterns in D-LA. Read them in their familiar order.

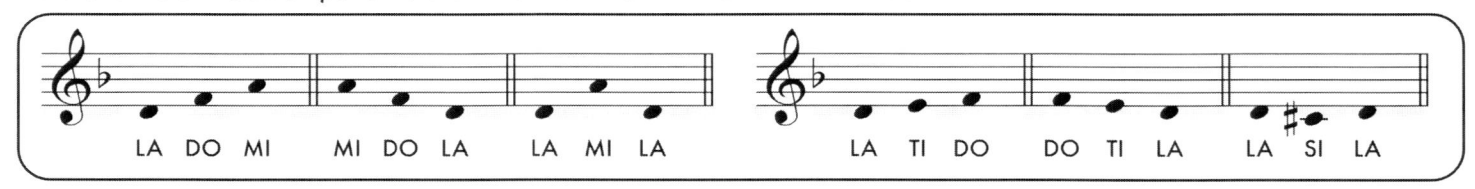

LA DO MI   MI DO LA   LA MI LA   LA TI DO   DO TI LA   LA SI LA

Read these familiar harmonic patterns in unfamiliar order in D-LA:

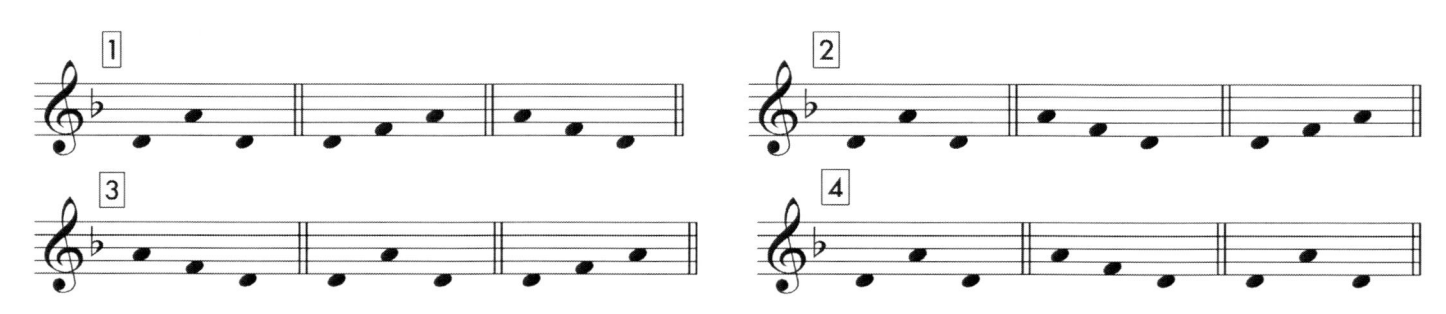

Read these familiar stepwise patterns in unfamiliar order in D-LA:

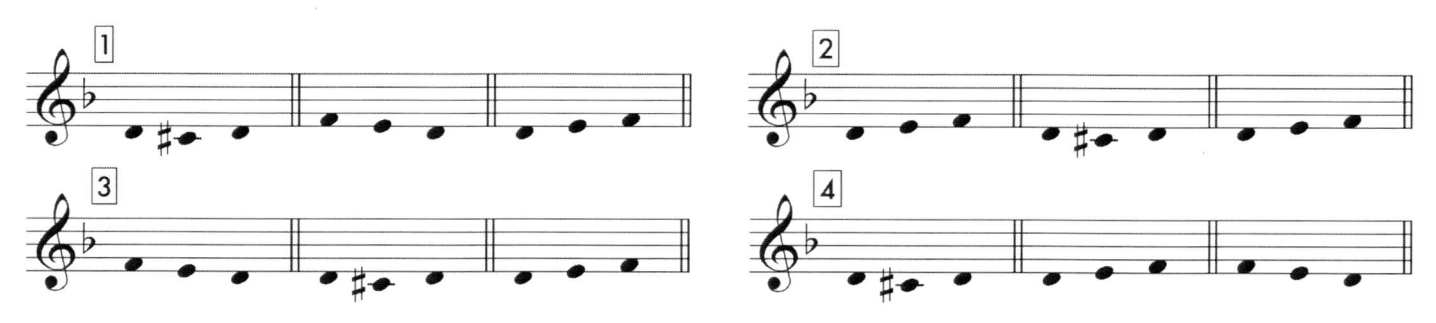

F-LA

Let's read in a new LA-signature: **F-LA**.

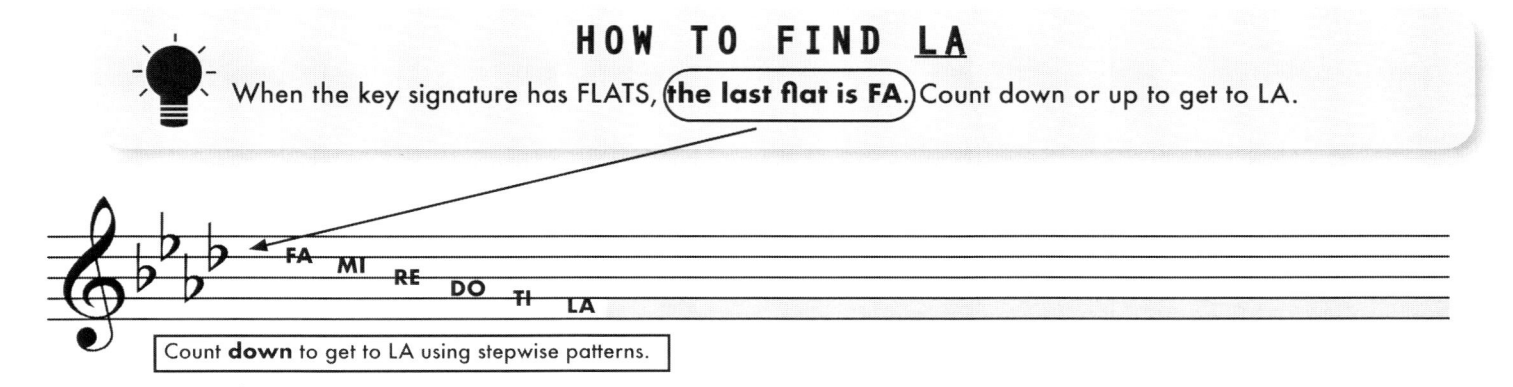

HOW TO FIND LA
When the key signature has FLATS, **the last flat is FA**. Count down or up to get to LA.

FA MI RE DO TI LA

Count **down** to get to LA using stepwise patterns.

FAMILIAR PATTERNS IN F-LA

Here are the six familiar patterns in D-LA. Read them in their familiar order.

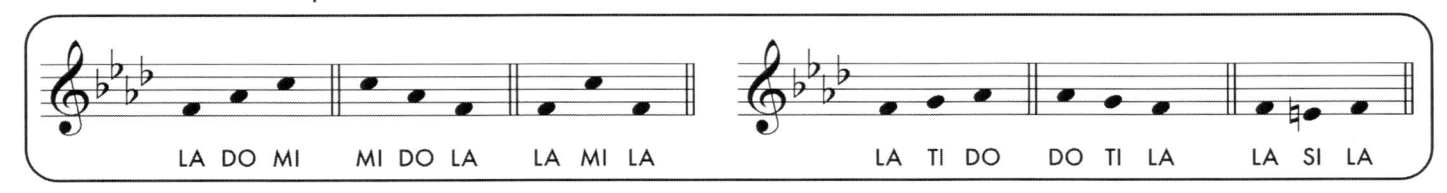

LA DO MI   MI DO LA   LA MI LA   LA TI DO   DO TI LA   LA SI LA

Read these familiar harmonic patterns in unfamiliar order in F-LA:

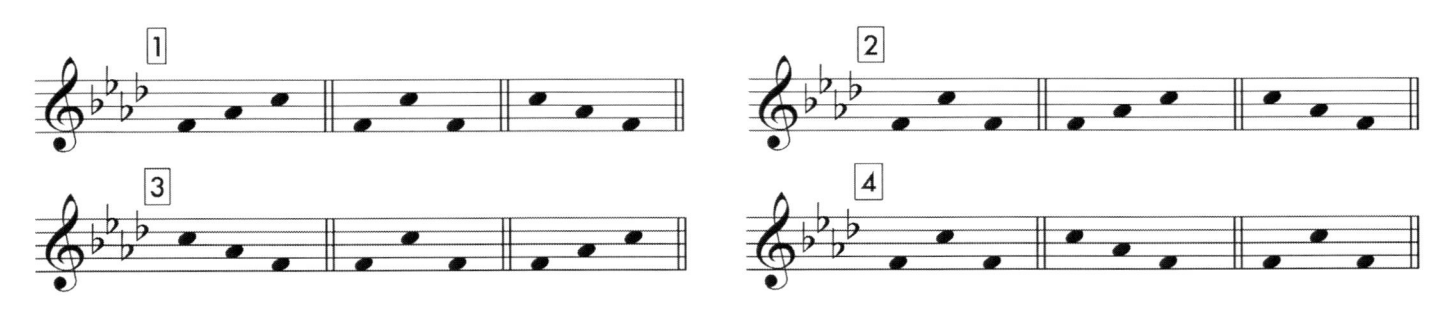

Read these familiar stepwise patterns in unfamiliar order in F-LA:

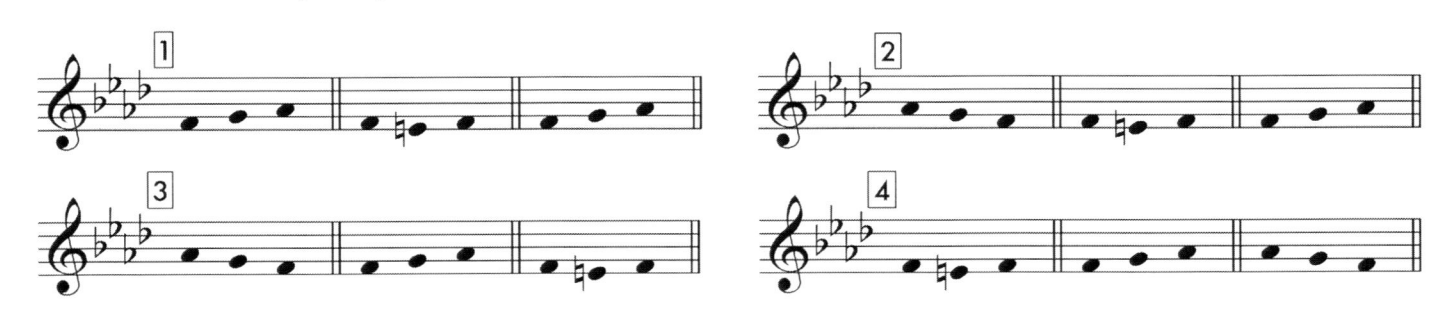

PREPARING FOR READING BENCHMARK 7D

Reading Benchmark 7D is a tricky one, mostly because the rhythm is challenging. You may wish to review the rhythm content, as well as Reading Benchmarks 6A and 7A before you tackle 7D. To prepare you for the tonal generalization that is required for 7B, try the exercises on the following page in C-LA, D-LA and F-LA. The final pattern will require generalization.

GENERALIZATION IN C-LA

Tonic Patterns

Stepwise Patterns

GENERALIZATION IN D-LA

Tonic Patterns

Stepwise Patterns

GENERALIZATION IN F-LA

Tonic Patterns

Stepwise Patterns

READING BENCHMARK 7D

Tonality = Minor
Pitches = Tonic; siLTD
Keys = Cm, Dm, Em, Fm, Gm

Meters = Duple and Triple
Time Signatures = 2/4, 4/4, 2/2; 6/8, 3/4
Functions = Macro/microbeat, divisions, elongations, division/elongations, macrobeat rests

Tonic Only

siLTD, Stepwise

READING SEQUENCE 8

SEQUENCE 8 AT A GLANCE

Reading Content	
TONAL	**RHYTHM**
• Tonality: Minor • Pitches: Tonic and siLTDRMF • Keys: Cm, Dm, Em, Fm, Gm, Am, Bm	• Meters: Duple and Triple • Functions: Macro/Microbeats, Divisions, Elongations, Division/Elongations, Macrobeat Rests, Microbeat Rests • Time Signatures: 2/4, 4/4, Cut Time; 6/8, 3/4

Lesson Sequence	
8.1 Tonal	Combining Harmonic and Stepwise Patterns
Reading Benchmark 8A • Minor; Tonic and siLTD; Keys: Cm, Dm, Em, Fm, Gm • Duple & Triple; Macro/Micro, Divisions, Elongations, Division/Elongations and Macrobeat Rests	
8.2 Tonal	New Stepwise Patterns in Minor Tonality (TDRM, MFM, MRDTL)
8.3 Tonal	Generalizing New Minor Stepwise Patterns (siLTDRMF)
Reading Benchmark 8B • Minor; siLTDRMF; Keys: Cm, Dm, Em, Fm, Gm • Macro/Micro, Divisions, Elongations	
8.4 Tonal	Two New LA-Signatures (B-LA and A-LA)
8.5 Tonal	Combining Stepwise and Harmonic Patterns
Reading Benchmark 8C • Minor; Tonic and siLTDRMF; Keys: Cm, Dm, Em, Fm, Gm, Am, Bm • Duple & Triple; Macro/Micro, Divisions, Elongations, Division/Elongations and Macrobeat Rests	
8.6 Rhythm	Microbeat Rests, Duple and Triple
8.7 Rhythm	Longer Rhythm Patterns
Reading Benchmark 8D • Major; Tonic/Dominant and tDRMFSL; Keys: Bb, C, D, Eb, F, G, A • Duple & Triple; Macro/Micro, Divisions, Elongations, Division/Elongations and Microbeat Rests	
Reading Benchmark 8E • Minor; Tonic and siLTDRMF; Keys: Cm, Dm, Em, Fm, Gm, Am, Bm • Duple & Triple; Macro/Micro, Divisions, Elongations, Division/Elongations and Microbeat Rests	

LESSON 8.1
COMBINING HARMONIC AND STEPWISE PATTERNS

Before we combine rhythm patterns **and unfamiliar** stepwise patterns and harmonic patterns in **Reading Benchmark 8A**, we will first combine **familiar** stepwise and harmonic patterns.

STEPS VS. LEAPS REVISITED

As we did with major, take note of the visual difference between a step and a leap. When you read by **step**, the notes are right next to each other (on a line, and then on a space, or on a space and then on a line). When you read by **leap**, you will skip either a line or a space.

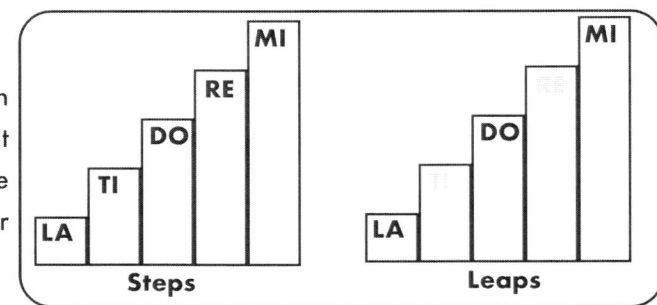

Read these **familiar** harmonic and stepwise patterns in all of our familiar LA-signatures.

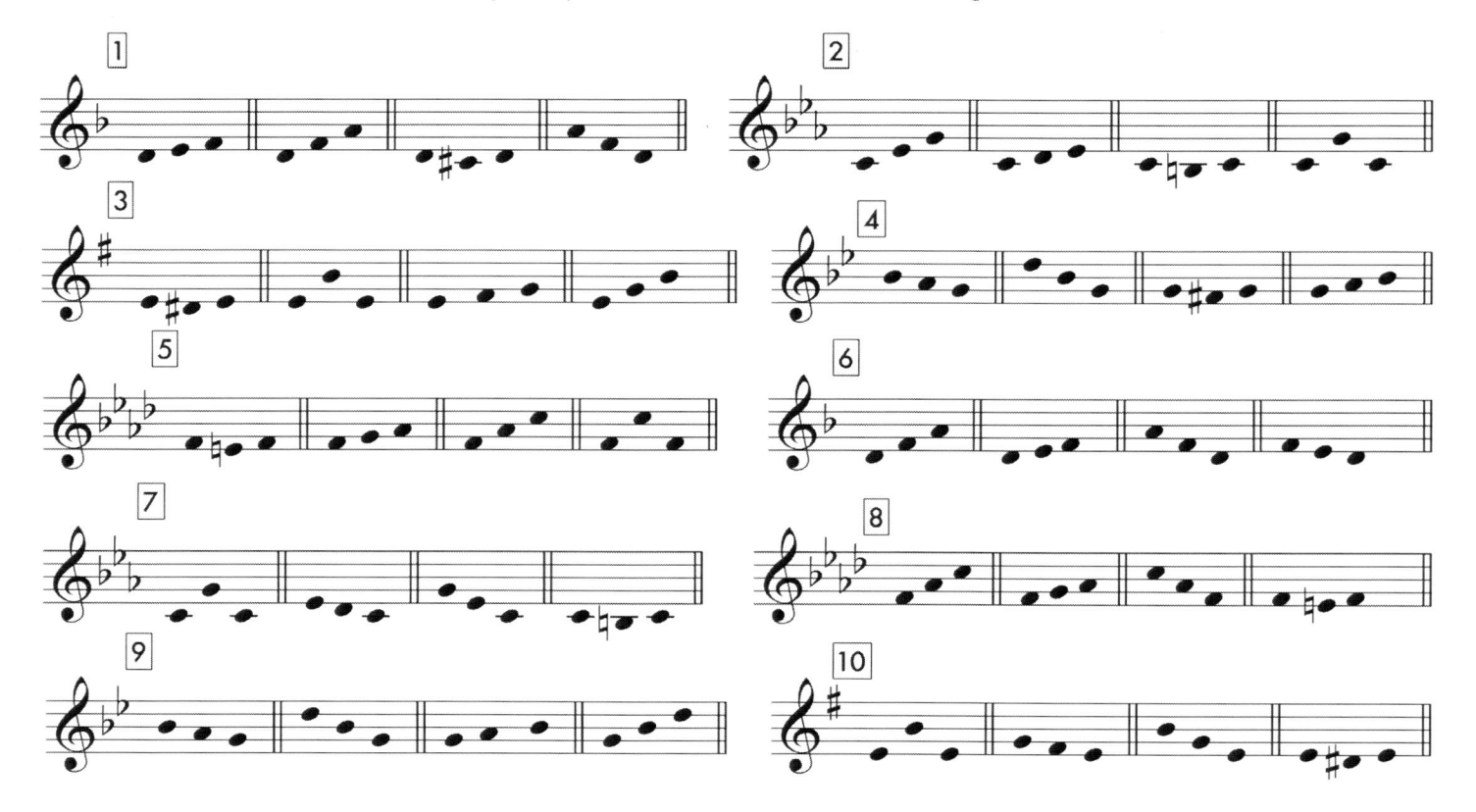

Read these familiar **and unfamiliar** harmonic and stepwise patterns in all of our familiar LA-signatures.

PREPARING FOR BENCHMARK 8A

As you approach the upcoming Reading Benchmarks, it may be a useful technique to continue to include some annotations in your tonal analysis. As you scan the pitches of the melody, be on the lookout for familiar and unfamiliar tonic patterns. You may wish to **circle** them. That way, you will know that everything else is merely a stepwise pattern. Look at the example below.

READING BENCHMARK 8A

Tonality = Minor
Pitches = Tonic and siLTD
Keys = Cm, Dm, Em, Fm, Gm

Meters = Duple and Triple
Time Signatures = 2/4, 4/4, 2/2; 6/8, 3/4
Functions = Macro/microbeat, divisions, elongations, division/elongations, macrobeat rests

More Difficult Exercises

LESSON 8.2
NEW STEPWISE PATTERNS IN MINOR TONALITY
TDRM, MFM, MRDTL

We will be learning to read two new pitches in minor tonality: RE and FA. Interestingly, you have already learned these pitches in major tonality. We will now learn them in the context of three familiar minor melodic patterns that we previously learned: TI DO RE MI, MI FA MI, and MI RE DO TI LA. Let's begin in the familiar key of G-LA.

TDRM, MFM, MRDTL IN G-LA

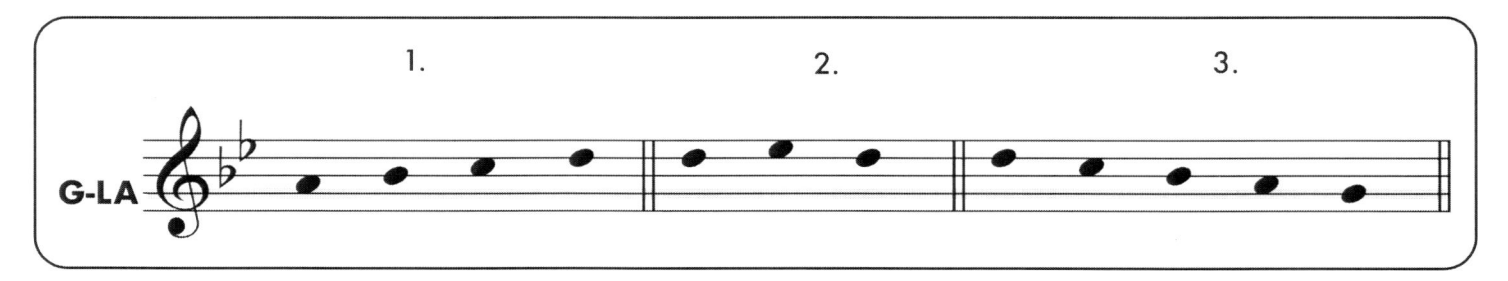

Before you sing these patterns, ground yourself in minor tonality by singing the Tonal Sequence (MI FA MI RE DO TI SI LA) and/or the first four harmonic patterns (LA DO, MI LA, SI TI, DO LA).

The first pattern is **TI DO RE MI**. Look at the notation, take a breath and sing **TI DO RE MI**. Just as you did when you echoed the patterns, keep the pitches separated. The second pattern is **MI FA MI**. Look at the notation, take a breath and sing **MI FA MI**. The third pattern is **MI RE DO TI LA**. Look at the notation, take a breath and sing **MI RE DO TI LA**.

Look at each of the patterns individually, and take note of where the first pitch of each pattern is **in relation to LA**. Visually recall the tonic chord, which will tell you where LA DO and MI are. If you ever get lost, you can always use the tonic chord as a visual problem-solving tool.

Minor Tonic

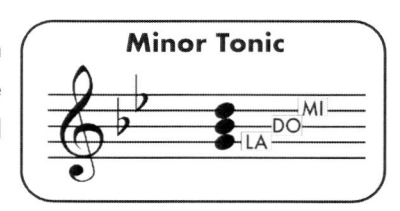

Look at each of the patterns individually, and take note of where the first pitch of each pattern is **in relation to LA**.

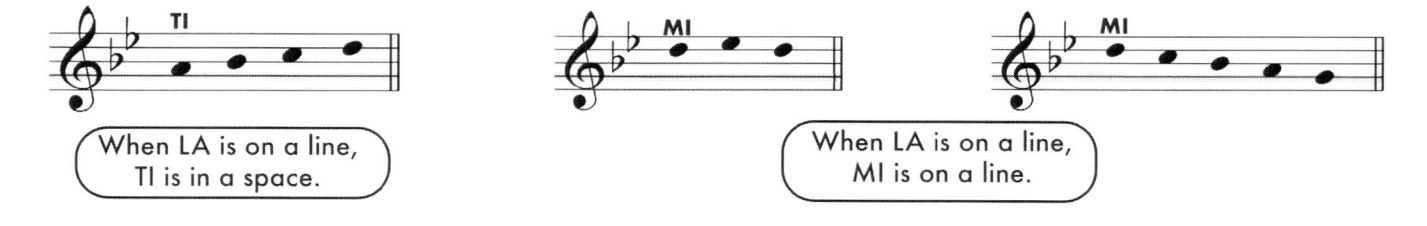

When LA is on a line, TI is in a space.

When LA is on a line, MI is on a line.

Read these three patterns, one after the other with a short pause in-between. These are **familiar patterns in a familiar order**. Also read them in **unfamiliar order** (3 2 1; 1 3 2; 2 3 1; 2 1 3; 3 1 2). Establishing tonality each time will help you maintain LA in your audiation.

! If you need an aural reminder of these three patterns, review them in the companion course videos. Remember: we are learning to read **familiar patterns**. !

COMBINING LTD, DTL, LsiL & TDRM, MFM, MRDTL IN G-LA

Read these patterns that combine our first set of stepwise patterns with our second set.

SAME PATTERNS IN OTHER KEYS

Let's look at our three new patterns in our other familiar keys. Let's begin with D-LA. Look at each of the patterns individually, and take note of where the **first pitch** of each pattern is **in relation to DO**. It will be different in D-LA since D is on a space.

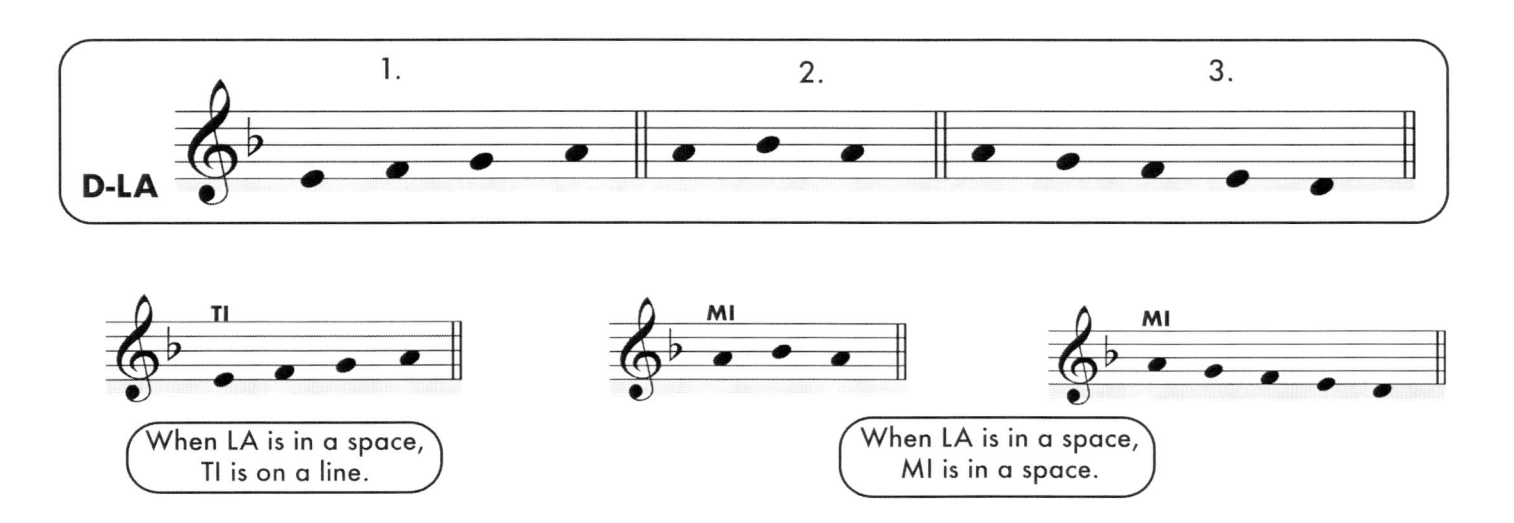

D-LA

When LA is in a space, TI is on a line.

When LA is in a space, MI is in a space.

Sing these patterns in both their familiar order and as many unfamiliar orders as you can. Establish tonality each time to keep LA in your audiation. Then, read the patterns on the following page which combine LTD, DTL, LsiL and TDRM, MFM, MRDTL in D-LA.

/ **242** The Literate Musician

COMBINING LTD, DTL, LsIL & TDRM, MFM, MRDTL IN D-LA

Since you have seen one key with LA on a line and one key with LA on a space, you should be able to make generalizations to the other keys below. **Be sure to establish tonality in each new key!**

COMBINING LTD, DTL, LsIL & TDRM, MFM, MRDTL IN E-LA

Here are our three familiar patterns in E-LA

COMBINING LTD, DTL, LsIL & TDRM, MFM, MRDTL IN F-LA

Here are our three familiar patterns in F-LA

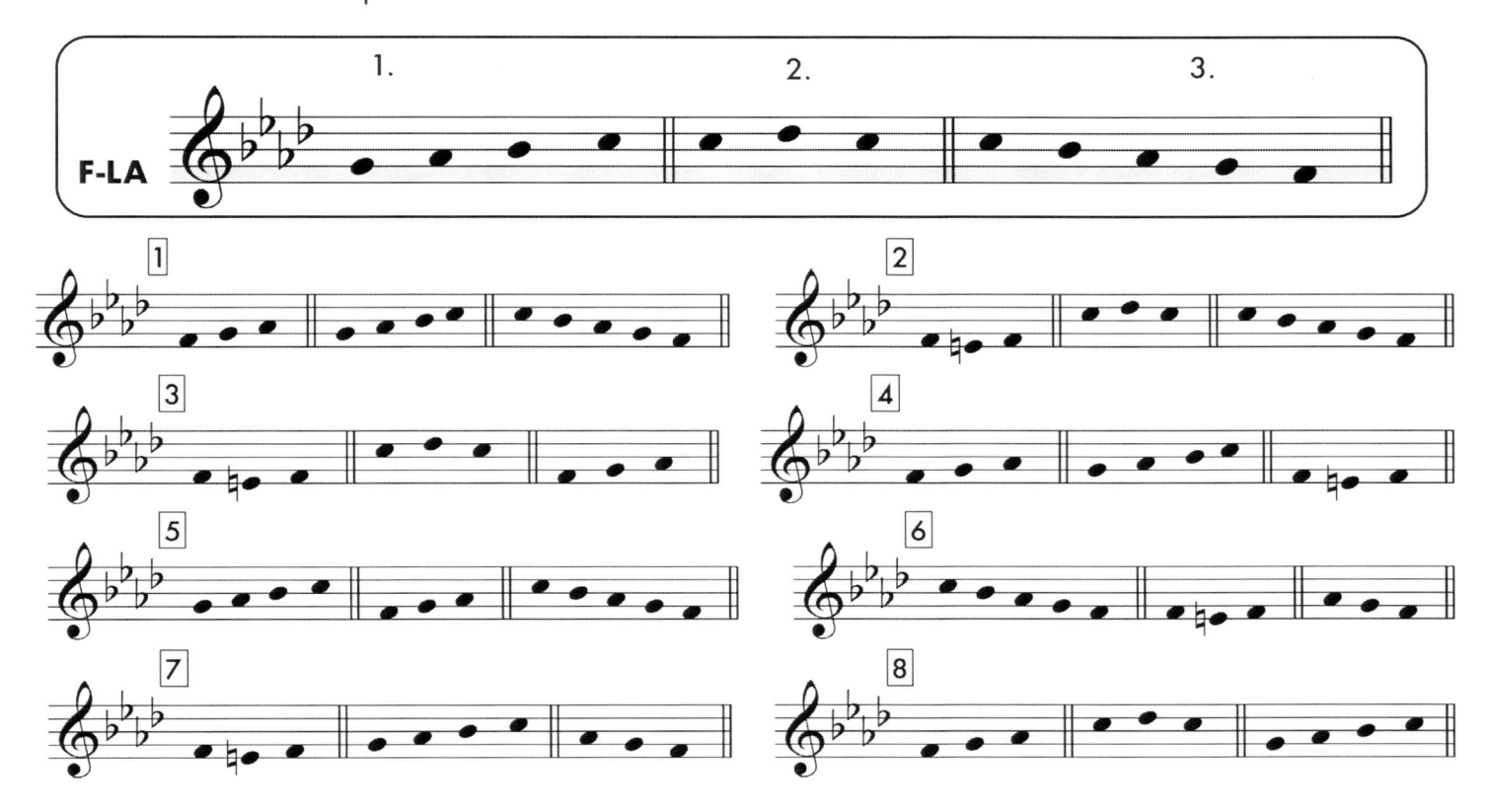

COMBINING LTD, DTL, LsIL & TDRM, MFM, MRDTL IN C-LA

Here are our three familiar patterns in C-LA

LESSON 8.3
GENERALIZATION IN MINOR TONALITY
SiLTDRMF

Now that we know how to read 6 familiar patterns, we can read seven pitches. These seven pitches compromise all of the pitches in minor tonality (LA TI DO RE MI FA and low SI). To prepare for all the possibilities of stepwise patterns that will appear in **Reading Benchmark 8B**, use the skill of generalization to read the pattern sets below. The final pattern will be unfamiliar, and will require generalization. **As we did in previous lessons, review translating patterns before you generalize notationally.**

GENERALIZATION IN G-LA

GENERALIZATION IN E-LA

GENERALIZATION IN D-LA

GENERALIZATION IN F-LA

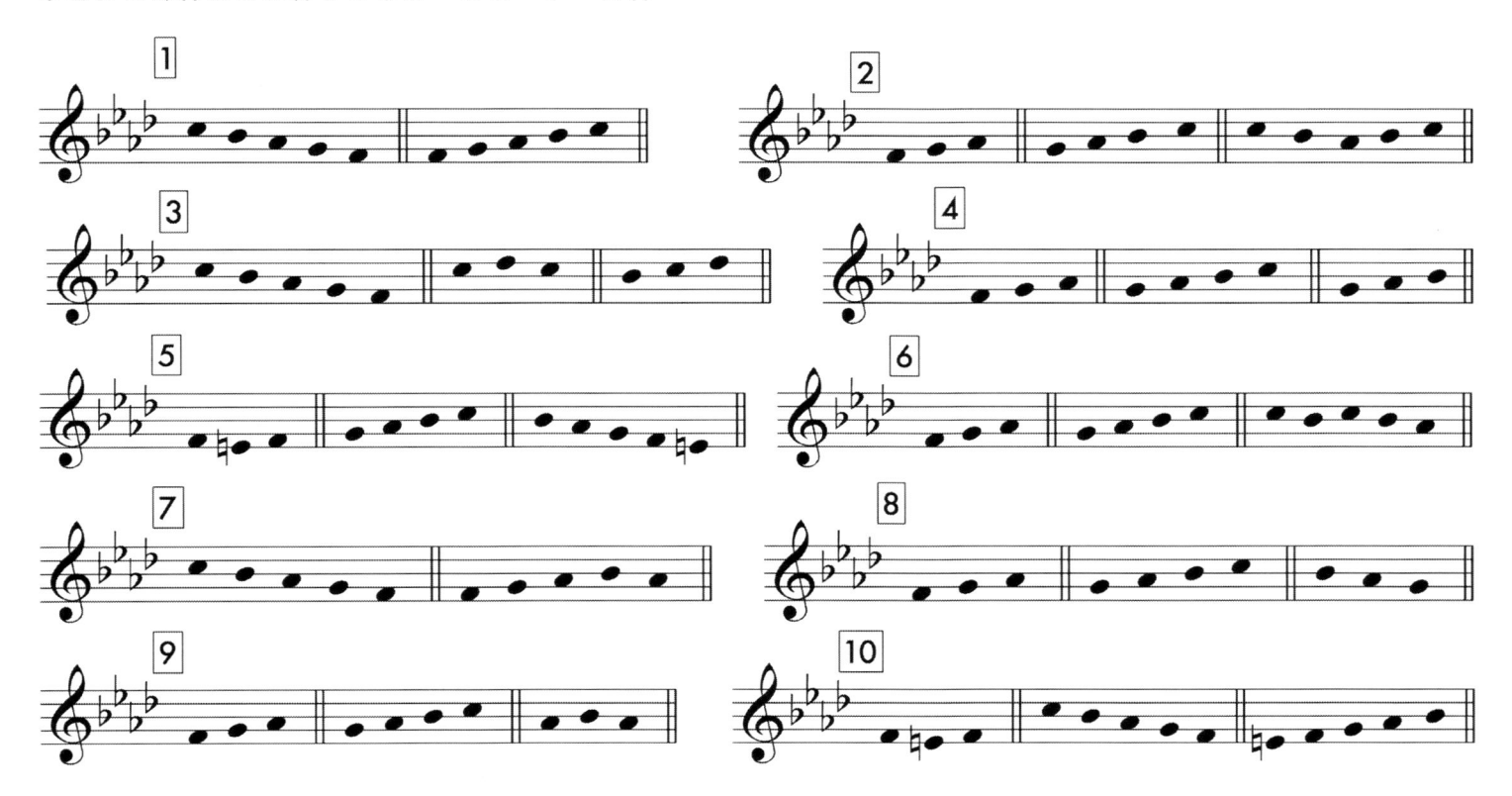

GENERALIZATION IN C-LA

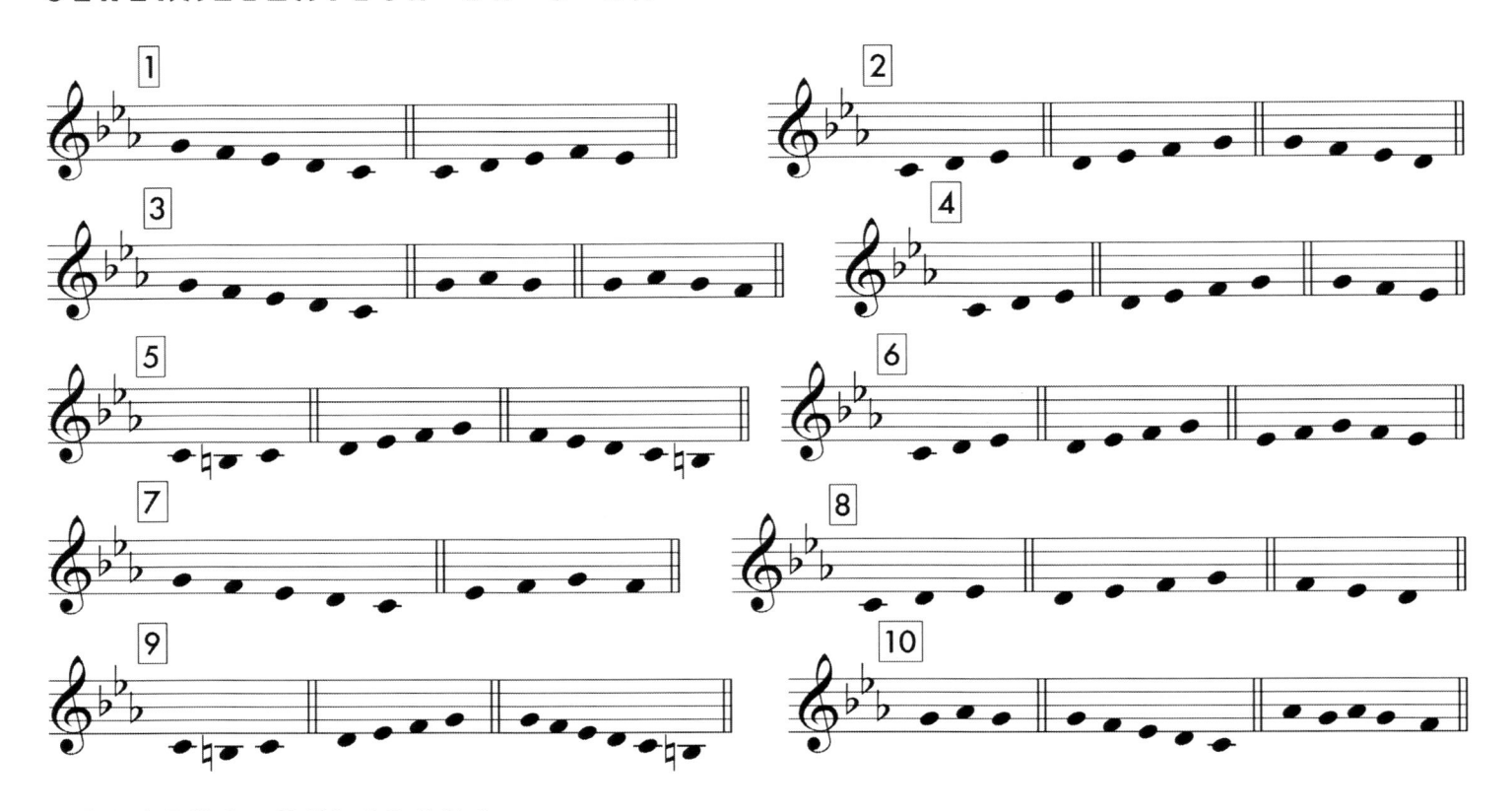

TRACING MELODIES

Trace the pitches in the below exercises. They all start and end on LA. The beams have been removed so you do not concern yourself with rhythm. Do these all in one breath. Follow along with your finger, as necessary.

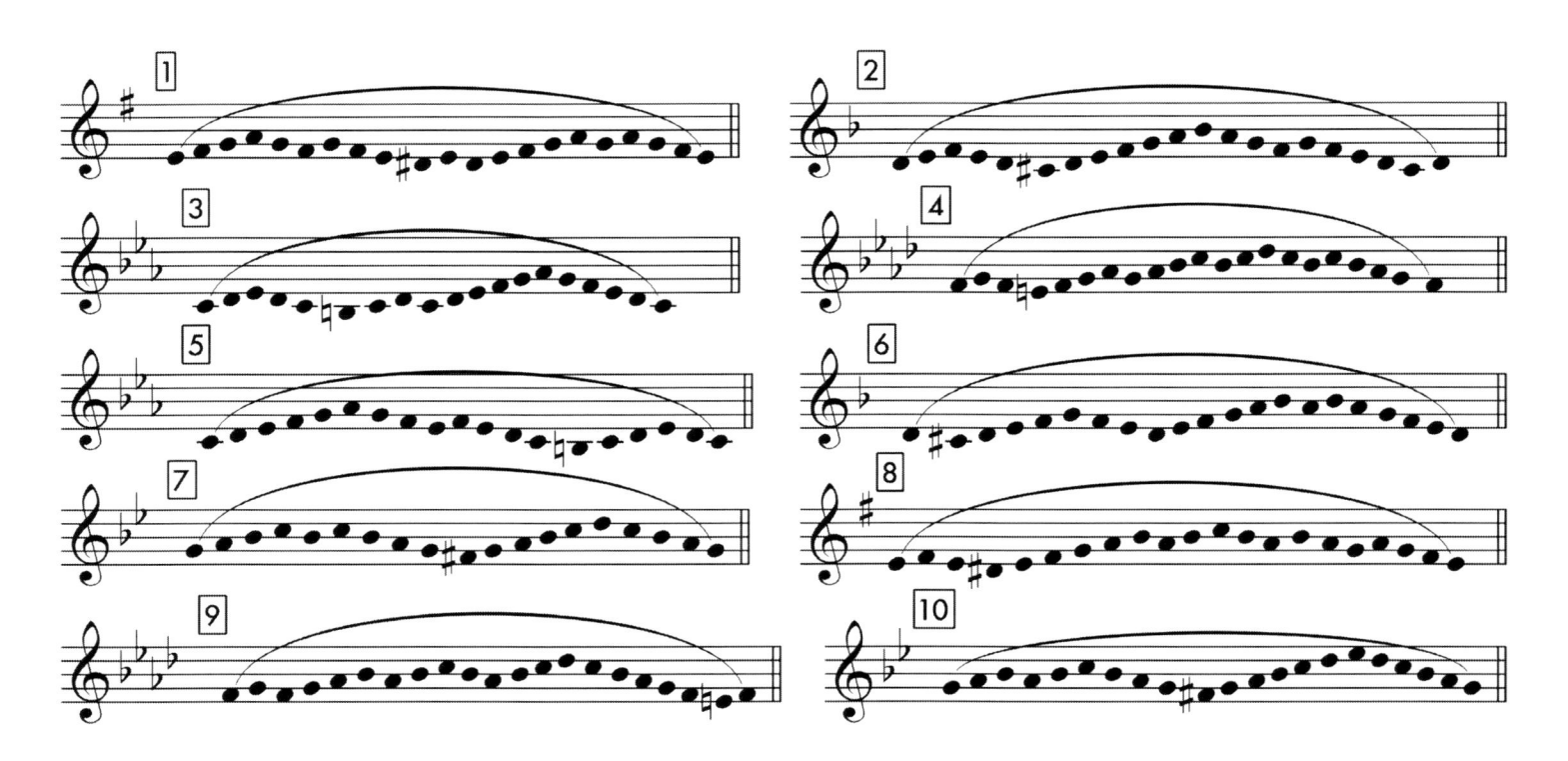

READING BENCHMARK 8B

Tonality = Minor	**Meters =** Duple and Triple
Pitches = siLTDRMF	**Time Signatures** = 2/4, 4/4, 2/2; 6/8, 3/4
Keys = Cm, Dm, Em, Fm, Gm	**Functions** = Macro/microbeat, divisions, elongations

More Difficult Exercises

LESSON 8.4
TWO NEW LA SIGNATURES
B-LA AND A-LA

B-LA

HOW TO FIND LA

When the key signature has SHARPS, **the last sharp is TI**. Count up or down to get to LA.

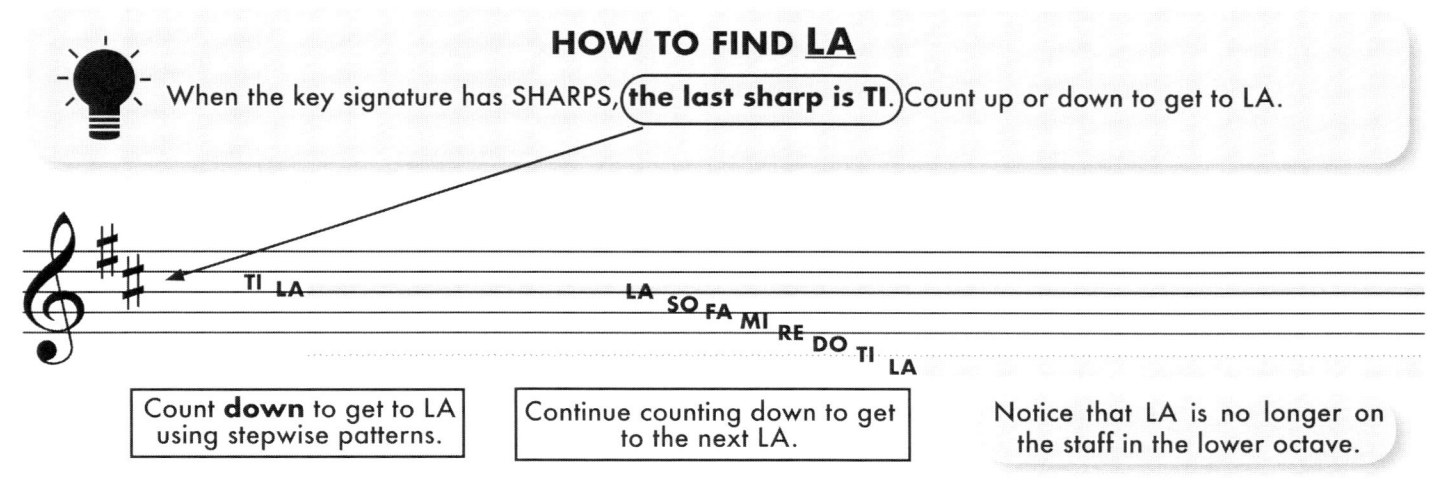

Count **down** to get to LA using stepwise patterns.

Continue counting down to get to the next LA.

Notice that LA is no longer on the staff in the lower octave.

Trace the pitches below in B-LA using solfege.

Read these familiar stepwise patterns in unfamiliar order in **B-LA**.

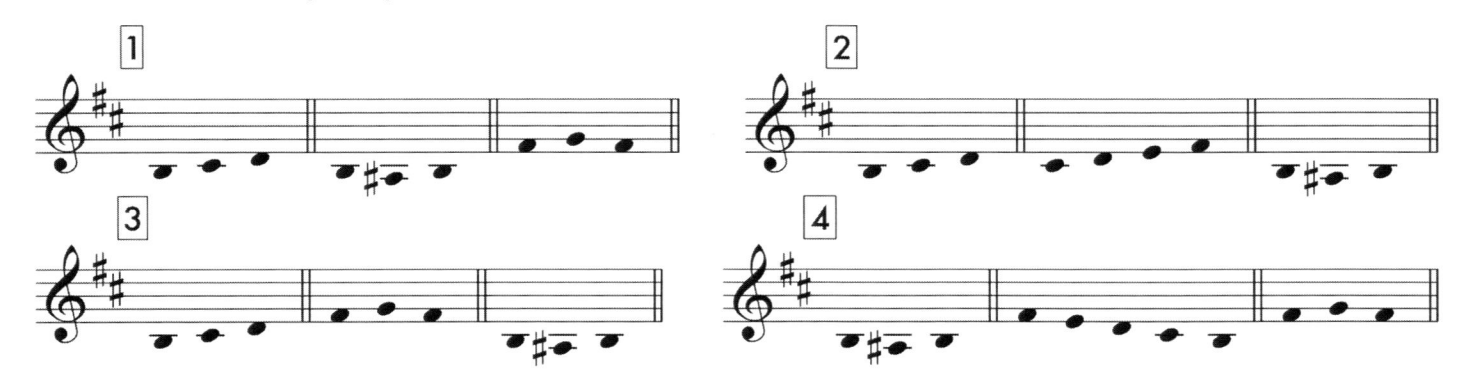

Read these familiar harmonic patterns in unfamiliar order in **B-LA.**

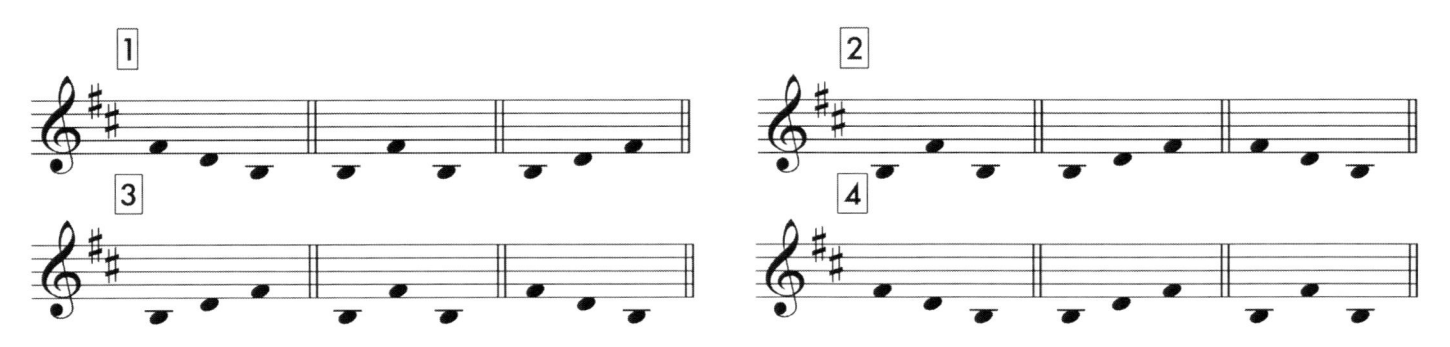

A-LA

HOW TO FIND A-LA

Since there are no sharps or flats, there is no trick to finding LA. You simply have to memorize this one.

A-LA is in the second space.

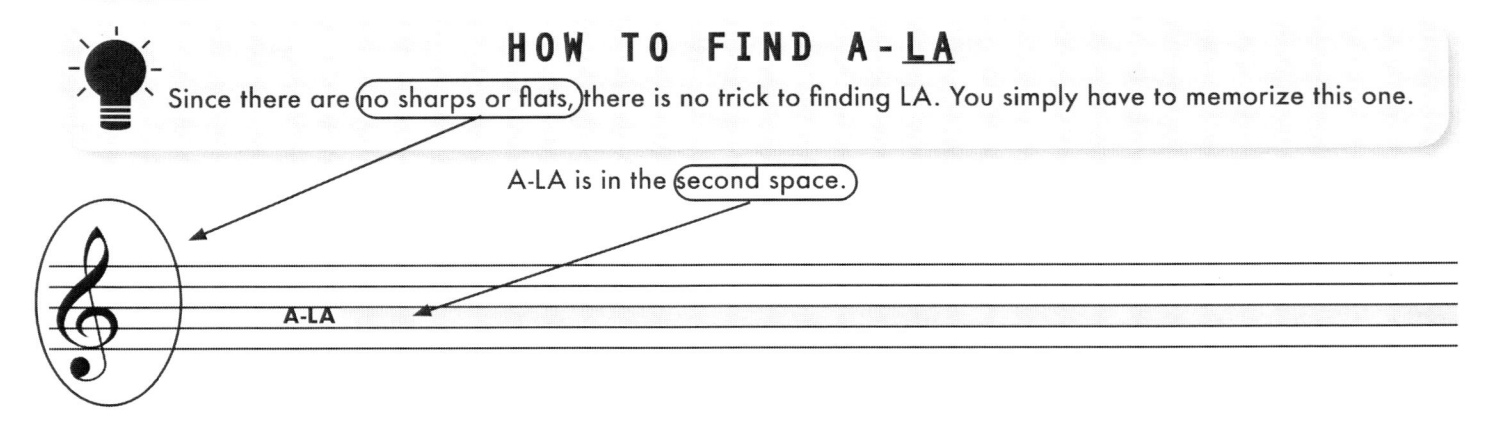

Trace the pitches below in A-LA using solfege.

Read these familiar stepwise patterns in unfamiliar order in **B-LA**.

1

2

3

4

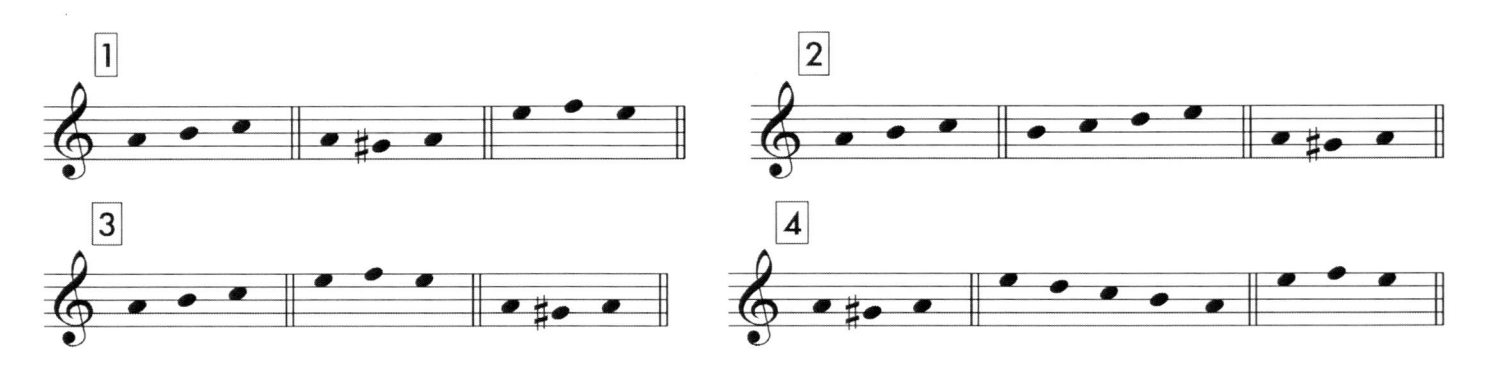

Read these familiar harmonic patterns in unfamiliar order in **B-LA**.

1

2

3

4

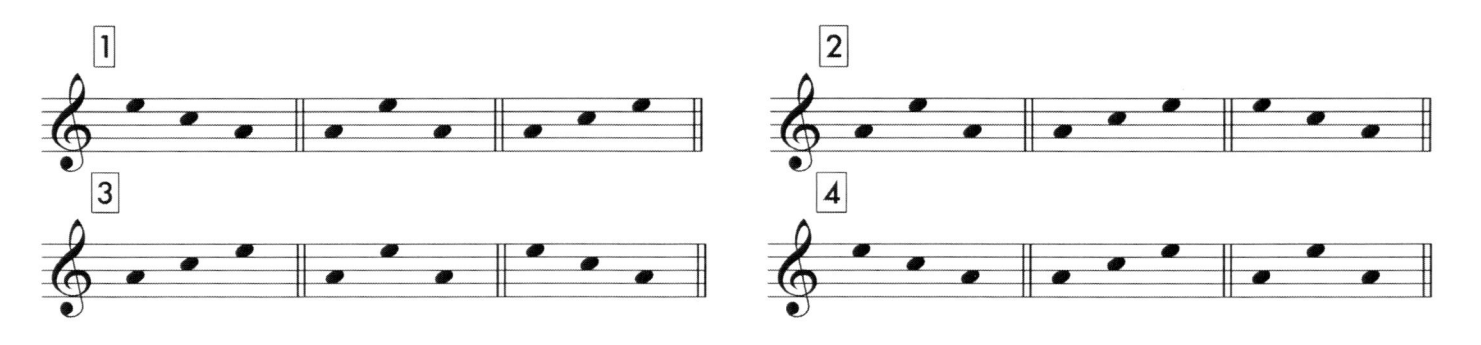

Try to play these patterns on the keyboard. Use the **Solfege** and/or **Minor I & V** Keyboard Card, lining up LA with B and then A.

LESSON 8.5
COMBINING STEPWISE AND HARMONIC PATTERNS
MINOR TONALITY

Before we combine rhythm patterns and unfamiliar melodic patterns and harmonic patterns in Reading Benchmark 8C, we will first combine **familiar** stepwise and harmonic patterns in the exercises below.

HOW TO FIND LA
When the key signature has FLATS, **the last flat is FA**. Count down or up to get to LA.
When the key signature has SHARPS, **the last sharp is TI**. Count up or down to get to LA.

Try writing these four pattern sequences in several different DO-signatures. Remember: audiate, read, remove them from your view, and then write **from your audiation**.

FAMILIAR AND UNFAMILIAR PATTERNS

Use the skill of generalization to read familiar and unfamiliar harmonic **and** melodic patterns in minor tonality.

More Difficult Exercises

LESSON 8.6
MICROBEAT RESTS, DUPLE & TRIPLE

Let's continue with our study of rests, this time focusing on **microbeat rests**. Learn the rhythm cells and then read the patterns.

DUPLE MICROBEAT RESTS IN 2/4 AND 4/4

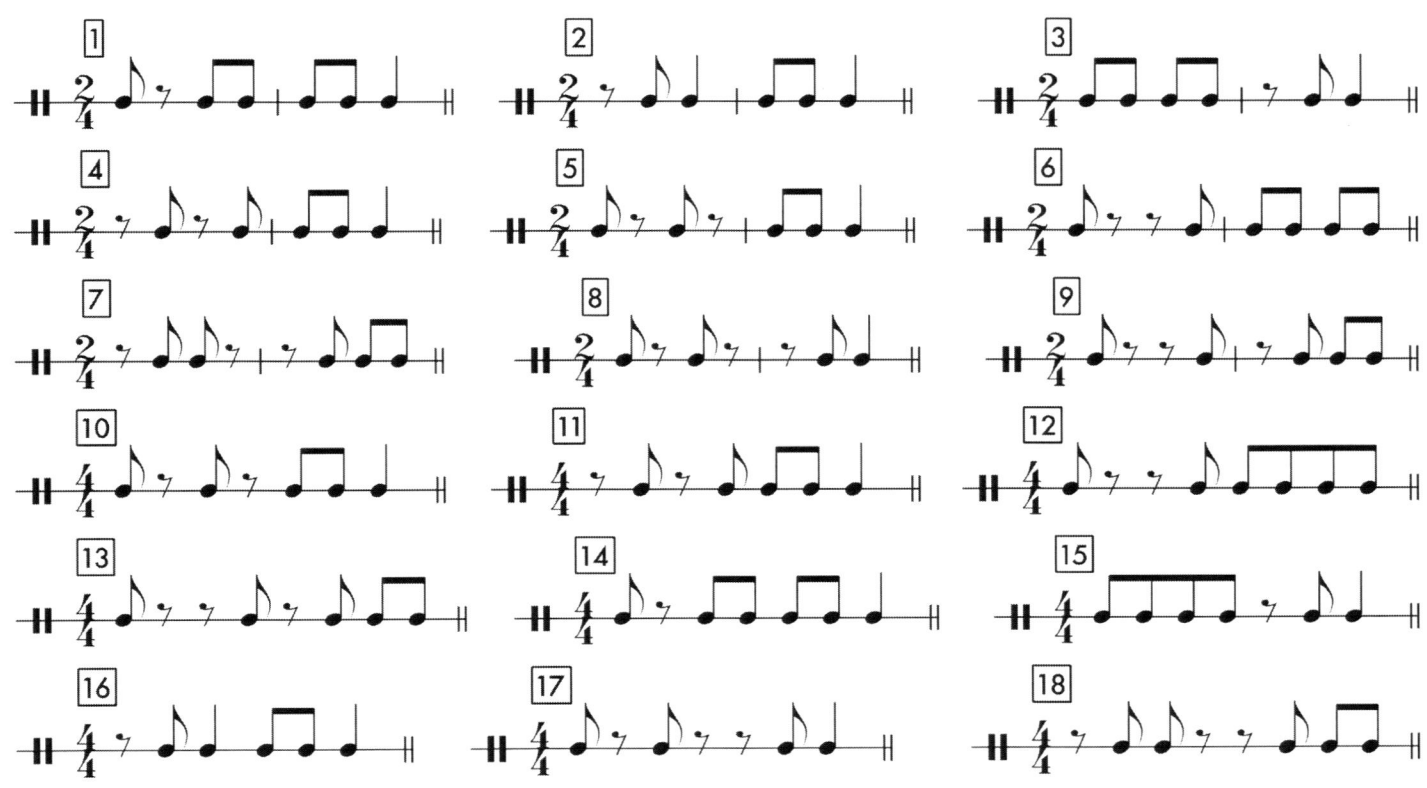

DUPLE MICROBEAT RESTS IN CUT TIME

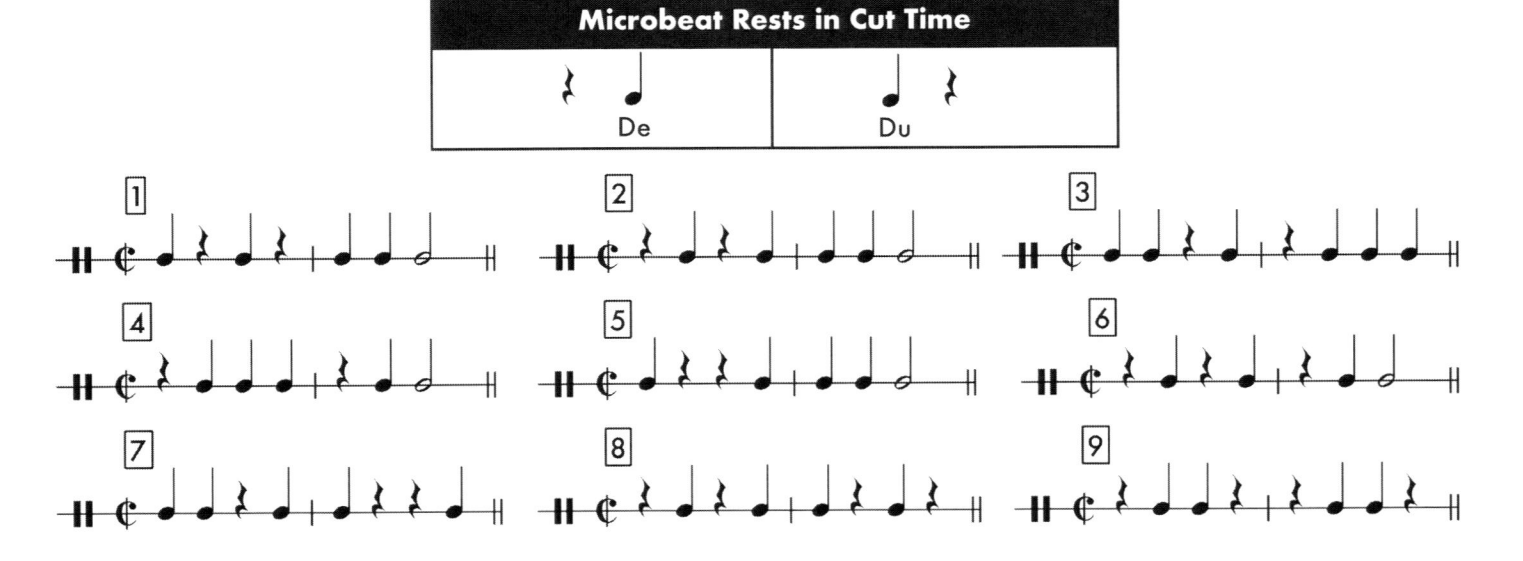

() # TRIPLE MICROBEAT RESTS IN 6/8

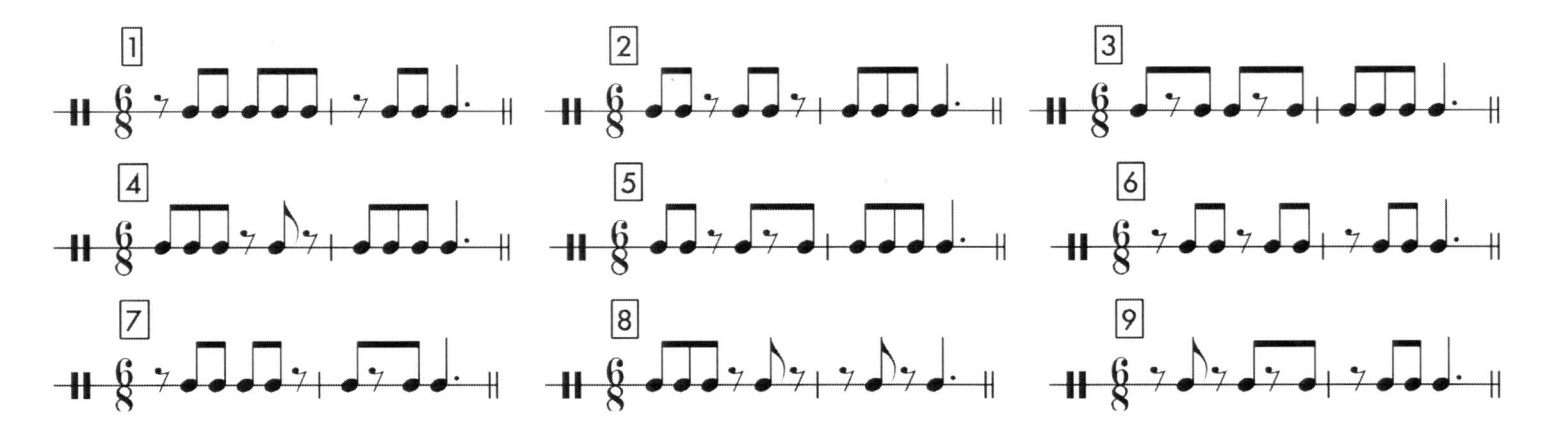

TRIPLE MICROBEAT RESTS IN 3/4

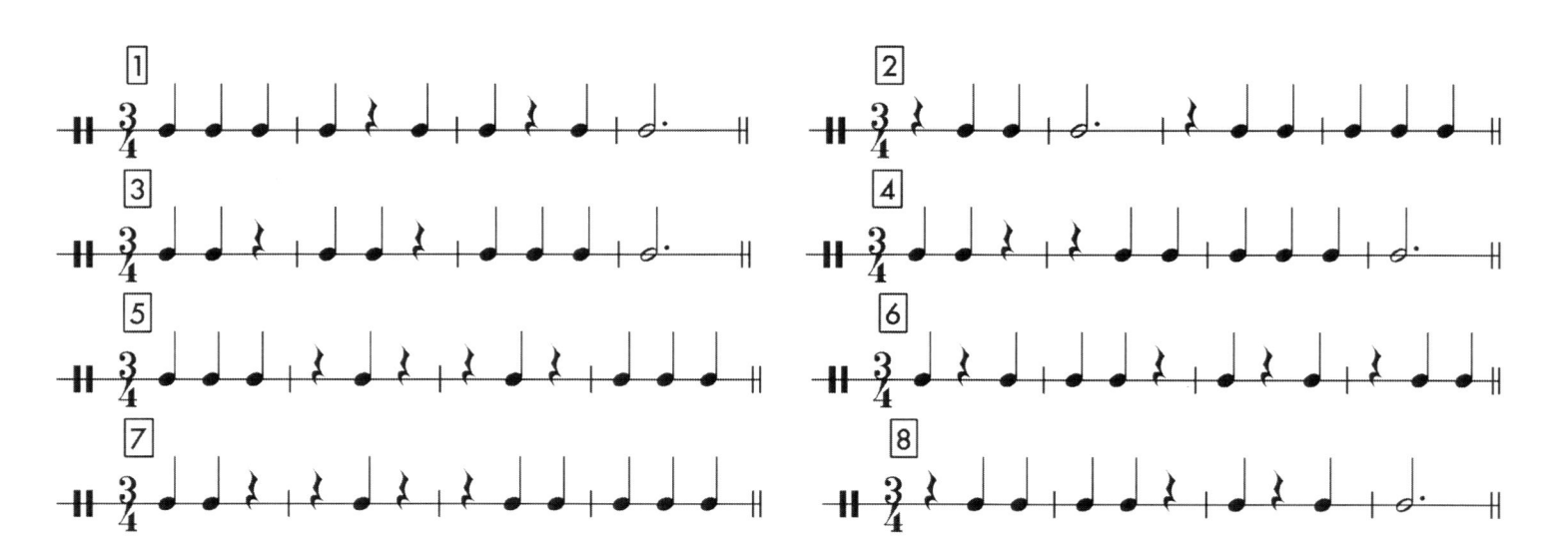

As usual, any time you learn to read a new rhythmic function, try writing both the individual rhythm cells and rhythm patterns **from your audiation**.

LESSON 8.7
LONGER RHYTHM PATTERNS

Before we combine tonal patterns and rhythms in **Reading Benchmark 8D** and **8E**, it is a good idea to review all of the new rhythm patterns we have learned. Read these longer rhythm patterns in all of our previously learned meters, time signatures with macrobeats, microbeats, divisions, elongations, division/elongations, and **rests**.

Add pitches to these longer rhythmic sentences and turn into composition.

READING BENCHMARK 8D

Tonality = Major
Pitches = Tonic/Dominant and tDRMFSL
Keys = C, D, Eb, F, G, A, Bb

Meters = Duple and Triple
Time Signatures = 2/4, 4/4, 2/2; 6/8, 3/4
Functions = Macro/microbeat, divisions, elongations, division/elongations, microbeat rests

More Difficult Exercises

READING BENCHMARK 8E

Tonality = Minor
Pitches = Tonic and siLTDRMF
Keys = Cm, Dm, Em, Fm, Gm, Am, Bm

Meters = Duple and Triple
Time Signatures = 2/4, 4/4, 2/2; 6/8, 3/4
Functions = Macro/microbeat, divisions, elongations, division/elongations, microbeat rests

More Difficult Exercises

READING SEQUENCE 9

SEQUENCE 9 AT A GLANCE

Reading Content	
TONAL	**RHYTHM**
• Tonality: Minor • Pitches: Tonic and siLTDRMF • Keys: Cm, Dm, Em, Fm, Gm, Am, Bm	• Meters: Duple and Triple • Functions: Macro/Microbeats, Divisions, Elongations, Division/Elongations, Macrobeat Rests, Microbeat Rests • Time Signatures: 2/4, 4/4, Cut Time; 6/8, 3/4

Lesson Sequence	
9.1 Tonal	Dominant Patterns, Minor Tonality
9.2 Tonal	Generalizing New Dominant Patterns, Minor Tonality
9.3 Tonal	Combining Familiar and Unfamiliar Tonic and Dominant Patterns, Minor Tonality
Reading Benchmark 9A • Minor; Tonic and Dominant Only; Keys: Cm, Dm, Em, Fm, Gm, Am, Bm • Duple & Triple; Macro/Micro, Divisions, Elongations, Division/Elongations and Macro/Microbeat Rests	
9.4 Tonal	Combining Stepwise and Harmonic Patterns
Reading Benchmark 9B • Minor; Tonic/Dominant and siLTDRMF; Keys: Cm, Dm, Em, Fm, Gm, Am, Bm • Duple & Triple; Macro/Micro, Divisions, Elongations, Division/Elongations and Macro/Microbeat Rests	
9.5 Rhythm	Ties, Duple and Triple
Reading Benchmark 9C • Major; Tonic/Dominant and tDRMFSL; Keys: Bb, C, D, Eb, F, G, A • Duple & Triple; Macro/Microbeats and Ties	
Reading Benchmark 9D • Minor; Tonic and Dominant Only; Keys: Cm, Dm, Em, Fm, Gm, Am, Bm • Duple & Triple; Macro/Microbeats and Ties	

LESSON 9.1
DOMINANT PATTERNS, MINOR TONALITY

INTRODUCTION

Just as we did with major tonic and dominant patterns, we can visualize minor dominant patterns in two different ways. First, we can think about them happening **vertically**, all at once, underneath the melody. Second, we can think of them moving **horizontally**, as if they were melody.

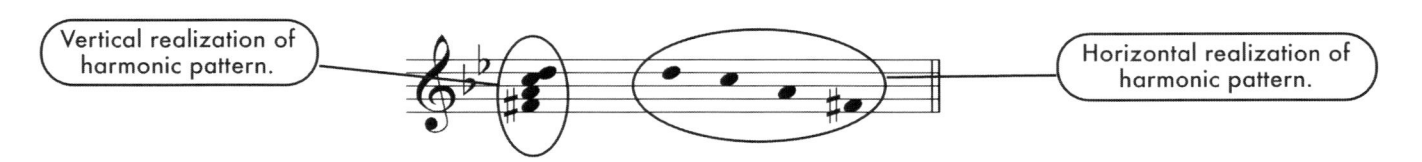

(Vertical realization of harmonic pattern.)   (Horizontal realization of harmonic pattern.)

THREE FAMILIAR DOMINANT PATTERNS: MTsi, siTM, MRTsi

We will learn dominant patterns in a very similar way that we learned tonic patterns. However, since dominant patterns feel unresolved, we will learn them in conjunction with familiar tonic patterns. We will begin by learning 3 familiar minor dominant patterns: MTsi, siTM, MRsiT. Begin by establishing minor tonality (MI FA MI RE DO TI SI LA) with G as LA.

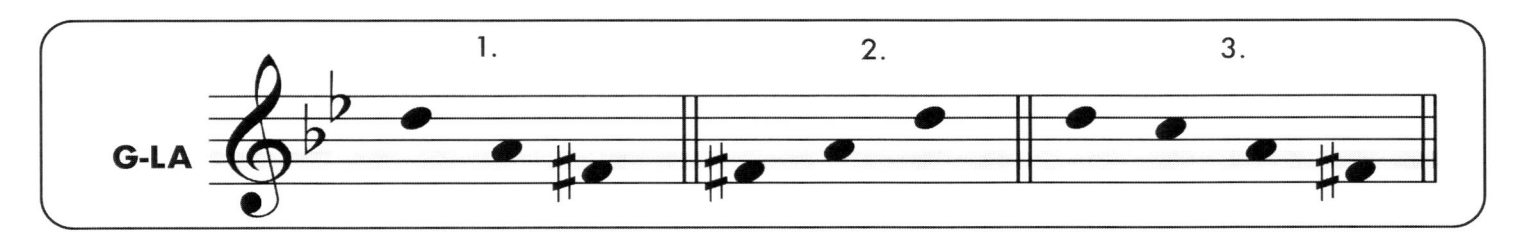

The first pattern is **MI TI SI**. Look at the notation, take a breath and sing **MI TI SI**. The second pattern is **SI TI MI**. Look at the notation, take a breath and sing **SI TI MI**. The third pattern is **MI RE TI SI**. Look at the notation, take a breath and sing **MI RE TI SI**.

! If you need an aural reminder of these 3 patterns, review them in the companion course !
videos. Remember: we are learning to read **familiar patterns**.

When you read a dominant pattern, take note of where each pitch is on the staff **in relation to LA**. You may want to review the first three minor stepwise patterns for a visual refresher of where TI and SI are in relation to LA.

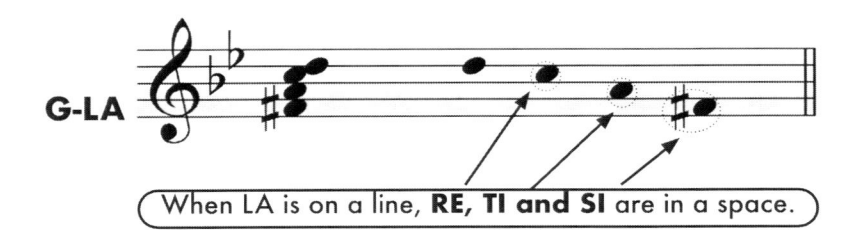

(When LA is on a line, **RE, TI and SI** are in a space.)

FAMILIAR i-V-i PATTERNS, UNFAMILIAR ORDER

Read the same 3 familiar dominant patterns, but this time, read them in an unfamiliar order in conjunction with familiar tonic chords in minor tonality. The first pattern will be a tonic chord, the second pattern will be one of our three familiar dominant chords, and the third chord will be another tonic chord.

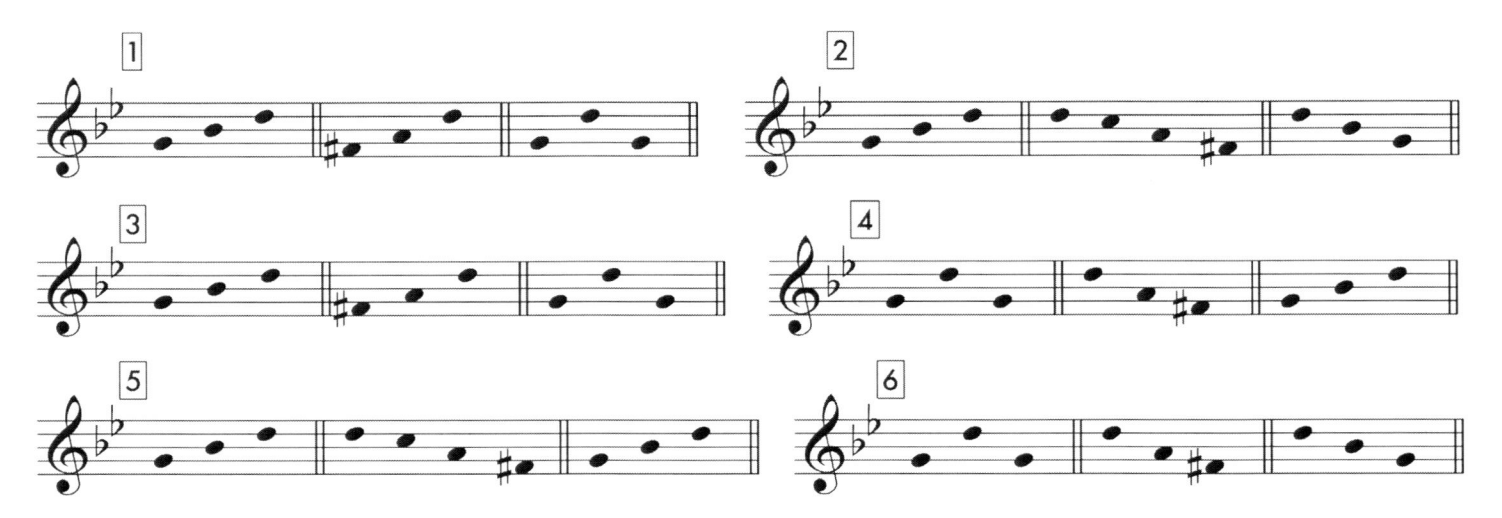

SAME PATTERNS IN DIFFERENT LA-SIGNATURES

Let's learn to read those same three dominant patterns in our familiar LA-signatures.

E-LA

Dominant Chord in E-LA

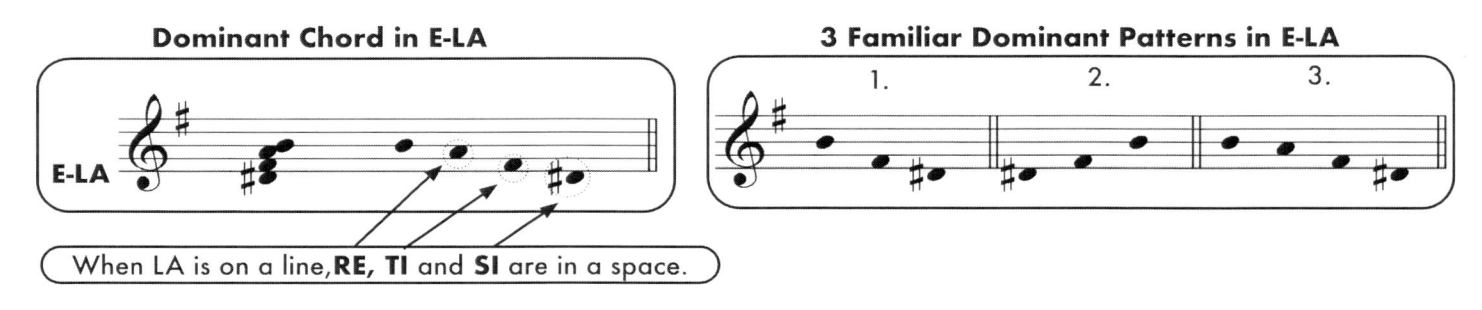

3 Familiar Dominant Patterns in E-LA

When LA is on a line, **RE, TI** and **SI** are in a space.

Read these familiar i-V-i harmonic patterns in unfamiliar order in **E-LA.**

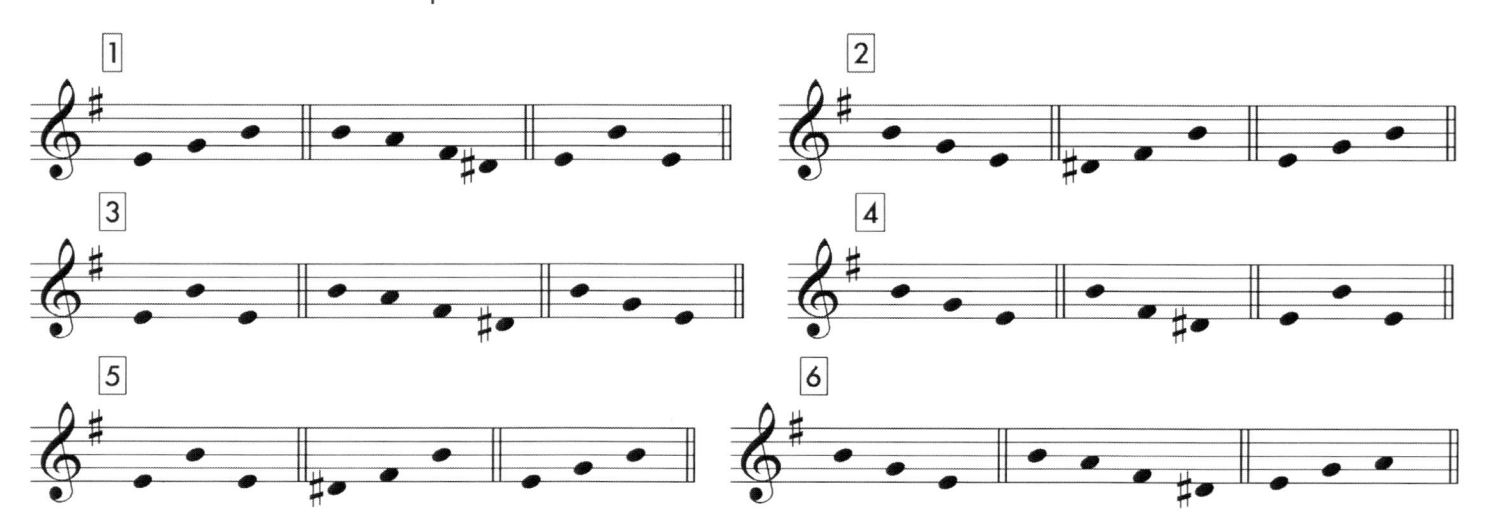

D - LA

Dominant Chord in D-LA

When LA is in a space, **RE, TI** and **SI** are on a line.

3 Familiar Dominant Patterns in D-LA

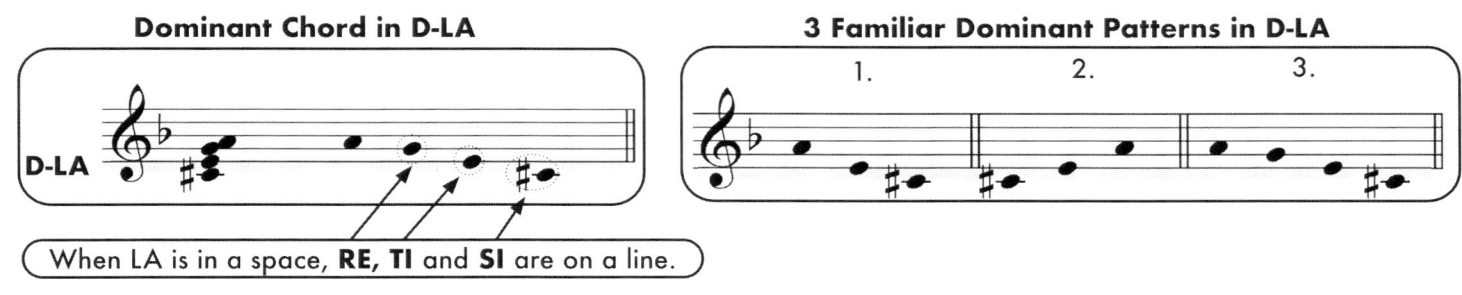

Read these familiar i-V-i harmonic patterns in unfamiliar order in **D-LA.**

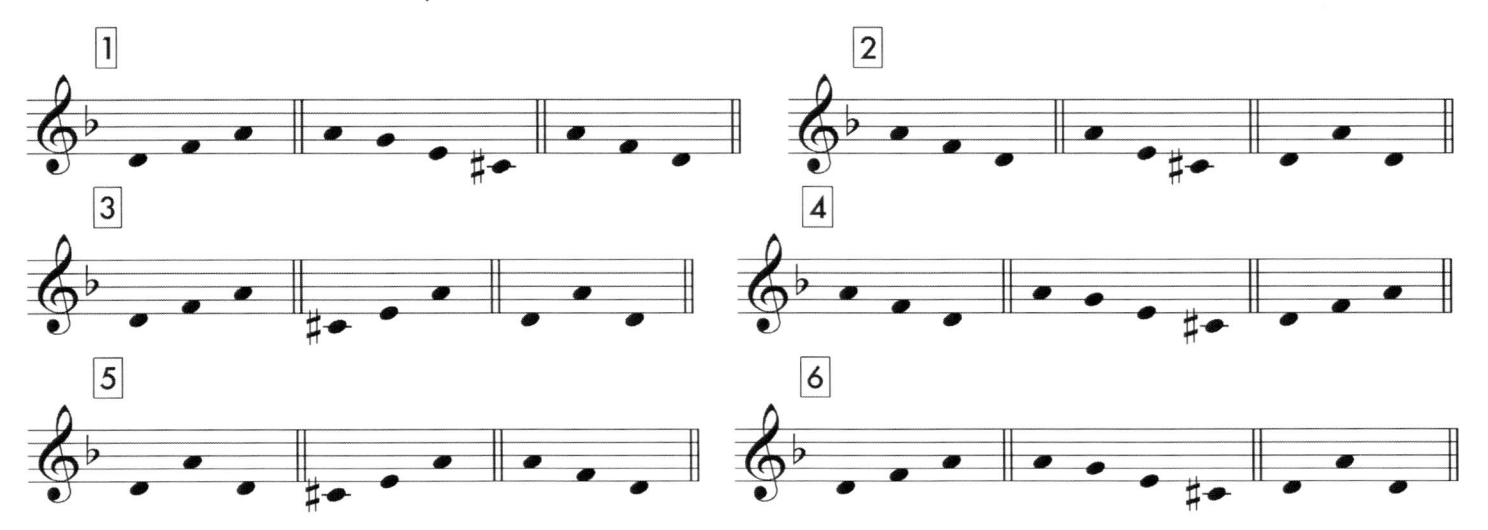

C - LA

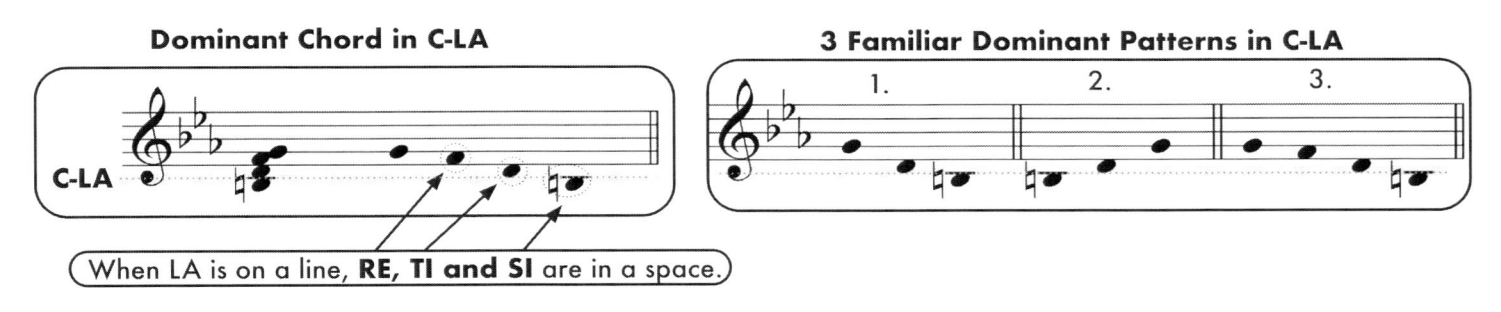

Dominant Chord in C-LA

When LA is on a line, **RE, TI** and **SI** are in a space.

3 Familiar Dominant Patterns in C-LA

Read these familiar i-V-i harmonic patterns in unfamiliar order in **C-LA**

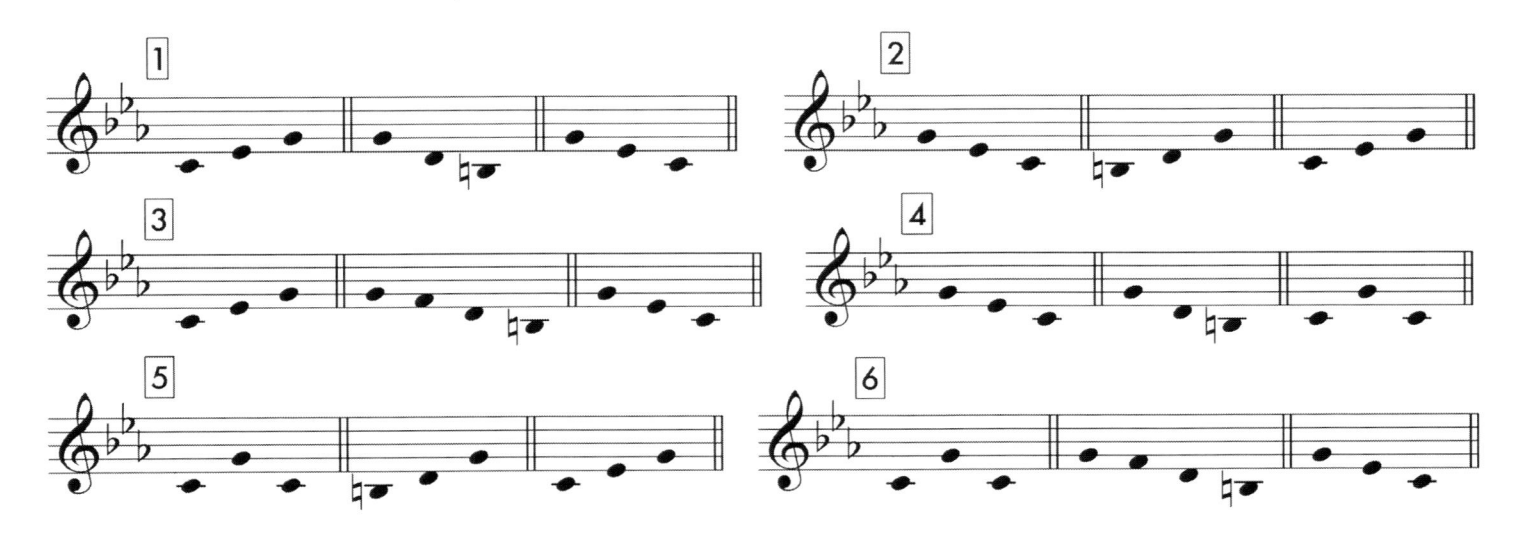

A - LA

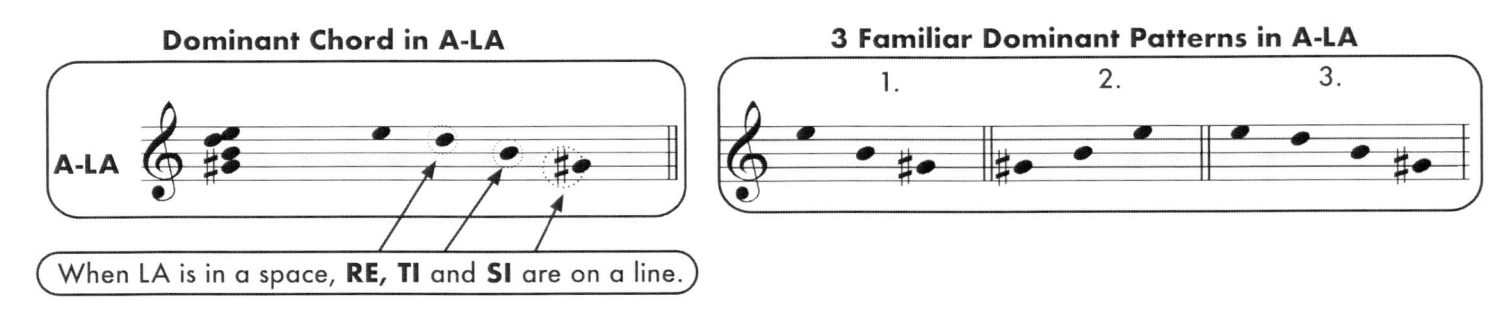

Dominant Chord in A-LA

3 Familiar Dominant Patterns in A-LA

When LA is in a space, **RE, TI** and **SI** are on a line.

Read these familiar i-V-i harmonic patterns in unfamiliar order in **A-LA**

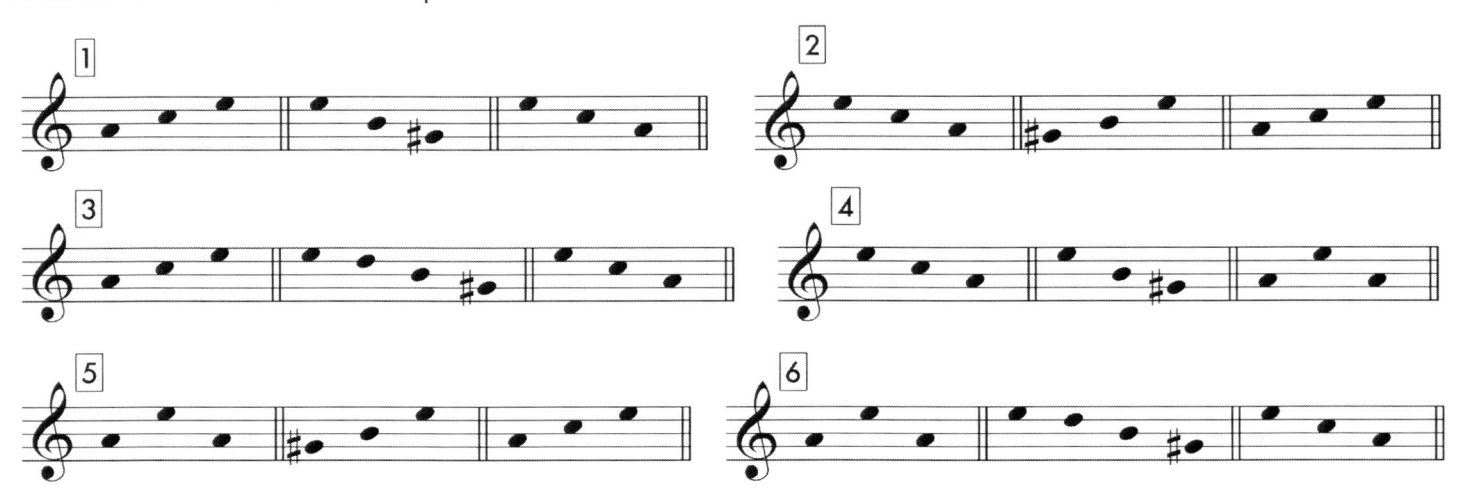

B - LA

Dominant Chord in B-LA

3 Familiar Dominant Patterns in B-LA

When LA is in a space, **RE, TI** and **SI** are on a line.

Read these familiar i-V-i harmonic patterns in unfamiliar order in **B-LA**

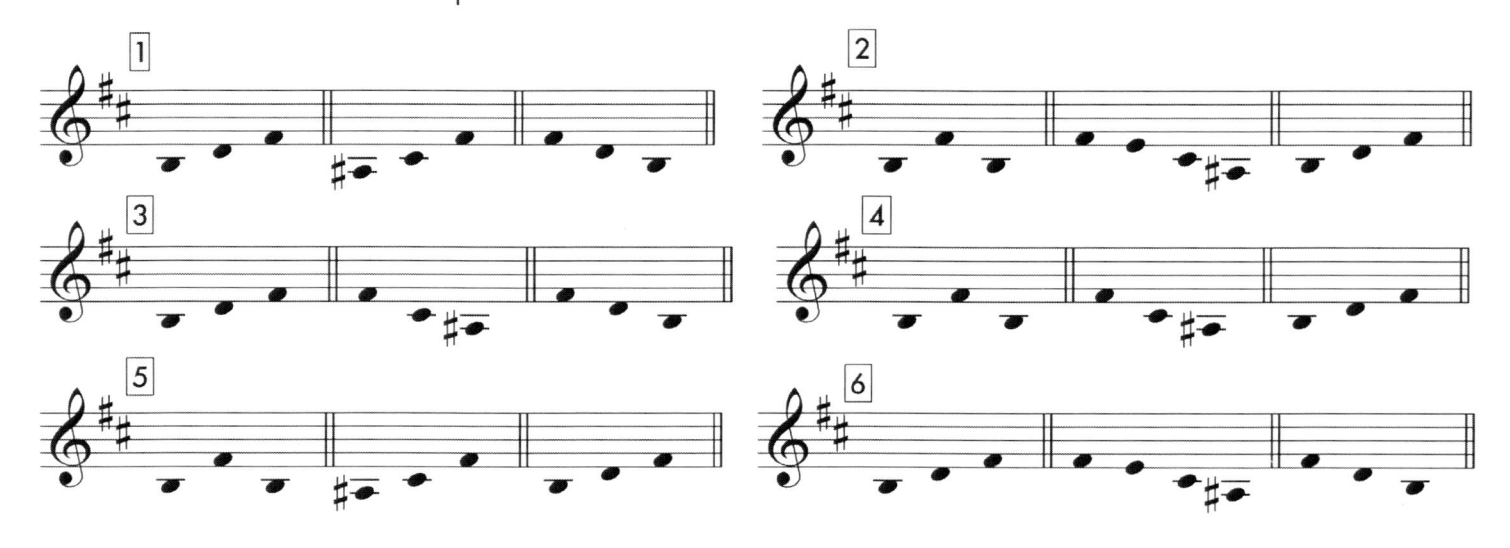

F - LA

Dominant Chord in F-LA

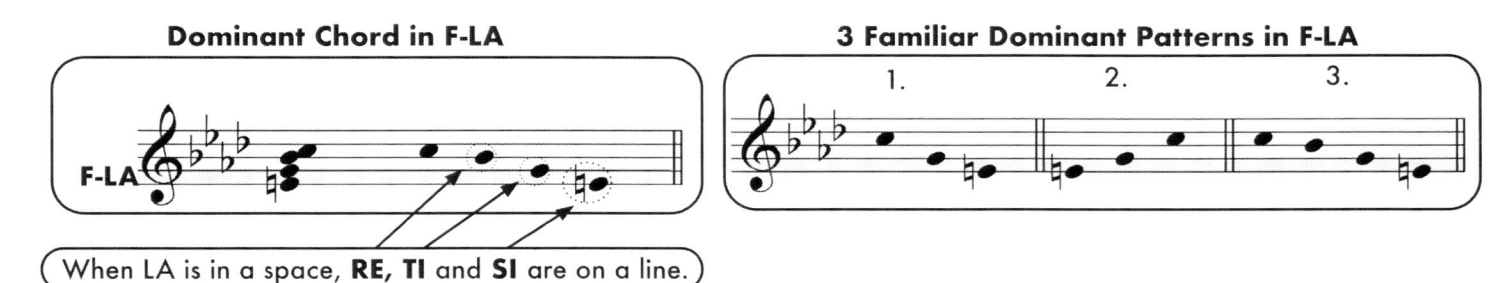

F-LA

When LA is in a space, **RE, TI** and **SI** are on a line.

3 Familiar Dominant Patterns in F-LA

1.   2.   3.

Read these familiar i-V-i harmonic patterns in unfamiliar order in **F-LA**

1 2

3 4

5 6

- Try writing these three pattern sequences in several different LA-signatures.

- This would be a perfect time to get the sound of a new function, Subdominant, in your audiation. **Spiral** to Lesson 10.1 for an aural introduction to the iv chord in minor tonality.

- Also play these patterns on the keyboard. Use the **Minor i & V** Keyboard Card.

LESSON 9.2
GENERALIZING NEW DOMINANT PATTERNS
MINOR TONALITY

Now that we have learned to read three familiar dominant patterns, we will harness the power of **generalization** to read more dominant patterns just as we did in major tonality. Some of the patterns will be familiar to you aurally from Part 1, while others will be brand new. **As we did in previous lessons, review translating patterns before you generalize notationally.**

GENERALIZING NEW PATTERNS

Look at the two patterns below in G-LA.

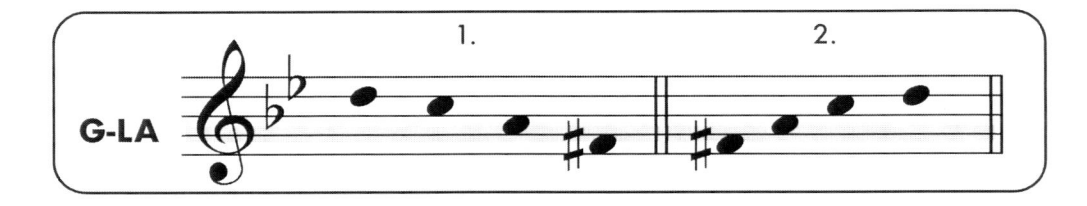

The first pattern (MI RE TI SI) is familiar to you. Using that knowledge, can you figure out the second pattern? Hopefully, you generalized that it was SI TI RE MI.

GENERALIZING DOMINANT PATTERNS IN G-LA

Use the skill of generalization to read these patterns. The final pattern in each example below will be unfamiliar. Tonic patterns are included to help you maintain a sense of tonality.

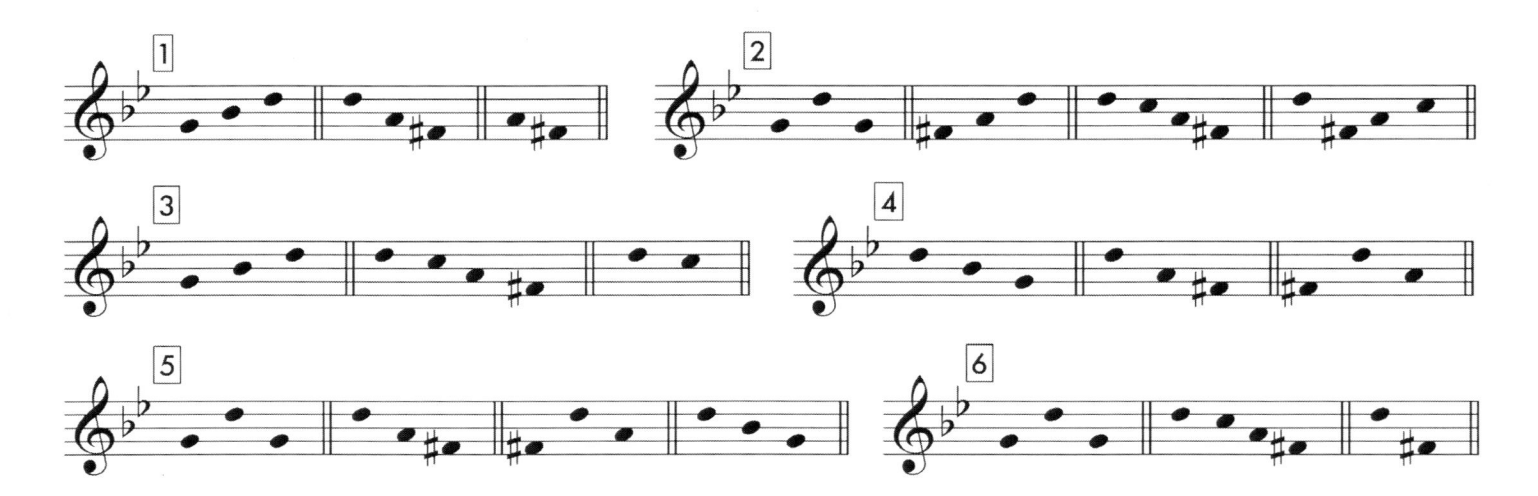

On the following pages, you will have the opportunity to generalize in all of our familiar keys. Be sure to establish tonality in each new key before you read the patterns. You can simply play a i-V-i in the new key. **If the notes are out of your vocal range, you may sing these in any comfortable octave.**

GENERALIZING DOMINANT PATTERNS IN E-LA

GENERALIZING DOMINANT PATTERNS IN D-LA

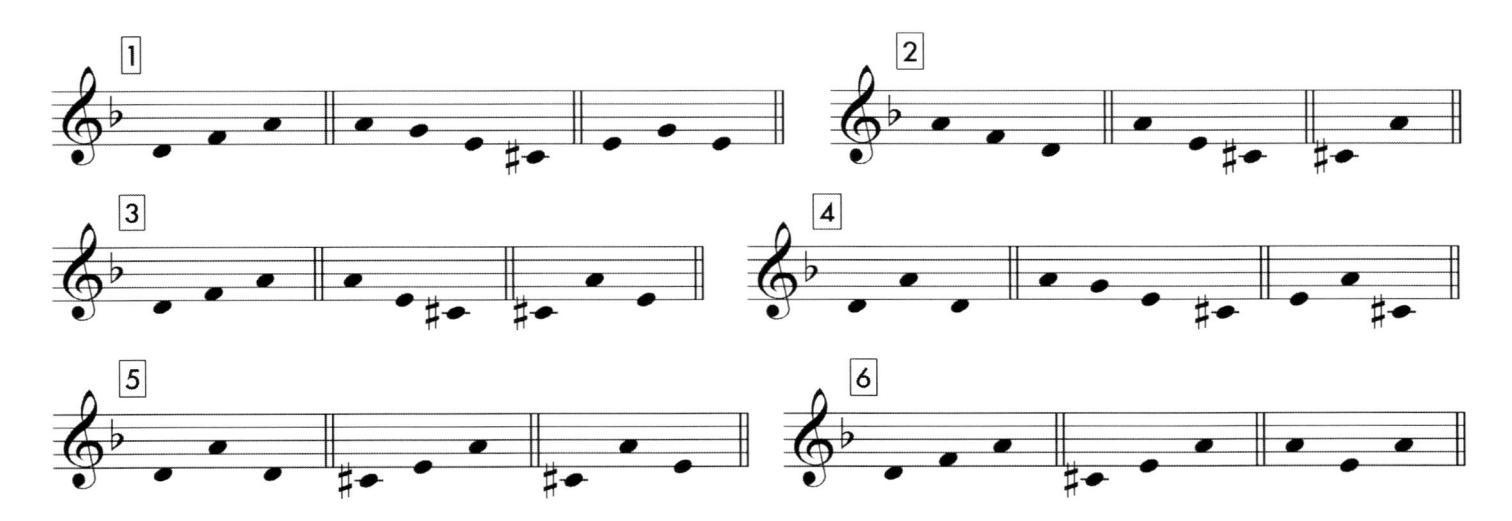

GENERALIZING DOMINANT PATTERNS IN C-LA

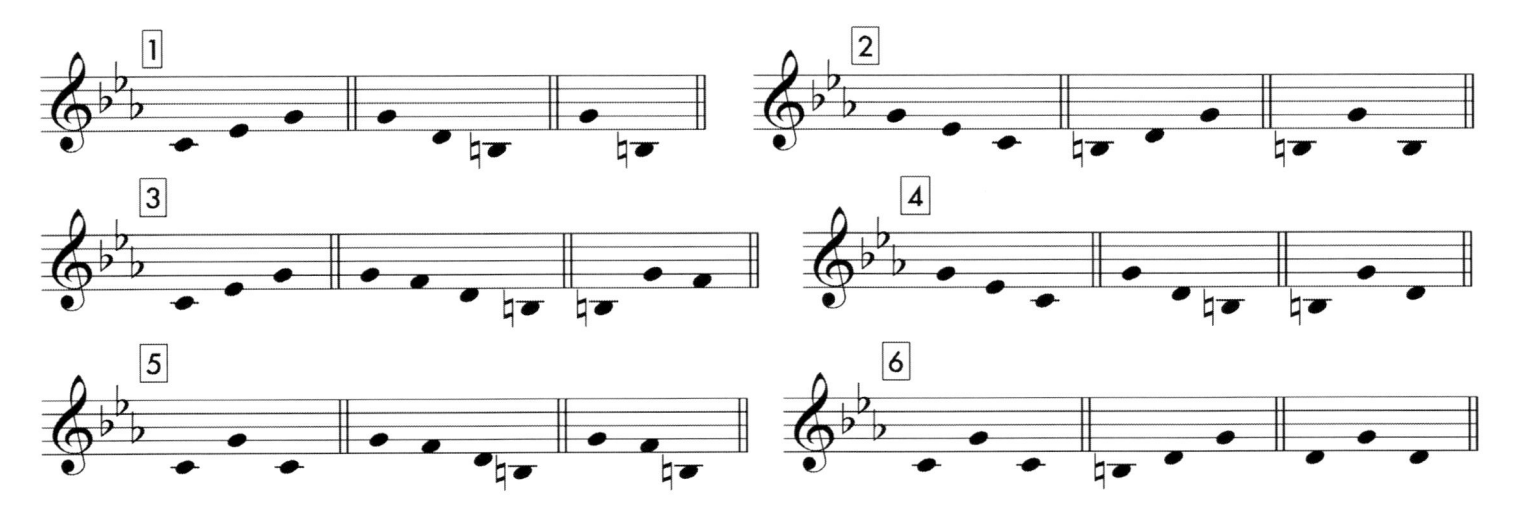

GENERALIZING DOMINANT PATTERNS IN A-LA

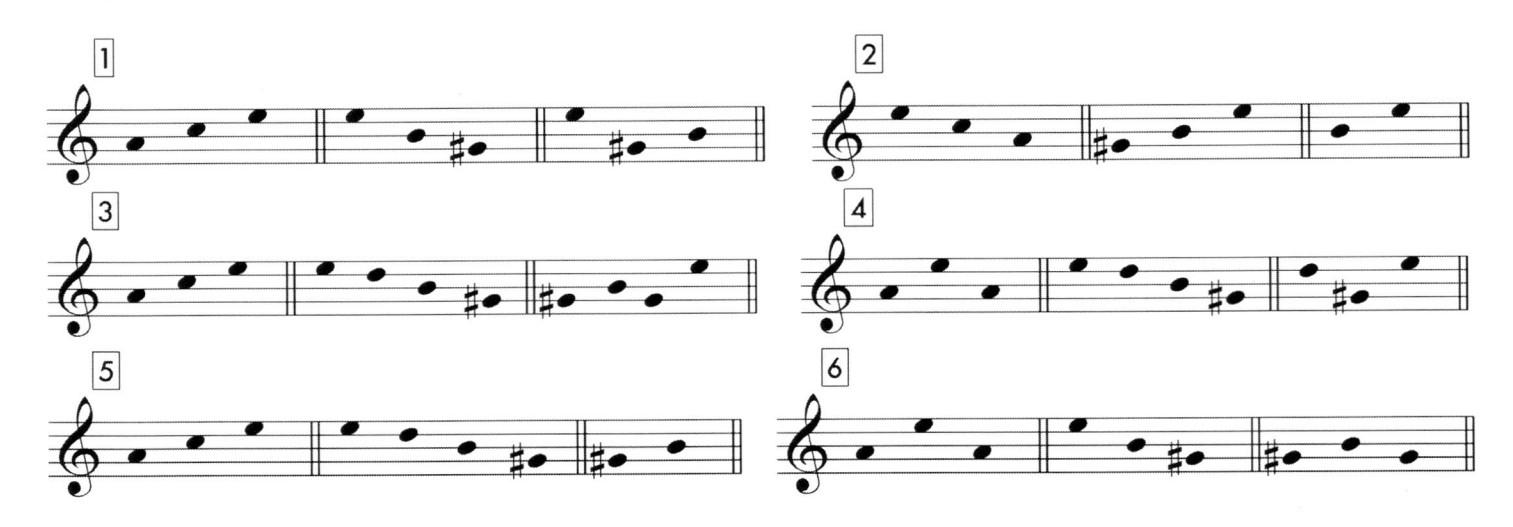

GENERALIZING DOMINANT PATTERNS IN B-LA

GENERALIZING DOMINANT PATTERNS IN F-LA

LESSON 9.3
COMBINING FAMILIAR AND UNFAMILIAR TONIC AND DOMINANT PATTERNS

FAMILIAR i&V PATTERNS, UNFAMILIAR ORDER

In preparation for **Reading Benchmark 9A**, read these **familiar** minor tonic and dominant patterns in all of our familiar key signatures in an unfamiliar order. Be sure to ground yourself in the key and tonality by playing a i-V-i on the keyboard before you read.

Try writing these four pattern sequences in several different LA-signatures. Remember: audiate, read, remove them from your view, and then write **from your audiation**.

FAMILIAR AND UNFAMILIAR i&V PATTERNS

Now, read these familiar **and unfamiliar** tonic and dominant patterns in all of our familiar key signatures in minor tonality. At least one pattern in each set will require generalization. Be patient with yourself, and remember that generalization is an inference skill, and will need persistence on your part.

READING BENCHMARK 9A

Tonality = Minor
Pitches = Tonic & Dominant only
Keys = Cm, Dm, Em, Fm, Gm, Am, Bm

Meters = Duple and Triple
Time Signatures = 2/4, 4/4, 2/2; 6/8, 3/4
Functions = Macro/microbeat, divisions, elongations, division/elongations, macro/microbeat rests

More Difficult Exercises

LESSON 9.4
COMBINING STEPWISE AND HARMONIC PATTERNS
MINOR TONALITY

FAMILIAR PATTERNS

Before we combine rhythm patterns and unfamiliar stepwise patterns **and** harmonic patterns in **Reading Benchmark 9B**, we will first combine **familiar** melodic and harmonic patterns in the exercises below.

Try writing these four pattern sequences in several different LA-signatures. Remember: audiate, read, remove them from your view, and then write **from your audiation**.

FAMILIAR AND UNFAMILIAR PATTERNS

Use the skill of generalization to read the patterns below. These examples will contain familiar **and unfamiliar** harmonic patterns, as well as familiar **and unfamiliar** stepwise patterns.

PREPARING FOR BENCHMARK 9B

As you did previously, you may wish to **circle tonic patterns**, and **square dominant patterns** like in the example below. If the melody is stepwise, leave it blank.

READING BENCHMARK 9B

Tonality = Minor
Pitches = Tonic/Dominant and siLTDRMF
Keys = Cm, Dm, Em, Fm, Gm, Am, Bm

Meters = Duple and Triple
Time Signatures = 2/4, 4/4, 2/2; 6/8, 3/4
Functions = Macro/microbeat, divisions, elongations, division/elongations, macro/microbeat rests

More Difficult Exercises

LESSON 9.5
TIES
DUPLE AND TRIPLE METERS

A **tie** is a special type of elongation which connects pairs of rhythm patterns (usually!) using a notational symbol, which is also called a tie. A tie can connect any note of any rhythmic function, and is only limited by a composer's audiation and imagination. For the purposes of this book, I will include only ties with macrobeats and microbeats in typical places where ties occur.

DUPLE TIE PATTERNS

In 2/4 ties often occur **between** measures. As in an elongation, audiate but do not perform the note after the tie.

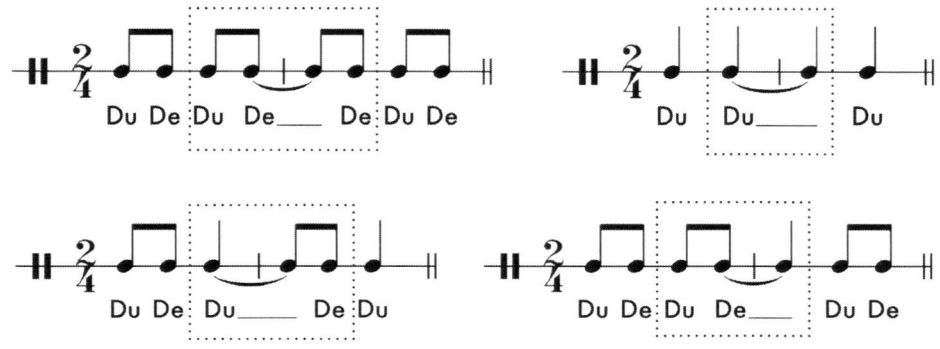

They can also occur in the middle of a measure, but only with advanced rhythm patterns where the combined value of the tied notes (See **Lesson 5.2, The Math of Music**) does not equal another standard note value.

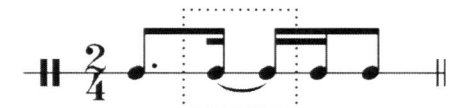

In 4/4 ties often occur either **in the middle** of a measure, or **between** measures.

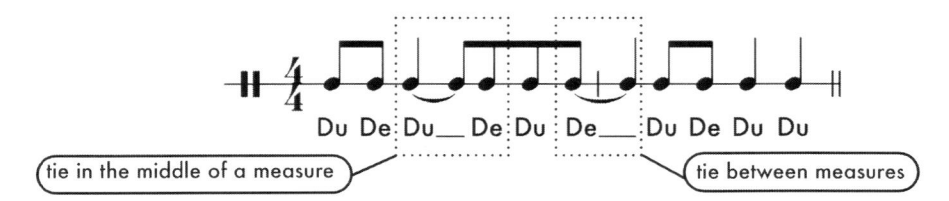

In Cut Time, ties often occur **between** measures (but, like 2/4, can occur in the middle of the measure, as well).

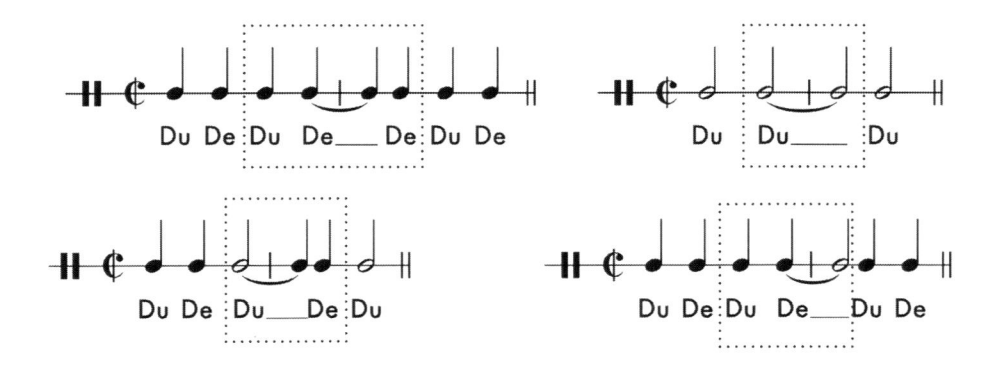

TRIPLE TIE PATTERNS

In 6/8 ties often occur either **in the middle** of a measure, or **between** measures.

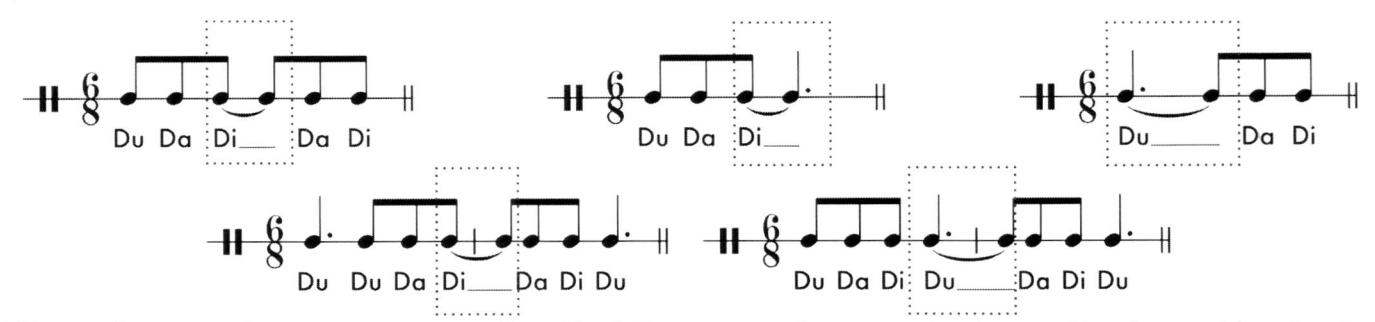

In 3/4 ties often occur **between** measures (but, like 2/4, can occur between microbeats with advanced functions).

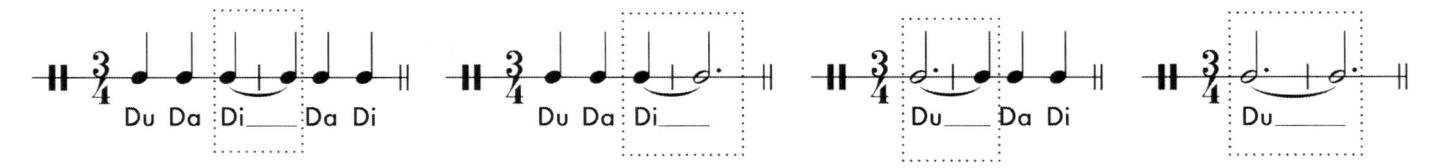

DUPLE AND TRIPLE TIE PATTERNS IN ACTION

In preparation for **Reading Benchmark 9C** and **9D**, read these longer patterns which have ties.

READING BENCHMARK 9C

Tonality = Major
Pitches = Tonic/Dominant and tDRMFSL
Keys = C, D, Eb, F, G, A, Bb

Meters = Duple and Triple
Time Signatures = 2/4, 4/4, 2/2; 6/8, 3/4
Functions = Macro/microbeat and ties

READING BENCHMARK 9D

Tonality = Minor
Pitches = Tonic/Dominant and siLTDRMF
Keys = Cm, Dm, Em, Fm, Gm, Am, Bm

Meters = Duple and Triple
Time Signatures = 2/4, 4/4, 2/2; 6/8, 3/4
Functions = Macro/microbeat and ties

READING SEQUENCE 10

SEQUENCE 10 AT A GLANCE

Reading Content	
TONAL	**RHYTHM**
• Tonality: Major and Minor • Pitches: Tonic, Dominant and Subdominant; Stepwise and Chord Roots • Keys: All	• Meters: Duple and Triple • Functions: All, including Upbeats • Time Signatures: All

Lesson Sequence	
10.1 Tonal	Major vs. Minor
Reading Benchmark 10A • Major/Minor; Tonic/Dominant and Stepwise; Keys: All • Duple & Triple; All Functions	
10.2 Tonal	Extending Into Other Octaves
Reading Benchmark 10B • Major; Tonic/Dominant and **slt**DRMFSL**TD**; Keys: All • Duple & Triple; All Functions	
Reading Benchmark 10C • Minor; Tonic/Dominant and **mf**siLTDRMF**siL**; Keys: All • Duple & Triple; All Functions	
10.3 Rhythm	Upbeats
Reading Benchmark 10D • Major/Minor; Tonic/Dominant and Stepwise; Keys: All • Duple & Triple; All Functions, Including **Upbeats**	
10.4 Tonal	Introduction to Subdominant
Reading Benchmark 10E • Major/Minor; Tonic/Dominant and Subdominant; Keys: All • Duple & Triple; Macrobeat and Microbeat	
10.5 Tonal	Crash Course in Chord Roots
Reading Benchmark 10F • Major/Minor; Tonic/Dominant and Subdominant **Chord Roots**; Keys: All • Duple & Triple; Macrobeat and Microbeat	

LESSON 10.1
MAJOR VS MINOR

Up to this point, you have always been told whether an exercise is in major or minor. When you leave the safe confines of this book, the world is harsh and cruel, and it's every musician for themselves! Here are some strategies to help you find what tonality a piece is in.

STRATEGIES

1. Find DO using the DO-signature using our tried-and true technique: **The last flat is FA; the last sharp is TI**. Count up or down to get to DO using stepwise patterns. Make note of its location.
2. Look at the **first and last note**. If it is also DO, you can bet it's probably major.
3. If it doesn't start and end on DO, there's a good chance it could be **minor**. Look to see if it starts and/or ends on LA (Count down DO-TI-LA). You can confirm this if there is n accidental (a sharp or a natural sign) on SO, changing it to SI. This is a good indication if it is in minor.
4. If none of these is true, it could be in another tonality! Consult p. 55 for the resting tones of each tonality.
5. Sing through the song, and identify familiar harmonic functions. This will add further clarification.

PRACTICE

Look at the eight exercises below, which will all be in either major or minor tonality. Make note of what you think they are, and check your answers below.

Answers: 1. Major 2. Minor 3. Major 4. Minor 5. Minor 6. Minor 7. Major 8. Minor

READING BENCHMARK 10A

Tonality = Major/Minor
Pitches = Tonic/Dominant and Stepwise
Keys = All

Meters = Duple and Triple
Time Signatures = 2/4, 4/4, 2/2; 6/8, 3/4
Functions = All

Bring tonal context to these exercises and then read them.

LESSON 10.2
EXTENDING INTO OTHER OCTAVES

So far, we have learned stepwise patterns from DO down to TI and from DO up to LA, as well as tonic and dominant patterns. A visual representation of the "tonal building" we have created appears to the right.

The final step in major tonality, at least in the course of this book, is to add the ability to "add more floors" above our current structure, as well as to "finish the basement." We will achieve this by learning our final stepwise pattern: SO LA TI DO.

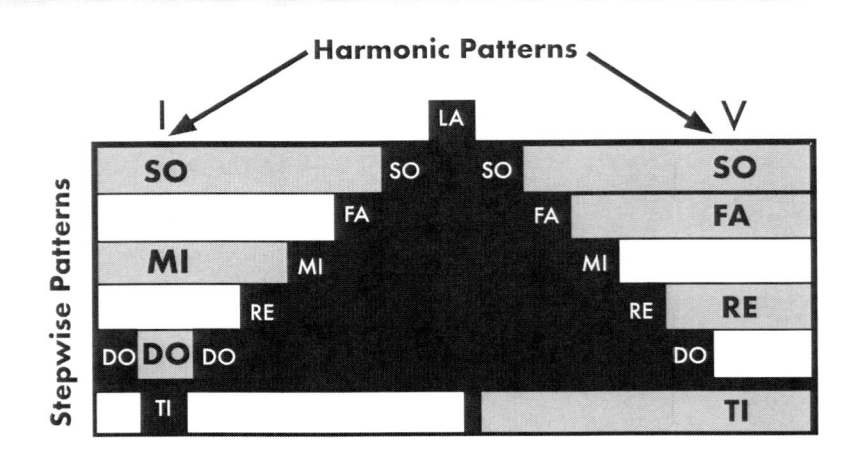

SO LA TI DO

Let's use a familiar harmonic pattern (DO MI SO) as an "elevator" to get us from DO up to SO. Let's begin in D-DO.

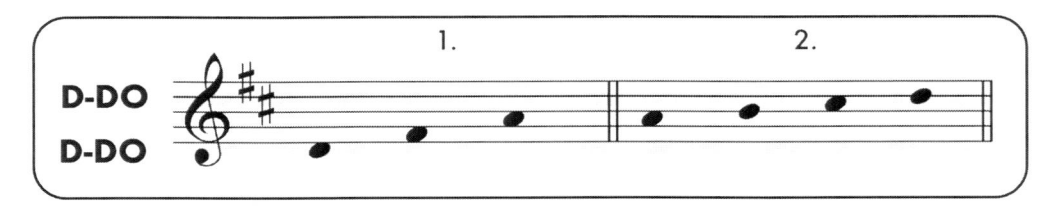

The first pattern is the familiar DO MI SO. The second pattern should be familiar to you from Part 1. It is **SO LA TI DO**. Take a breath and sing SO LA TI DO. Notice that the first pattern **begins** on DO, and the second pattern **ends** on DO. Notice also that it is an **octave higher** than the other DO. There are always multiple DOs in music you will encounter.

Below you will find the same patterns in a few other keys. Notice the distance an octave comprises.

Once we have connected one DO to the next higher DO, we can conceivably continue to read our stepwise and harmonic patterns in the next higher octave.

The diagram to the right is a visual representation of what that might look like.

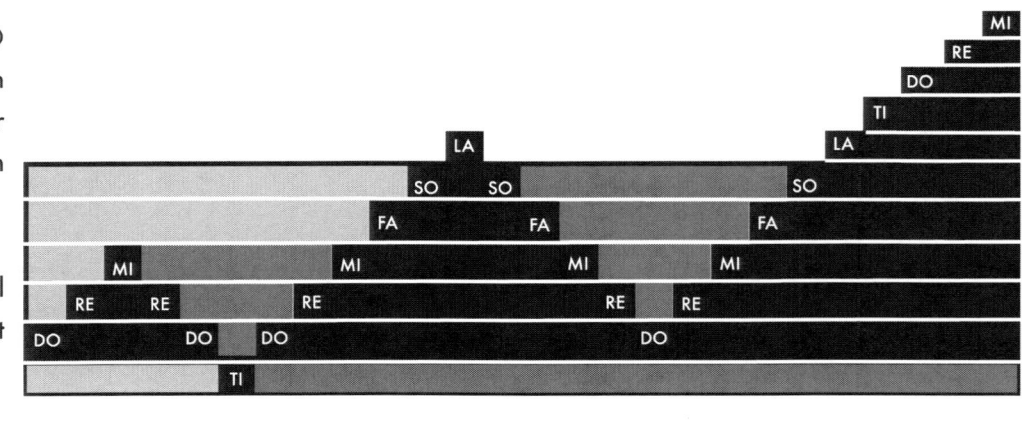

Here are some extended patterns utilizing the pattern SO LA TI DO as a pathway to the next higher DO:

D-DO **C-DO**

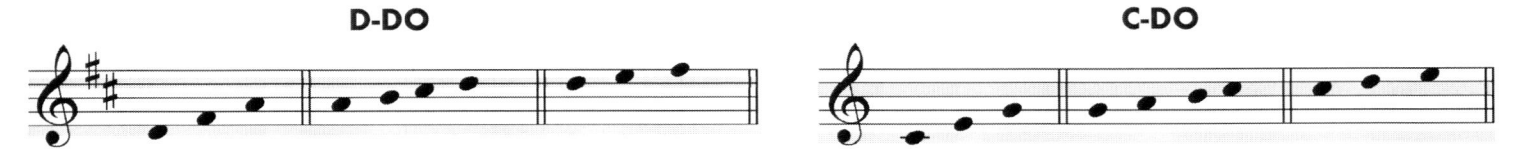

GENERALIZATION

If you know the pattern SO LA TI DO, you can use the power of generalization to teach yourself some more patterns. Pattern 1 is SO LA TI DO. Can you generalize the rest of the patterns?

Bb-DO

Generalize these patterns:

These are the same pitches, just in different octaves.

You can also use generalization to read the notes **below** DO.

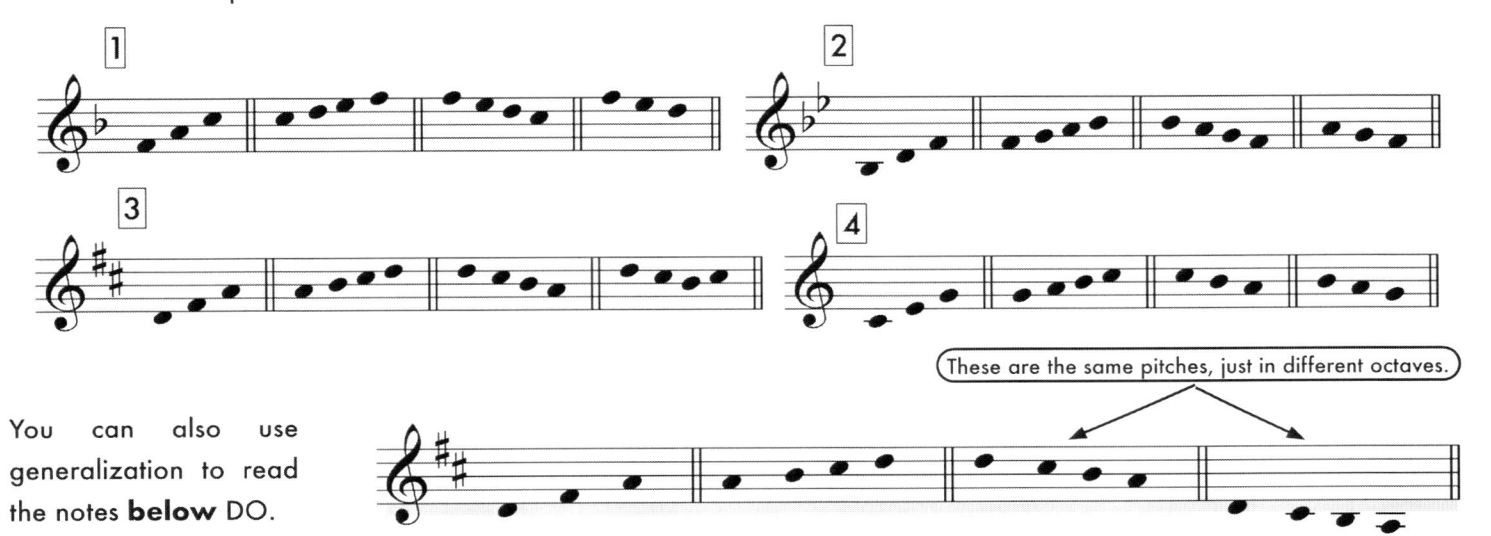

Trace all of the notes below. They all start and end on DO.

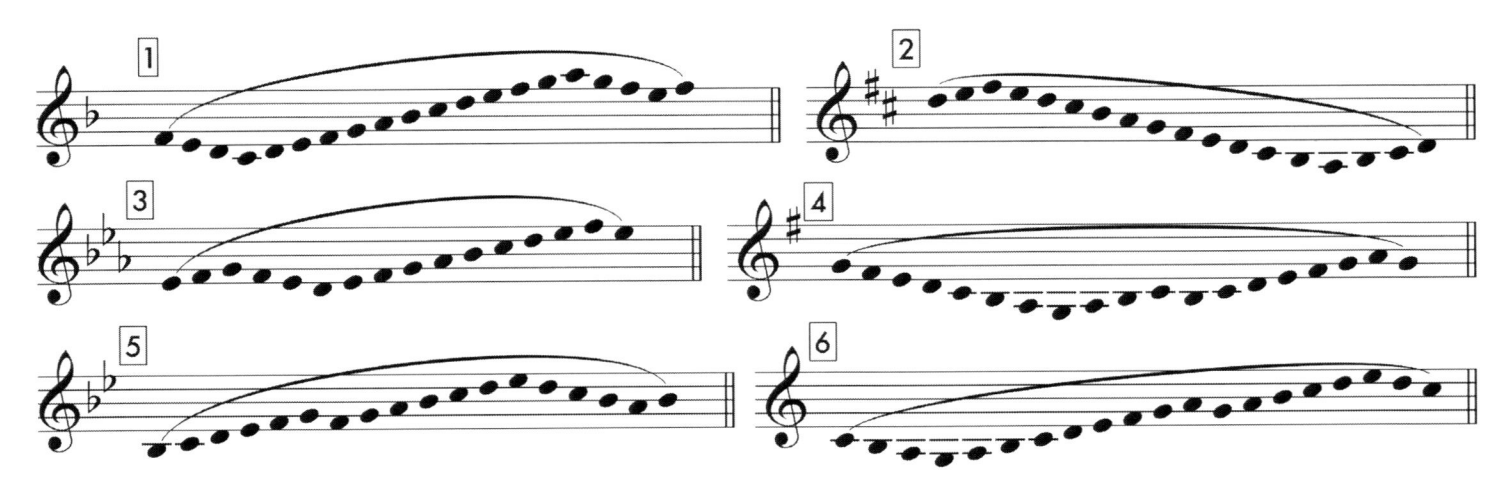

In **Reading Benchmark 10B**, you will read DO RE ME FA SO LA TI DO in multiple octaves. Can you generalize that information and apply it to minor tonality in **Reading Benchmark 10C**?

You may also wish to **spiral** to Reading Sequence 10.4 and learn tonic, dominant and subdominant tonal patterns which extend into the higher octave.

READING BENCHMARK 10B

Tonality = Major
Pitches = **sl**tDRMFSL**TD** and I/V
Keys = All

Meters = Duple and Triple
Time Signatures = 2/4, 4/4, 2/2; 6/8, 3/4
Functions = All

READING BENCHMARK 10C

Tonality = Major
Pitches = **mf**siLTDRMF**siL** and i/V
Keys = All

Meters = Duple and Triple
Time Signatures = 2/4, 4/4, 2/2; 6/8, 3/4
Functions = Macrobeat and microbeat

LESSON 10.3
UPBEATS

The final rhythm pattern that we will cover in this book is **upbeats**. In an upbeat, part of the rhythm pattern occurs before the first measure, or the pattern it precedes. An upbeat is only limited by a composer's audiation and imagination, but for the purposes of this book, we will look at a few typical upbeat patterns with macrobeats and microbeats only.

DUPLE UPBEAT PATTERNS

Here are three macro/microbeat upbeat patterns in 2/4:

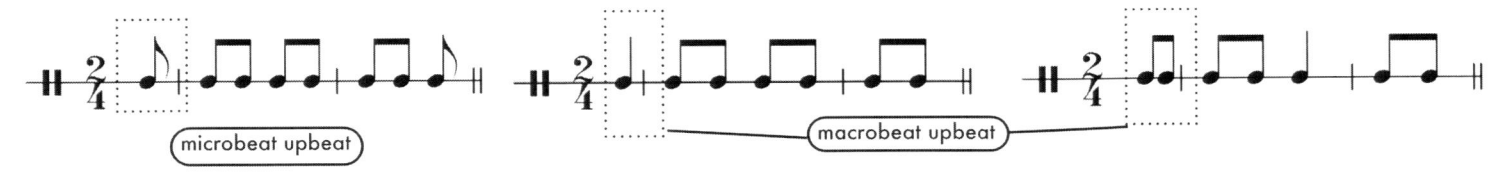

Here are two macro/microbeat upbeat patterns in 4/4:

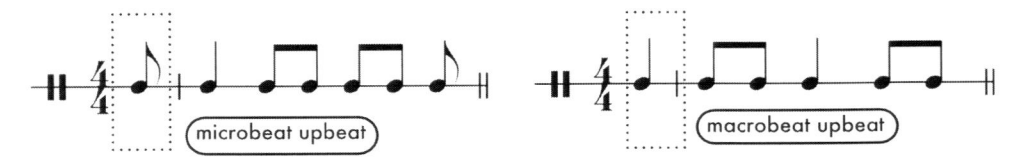

Here are three macro/microbeat upbeat patterns in Cut Time:

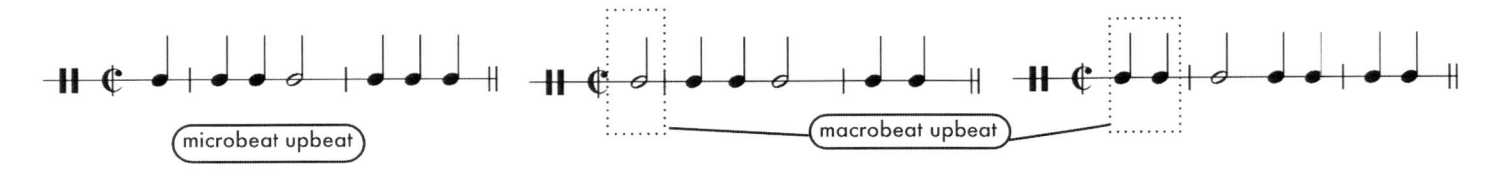

TRIPLE UPBEAT PATTERNS

Here are two macro/microbeat upbeat patterns in 6/8:

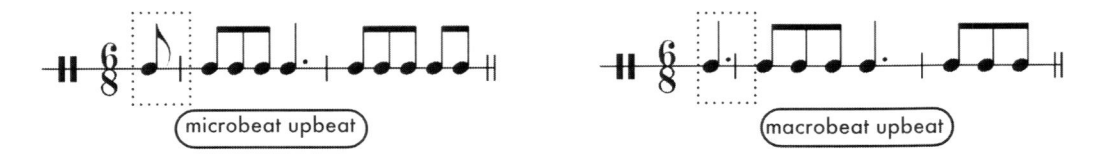

Here is one possible microbeat upbeat pattern in 3/4:

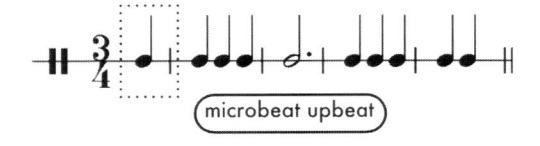

Try reading the exercises in **Reading Benchmark 10D** with rhythm only first. Then try to add the pitches.

READING BENCHMARK 10D

Tonality = Major/Minor
Pitches = Tonic/Dominant and Stepwise
Keys = All

Meters = Duple and Triple
Time Signatures = 2/4, 4/4, 2/2; 6/8, 3/4
Functions = All, including Upbeats

LESSON 10.4
INTRODUCTION TO SUBDOMINANT (THE IV CHORD)

When you think about the possibilities that exist with harmony, we really have just begun! We have focused our attention thus far on tonic and dominant (I and V) in major and minor. So, you might be asking yourself, what happened to 2, 3 and 4? Is there a "2" chord? A "3" chord? A "4" chord? The answer is yes! When you begin to study functional harmony, you'll discover a whole new world. We are laying the foundation of I and V in this book which will set you up for your future study of harmony.

CRASH COURSE IN ADVANCED HARMONY

There is actually a chord built on each scale degree. The tonic chord is built on DO, whereas the dominant chord is built on SO. If we use the keyboard as a visual, you will be able to see all of the chords in major tonality.

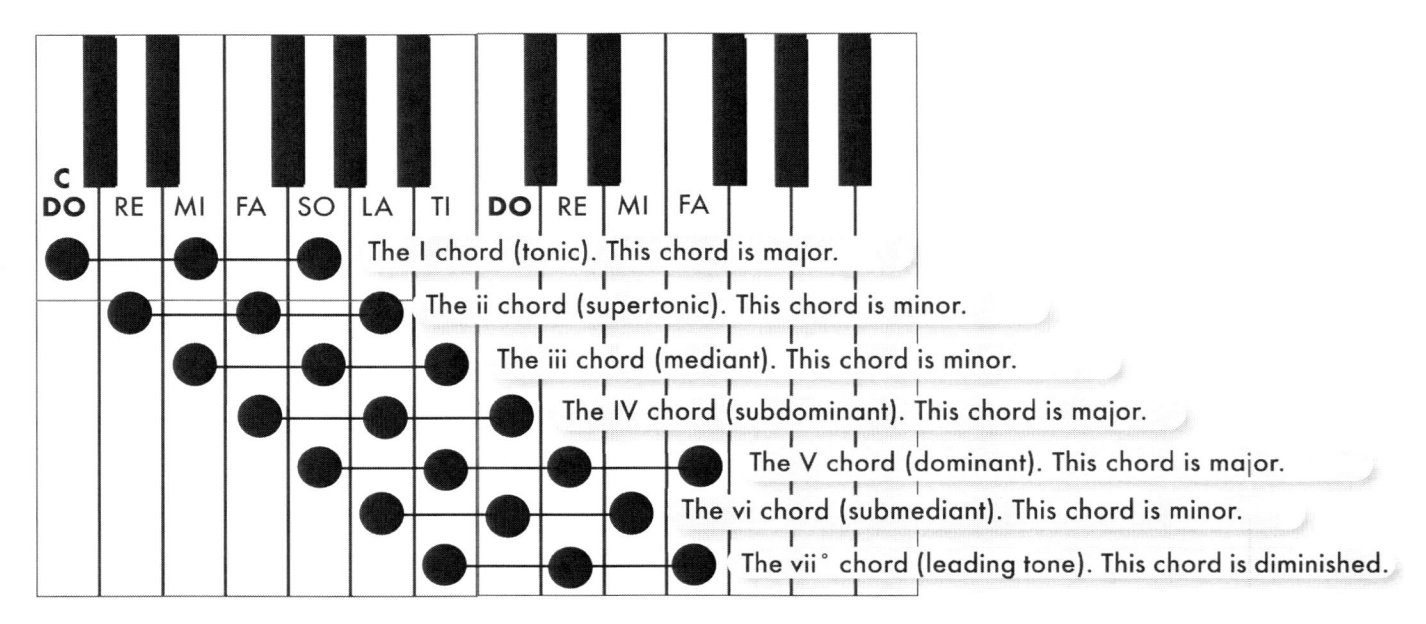

- The I chord (tonic). This chord is major.
- The ii chord (supertonic). This chord is minor.
- The iii chord (mediant). This chord is minor.
- The IV chord (subdominant). This chord is major.
- The V chord (dominant). This chord is major.
- The vi chord (submediant). This chord is minor.
- The vii° chord (leading tone). This chord is diminished.

Many (most?) songs make primary use of the I, IV and V chords, and, as such, will be the limit of this book.

MAJOR SUBDOMINANT

The major subdominant, or, the IV chord, is any combination of the pitches **FA, LA and DO**. We can put those in any order to create any number of subdominant chords.

On the following page, you will see subdominant FPIFO for your reference. Be sure to listen to the patterns first with a neutral syllable and then add the verbal association. (Whenever we learn a new function, we need to experience the patterns first at the Aural/Oral level.) Try all of the same techniques you used to learn tonic and dominant. Solfege is included for your reference.

	Tonic (I)	Subdominant (IV)	Dominant (V)
RE			RE
DO		DO	
TI			TI
LA		LA	
SO	SO		SO
FA		FA	
MI	MI		
RE			
DO	DO		

Major Subdominant FPIFO

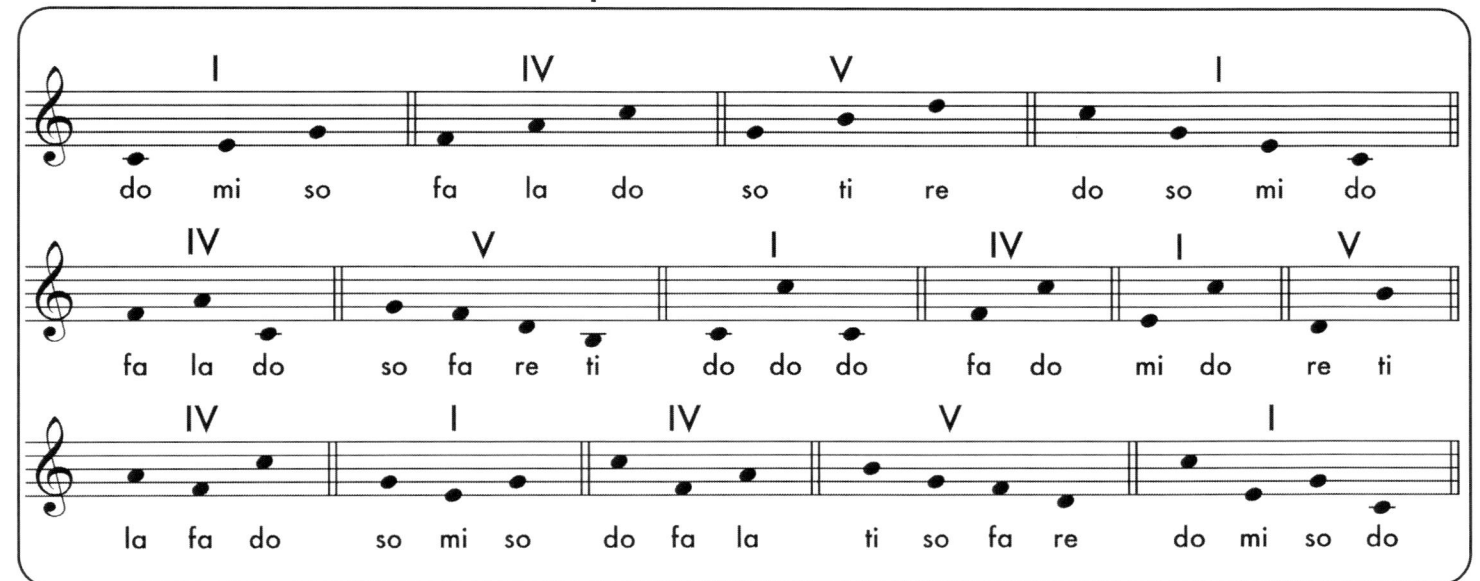

I	IV	V	I
do mi so	fa la do	so ti re	do so mi do

IV	V	I	IV	I	V
fa la do	so fa re ti	do do do	fa do	mi do	re ti

IV	I	IV	V	I
la fa do	so mi so	do fa la	ti so fa re	do mi so do

MINOR SUBDOMINANT

The minor subdominant, or, the iv chord, is any combination of the pitches **RE FA and LA**. We can put those in any order to create any number of subdominant chords.

Below, you will see minor subdominant FPIFO for your reference. Again, be sure to listen to the patterns first with a neutral syllable and then add the verbal association. Solfege is included for your reference.

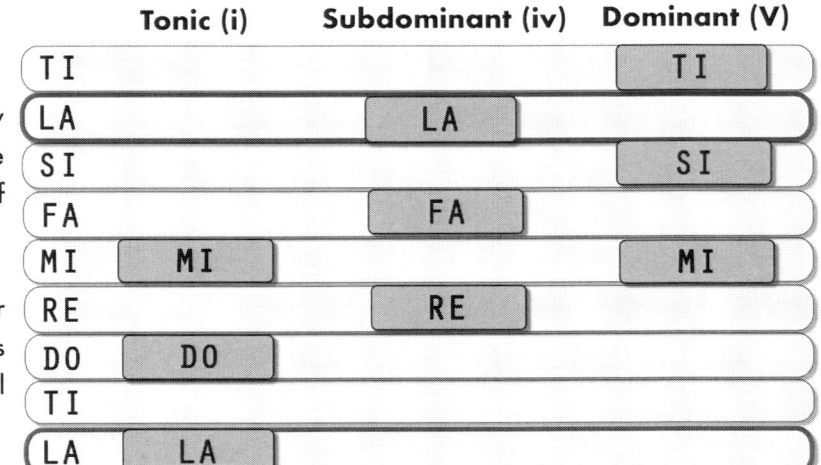

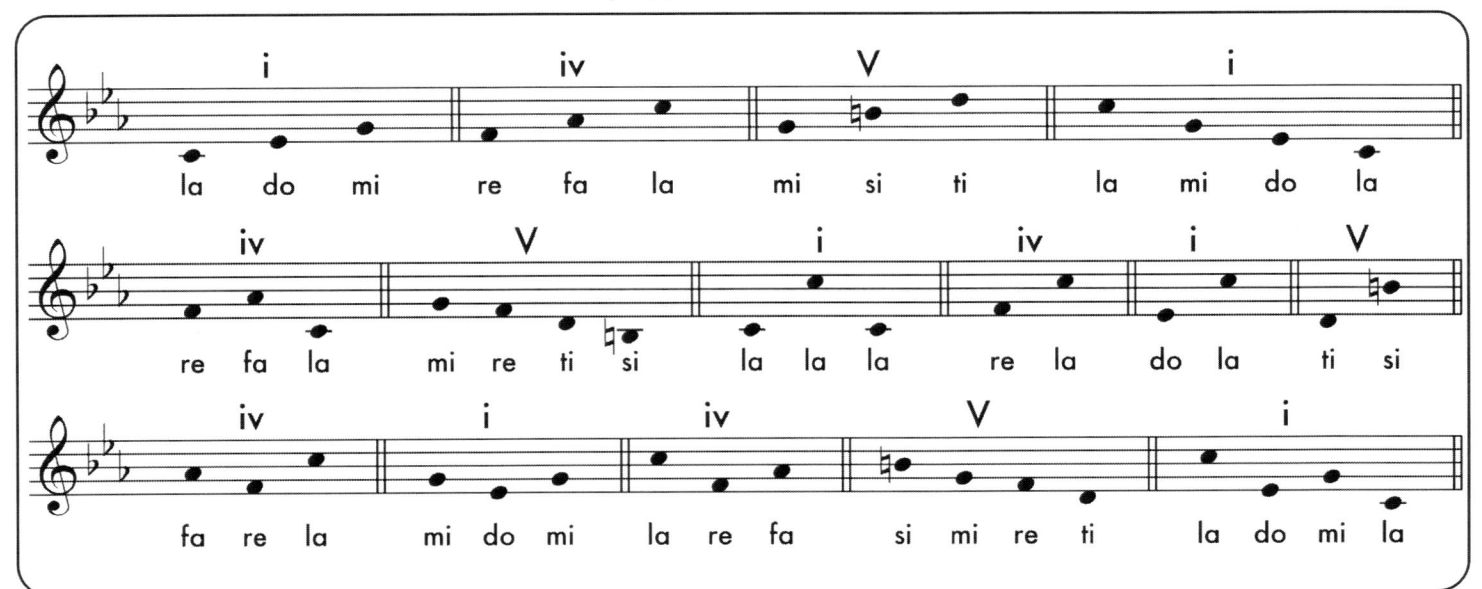

	Tonic (i)	Subdominant (iv)	Dominant (V)
TI			TI
LA		LA	
SI			SI
FA		FA	
MI	MI		MI
RE		RE	
DO	DO		
TI			
LA	LA		

Minor Subdominant FPIFO

i	iv	V	i
la do mi	re fa la	mi si ti	la mi do la

iv	V	i	iv	i	V
re fa la	mi re ti si	la la la	re la	do la	ti si

iv	i	iv	V	i
fa re la	mi do mi	la re fa	si mi re ti	la do mi la

INSTRUMENTAL ASSOCIATION

Play a simple I-IV-V progression in the key of C major on the keyboard, as indicated by the digram below. Make an **instrumental association** to where the notes fall on the staff in relation to the keyboard

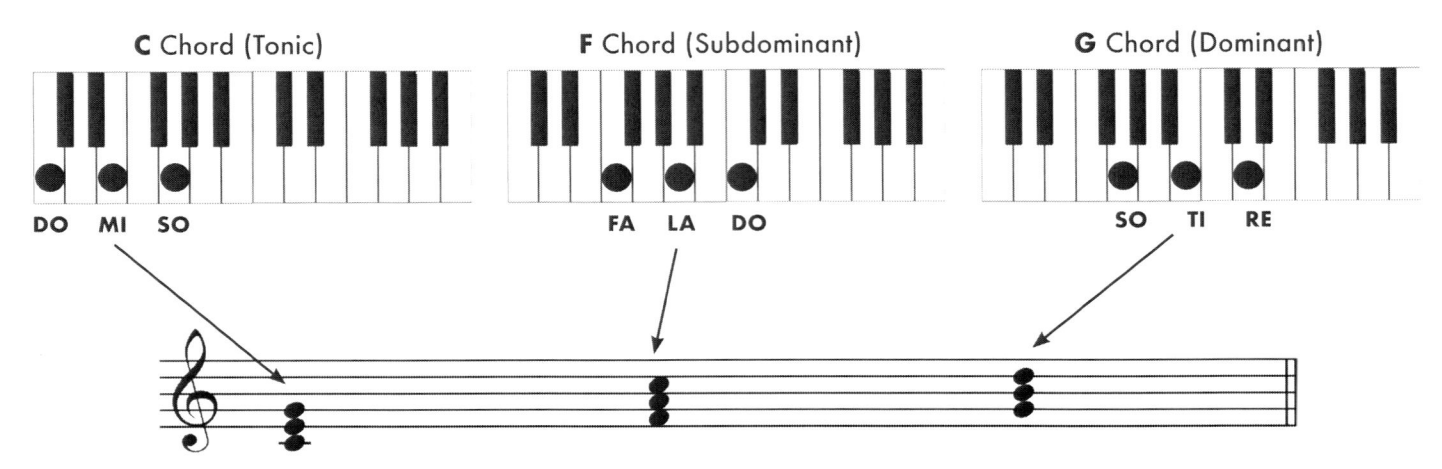

C Chord (Tonic) — DO MI SO

F Chord (Subdominant) — FA LA DO

G Chord (Dominant) — SO TI RE

Play a simple i-iv-V progression in the key of C minor on the keyboard, as indicated by the digram below. Take note of how you turn a major chord into a minor chord on the keyboard.

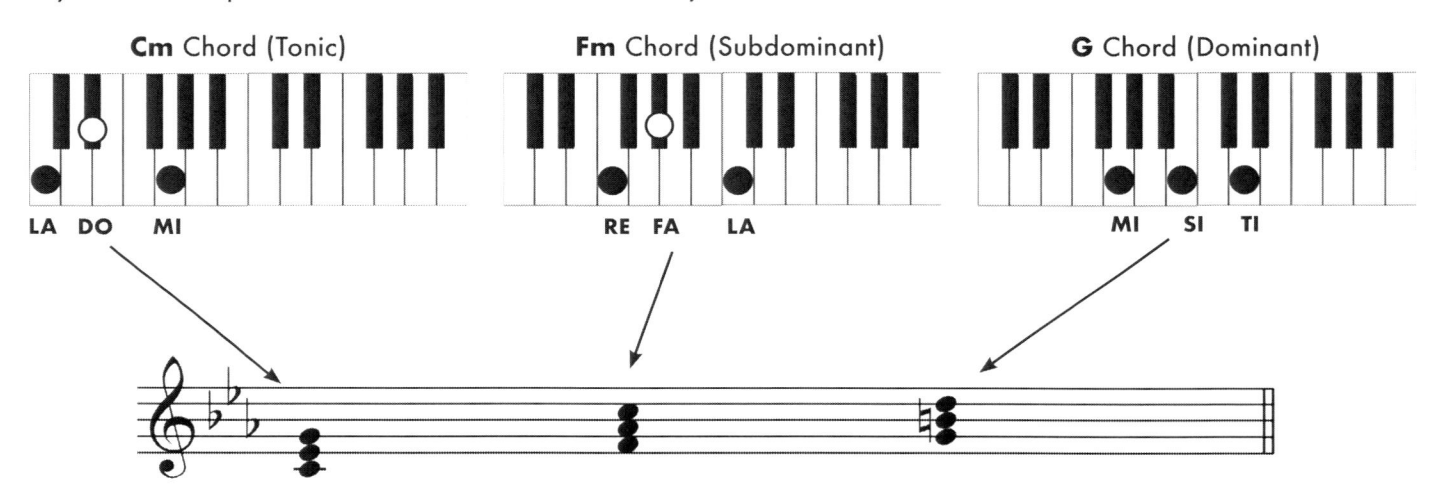

Cm Chord (Tonic) — LA DO MI

Fm Chord (Subdominant) — RE FA LA

G Chord (Dominant) — MI SI TI

Try this in different keys. You may wish to use the **Solfege Keyboard Card** (See appendix for the full size version) to assist you. This is what I, IV and V look like in D-DO, for example.

Line up DO on the Keyboard Card with any key, and the card will show you where each solfege note is in that key.

SOLFEGE KEYBOARD CARD

Major Tonality
Resting Tone = DO
Tonic Chord (I) = DO MI SO
Dominant Chord (V) = SO FA RE TI

Where is DO?
C D E F G A B

Minor Tonality
Resting Tone = LA
Tonic Chord (i) = LA DO MI
Dominant Chord (V) = MI RE TI

Si LA TI DO RE MI FA SO SI LA TI DO RE

D Chord (Tonic)
G Chord (Subdominant)
A Chord (Dominant)

READING BENCHMARK 10E

Tonality = Major/Minor
Pitches = Tonic/Dominant and Subdominant
Keys = All
Meters = Duple and Triple
Time Signatures = 2/4, 4/4, 2/2; 6/8, 3/4
Functions = Macrobeat and microbeat

Major - I, IV & V

Minor - i, iv & V

LESSON 10.5
CRASH COURSE IN CHORD ROOTS

Up to this point, we have read for the most part in treble clef. However, we can also read in **bass clef.** If we were to read **Chord Roots**, they would most likely be notated using the bass clef because that is where their low range is represented on the grand staff.

INSTRUMENTAL ASSOCIATION

Play a simple I-IV-V progression in the key of C on the keyboard, as indicated by the digram below. Take note of what they left hand is playing (DO, FA, SO). Make an **instrumental association** to where those notes fall on the staff.

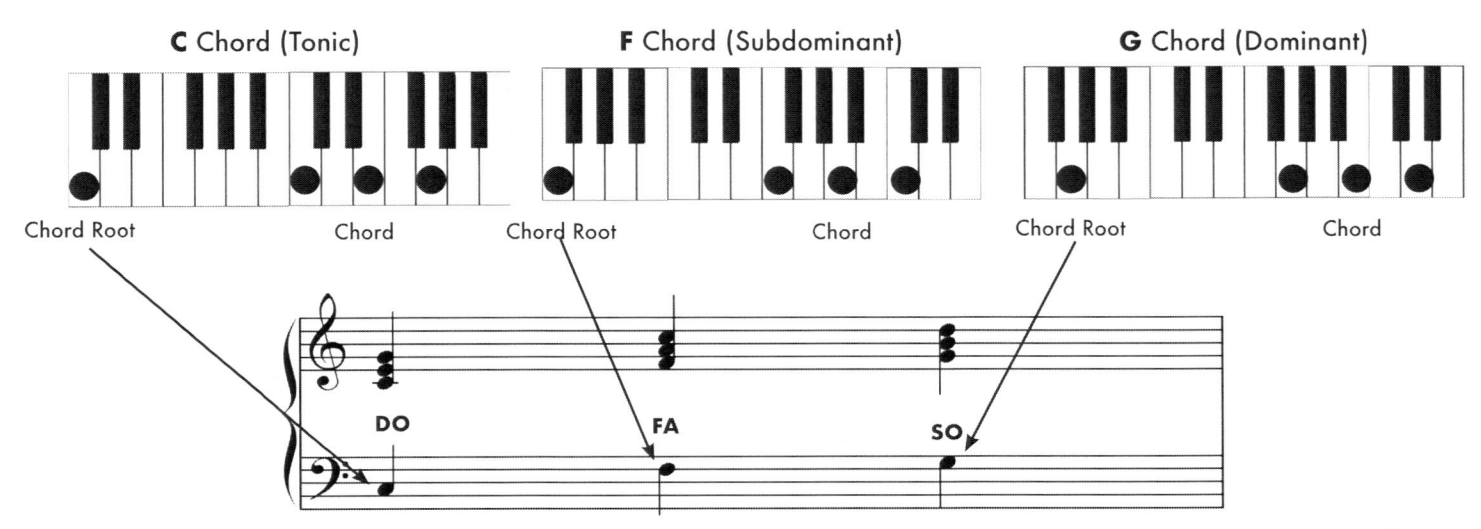

C Chord (Tonic)   **F Chord (Subdominant)**   **G Chord (Dominant)**

DO is the chord root of tonic; FA is the chord root of subdominant; SO is the chord root of dominant. You may wish to use the **Chord Root Keyboard Card** to assist you.

READING CHORD ROOTS

This is where the **major tonality** chord roots DO (Tonic), FA (Subdominant) and SO (Dominant) appear on the staff in various keys. Note that there are two possibilities for each note.

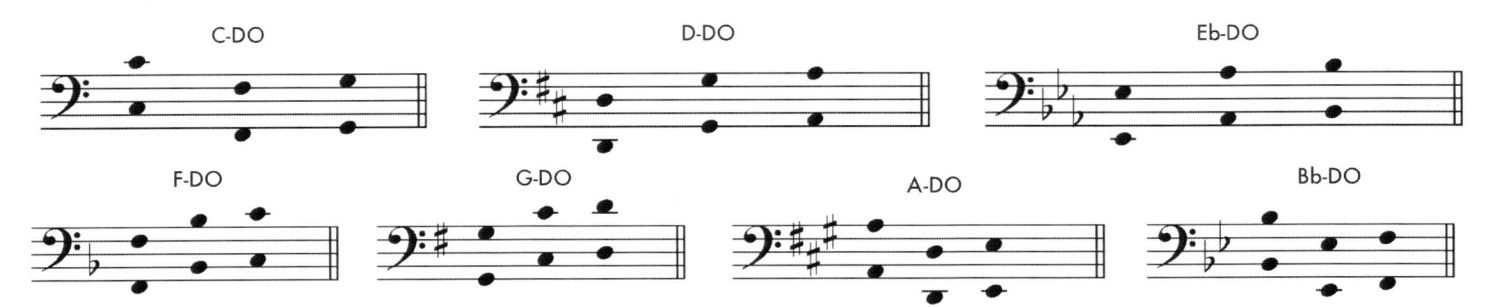

C-DO   D-DO   Eb-DO

F-DO   G-DO   A-DO   Bb-DO

Can you make generalizations to **minor tonality** with the chord roots LA, RE and MI? LA is the chord root of tonic; RE is the chord root of subdominant; MI is the chord root of dominant.

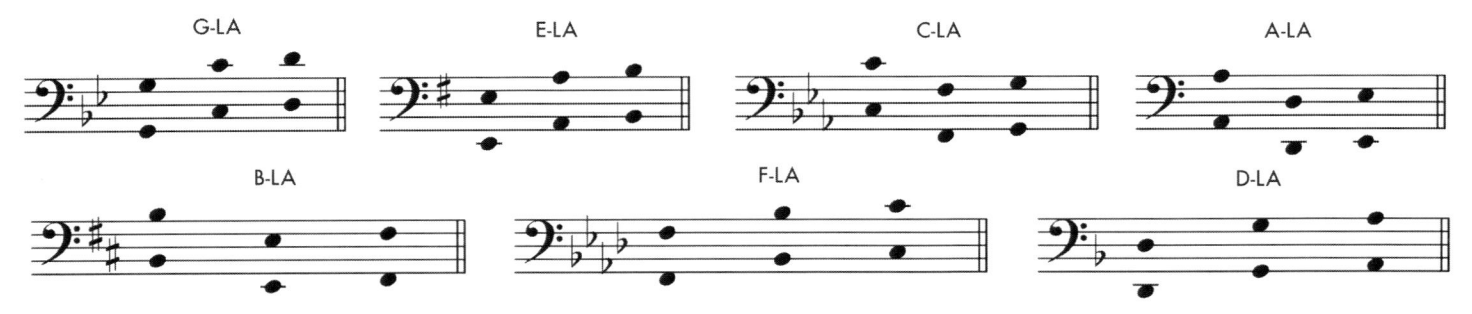

G-LA   E-LA   C-LA   A-LA

B-LA   F-LA   D-LA

READING BENCHMARK 10F

Tonality = Major/Minor
Pitches = I, IV, V Chord Roots
Keys = All

Meters = Duple and Triple
Time Signatures = 2/4, 4/4, 2/2; 6/8, 3/4
Functions = Macrobeat and microbeat

APPENDICES

MUSICIANSHIP CHEAT SHEET

TONAL

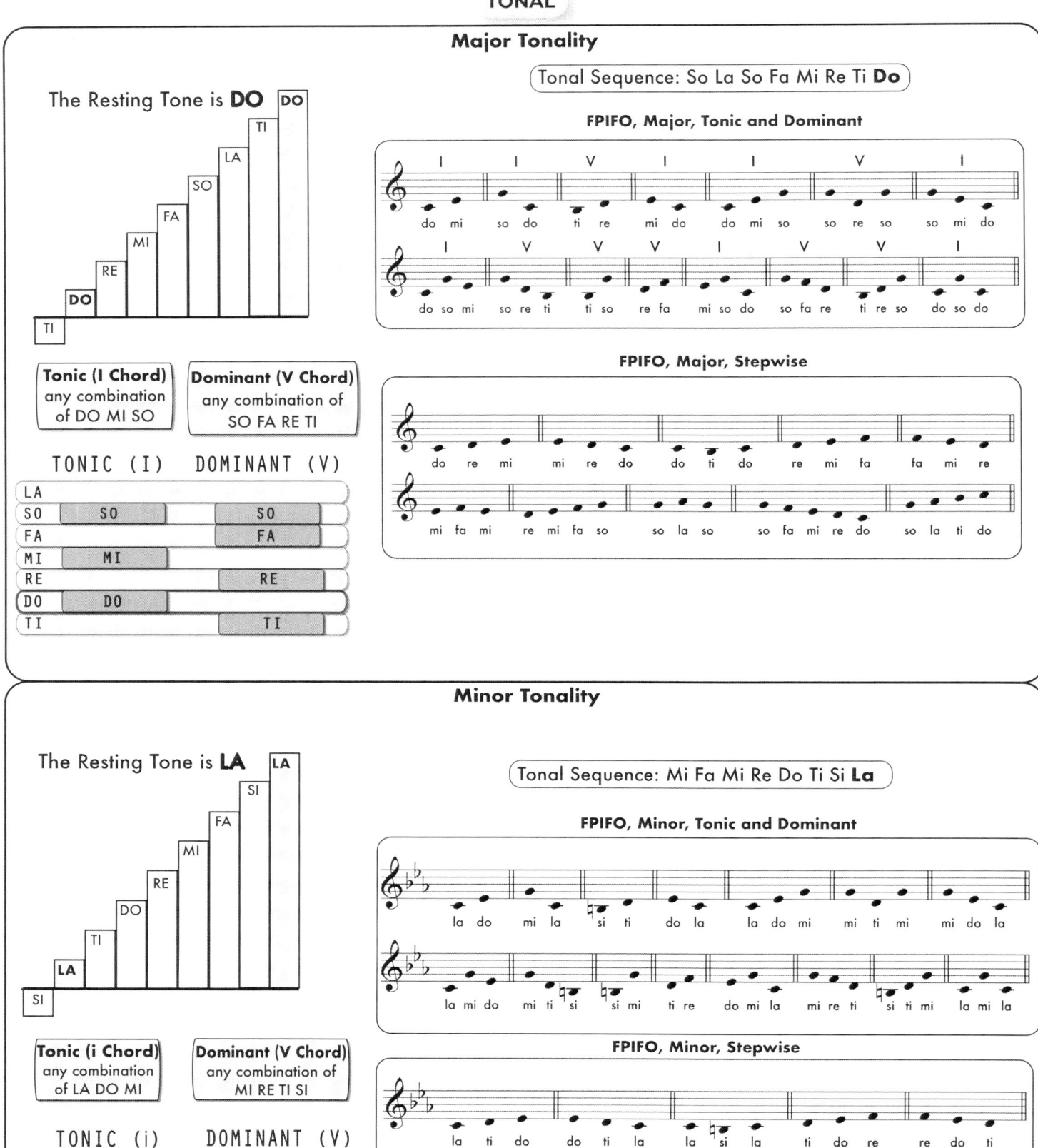

Major Tonality

Tonal Sequence: So La So Fa Mi Re Ti **Do**

The Resting Tone is **DO**

Staircase (ascending): TI, DO, RE, MI, FA, SO, LA, TI, DO

Tonic (I Chord) any combination of DO MI SO

Dominant (V Chord) any combination of SO FA RE TI

TONIC (I)	DOMINANT (V)
LA	
SO — SO	SO
FA	FA
MI — MI	
RE	RE
DO — DO	
TI	TI

FPIFO, Major, Tonic and Dominant

I — I V I I V I
do mi so — do ti re — mi do — do mi so — so re so — so mi do
I V V V I V V I
do so mi — so re ti — ti so re fa — mi so do — so fa re — ti re so — do so do

FPIFO, Major, Stepwise

do re mi — mi re do — do ti do — re mi fa — fa mi re
mi fa mi — re mi fa so — so la so — so fa mi re do — so la ti do

Minor Tonality

Tonal Sequence: Mi Fa Mi Re Do Ti Si **La**

The Resting Tone is **LA**

Staircase (ascending): SI, LA, TI, DO, RE, MI, FA, SI, LA

Tonic (i Chord) any combination of LA DO MI

Dominant (V Chord) any combination of MI RE TI SI

TONIC (i)	DOMINANT (V)
FA	
MI — MI	MI
RE	RE
DO — DO	
TI	TI
LA — LA	
SI	SI

FPIFO, Minor, Tonic and Dominant

la do mi la — si ti do la — la do mi — mi ti mi — mi do la
la mi do — mi ti si — si mi ti re — do mi la — mi re ti — si ti mi — la mi la

FPIFO, Minor, Stepwise

la ti do — do ti la — la si la — ti do re — re do ti
do re do — ti do re mi — mi fa mi — mi re do ti la — mi fa si la

MUSICIANSHIP CHEAT SHEET

RHYTHM

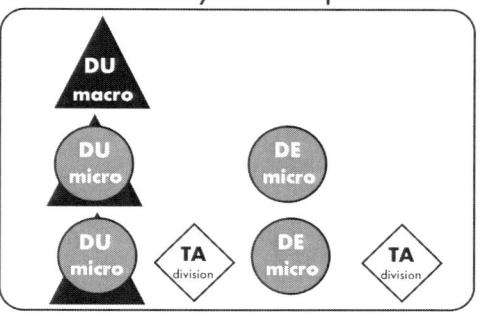

Duple Meter

3 Levels of Rhythm in Duple Meter

- DU macro
- DU micro / DE micro
- DU micro, TA division / DE micro, TA division

3 Duple Division Patterns

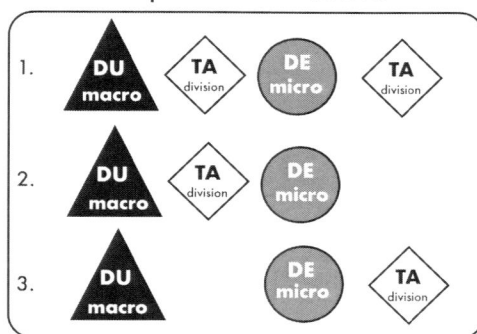

1. DU macro — TA division — DE micro — TA division
2. DU macro — TA division — DE micro
3. DU macro — DE micro — TA division

Time Signature	Macrobeats	Microbeats	Divisions Patterns		
2/4 4/4	♩ Du	♫ Du De	♬♬ Du Ta De Ta	♬♩ Du Ta De	♩♬ Du De Ta
¢	♩ Du	♩♩ Du De	♫♫ Du Ta De Ta	♫♩ Du Ta De	♩♫ Du De Ta

Triple Meter

3 Levels of Rhythm in Triple Meter

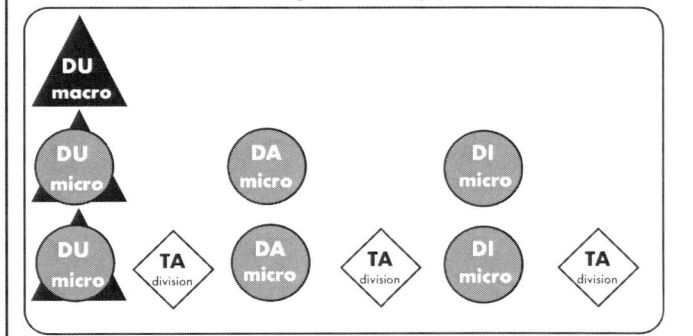

- DU macro
- DU micro / DA micro / DI micro
- DU micro, TA division / DA micro, TA division / DI micro, TA division

4 Triple Division Patterns

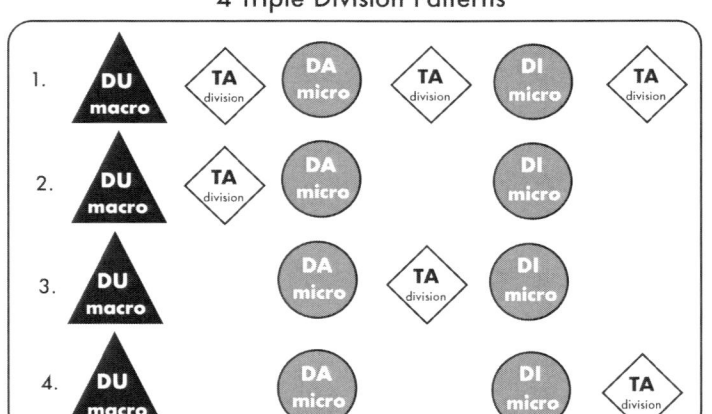

1. DU macro — TA division — DA micro — TA division — DI micro — TA division
2. DU macro — TA division — DA micro — DI micro
3. DU macro — DA micro — TA division — DI micro
4. DU macro — DA micro — DI micro — TA division

Time Signature	Macrobeats	Microbeats	Divisions			
6/8	♩. Du	♪♪♪ Du Da Di	Du Ta Da Ta Di Ta	Du Ta Da Di	Du Da Ta Di	Du Da Di Ta
3/4	♩. Du	♩♩♩ Du Da Di	Du Ta Da Ta Di Ta	Du Ta Da Di	Du Da Ta Di	Du Da Di Ta

KEYBOARD CHEAT SHEET

BASICS

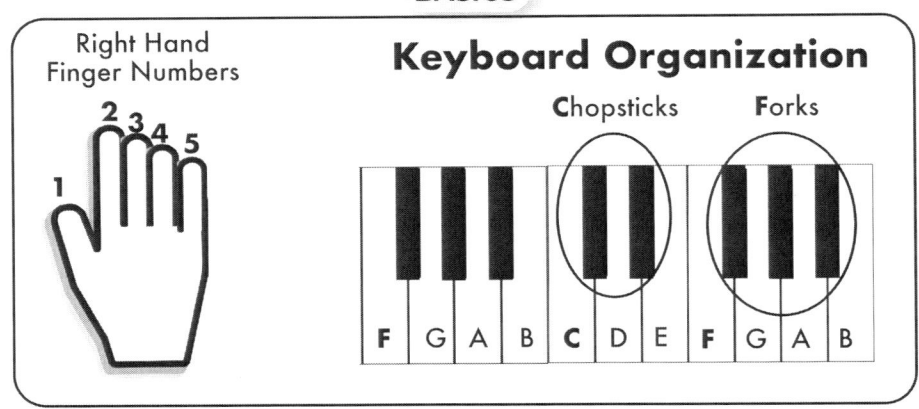

Right Hand Finger Numbers
1, 2, 3, 4, 5

Keyboard Organization
- Chopsticks
- Forks

F G A B C D E F G A B

C-DO

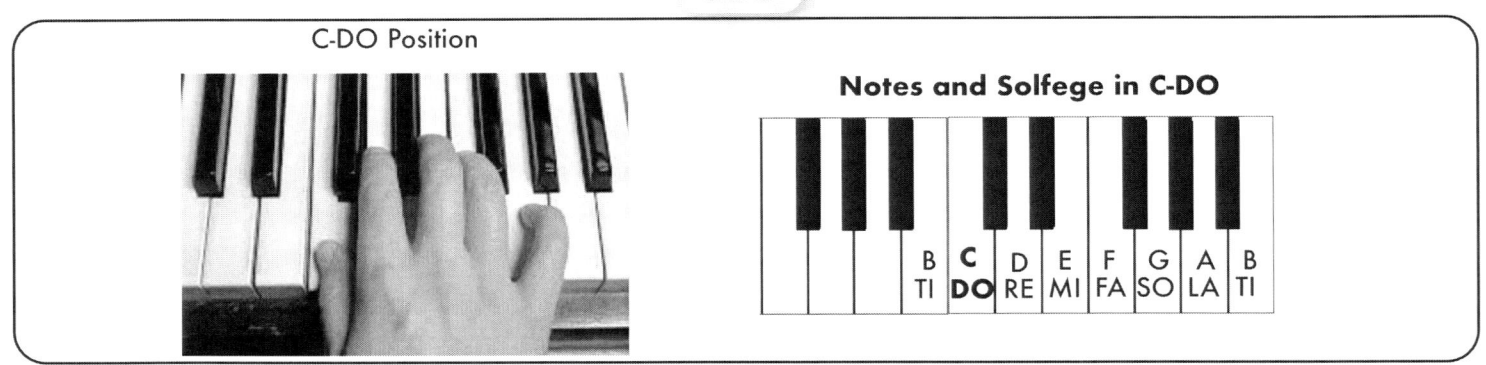

C-DO Position

Notes and Solfege in C-DO

B	C	D	E	F	G	A	B
TI	DO	RE	MI	FA	SO	LA	TI

LINES & SPACES

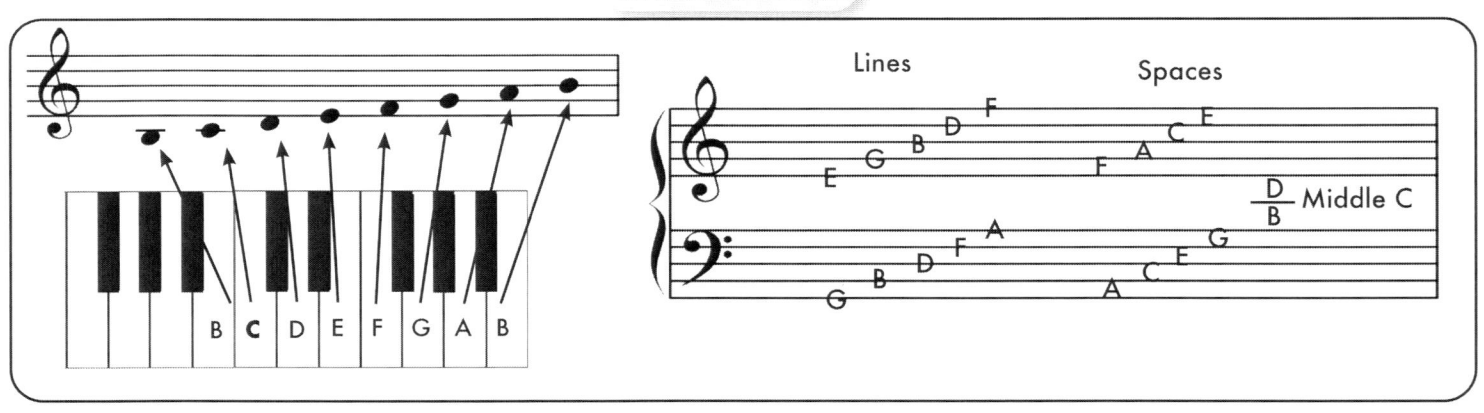

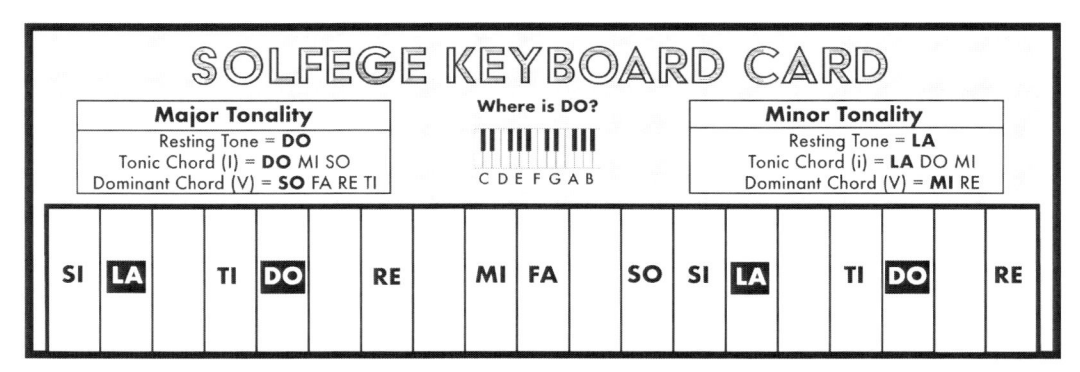

B C D E F G A B

Lines — E G B D F (treble), G B D F A (bass)
Spaces — F A C E (treble), A C E G (bass)
D/B Middle C

SOLFEGE KEYBOARD CARD

Major Tonality	Where is DO?	Minor Tonality
Resting Tone = **DO**	C D E F G A B	Resting Tone = **LA**
Tonic Chord (I) = **DO** MI SO		Tonic Chord (i) = **LA** DO MI
Dominant Chord (V) = **SO** FA RE TI		Dominant Chord (V) = **MI** RE

SI | LA | TI | DO | RE | MI | FA | SO | SI | LA | TI | DO | RE

To print out this **Keyboard Card** (and many others!), go to this webpage: www.shorturl.at/irEIU
Be sure to check that your printer is printing at 100% or they will not line up with the keyboard.

HARMONIC FUNCTIONS CHEAT SHEET

Major Tonality

Functions Key	I	ii	iii	IV	V	vi	vii°
C	C	Dm	Em	F	G	Am	B°
C#	C#	D#m	E#m	F#	G#	A#m	B#°
D	D	Em	F#m	G	A	Bm	C#°
Eb	Eb	Fm	Gm	Ab	Bb	Cm	D°
E	E	F#m	G#m	A	B	C#m	D#°
F	F	Gm	Am	Bb	C	Dm	E°
F#	F#	G#m	A#m	B	C#	D#m	E#°
G	G	Am	Bm	C	D	Em	F#°
Ab	Ab	Bbm	Cm	Db	Eb	Fm	G°
A	A	Bm	C#m	D	E	F#m	G#°
Bb	Bb	Cm	Dm	Eb	F	Gm	A°
B	B	C#m	D#m	E	F#	G#m	A#°

Minor Tonality

Functions Key	i	ii°	III	iv	V	VI	vii°
C	Cm	D°	Eb	Fm	G	Ab	B♮°
C#	C#m	D#°	E	F#m	G#	A	B#°
D	Dm	E°	F	Gm	A	Bb	C#°
Eb	Ebm	F°	Gb	Abm	Bb	C	D♮°
E	Em	F#°	G	Am	B	C	D#°
F	Fm	G°	Ab	Bbm	C	Db	E♮°
F#	F#m	G#°	A	Bm	C#	D	E#°
G	Gm	A°	Bb	Cm	D	Eb	F#°
G#	G#m	A#°	B	C#m	D#	E	F#
A	Am	B°	C	Dm	E	F	G#°
Bb	Bbm	C°	Db	Ebm	F	Gb	A♮°
B	Bm	C#°	D	Em	F#	G	A#°

Dorian Tonality

Functions Key	i	ii	III	IV	v	vi°	VII
C	Cm	Dm	E	F	Gm	A°	B
C#	C#m	D#m	E#	F#	G#m	A#°	B#
D	Dm	Em	F#	G	Am	B°	C#
Eb	Ebm	Fm	G	Ab	Bbm	C°	D
E	Em	F#m	G#	A	Bm	C#°	D#
F	Fm	Gm	A	Bb	Cm	D°	E
F#	F#m	G#m	A#	B	C#m	D#°	E#
G	Gm	Am	B	C	Dm	E°	F#
Ab	Abm	Bbm	C	Db	Ebm	F°	G
A	Am	Bm	C#	D	Em	F#°	G#
Bb	Bbm	Cm	D	Eb	Fm	G°	A
B	mB	C#m	D#	E	F#m	G#°	A#

Mixolydian Tonality

Functions Key	I	ii	iii°	IV	v	vi	VII
C	C	Dm	E°	F	Gm	Am	B
C#	C#	D#m	E#°	F#	G#m	A#m	B#
D	D	Em	F#°	G	Am	Bm	C#
Eb	Eb	Fm	G°	Ab	Bbm	Cm	D
E	E	F#m	G#°	A	Bm	C#m	D#
F	F	Gm	A°	Bb	Cm	Dm	E
F#	F#	G#m	A#°	B	C#m	D#m	E#
G	G	Am	B°	C	Dm	Em	F#
Ab	Ab	Bbm	C°	Db	Ebm	Fm	G
A	A	Bm	C#°	D	Em	F#m	G#
Bb	Bb	Cm	D°	Eb	Fm	Gm	A
B	B	C#m	D#°	E	F#m	G#m	A#

Phrygian Tonality

Functions Key	i	bII	III	iv	v°	VI	vii
C	Cm	D	E	Fm	G°	A	Bm
C#	C#m	D#	E#	F#m	G#°	A#	B#m
D	Dm	E	F#	Gm	A°	B	C#m
Eb	Ebm	F	G	Abm	Bb°	C	Dm
E	Em	F#	G#	Am	B°	C#	D#m
F	Fm	G	A	Bbm	C°	D	Em
F#	F#m	G#	A#	Bm	C#°	D#	E#m
G	Gm	A	B	Cm	D°	E	F#m
Ab	Abm	Bb	C	Dbm	Eb°	F	Gm
A	Am	B	C#	Dm	E°	F#	G#m
Bb	Bbm	Cb	D	Ebm	F°	G	Am
B	Bm	C#m	D#	Em	F#°	G	A#m

Lydian Tonality

Functions Key	I	II	iii	iv°	V	vi	vii
C	C	D	Em	F°	G	Am	Bm
C#	C#	D#	E#m	F#°	G#	A#m	B#m
D	D	E	F#m	G°	A	Bm	C#
Eb	Eb	F	Gm	Ab°	Bb	Cm	Dm
E	E	F#	G#m	A°	B	C#m	D#m
F	F	G	Am	Bb°	C	Dm	Em
F#	F#	G#	A#m	B°	C#	D#m	E#m
G	G	A	Bm	C°	D	Em	F#m
Ab	Ab	Bb	Cm	Db°	Eb	Fm	Gm
A	A	B	C#m	D°	E	F#m	G#m
Bb	Bb	C	Dm	Eb°	F	Gm	Am
B	B	C#	D#m	E°	F#	G#m	A#m

Aeolian Tonality

Functions Key	i	ii°	III	iv	v	VI	VII
Cm	Cm	D°	Eb	Fm	Gm	Ab	Bb
C#m	C#m	D#°	E	F#m	G#m	A	B
Dm	Dm	E°	F	Gm	Am	Bb	C
Ebm	Ebm	F°	Gb	Abm	Bbm	C	Db
Em	Em	F#°	G	Am	Bm	C	D
Fm	Fm	G°	Ab	Bbm	Cm	Db	Eb
F#m	F#m	G#°	A	Bm	C#m	D	E
Gm	Gm	A°	Bb	Cm	Dm	Eb	F
G#m	G#m	A#°	B	C#m	D#m	E	F#
Am	Am	B°	C	Dm	Em	F	G
Bbm	Bbm	C°	Db	Ebm	Fm	Gb	Ab
Bm	Bm	C#°	D	Em	F#m	G	A

Locrian Tonality

Functions Key	i°	II	iii	iv	V	VI	vii
Cm	C°	D	Ebm	Fm	Gb	Ab	Bbm
C#m	C#°	D#	Em	F#m	G	A	Bm
Dm	D°	E	Fm	Gm	Ab	Bb	Cm
Ebm	Eb°	F	Gbm	Abm	Bbb	C	Dbm
Em	E°	F#	Gm	Am	Bb	C	Dm
Fm	F°	G	Abm	Bbm	Cb	Db	Ebm
F#m	F#°	G#	Am	Bm	C	D	Em
Gm	G°	A	Bbm	Cm	Db	Eb	Fm
G#m	G#°	A#	Bm	C#m	D	E	F#m
Am	A°	B	Cm	Dm	Eb	F	Gm
Bbm	Bb°	C	Dbm	Ebm	Fb	Gb	Abm
Bm	B°	C#	Dm	Em	F	G	Am

GORDON'S SKILL LEARNING SEQUENCE

DISCRIMINATION LEARNING	INFERENCE LEARNING
• Students are taught, and they learn • Information is acquired • Familiar patterns, familiar or unfamiliar order	• Students are guided in how to teach themselves • Students infer the unfamiliar on the basis of the familiar • Familiar and unfamiliar patterns in unfamiliar order
Aural/Oral • The most fundamental level of music. • Students listen and imitate. • Neutral syllables. • Students move to music.	**Generalization** • Students can identify if something is the same or different. • Students can translate patterns from a neutral syllable to solfege. • Students can identify familiar and unfamiliar harmonic and rhythmic functions. • Students can read familiar and unfamiliar music. • Students can identify the tonality or meter of an unfamiliar song.
Verbal Association • Students label the aural sounds from A/O. • Tonal and rhythm solfege is used to organize sounds. • Students label sounds of harmonic and rhythmic functions.	**Creativity/Improvisation** • Students can make up endings to songs. • Students can have tonal or rhythmic conversations. • Students can improvise over chord changes. • Students can compose their own music.
Partial Synthesis • Students are taught how to discriminate between contexts (tonalities and meters).	**Theoretical Understanding** • The "why" of music. • Students learn the "grammar" of music. • Students learn technical information (lines and spaces, letter names, types of cadences, etc.)
Symbolic Association • Reading and writing at the word level. • Students learn to read and write the same patterns they were taught at the Verbal Association levels.	
Composite Synthesis • Reading and writing at the sentence level. • Reading and writing with comprehension. • Students learn how to chain patterns together to read and write longer musical statements. • Students can recognize the tonality and meter of written music.	

4 PART VOICINGS

Try to sing these harmonizations in small groups. Assign each person to a voice, with the bass part being optional. Have each person try all three voice parts.

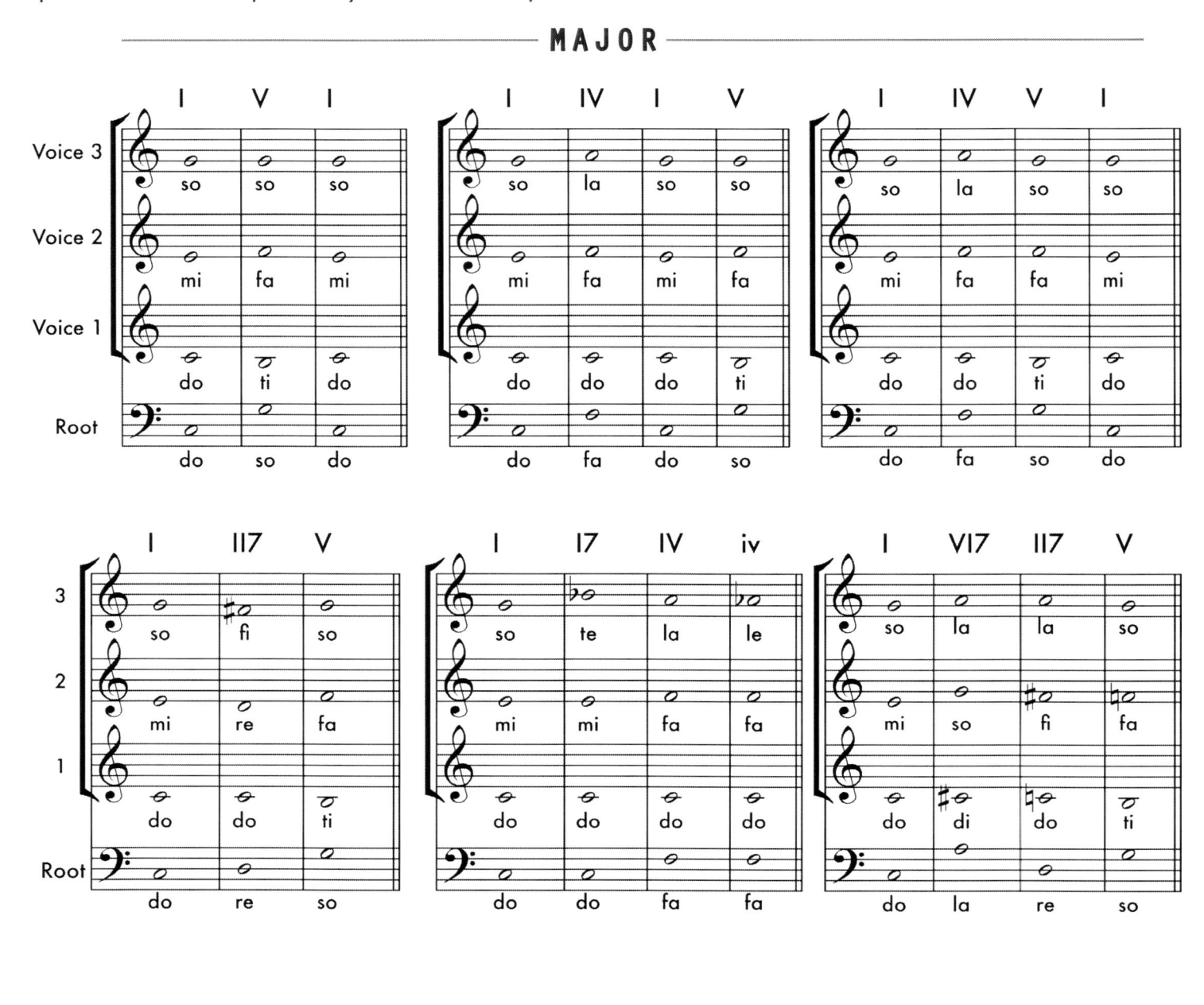

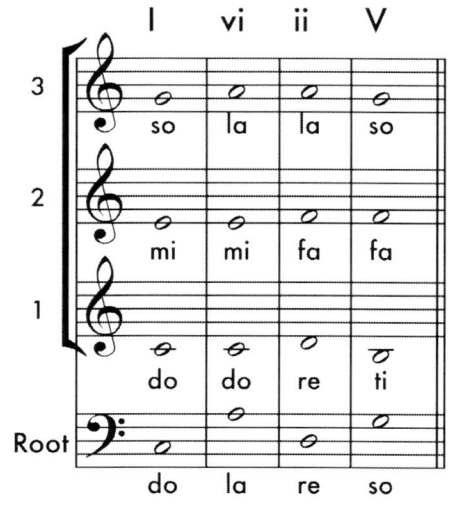

MAJOR

I V I
- Voice 3: so so so
- Voice 2: mi fa mi
- Voice 1: do ti do
- Root: do so do

I IV I V
- Voice 3: so la so so
- Voice 2: mi fa mi fa
- Voice 1: do do do ti
- Root: do fa do so

I IV V I
- Voice 3: so la so so
- Voice 2: mi fa fa mi
- Voice 1: do do ti do
- Root: do fa so do

I II7 V
- 3: so fi so
- 2: mi re fa
- 1: do do ti
- Root: do re so

I I7 IV iv
- 3: so te la le
- 2: mi mi fa fa
- 1: do do do do
- Root: do do fa fa

I VI7 II7 V
- 3: so la la so
- 2: mi so fi fa
- 1: do di do ti
- Root: do la re so

I vi ii V
- 3: so la la so
- 2: mi mi fa fa
- 1: do do re ti
- Root: do la re so

I III7 vi IV
- 3: so si la la
- 2: mi re mi fa
- 1: do ti do do
- Root: do mi la fa

I I7 IV I II7 V
- 3: so te la so fi so
- 2: mi mi fa mi re fa
- 1: do do do do do ti
- Root: do do fa do re so

MINOR

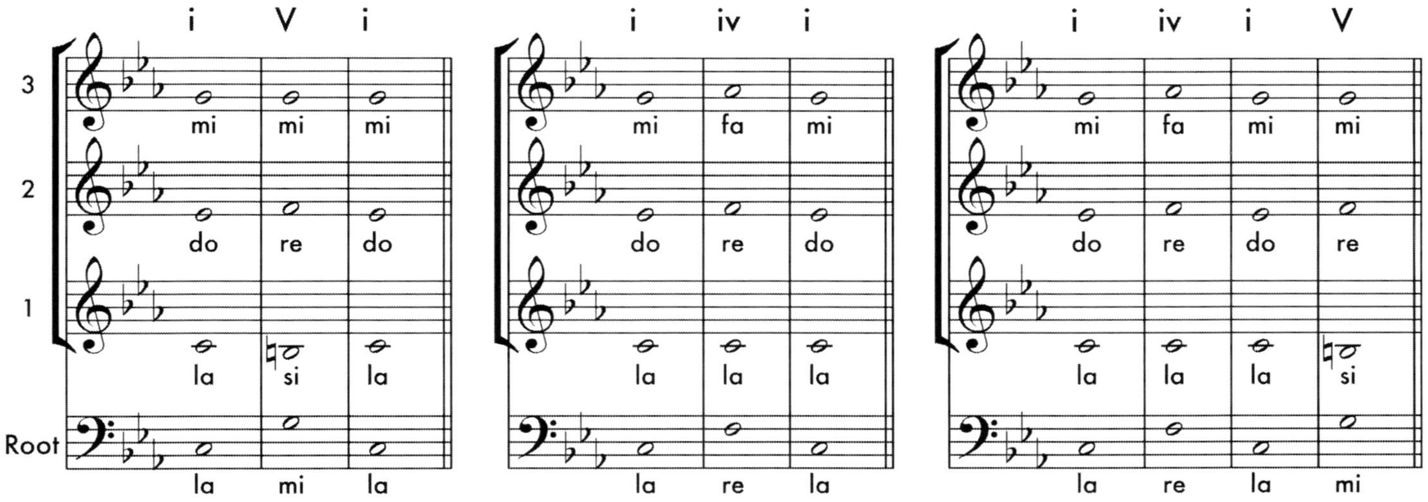

DORIAN

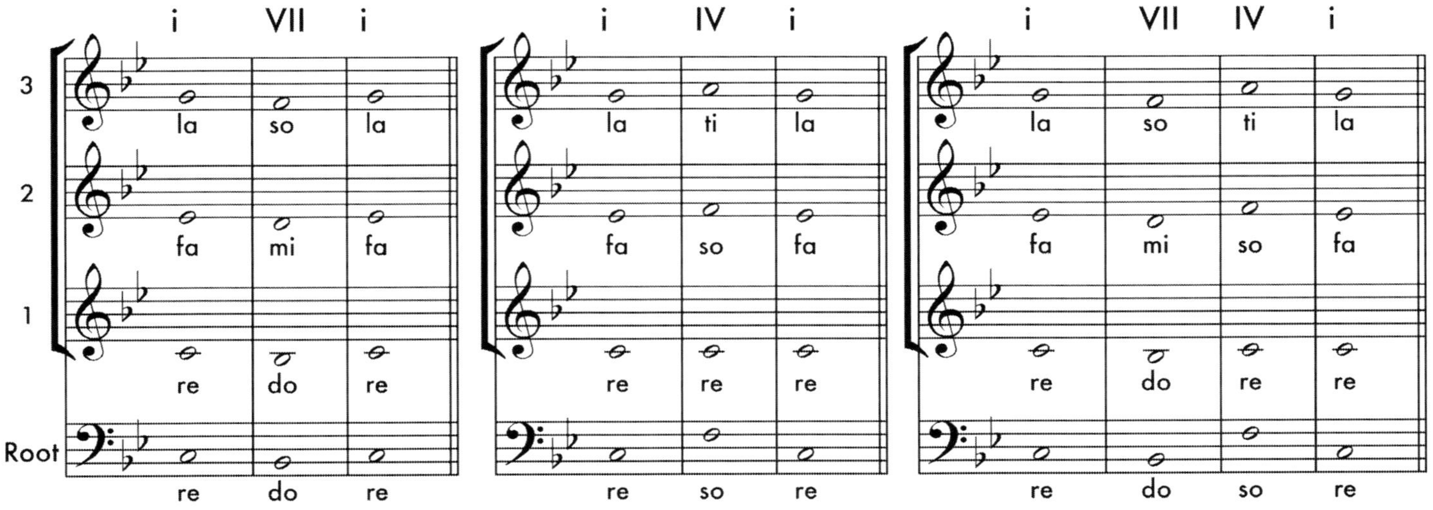

MIXOLYDIAN

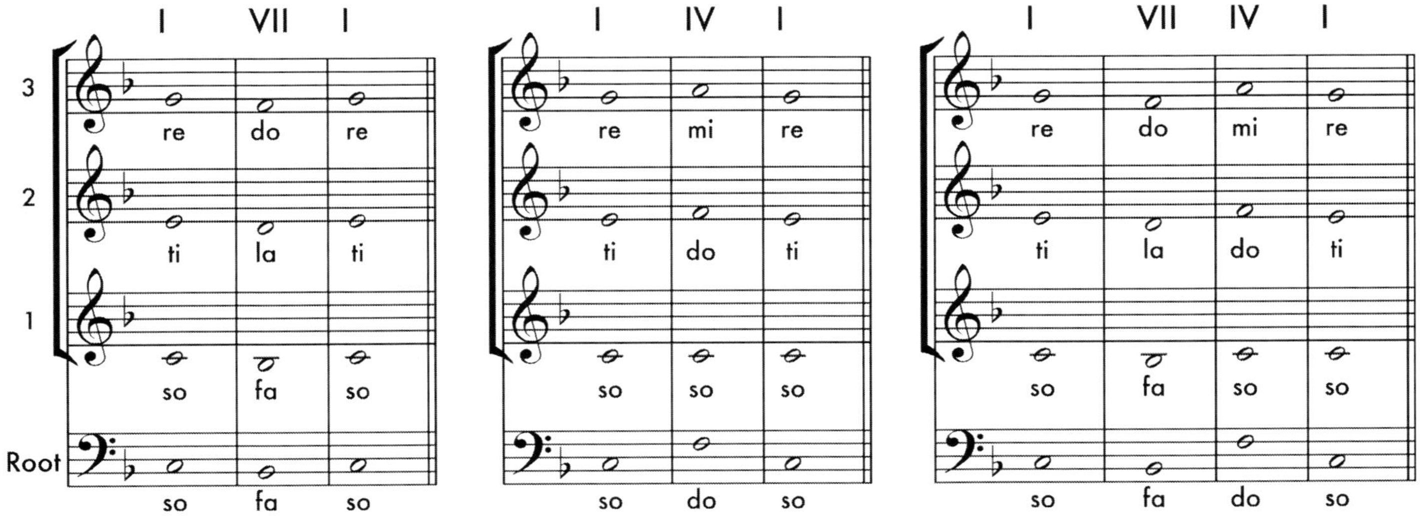

LYDIAN

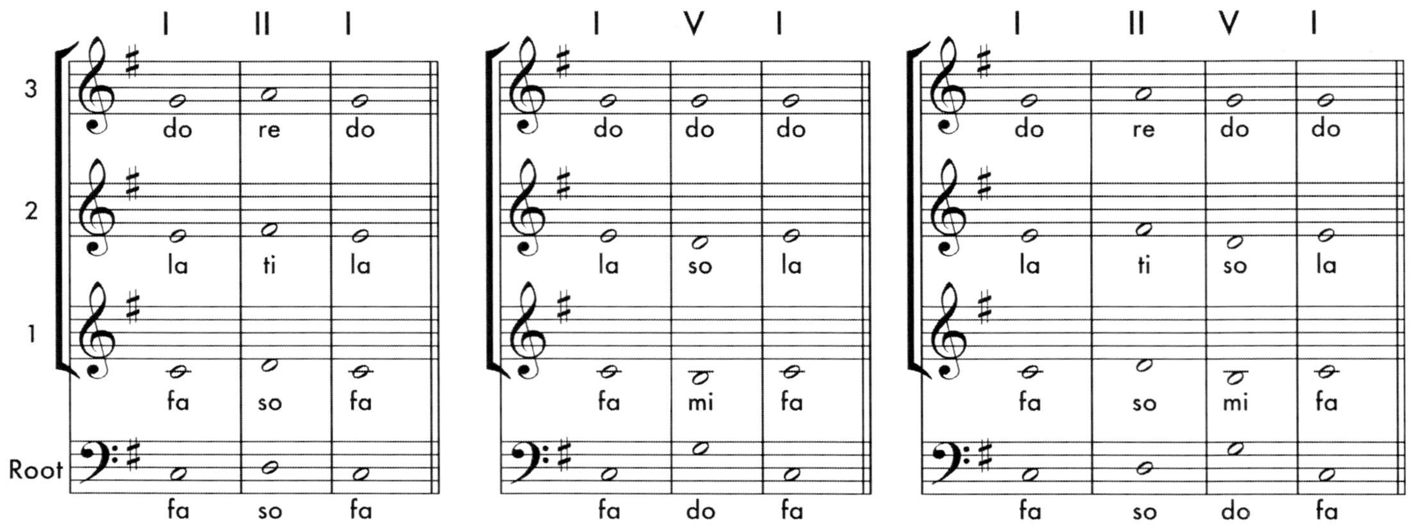

PHRYGIAN

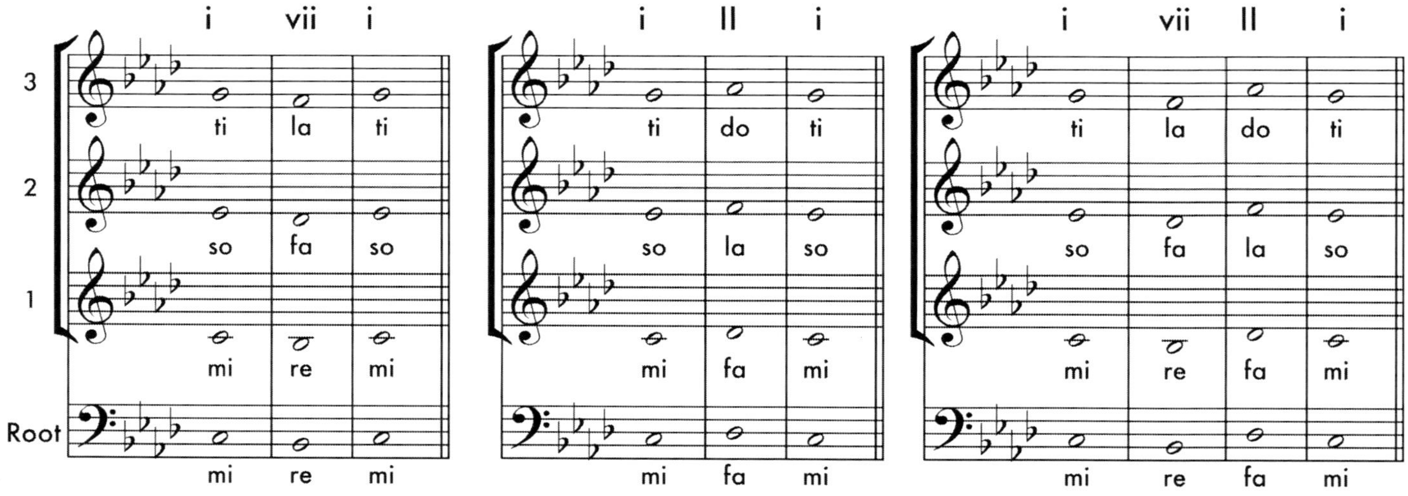

AEOLIAN

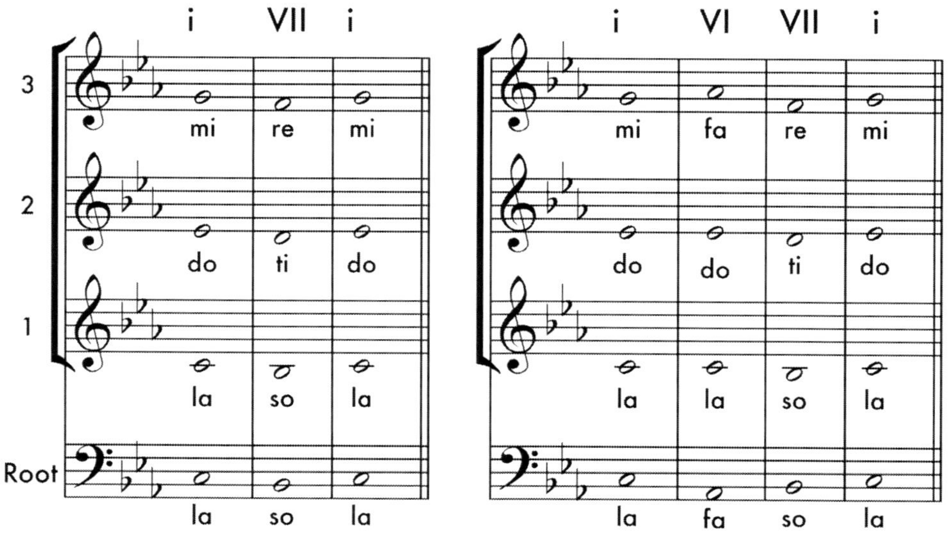

LOCRIAN

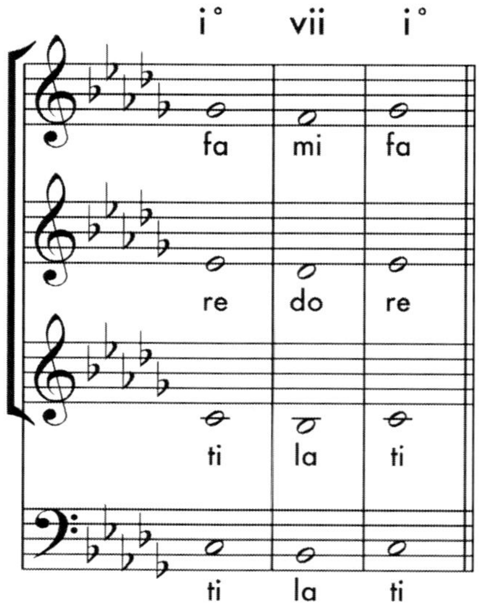

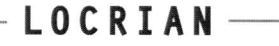

UKULELE CHORDS

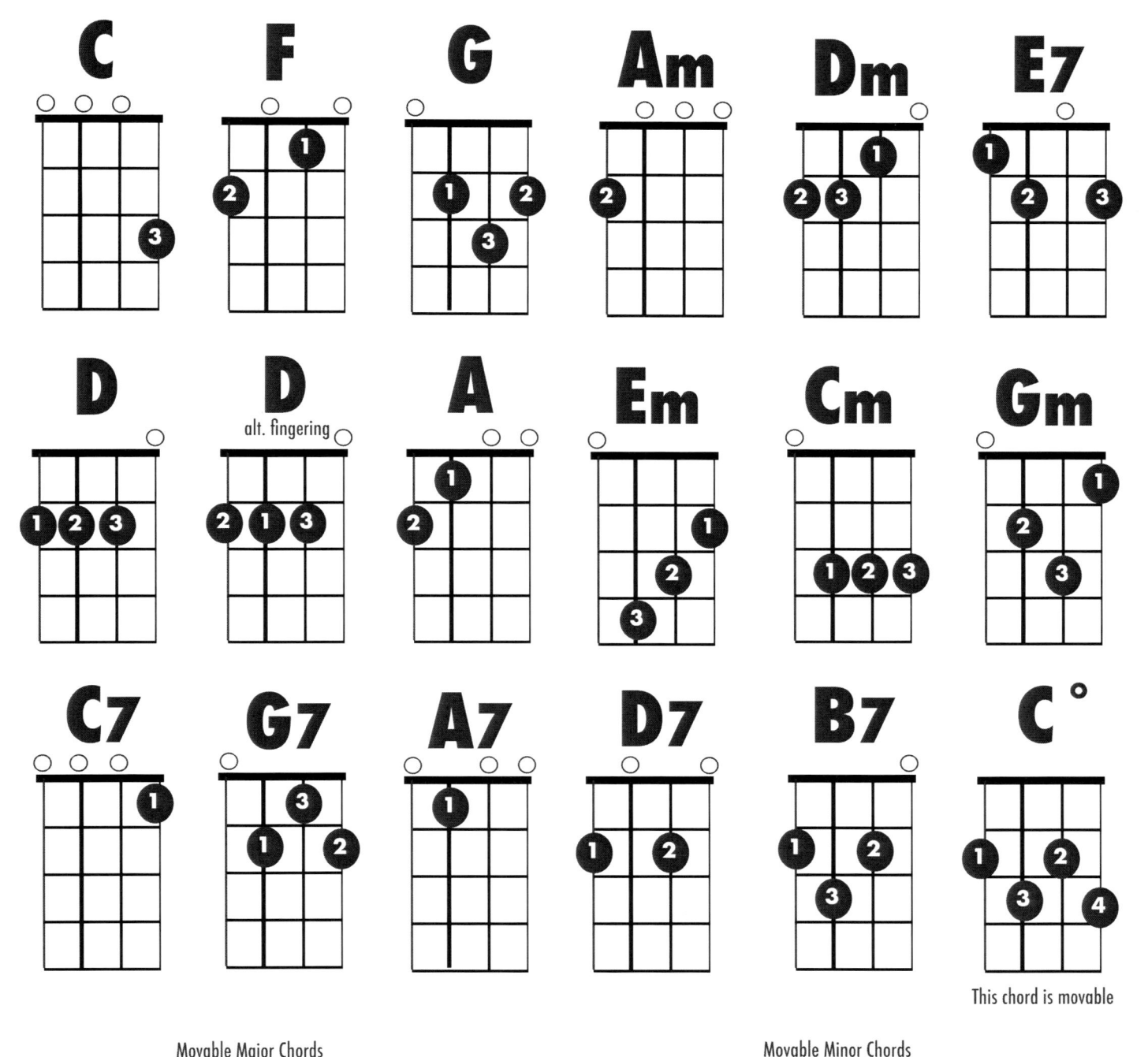

C **F** **G** **Am** **Dm** **E7**

D **D** alt. fingering **A** **Em** **Cm** **Gm**

C7 **G7** **A7** **D7** **B7** **C°**

This chord is movable

Movable Major Chords

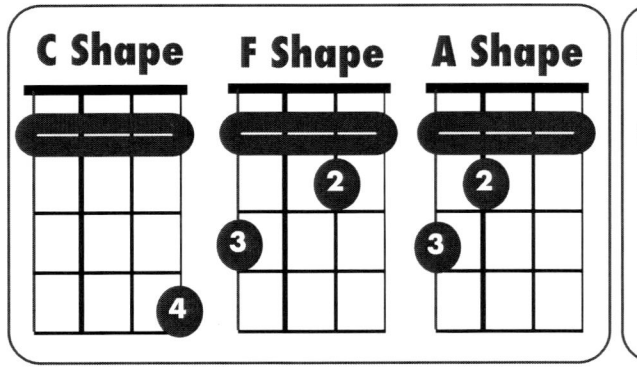

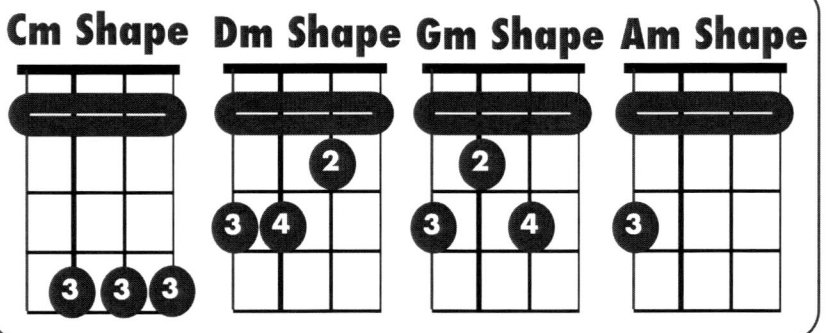

C Shape **F Shape** **A Shape**

Movable Minor Chords

Cm Shape **Dm Shape** **Gm Shape** **Am Shape**

END NOTES & REFERENCES

The majority of the content of this book can be attributed to general pedagogy of Music Learning Theory, developed by Dr. Edwin E. Gordon. For a thorough explanation of Music Learning Theory and its practical applications, read the following book: *Learning Sequences in Music: A Contemporary Music Learning Theory* by Dr. Edwin E. Gordon. It is published by GIA Publications. I have also no doubt been heavily influenced by all of the conferences, classes and workshops I have attended by other MLT practitioners. Specific references appear below:

PART I: FOUNDATIONS OF MUSICAL THOUGHT

Section 1
- The reference information for each tonality and meter is inspired by Dr. Beth Bolton's book, *Musicianship*. Beth's creative compositions are always part of an MLT teacher's repertoire.
- "Acculturation" is a term used by Dr. Gordon in his book *A Music Learning Theory for Newborn and Young Children*. Teaching ideas for acculturation were also inspired by certification courses in Early Childhood Music with The Gordon Institute for Music Learning (GIML).

Section 2
- Most of the ideas for the practical applications of pattern teaching come from Dr. Gordon's book, *Reference Handbook for Learning Sequence Activities*, as well as certification courses in Elementary General Music with The Gordon Institute for Music Learning (GIML).
- Dr. Gordon did not advocate for students to see solfege (DU, DU DE; DO RE MI, etc.) written out. However, the research that supported those claims was done many years ago when students were not so visually attached to electronic devices. More research needs to be done with students of this current technologically-dependent generation.
- Lesson 10: Many of my thoughts about the higher skill levels and their practical applications were shaped and refined by Jennifer Bailey, Dr. Jill Reese, Dr. Cynthia Taggart and Dr. Heather Shouldice, the instructors of Elementary General Level 2, a certification course with GIML. In particular, Jill's notions about the importance of "the struggle" in inference learning, Jennifer's ideas about Partial Synthesis, Cindy's use of skills as problem solving tools, and Heather's navigation of the Skill Learning Sequence found particular resonance with me, and are represented in this book with gratitude.
- The tests I use are based on Dr. Gordon's *Iowa Tests of Music Literacy*. They are published by GIA.

Section 3
- The technique of singing bass lines was created by Dr. Gordon who was himself a bass player. These ideas were developed further by Dr. Richard Grunow and Dr. Christopher Azzara in their series *Developing Musicianship Through Improvisation*. This series is published by GIA.
- Some of the techniques for giving students options for making improvisational choices were borrowed from Dr. Heather Shouldice in informal discussions in the Facebook group, *MLT Classroom Teachers*. Heather's creative teaching has been a consistent source of inspiration for many aspiring MLT teachers.

END NOTES & REFERENCES

Section 4

- The idea of stepwise, diatonic patterns was inspired by the pioneering music literacy techniques of Zoltan Kodály, which were further developed and Americanized by Dr. John Feierabend in his excellent series *Conversational Solfege*, which is in itself a realization of Gordon's Music Learning Theory. Dr. Feierabend's ideas about connecting the Kodály approach and Music Learning Theory can be found in his chapter "Integrating Music Learning Theory into the Kodály Curriculum" in *Readings in Music Learning Theory*, a collection of articles edited by Darrel L. Walters and Cynthia Taggart. It was originally published by GIA.
- Dr. Gordon referred to "DO RE MI" patterns as "multiple patterns," in that they encompassed multiple harmonic functions. He advocated that they be taught far later in his sequence. In this book, I am proposing that they be taught far sooner in the tonal sequence. Additionally, I make more overt connections between melody and harmony in my practical applications than has been previously brought forth by Music Learning Theory pedagogy.
- The idea of creating very simple tunes in tonal/rhythm combinations came from *Jump Right In: The Instrumental Series*.
- Many of the ideas in this section about improvisation are inspired by Dr. Richard Grunow and Dr. Christopher Azzara in their series *Developing Musicianship Through Improvisation*. In particular, the idea of using songs and repertoire as the basis of creativity and improvisation, as well as finding connections between harmonic functions can be found in this series. It is published by GIA.

PART II: READING MUSICAL THOUGHT

- Many of the basic ideas about the practical applications of Music Learning Theory as they apply to reading are attributed to the faculty of Elementary General Level 1 at Temple University in 2016. In particular, the concept of providing students with succinct, verb-focused directions prior to pattern instruction are attributed to Dr. Alison Reynolds and Dr. Suzanne Burton, both of who taught the course. Dr. Jill Reese is also acknowledged as having contributed to the text of the course, the contents of which are included in her book with GIA called *Navigating Music Learning Theory: A Guide for General Music Teachers* (2019).
- The concepts of "familiar patterns in familiar and unfamiliar order" were originated by Dr. Gordon, and were further developed by Dr. Richard Grunow and Dr. Christopher Azzara in *Jump Right In: The Instrumental Series*. It is published by GIA.
- The technique of using the last flat and sharp to find DO was learned from Amy J. Beresik in her presentation entitled "Taking The Pain Out of Sight-Singing" at the 5th International Conference of Music Learning Theory.

Appendices

- Many of the voicings for advanced harmonizations were learned from Dr. Heather Shouldice at the GIML Elementary General Level 2 PDLC.
- The idea for the Solfege Keyboard card was borrowed from the pedagogy of Little Kids Rock. They call them "Jam Cards" and offer them for free in the teacher's section of their website, www.LittleKidsRock.org.

ABOUT THE AUTHOR

ANDY MULLEN is a teacher, folk musician, multi-instrumentalist, recovering singer-songwriter, voice actor, blogger, desktop publisher, and lifelong learner. He has taught all levels of students in a number of subjects, and is currently a middle school general music and chorus teacher in Burlington, Massachusetts. Mr. Mullen holds Masters degrees in Music Education and School Administration, as well as certification from the Gordon Institute of Music Learning (GIML) in Elementary General Level 2 and Early Childhood Music. He is the author of *Fifty Tunes for Teaching*, *About a Hundred Fiddle Tunes*, *MLT Any Music Teacher Can Du...De*, and the creator of www.TheImprovingMusician.com.

OTHER RESOURCES FROM THE IMPROVING MUSICIAN

MLT Any Music Teacher Can Du...De

For teachers interested in teaching *The Literate Musician*, a teacher's edition is now available! This long awaited book delves into the theory and practical applications of Music Learning Theory, and demonstrates how to bring it alive in the classroom. A must have for any general music, band, choir or orchestra teacher interested in MLT!

Also Available: **The Literate Musician Teacher Slideshows** with over 1000 slides for teacher use.

Fifty Tunes for Teaching

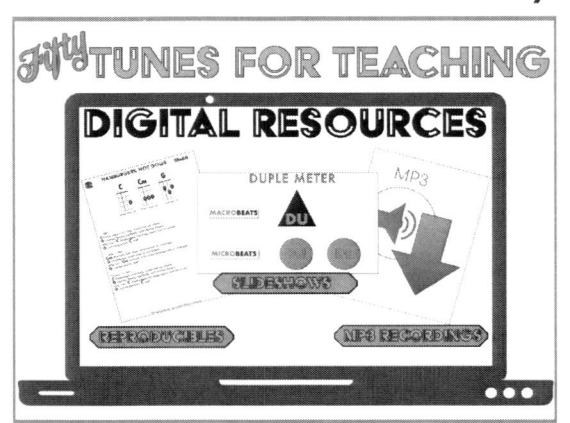

New songs with and without words to use in the general music classroom! These 50 songs contain lyrics, chord symbols, harmonic functions, as well as teaching ideas from all levels of Dr. Edwin E. Gordon's Skill Learning Sequence.

A **Digital Resources Pack** is also available, which contains reproducibles, mp3 recordings of all the tunes, XML files, and slideshows for classroom use.

Teacher Pattern Pack, vol. 1

This new resource for teachers contains over 50 mp3s to use for in-person, remote or hybrid teaching. While they cannot replace a face-to-face teacher, these virtual tonal and rhythm pattern exercises are a wonderful substitute when in-person singing is not allowed. Tonal patterns include Learning Sequence Activities with tonic and dominant functions in Major and Minor tonalities. Rhythm patterns include Learning Sequence Activities with macrobeats, microbeats and divisions in Duple and Triple meters.

Made in United States
Cleveland, OH
28 March 2025